P9-EFG-044

DEATH AND DYING

WHO DECIDES?

ISSN 1532-2726

DEATH AND DYING

WHO DECIDES?

Barbara Wexler

INFORMATION PLUS® REFERENCE SERIES
Formerly published by Information Plus, Wylie, Texas

GALE®

THOMSON

GALE

Detroit • New York • San Diego • San Francisco • Cleveland • New Haven, Conn. • Waterville, Maine • London • Munich

THOMSON
★
GALE

Death and Dying: Who Decides?
Barbara Wexler

Project Editor
Ellice Engdahl

Editorial
Paula Cutcher-Jackson, Kathleen Edgar, Christy Justice, Debra Kirby, Prindle LaBarge, Elizabeth Manar, Kathleen Meek, Charles B. Montney, Heather Price

Permissions
Shalice Shah-Caldwell

Imaging and Multimedia
Robert Duncan, Lezlie Light, Dan Newell, Kelly A. Quin

Product Design
Michael Logusz

Composition and Electronic Prepress
Evi Seoud

Manufacturing
Keith Helmling

© 2003 by Gale. Gale is an imprint of The Gale Group, Inc., a division of Thomson Learning, Inc.

Gale and Design™ and Thomson Learning™ are trademarks used herein under license.

For more information, contact
The Gale Group, Inc.
27500 Drake Rd.
Farmington Hills, MI 48331-3535
Or you can visit our Internet site at
http://www.gale.com

ALL RIGHTS RESERVED
No part of this work covered by the copyright hereon may be reproduced or used in any form or by any means—graphic, electronic, or mechanical, including photocopying, recording, taping, Web distribution, or information storage retrieval systems—without the written permission of the publisher.

For permission to use material from this product, submit your request via Web at http://www.gale-edit.com/permissions, or you may download our Permissions Request form and submit your request by fax or mail to:

The Gale Group, Inc.
27500 Drake Rd.
Farmington Hills, MI 48331-3535
Permissions Hotline: 248-699-8006 or 800-877-4253, ext. 8006
Fax: 248-699-8074 or 800-762-4058

Cover photograph reproduced by permission of PhotoDisc.

Since this page cannot legibly accommodate all copyright notices, the acknowledgments constitute an extension of the copyright notice.

While every effort has been made to ensure the reliability of the information presented in this publication, The Gale Group, Inc. does not guarantee the accuracy of the data contained herein. The Gale Group, Inc. accepts no payment for listing; and inclusion in the publication of any organization, agency, institution, publication, service, or individual does not imply endorsement of the editors or publisher. Errors brought to the attention of the publisher and verified to the satisfaction of the publisher will be corrected in future editions.

LIBRARY OF CONGRESS CATALOGING-IN-PUBLICATION DATA

ISBN 0-7876-5103-6 (set)
ISBN 0-7876-6063-9
ISSN 1532-2726

Printed in the United States of America
10 9 8 7 6 5 4 3 2 1

TABLE OF CONTENTS

CHAPTER 1

Death Through the Ages—A Brief Overview. 1

Different cultures have reacted to death in different ways. This chapter examines beliefs and rituals spanning 3 million years of human history. Particular attention is paid to modern approaches to death, including the option of hospice.

CHAPTER 2

Redefining Death 9

The definition of death has changed significantly throughout and since the last quarter of the twentieth century. Medical institutions and the federal government have presented their own definitions, garnering disagreement among the medical community. Controversy also surrounds the validity of the near-death experience.

CHAPTER 3

The End of Life—Ethical Considerations 13

All major religions consider life sacred, but religions differ in the way they view death. Doctors and patients may also have differing thoughts on end-of-life care. Topics such as patient involvement in decision-making and ethical issues concerning the treatment of AIDS are discussed.

CHAPTER 4

The End of Life—Medical Considerations. 23

There are numerous medical considerations as one approaches the end of life. This chapter examines the leading causes of death, how end-of-life care sometimes falls short (as demonstrated by the SUPPORT study), and life-sustaining treatments. Also discussed in depth are persistent vegetative state (PVS) and organ donation.

CHAPTER 5

Seriously Ill Children 41

Children generally outlive their parents. Unfortunately, some parents must address end-of-life issues for their children. This chapter discusses the types of medical concerns found in children, with heavy coverage of birth defects. The roles of parents, guardians, courts, and the medical community in caring for critically ill children are also examined.

CHAPTER 6

Euthanasia and Assisted Suicide 57

Some people choose to die by asking for assistance in their deaths or by taking their own lives. Religions, cultures, special interest groups, nurses, and physicians view these end-of-life issues in different ways. Federal and state laws fall on both ends of the spectrum. Specific details on Oregon's Death with Dignity Act and the Netherlands' legal euthanasia policy are provided.

CHAPTER 7

Advance Directives. 77

All adults have the right to decide in advance what medical treatment they want to receive in the event they become physically or mentally unable to communicate their wishes. The two types of advance directives, living wills and durable powers of attorney for health care, are explained, as are the legal, historical, and practical effectiveness of advance directives.

CHAPTER 8

Courts and the End of Life 99

This chapter examines the legal ramifications of end of life issues. Legal decisions concerning patients, guardians, physicians, hospitals, and nursing homes are presented.

CHAPTER 9

The Cost of Health Care 113

Public and private health care plans carry the burden of providing high-quality care, but high-quality care comes at an increasingly high cost. This chapter explores the types of health care plans available, as well as their coverage of services such as hospice, in-home care, nursing home care, and care for terminal patients.

CHAPTER 10

Older Adults. 131

Americans are living increasingly long lives, creating a population that is older on average than ever before. This chapter discusses the health problems that afflict the elderly. Also touched upon are geriatricians, the doctors that treat older patients.

CHAPTER 11

Public Opinion About Life and Death 147

People have varying concerns about getting older and dying. In this chapter, selected opinion polls illustrate some of the concerns about and attitudes toward end-of-life issues.

PREFACE

Death and Dying: Who Decides? is one of the latest volumes in the Information Plus Reference Series. Previously published by the Information Plus company of Wylie, Texas, the Information Plus Reference Series (and its companion set, the Information Plus Compact Series) became a Gale Group product when Gale and Information Plus merged in early 2000. Those of you familiar with the series as published by Information Plus will notice a few changes from the 2000 edition. Gale has adopted a new layout and style that we hope you will find easy to use. Other improvements include greatly expanded indexes in each book, and more descriptive tables of contents.

While some changes have been made to the design, the purpose of the Information Plus Reference Series remains the same. Each volume of the series presents the latest facts on a topic of pressing concern in modern American life. These topics include today's most controversial and most studied social issues: abortion, capital punishment, care for the elderly, crime, health care, the environment, immigration, minorities, social welfare, women, youth, and many more. Although written especially for the high school and undergraduate student, this series is an excellent resource for anyone in need of factual information on current affairs.

By presenting the facts, it is Gale's intention to provide its readers with everything they need to reach an informed opinion on current issues. To that end, there is a particular emphasis in this series on the presentation of scientific studies, surveys, and statistics. These data are generally presented in the form of tables, charts, and other graphics placed within the text of each book. Every graphic is directly referred to and carefully explained in the text. The source of each graphic is presented within the graphic itself. The data used in these graphics are drawn from the most reputable and reliable sources, in particular from the various branches of the U.S. government and from major independent polling organizations.

Every effort has been made to secure the most recent information available. The reader should bear in mind that many major studies take years to conduct, and that additional years often pass before the data from these studies is made available to the public. Therefore, in many cases the most recent information available in 2002 dated from 1999 or 2000. Older statistics are sometimes presented as well, if they are of particular interest and no more recent information exists.

Although statistics are a major focus of the Information Plus Reference Series, they are by no means its only content. Each book also presents the widely held positions and important ideas that shape how the book's subject is discussed in the United States. These positions are explained in detail and, where possible, in the words of their proponents. Some of the other material to be found in these books includes: historical background; descriptions of major events related to the subject; relevant laws and court cases; and examples of how these issues play out in American life. Some books also feature primary documents, or have pro and con debate sections giving the words and opinions of prominent Americans on both sides of a controversial topic. All material is presented in an even-handed and unbiased manner; the reader will never be encouraged to accept one view of an issue over another.

HOW TO USE THIS BOOK

Death is one of the universal human experiences. This and its ultimately unknowable nature combine to make it a topic of great interest to most Americans. How we die and how we deal with the deaths of others evokes profound religious and/or ethical issues about which many people hold very strong beliefs. When these beliefs are in conflict with those of others, they can result in some of the most serious and divisive controversies in the modern United States. This book examines how Americans deal with death, with a particular focus on the highly charged political and moral issues of living wills, life-sustaining treatments, end-of-life care funding, and physician-assisted suicide.

Death and Dying: Who Decides? consists of eleven chapters and three appendices. Each of the chapters is devoted to a particular aspect of death and dying in the United States. For a summary of the information covered in each chapter, please see the synopses provided in the Table of Contents at the front of the book. Chapters generally begin with an overview of the basic facts and background information on the chapter's topic, then proceed to examine sub-topics of particular interest. For example, Chapter 6: Euthanasia and Assisted Suicide begins with background information on how suicide and euthanasia have been regarded by different cultures throughout history. The chapter then moves on to deal with suicide and euthanasia in the United States more specifically, including how many Americans commit suicide. Outlined next are the stances of major political figures and organizations involved in the controversies surrounding euthanasia and assisted suicide. Finally, legal physician-assisted suicide, as practiced in the state of Oregon and in the Netherlands, is scrutinized. Readers can find their way through a chapter by looking for the section and sub-section headings, which are clearly set off from the text. Or, they can refer to the book's extensive index if they already know what they are looking for.

Statistical Information

The tables and figures featured throughout *Death and Dying: Who Decides?* will be of particular use to the reader in learning about this issue. These tables and figures represent an extensive collection of the most recent and important statistics on death, as well as related issues—for example, graphics in the book cover death rates for suicide; reasons for choosing hospice care; Medicare coverage of various end-of-life needs; the rise in life expectancy over the last century; and public opinion about the most fearful aspects of death. Gale believes that making this information available to the reader is the most important way in which we fulfill the goal of this book: to help readers understand the issues and controversies surrounding death and dying in the United States and reach their own conclusions.

Each table or figure has a unique identifier appearing above it, for ease of identification and reference. Titles for the tables and figures explain their purpose. At the end of each table or figure, the original source of the data is provided.

In order to help readers understand these often complicated statistics, all tables and figures are explained in the text. References in the text direct the reader to the relevant statistics. Furthermore, the contents of all tables and figures are fully indexed. Please see the opening section of the index at the back of this volume for a description of how to find tables and figures within it.

Appendices

In addition to the main body text and images, *Death and Dying: Who Decides?* has three appendices. The first is the Important Names and Addresses directory. Here the reader will find contact information for a number of government and private organizations that can provide further information on aspects of death and dying. The second appendix is the Resources section, which can also assist the reader in conducting his or her own research. In this section, the author and editors of *Death and Dying: Who Decides?* describe some of the sources that were most useful during the compilation of this book. The final appendix is the index. It has been greatly expanded from previous editions, and should make it even easier to find specific topics in this book.

ADVISORY BOARD CONTRIBUTIONS

The staff of Information Plus would like to extend their heartfelt appreciation to the Information Plus Advisory Board. This dedicated group of media professionals provides feedback on the series on an ongoing basis. Their comments allow the editorial staff who work on the project to continually make the series better and more user-friendly. Our top priorities are to produce the highest-quality and most useful books possible, and the Advisory Board's contributions to this process are invaluable.

The members of the Information Plus Advisory Board are:

- Kathleen R. Bonn, Librarian, Newbury Park High School, Newbury Park, California

- Madelyn Garner, Librarian, San Jacinto College—North Campus, Houston, Texas

- Anne Oxenrider, Media Specialist, Dundee High School, Dundee, Michigan

- Charles R. Rodgers, Director of Libraries, Pasco-Hernando Community College, Dade City, Florida

- James N. Zitzelsberger, Library Media Department Chairman, Oshkosh West High School, Oshkosh, Wisconsin

COMMENTS AND SUGGESTIONS

The editors of the Information Plus Reference Series welcome your feedback on *Death and Dying: Who Decides?* Please direct all correspondence to:

Editors
Information Plus Reference Series
27500 Drake Rd.
Farmington Hills, MI 48331-3535

ACKNOWLEDGMENTS

The editors wish to thank the copyright holders of material included in this volume and the permissions managers of many book and magazine publishing companies for assisting us in securing reproduction rights. We are also grateful to the staffs of the Detroit Public Library, the Library of Congress, the University of Detroit Mercy Library, Wayne State University Purdy/Kresge Library Complex, and the University of Michigan Libraries for making their resources available to us.

Following is a list of the copyright holders who have granted us permission to reproduce material in Information Plus: Death and Dying. *Every effort has been made to trace copyright, but if omissions have been made, please let us know.*

For more detailed source citations, please see the sources listed under each individual table and figure.

Alliance for Aging Research: Figure 11.11, Figure 11.12, Figure 11.13

American Cancer Society, Inc.: Table 10.5, Table 10.6

American Medical Association: Figure 3.1

Centers for Disease Control and Prevention: Figure 1.2, Table 1.2, Table 1.3, Table 4.1, Table 4.2, Table 4.3, Table 4.4, Figure 5.1, Figure 5.2, Table 5.1, Table 5.2, Table 5.3, Table 5.4, Table 5.5, Table 5.6, Table 5.7, Figure 6.1, Table 6.1, Table 6.2, Table 6.3, Figure 9.3, Table 9.2, Table 9.3, Table 9.4, Table 9.11, Table 9.12, Table 10.3, Table 10.4, Table 10.7, Table 10.9

Centers for Medicare & Medicaid Services: Figure 9.1, Table 9.1

The Harris Poll: Table 11.1

Health Care Financing Administration: Figure 9.4

The Hemlock Society: Table 6.6

Hospice Association of America: Table 1.1, Table 9.5, Table 9.7, Table 9.8, Table 9.9

National Association for Home Care: Table 9.6

National Conference of State Legislatures: Table 7.1

National Right to Life Committee (NRLC): Figure 7.4

The New England Journal of Medicine: Figure 3.2, Table 3.1, Table 3.2, Figure 4.2, Table 4.5, Table 6.4, Table 6.5, Table 6.7

Partnership for Caring, Inc.: Figure 4.1, Figure 7.1, Figure 7.2, Figure 7.6, Figure 7.7, Figure 7.8

The Roper Center for Public Opinion Research: Figure 11.1, Figure 11.2, Figure 11.3, Figure 11.4, Figure 11.5, Figure 11.6, Figure 11.7, Figure 11.8, Figure 11.9, Figure 11.10, Figure 11.14, Figure 11.15, Figure 11.16, Figure 11.17

United Network for Organ Sharing: Table 4.6, Table 4.7, Table 4.9

U.S. Census Bureau: Table 10.1, Table 10.2, Table 10.10

U.S. Department of Health and Human Services, Health Resources and Services Administration, Division of Transplantation: Figure 4.3, Figure 4.4, Figure 4.5, Table 4.8

U.S. Department of Health and Human Services, Health Resources and Services Administration, HIV/AIDS: Table 9.13, Table 9.14

U.S. Department of Health and Human Services, National Institutes of Health, National Institute on Aging: Figure 9.5

U.S. General Accounting Office: Figure 7.3, Figure 7.5, Figure 9.2, Table 9.10, Table 10.8

U.S. Government Printing Office: Figure 1.1, Figure 2.1

Weekly Compilation of Presidential Documents: Figure 6.2

CHAPTER 1
DEATH THROUGH THE AGES—A BRIEF OVERVIEW

Strange, is it not? That of the myriads who
Before us passed the door of Darkness through,
Not one returns to tell us of the road,
Which to discover we must travel too.
—Omar Khayyám

Death is the inevitable conclusion of life, a universal destiny all share. Although all societies since the dawn of history have realized that death is mankind's certain fate, different cultures have reacted to death in different ways. Through the ages, attitudes toward death and dying have changed, and they continue to change, shaped by religious beliefs and philosophical traditions. In modern times, advances in medical science and technology further influence attitudes toward death and dying.

ANCIENT TIMES

Archaeologists have found that as early as the Paleolithic period (about 2.5 to 3 million years ago), humans held specific beliefs about death and dying. Tools and ornaments excavated at burial sites suggest that our earliest ancestors believed some element of a person survived the dying experience.

Ancient Hebrews (circa 1020–586 B.C.E.), while acknowledging the existence of the soul, were not preoccupied with the afterlife. They lived according to the commandments of their God, to whom they entrusted their eternal destiny. Early Egyptians (circa 2900–950 B.C.E.), on the other hand, thought that preservation of the dead body (mummification) guaranteed a happy afterlife. They believed that a person had a dual soul—the *ka* and the *ba*. The *ka* was the spirit that dwelled near the body, while the *ba* was the vitalizing soul that lived on in the netherworld. Similarly, the ancient Chinese (circa 2500–1000 B.C.E.) also believed in a dual soul, one part of which continued to exist after the death of the body. It was this spirit that the living venerated during ancestor worship.

Among the ancient Greeks (circa 2600–1200 B.C.E.), death was greatly feared. Greek mythology—full of tales of gods and goddesses who exacted punishment—caused the living to meticulously follow rituals when burying their dead so as not to displease the gods. Although reincarnation is usually associated with Asian religions, some Greeks were followers of Orphism, a religion that taught that the soul underwent numerous reincarnations until purification was achieved.

CLASSICAL PERIOD

Mythological beliefs among the ancient Greeks persisted in the classical age. The Greeks believed that after death the psyche, or vital essence of a person, lived on in the underworld. The renowned Greek writer Homer (circa 800–700 B.C.E.) greatly influenced classical Greek attitudes toward death through his epic poems the *Iliad* and the *Odyssey*. Greek mythology was freely interpreted by writers following Homer, and belief in eternal judgment and retribution continued to evolve throughout this period.

Certain Greek philosophers also influenced people's outlook about death. Pythagoras (circa 580–500 B.C.E.), for example, advocated Orphic teachings about the cycle of birth and death. He opposed euthanasia ("good death," or mercy killing) because it disturbed the soul's journey toward final purification as planned by the gods. On the other hand, Socrates (circa 470–399 B.C.E.) and Plato (circa 428–347 B.C.E.) believed that people could choose to end their lives if they were no longer useful to themselves or the state.

Like Socrates and Plato, the classical Romans (circa 509–264 B.C.E.) believed that a person suffering from intolerable pain or an incurable illness should have the right to choose a "good death." Classical Greeks and Romans considered euthanasia a "mode of dying" that took into consideration a person's right to take control of an intolerable situation. They distinguished it from suicide, an act considered to be a shirking of responsibilities to one's family and to humankind.

THE MIDDLE AGES

During the Middle Ages in Europe (circa 500–1485), death—with its accompanying agonies—was accepted as a destiny everyone shared, but was still feared. As a defense against this phenomenon that could not be explained, medieval people confronted the death of a loved one together, as a community. Because medical practices in this era were crude and imprecise, the ill and dying person often endured prolonged suffering. However, this gave the dying individual an opportunity to put his or her affairs in order and confess sins. Then, with family and friends close by, the dying person bore death pains, because that was believed to be conduct befitting a good Christian.

Since dying was often a drawn-out process, medieval people sincerely believed they possessed supernatural premonitions about their own deaths. Dying persons often declared "I will die soon," and were said to have been warned about their impending deaths. When a person died suddenly, the death was considered uncommon and had very negative connotations. Since the whole community shared the experience of dying, sudden deaths jarred the accepted pattern of an already grim existence.

By the late Middle Ages the fear of death had intensified. The Black Death, the plague of 1347–51, wiped out more than 25 million people in Europe alone. Commoners watched not just their own kind stricken, but also saw church officials and royalty struck down: Queen Eleanor of Aragon and King Alfonso XI of Castile in France met with untimely deaths, and so did many at the papal court at Avignon, France. With their perceived "proper order" of existence shaken, the common people became increasingly preoccupied with their own deaths and the Last Judgment, God's final and certain determination of the character of each individual. Since the Last Judgment was closely linked to an individual's disposition to heaven or hell, it was frightening for those unprepared for sudden deaths.

THE RENAISSANCE

Obsession with death did not diminish with the "rebirth" of Western culture during the mid-fourteenth century. The new self-awareness and emphasis on man as the center of the universe further fueled the fear of dying. Rebelling against religion, people distanced themselves from the somewhat comforting concept of forewarning and the communally shared experience of death.

By the sixteenth century many individuals had stopped relying on church, family, and friends to help ease their passage to the next life. The religious upheaval of the Protestant Reformation of 1520, which emphasized

the individual nature of salvation, caused further uncertainties about death and dying.

The seventeenth century marked a shift from a religious to a more scientific exploration of death and dying. Lay people drifted away from the now disunited Christian Church toward the medical profession, seeking answers in particular to the question of "apparent death." In many cases, unconscious patients were mistakenly believed to be dead and were hurriedly prepared for burial by the clergy, only to "come back to life" during burial or while being transported to the cemetery.

But even physicians disagreed about what happened after death. Some believed that the body retained some kind of "sensibility," a belief shared by many in the general population, who preserved cadavers so that the bodies could "live on." On the other hand, physicians who ascribed to the teachings of the Catholic Church claimed that once the body was dead, the soul proceeded to its eternal fate. Since the body could not survive without the soul, these physicians would pronounce the cadaver permanently dead.

THE EIGHTEENTH CENTURY

The sensuousness that characterized the Baroque Period (circa 1550–1750) was often mirrored in people's fascination with the juxtaposition of love with death. In what was called "macabre eroticism," much art and literature of the time flamboyantly portrayed necrophilia (sexual intercourse by the living with the dead), although no historian ever confirmed such incidents.

The fear of apparent death that took root in the seventeenth century resurfaced with great intensity during the eighteenth century. Coffins were built with contraptions to enable any prematurely buried person to survive and communicate from the grave. (See Figure 1.1.)

For the first time, the Christian Church was blamed for hastily burying its "living dead," particularly as it had admonished the general population to abandon "pagan" burial traditions such as protracted mourning rituals. Such traditions were revived in the wake of apparent death incidents.

The Romantic Era

By the late eighteenth century, the European popular notion about death, with its accompanying terror and morbidity, underwent a transformation. Death became romantic and exotic. Influenced by the literary and artistic movements of the time, the concept of death left out the possibility of eternal damnation and came to be viewed as a passage to a utopian world where no evil existed.

THE NINETEENTH CENTURY

The beginning of the nineteenth century witnessed yet another shift in the attitude toward death and dying.

This change was partly a holdover from late eighteenth-century Romanticism, and partly due to the eighteenth-century Enlightenment. New ideas ushered in by Enlightenment thinkers changed people's outlook about their families. People began to think less about their own deaths and more about the deaths of their loved ones.

Bonds between family members grew stronger, and parents began the practice of naming their newborns. (Because the life expectancy of infants was short, children had previously seldom been given names at birth.) That, coupled with the romantic belief that families would reunite in the afterlife, meant that the death of a loved one, although still a cause for great sadness, was no longer thought to be such a dreaded event.

Concept of Death in America

The Europeans who settled in the New World brought with them many beliefs about death and dying. Death was accepted as a harsh fact of life. Even as family and friends were dying, the survivors went on with their lives. In the 1800s many Americans continued the practice of not naming their infants at birth because, just as in Europe, infant mortality was high.

Similar to the way it was thought of during the period of Romanticism (1795–1805), death was viewed as leading to another existence where the departed happily waited for the arrival of family and friends. Mourning was not so much for the dead, but for the indefinite length of separation until that final reunion. During this period, no mention was made of eternal rewards or of retribution, although the dying gave themselves gladly to God.

SPIRITUALISM. By the mid-nineteenth century, romantic solicitude for the deceased had taken on a new twist. In 1848 Maggie and Katie Fox of Hydesville, New York, claimed to have communicated with the spirit of a man murdered by a former tenant in their house. The practice of conducting "sittings" to contact the dead gained instant popularity. Mediums, such as the Fox sisters, were supposedly sensitive to "vibrations" from the disembodied spirits that temporarily lived in that part of the spirit world just outside the earth's limits.

This was not the first time people had tried to communicate with the dead, however. Spiritualism has been practiced in cultures all over the world. For example, many Native Americans believe shamans (priests or medicine men) have the power to communicate with the spirits of the dead. The Old Testament (I Samuel 28:7–19) recounts the visit of King Saul to a medium at Endor who summoned the spirit of the prophet Samuel, which predicted the death of Saul and his sons.

The mood in the United States in the 1860s and 1870s was ripe for Spiritualist seances. Virtually everyone had lost a son, husband, or other loved one during the Civil War

FIGURE 1.1

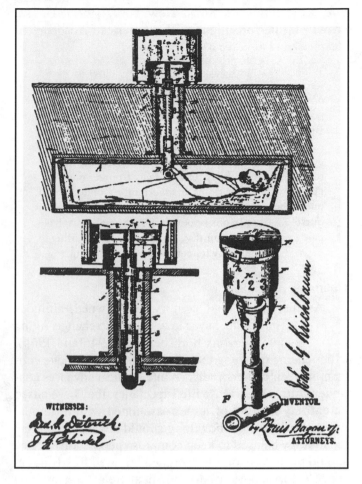

The 1882 patent sketch of a device for indicating life in buried people. *"Defining Death: Medical, Legal and Ethical Issues in the Determination of Death," U.S. Government Printing Office, Washington, DC, 1981*

(1861–65). Some survivors wanted assurances that their loved ones were all right; others were simply curious about life after death. Those who had drifted away from traditional Christianity embraced this new Spiritualism, which claimed scientific proof of survival after bodily death.

THE MODERN AGE

Modern medicine has played a vital role in the way a person dies and, consequently, the manner in which the dying process of a loved one affects relatives and friends. With advancements in medical technology, the dying process has become depersonalized, as it moves away from the familiar surroundings of home and family to the less familiar and sterile world of hospitals and strangers. Certainly, the institutionalization of death has not diminished the fear of dying. Now the fear of death also involves the fear of separation: for the living, the fear of not being present when a loved one dies, and for the dying, the prospect of facing death without the comforting presence of a loved one.

In *Dying Well: The Prospect for Growth at the End of Life* (G.P. Putnam's Sons, New York, 1997), Dr. Ira Byock, former president of the American Academy of Hospice and Palliative Medicine, noted:

> While death may cast a long shadow upon us as we journey through life, Americans typically refuse to notice.... We make jokes about death to diminish its power, using laughter to insulate ourselves from fear. But, then, when death approaches, we are stunned and feel unprepared to deal with the situation we face. We don't know the right thing to do or say, and so we may retreat.... In reflexively turning away from reminders of death, we have at times inadvertently isolated loved ones who needed our presence, and we [have] robbed ourselves of precious opportunities. Socially, we have paid dearly, and culturally, we are poorer for failing to explore the inherently human experience of dying.

Changing Attitudes

As the twenty-first century has dawned, attitudes about death and dying have slowly begun to change. Aging baby boomers (persons born between 1946 and 1964), experiencing or facing the death of their parents, are confronting their own mortality. While medical advances continue to strive to increase life expectancy, they have raised an entirely new set of issues associated with death and dying. For example, how long should advanced medical technology be used to keep comatose people alive? How should the elderly or incapacitated be cared for? Is it reasonable for people to stop medical treatment, or even actively end their lives, if that is what they wish?

The works of psychiatrist Dr. Elisabeth Kübler-Ross, including the pioneering book *On Death and Dying* (Macmillan Publishing Company, New York, 1969), have helped individuals from all walks of life confront the reality of death, and helped restore dignity to people who are dying. One of the most respected authorities on death, grief, and bereavement, Kübler-Ross and her theories have influenced medical practices undertaken at the end of life, as well as the attitudes of physicians, nurses, clergy, and others who care for the dying.

During the late 1960s, medical education was revealed to be seriously deficient in areas related to death and dying. However, initiatives underway in the late twentieth and early twenty-first centuries offer more comprehensive training about end-of-life care. With the introduction of in-home hospice care, more terminally ill people have the option of spending their final days at home with their loved ones. With the veil of secrecy lifted and open public discussions about issues related to the end of life, Americans appear more ready to learn about death, and learn from the dying.

Hospice Care

In medieval times, hospices were refuges for the sick, the needy, and travelers. The modern hospice movement developed in response to the need to provide humane care to terminally ill patients, while at the same time lending support to their families. An English physician, Dame Cicely Saunders, introduced the hospice concept in the United States. The care provided by hospice workers is called palliative care, and it aims to relieve patients' pain and the accompanying symptoms of terminal illness.

Hospice may refer to a place—a freestanding facility or designated floor in a hospital or nursing home—or to a program such as hospice-home care, where a team of health professionals helps the dying patient and family at home. Hospice teams may involve physicians, nurses, social workers, pastoral counselors, and trained volunteers.

WHY DO MANY CHOOSE HOSPICE? Hospice workers consider the patient and family the "unit of care" and focus their efforts on attending to emotional, psychological, and spiritual needs as well as physical comfort and well-being. Dr. Ira Byock, former president of the American Academy of Hospice and Palliative Medicine, explains the concept of hospice care in *Dying Well: The Prospect for Growth at the End of Life* (G.P. Putnam's Sons, New York, 1997):

> Hospice care differs noticeably from the modern medical approach to dying. Typically, as a hospice patient nears death, the medical details become almost automatic and attention focuses on the personal nature of this final transition—what the patient and family are going through emotionally and spiritually. In the more established system, even as people die, medical procedures remain the first priority. With hospice, they move to the background as the personal comes to the fore.

In Table 1.1, the Hospice Association of America, the largest lobbying group for hospice, lists the reasons for choosing hospice care.

Studies show that about 80 percent of terminally ill patients die in a hospital or a nursing home, many of them the object of over-treatment. The Institute of Medicine's Committee on Care at the End of Life described this over-treatment as involving both care that is inappropriate and care that is not wanted by the patient, even if some clinical benefit might be expected.

THE POPULATION SERVED. Hospice facilities served 393,200 people in 1995–96; of these, 82 percent eventually died. (See Figure 1.2.) About 67 percent of hospice patients were 65 years of age and older, and nearly 29 percent were 80 years of age or older. Male hospice patients numbered 197,700, while 195,500 were female. The vast majority were white (79 percent). (See Table 1.2.)

Although more than two-thirds (70.6 percent) of those admitted to hospice had cancer (neoplasms), patients with neurological diseases such as Alzheimer's disease, as well as people with heart, respiratory, and kidney diseases, were also served by hospice. (See Table 1.3.)

TABLE 1.1

Top ten reasons for choosing hospice

1. Holistic care. Hospice provides a comprehensive continuum of services, including nursing care; medical social services; physician services; counseling (including dietary, pastoral, and other); home care aide and homemaker services; short-term inpatient care (including both respite care and procedures necessary for pain control and symptom management); medical appliances and supplies (including drugs and biologicals); and physical, occupational, and speech therapies.

2. Patient-family focus. Hospice care differs from other forms of health care in that it focuses on the family and not just the terminally ill patient. Hospice provides palliative medical care for the patient, as well as psychological, social, and spiritual support for the patient and his or her family.

3. Cost effectiveness. Approximately 90% of hospice services are delivered in the home. Care delivered in the home, where a family member or friend is the primary caregiver, has been proven time and time again to be less expensive than hospitals or nursing homes.

4. Primary goal of pain relief. One of the largest fears of terminally ill patients is the pain associated with the illness. Hospice staff are trained specifically in palliative care or symptom control and comfort care. Through the effective combination of medication, equipment, and supplies, hospice is able to help the patient live his or her final days as peacefully and pain free as possible.

5. The people's choice. According to a 1993 study conducted by Louis Harris and Associates, Inc., Americans prefer the type of in-home care most associated with hospice over nursing home care by an overwhelming 79% to 14% margin. In 1996 a Gallup poll conducted for the National Hospice Organization reaffirmed the 1993 results: 7 in 10 adults reported they would seek a hospice program, if terminally ill, until death occurred naturally.

6. Medicare savings. In 1995 Lewin-VHI, Inc., conducted a study that found hospice beneficiaries who enrolled in hospice during the last month of life cost Medicare $2,884 less than the non-users. The study also concluded that Medicare's hospice program saves an estimated $1.68 for every dollar spent in the last month of life.

7. Bereavement services. Hospice realizes that care and support for the family does not end after the loss of a loved one. Specially trained counselors are available for family members and friends for up to 13 months following the patient's death.

8. Humane, compassionate care. More compelling than the amount of money saved is the fact that hospice is a humane and compassionate way to deliver health care and supportive services. Common among all hospices is the philosophy that every individual has the right to spend his or her last days in peace, comfort, and dignity. To assure this, hospice cares for the whole patient—emotionally, spiritually, and physically—as well as the patient's family.

9. Reduction of fear. All humans face death and most fear it. Hospice seeks to alleviate the fears most commonly associated with the prognosis of a terminal illness—the fear of pain related to the illness, the fear of becoming a burden to the family, and the fear of overwhelming medical costs.

10. Health care accessibility. As a majority of the services provided by hospice are delivered in the home, health care accessibility is easy for those who have no or limited means of traveling to and from a doctor's office, hospital, or other health care facility.

SOURCE: *Information About Hospice: A Consumer's Guide, Hospice Association of America* Washington, D.C., n.d.

TABLE 1.2

Number and percent distribution of home health and hospice care discharges by age, sex, race, and marital status, according to type of care received, 1995–1996

Discharge characteristic	All discharges	Type of care		All discharges	Type of care	
		Home health	Hospice		Home health	Hospice
		Number			Percent distribution	
Total	8,168,900	7,775,700	393,200	100.0	100.0	100.0
Age at admission						
Under 45 years	1,549,800	1,518,100	31,700	19.0	19.5	8.1
45-54 years.	493,700	462,600	31,200	6.0	5.9	7.9
55-64 years	710,500	652,400	58,200	8.7	8.4	14.8
65 years and over	5,402,700	5,137,500	265,200	66.1	66.1	67.5
65-69 years	874,500	840,400	34,100	10.7	10.8	8.7
70-74 years	1,085,900	1,024,600	61,300	13.3	13.2	15.6
75-79 years	1,024,400	967,400	57,000	12.5	12.4	14.5
80-84 years	1,152,600	1,104,300	48,300	14.1	14.2	12.3
85 years and over	1,265,400	1,200,900	64,500	15.5	15.4	16.4
Unknown	*	*	*	*	*	*
Sex						
Male	3,038,000	2,840,300	197,700	37.2	36.5	50.3
Female	5,131,000	4,935,400	195,500	62.8	63.5	49.7
Race						
White	5,190,800	4,880,500	310,300	63.5	62.8	78.9
Black and other	825,400	776,900	48,500	10.1	10.0	12.3
Black	620,200	576,300	43,900	7.6	7.4	11.2
Unknown	2,152,800	2,118,300	34,500	26.4	27.2	8.8
Marital status at discharge						
Married	3,064,700	2,874,400	190,300	37.5	37.0	48.4
Widowed	2,029,800	1,914,100	115,600	24.8	24.6	29.4
Divorced or separated	411,400	385,900	25,500	5.0	5.0	6.5
Single or never married	1,470,400	1,433,900	36,500	18.0	18.4	9.3
Unknown	1,192,600	1,167,300	25,300	14.6	15.0	6.4

*Figure does not meet standards of reliability or precision.

NOTES: Numbers may not add to totals because of rounding. Percents are based on the unrounded figures.

SOURCE: Barbara J. Haupt, "Table 6: Number and percent distribution of home health and hospice care discharges by age, sex, race, and marital status, according to type of care received: United States, 1995–96," *An Overview of Home Health and Hospice Care Patients: 1996 National Home and Hospice Care Survey,* Advance Data no. 297, Centers for Disease Control and Prevention, National Center for Health Statistics, Hyattsville, MD, 1998.

FIGURE 1.2

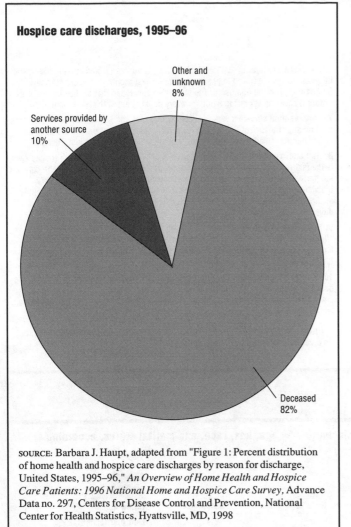

Hospice care discharges, 1995–96

Other and unknown 8%

Services provided by another source 10%

Deceased 82%

SOURCE: Barbara J. Haupt, adapted from "Figure 1: Percent distribution of home health and hospice care discharges by reason for discharge, United States, 1995–96," *An Overview of Home Health and Hospice Care Patients: 1996 National Home and Hospice Care Survey,* Advance Data no. 297, Centers for Disease Control and Prevention, National Center for Health Statistics, Hyattsville, MD, 1998

THE NATIONAL HOSPICE ORGANIZATION OPPOSES PHYSICIAN-ASSISTED SUICIDE. In 1996 the National Hospice Organization, or NHO (now known as the National Hospice and Palliative Care Organization, or NHPCO), a nonprofit organization created two decades earlier to champion the concept of death with dignity, reaffirmed a 1990 resolution opposing physician-assisted suicide. Responding to the 1997 Supreme Court rulings on physician-assisted suicide, John J. "Jay" Mahoney, then-president of the NHO, stated:

> A stark, and frankly incomplete, picture of end-of-life care has been presented to the public during the debate of assisted suicide. There is a perception that a terminally ill patient must choose between a painful existence devoid of value on one hand and assisted suicide on the other; however, there is another, more appropriate option—hospice care. People cannot make an informed choice unless they fully understand their options. Unfortunately, in the debate about assisted suicide, the option of hospice care is often overlooked.

HOSPICE ISN'T THE ANSWER FOR EVERYONE. Hospice, however, is not for everyone. To some, resorting to hospice seems like giving up hope and succumbing to death. Others might wish to endure their pain and suffering due to their religious or philosophical convictions. Still others might opt for quantity rather than quality of life. This phenomenon was reported by Joel Tsevat, et al., in "Health Values of Hospitalized Patients 80 Years or Older" (*The Journal of the American Medical Association,* vol. 279, no. 5, February 4, 1998). In this study, 414 hospitalized patients ages 80–98 were interviewed. Nearly 41 percent of patients were unwilling to exchange any time in their current state of health for a shorter life in excellent health.

TABLE 1.3

Number and percent distribution of home health and hospice care discharges by first-listed and all-listed diagnoses at admission, according to type of care received, 1995–96

	Primary diagnosis			All-listed diagnoses		
		Type of care			Type of care	
Admission diagnosis	All discharges	Home health	Hospice	All discharges	Home health	Hospice
	Number					
Total	8,168,900	7,775,700	393,200	21,953,900	21,089,100	864,800
Infectious and parasitic diseases	166,400	*151,200	*15,200	385,700	362,500	*23,200
Human immunodeficiency virus (HIV) disease	*36,700	*	*11,500	*57,200	*	*13,806
Neoplasms	948,200	670,700	277,500	1,661,300	1,228,800	432,500
Malignant neoplasms	923,000	649,000	274,000	1,560,600	1,131,700	428,900
Malignant neoplasm of trachea, bronchus, and lung	127,800	*41,700	86,000	213,800	110,000	103,800
Malignant neoplasm of breast	*175,600	*	17,300	*233,300	*204,600	18,700
Malignant neoplasm of prostate	34,600	*	12,900	*82,700	67,700	15,000
Endocrine, nutritional, and metabolic diseases and immunity disorders.	456,200	454,000	*	1,912,300	1,884,600	27,600
Diabetes mellitus	333,400	332,200	*	1,256,600	1,241,700	14,800
Diseases of the blood and blood-forming organs	*130,500	*129,700	*	488,500	482,800	*5,700
Mental disorders	138,800	133,800	*	728,400	707,000	21,400
Diseases of the nervous system and sense organs	271,700	259,200	*12,500	870,800	836,300	34,500
Diseases of the circulatory system	1,776,900	1,739,300	37,600	5,779,300	5,631,000	148,300
Essential hypertension	260,700	260,400	*	1,717,400	1,691,600	25,800
Heart disease	999,100	972,100	26,900	2,884,400	2,810,300	74,100
Diseases of the respiratory system	639,200	618,700	20,500	1,369,200	1,315,500	53,600
Diseases of the digestive system	314,100	310,800	*	973,700	958,200	15,500
Diseases of the genitourinary system	181,300	172,000	9,300	711,100	692,600	18,500
Diseases of the skin and subcutaneous tissue	190,100	189,400	*	421,800	417,200	*
Diseases of the musculoskeletal system and connective tissue	629,200	628,300	*	1,617,600	1,600,700	*16,800
Symptoms, signs, and ill-defined conditions	578,000	575,500	*	1,853,900	1,814,800	39,000
Injury and poisoning	974,400	974,300	*	1,343,800	1,338,200	*
Supplementary classification	565,500	565,200	*	1,420,200	1,407,200	13,100
All other diagnoses	174,900	171,200	*	416,500	411,700	*
Unknown or no diagnosis	*	*	*	...	...	...
	Percent distribution					
Total	100.0	100.0	100.0	100.0	100.0	100.0
Infectious and parasitic diseases	2.0	*1.9	*3.9	1.8	1.7	*2.7
Human immunodeficiency virus (HIV) disease	*0.4	*	*2.9	*0.3	*	*1.6
Neoplasms	11.6	8.6	70.6	7.6	5.8	50.0
Malignant neoplasms	11.3	8.3	69.7	7.1	5.4	49.6
Malignant neoplasm of trachea, bronchus, and lung	1.6	*0.5	21.9	1.0	0.5	12.0
Malignant neoplasm of breast	*2.1	*	4.4	*1.0	*1.0	2.2
Malignant neoplasm of prostate	0.4	*	3.3	*0.4	*0.3	1.7
Endocrine, nutritional, and metabolic diseases and immunity disorders	5.6	5.8	*	8.7	8.9	3.2
Diabetes mellitus	4.1	4.3	*	5.7	5.9	1.7
Diseases of the blood and blood-forming organs	*1.6	*1.7	*	2.2	2.3	*0.7
Mental disorders	1.7	1.7	*	3.3	3.4	2.5
Diseases of the nervous system and sense organs	3.3	3.3	*3.2	4.0	4.0	4.0
Diseases of the circulatory system	21.8	22.4	9.6	26.3	26.7	17.1
Essential hypertension	3.2	3.3	*	7.8	8.0	3.0
Heart disease	12.2	12.5	6.8	13.1	13.3	8.6
Diseases of the respiratory system	7.8	8.0	5.2	6.2	6.2	6.2
Diseases of the digestive system	3.8	4.0	*	4.4	4.5	1.8
Diseases of the genitourinary system	2.2	2.2	*2.4	3.2	3.3	2.1
Diseases of the skin and subcutaneous tissue	2.3	2.4	*	1.9	2.0	*
Diseases of the musculoskeletal system and connective tissue	7.7	8.1	*	7.4	7.6	*1.9
Symptoms, signs, and ill-defined conditions	7.1	7.4	*	8.4	8.6	4.5
Injury and poisoning	11.9	12.5	*	6.1	6.3	*
Supplementary classification	6.9	7.3	*	6.5	6.7	1.5
All other diagnoses	2.1	2.2	*	1.9	2.0	*
Unknown or no diagnosis	*	*	*	...	...	...

*Figure does not meet standard of reliability or precision.

... Category not applicable.

NOTES: Numbers may not add to totals because of rounding. Percents are based on the unrounded figures.

SOURCE: Adapted from Barbara J. Haupt, "Table 8: Number and percent distribution of home health and hospice care discharges by first-listed and all-listed diagnoses at admission…," *An Overview of Home Health and Hospice Care Patients: 1996 National Home and Hospice Care Survey,* Advance Data no. 297, Centers for Disease Control and Prevention, National Center for Health Statistics, Hyattsville, MD, 1998.

CHAPTER 2

REDEFINING DEATH

TRADITIONAL DEFINITION OF DEATH

The processes of human life are sustained by oxygen. Respiration and blood circulation provide the body's cells with the oxygen needed to perform their life functions. When an injury or a disease compromises respiration and circulation, a breakdown in oxygen supply occurs. As a result, the cells, deprived of essential life-sustaining oxygen, deteriorate. Using these criteria, defining death was once quite simple—a person was considered dead once he or she stopped breathing or was without a detectable heartbeat.

A NEW CRITERION FOR DEATH

Advances in medical science have complicated the definition of death. Life-saving measures such as cardiopulmonary resuscitation (CPR) or defibrillation (electrical shock) can restart cardiac activity. The development of the mechanical respirator in the 1950s also prompted a change in the concept of death. An unconscious patient, unable to breathe without assistance, could be kept alive with a respirator and, based on the heart-and-lung criterion, the patient could not be declared dead.

Further complicating the issue was the transplantation of the first human heart. Experimental organ transplantation had been performed since the early 1900s. In the 1960s, transplantation of organs such as kidneys became routine practice. Kidneys could be harvested from a patient whose heart had stopped and who therefore could be declared legally dead. A successful heart transplant, on the other hand, required a beating heart from a "dead" donor. On December 3, 1967, South African surgeon Christiaan Barnard transplanted a heart from a fatally injured accident victim into Louis Washkansky.

Physicians who had been debating how to best handle patients whose life functions were supported mechanically now faced a new dilemma. With the first successful heart transplant, such patients now became potential heart donors, and it became necessary to ensure that a patient was truly dead before the heart was actually removed. Thus physicians proposed a new criterion for death—irreversible cessation of brain activity, or what many termed "brain death."

The Harvard Criteria

In 1968 the Ad Hoc Committee of the Harvard Medical School to Examine the Definition of Brain Death was organized. Also known as the Harvard Brain Death Committee, its goal was to redefine death. On August 5, 1968, the committee published its report, "A Definition of Irreversible Coma," in *The Journal of the American Medical Association.*

This landmark report, known as the Harvard Criteria, listed the following guidelines for identifying irreversible coma:

• Unreceptivity and unresponsivity—the patient is completely unaware of externally applied stimuli and inner need. He/she does not respond even to intensely painful stimuli.

• No movements or breathing—the patient shows no sign of spontaneous movements and spontaneous respiration and does not respond to pain, touch, sound, or light.

• No reflexes—the pupils of the eyes are fixed and dilated. The patient shows no eye movements even when the ear is flushed with ice water or the head is turned. He/she does not react to harmful stimuli and exhibits no tendon reflexes.

• Flat electroencephalogram (EEG)—this shows lack of electrical activity in the cerebral cortex.

The Harvard Criteria could not be used unless reversible causes of brain dysfunction, such as drug intoxication and hypothermia (abnormally low body temperature—below 32.2 degrees centigrade or 89.96 degrees

Fahrenheit core temperature), had been ruled out. The committee further recommended that the four tests be repeated 24 hours after the initial test.

Although the Harvard committee stated, "Our primary purpose is to define irreversible coma as a new criterion for death," it really did not redefine death. The committee, made up mostly of physicians, simply declared that brain death was the new criterion for death. A patient who met the four guidelines could be declared dead, and his or her respirator could be withdrawn. The committee added, however, "We are concerned here only with those comatose individuals who have no discernible central nervous system activity." Persons in a persistent vegetative state were not included because they can breathe on their own, while brain-dead persons can breathe only with the help of a respirator.

Criticisms of the Harvard Criteria

In 1981 then-President Ronald Reagan assigned a national commission to study the task of defining death. The President's Commission for the Study of Ethical Problems in Medicine and Biomedical and Behavioral Research reported that "the 'Harvard Criteria' have been found to be quite reliable. Indeed, no case has yet been found that met these criteria and regained any brain functions despite continuation of respirator support."

The President's Commission, however, noted the following deficiencies of the Harvard Criteria:

- The phrase "irreversible coma" is misleading. Coma is a condition of a living person. A person lacking in brain functions is dead and, therefore, beyond the condition called coma.

- The Harvard Brain Death Committee failed to realize that spinal cord reflexes can continue or resume activity even after the brain stops functioning.

- "Unreceptivity" cannot be tested in an unresponsive person who has lost consciousness.

- The committee had not been "sufficiently explicit and precise" in expressing the need for adequate testing of brainstem reflexes, especially apnea (absence of the impulse to breathe, leading to an inability to breathe spontaneously). Adequate testing to eliminate drug and metabolic intoxication as possible causes of the coma had also not been spelled out explicitly. Metabolic intoxication refers to the accumulation of toxins (poisons) in the blood resulting from kidney or liver failure. Though these toxins can severely impair brain functioning and cause coma, the condition is potentially reversible.

- Although all persons who satisfy the Harvard Criteria are dead (with irreversible cessation of whole-brain functions), many dead individuals cannot maintain circulation long enough for re-testing after a 24-hour interval.

THE GOVERNMENT REDEFINES DEATH

In 1981, pursuant to the provision of Public Law 95-622, the President's Commission published *Defining Death: A Report on the Medical, Legal and Ethical Issues in the Determination of Death* (U.S. Government Printing Office, Washington, D.C.). In its report to President Ronald Reagan and the Congress, the Commission proposed a model statute, the Uniform Determination of Death Act, the guidelines of which would be used to define death:

- [Determination of Death.] An individual who has sustained either (1) irreversible cessation of circulation and respiratory functions, or (2) irreversible cessation of all functions of the entire brain, including the brain stem, is dead. A determination of death must be made in accordance with accepted medical standards.

- [Uniformity of Construction and Application.] This act shall be applied and construed to effectuate its general purpose to make uniform the law with respect to the subject of this Act among states enacting it.

Brain Death

The President's Commission incorporated two formulations or concepts of the "whole-brain definition" of death. The Commission claimed that these two concepts were "actually mirror images of each other. The Commission has found them to be complementary; together they enrich one's understanding of the 'definition' [of death]."

The first whole-brain formulation states that death occurs when the three major organs—the heart, lungs, and brain—suffer an irreversible functional breakdown. These organs are closely interrelated, so that if one stops functioning permanently, the other two would also stop working. While traditionally, the absence of the "vital signs" of respiration and circulation have signified death, they are simply a sign that the brain, the core organ, has permanently ceased to function. Even if individual cells or organs continue to live, the body as a whole cannot survive for long. Therefore, death can be declared even before the whole system shuts down.

The second whole-brain formulation "identifies the functioning of the whole brain as the hallmark of life because the brain is the regulator of the body's integration." Since the brain is the seat of consciousness and the director of all bodily functions, when the brain dies, the person is considered dead.

Reason for Two Definitions of Death

The President's Commission claimed that, in redefining death, its aim was to "supplement rather than supplant [take the place of] the existing legal concept." The brain-death criteria were not being introduced to define a new kind of death. In most cases, the cardiopulmonary definition of death would be sufficient. Only comatose patients on respirators would be diagnosed using the brain-death criteria.

Criteria for Determination of Death

The Commission did not include in the proposed Uniform Determination of Death Act any specific medical criteria for diagnosing brain death. Instead it had a group of medical consultants develop a summary of currently accepted medical practices. The Commission stated that "such criteria—particularly as they relate to diagnosing death on neurological grounds—will be continually revised by the biomedical community in light of clinical experience and new scientific knowledge." These Criteria for Determination of Death read as follows (with medical details omitted here):

1. An individual with irreversible cessation of circulatory and respiratory functions is dead. A) Cessation is recognized by an appropriate clinical examination. B) Irreversibility is recognized by persistent cessation of functions during an appropriate period of observation and/or trial of therapy.

2. An individual with irreversible cessation of all functions of the entire brain, including the brainstem, is dead. A) Cessation is recognized when evaluation discloses that cerebral cortical and brainstem functions are absent. B) Irreversibility is recognized when evaluation discloses that: the cause of coma is established and is sufficient to account for the loss of brain functions; the possibility of recovery of any brain functions is excluded; and the cessation of all brain functions persists for an appropriate period of observation and/or trial of therapy.

The Criteria for Determination of Death further warn that conditions such as drug intoxication, metabolic intoxication, and hypothermia may be confused with brain death. Physicians should practice caution when dealing with young children and persons in shock. Infants and young children, who have more resistance to neurological damage, have been known to recover brain functions. Shock victims, on the other hand, might not test well due to a reduction in blood circulation to the brain.

Since the development of these criteria, most countries have adopted the brain death concept of death. Some countries have not done so because the definition is contrary to cultural or religious beliefs. For example, in Japan it is believed that the soul lingers in the body for some time after death. Traditional respect for elders has also precluded consent to donate their organs, especially if the brain-dead person is still breathing.

Brain Death and Persistent Vegetative State

In the past, persons who suffered severe head injuries usually died from apnea (absence of the impulse to breathe, leading to an inability to breathe spontaneously).

FIGURE 2.1

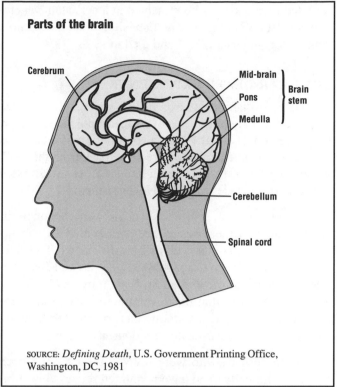

Parts of the brain

SOURCE: *Defining Death,* U.S. Government Printing Office, Washington, DC, 1981

Today, rapid emergency medical intervention allows such persons to be placed on respirators before breathing stops. In some cases, the primary brain damage may be reversible, and unassisted breathing eventually resumes. In many cases, however, brain damage is irreversible, and if the respirator is not disconnected, it will continue to pump blood to the dead brain.

The brain stem, traditionally called the lower brain, is usually more resistant to oxygen deprivation, or anoxia. Less serious brain injury may cause irreversible damage to the cerebrum, or higher brain, but may spare the brain stem. (See Figure 2.1.) When this occurs, the patient goes into a persistent vegetative state (PVS), also called persistent noncognitive state. PVS patients, lacking in the higher-brain functions, are "awake but unaware." They swallow, grimace when in pain, yawn, open their eyes, and may even breathe without a respirator.

The case of Karen Ann Quinlan has called attention to the ramifications of the persistent vegetative state. In 1975 Quinlan suffered a cardiopulmonary arrest after ingesting a combination of alcohol and drugs. In 1976 Joseph Quinlan was granted court permission to discontinue artificial respiration for his then-comatose daughter. Even after life support was removed, Karen remained in a persistent vegetative state until she died of multiple infections in 1985.

Patients in a persistent vegetative state are not dead, and so the brain-death criteria do not apply to them. They can survive for years with artificial feeding and antibiotics for possible infections. The President's Commission reported on a patient who remained in a persistent vegetative state for 37 years: Elaine Esposito, who lapsed into a coma after surgery in 1941 and died in 1978.

THE NEAR-DEATH EXPERIENCE

The term "near-death experience" was first used by Dr. Raymond Moody in *Life After Life* (Stackpole Books, Harrisburg, Pennsylvania, 1976), a compilation of interviews with people who claimed to have come back from the dead. A decade earlier, Dr. Elizabeth Kübler-Ross investigated out-of-body episodes recounted by her patients.

The near-death experience is not a phenomenon limited to modern times. It has been recounted in various forms of mysticism, as well as by well-known historical figures such as Plato (circa 428–347 B.C.E.) and Benedictine historian and theologian St. Bede (circa 672–735). It appears, however, that the development and administration of emergency resuscitation has contributed to widespread reports of near-death experiences.

Some persons who were revived after having been declared clinically dead have recounted remarkably similar patterns of experiences. They reported leaving their body and watching, in a detached manner, while others tried to save that body. They felt no pain, but rather complete serenity. After traveling through a tunnel, they encountered a radiant light and a magnificent spiritual being. Some claimed they had met friends and relatives who had died; many attested to seeing their whole lives replayed and of ultimately being given either a choice or a command to return to their bodies.

Many people who have had a near-death experience believe that they have experienced a spiritual event of great importance. For example, they may believe that they saw, or even entered, the afterlife. Skeptics, however, attribute the near-death phenomenon to brain malfunction in someone who is near death or, if the person has been on medication, to the effects of drugs. Studies conducted during the 1990s indicated that the near-death experience might be related to one or more physical changes in the brain. These changes include the gradual onset of anoxia (oxygen deprivation) in the brain; residual electrical activity in the brain; the release of endorphins in response to stress; or drug-induced hallucinations produced by drug therapies used during resuscitation attempts or resulting from prior drug abuse.

CHAPTER 3
THE END OF LIFE—ETHICAL CONSIDERATIONS

Defining death has become a complex matter. Innovative medical technology, while saving many lives, has also blurred the lines between life and death. The controversy about the definition of death is but one of the ethical issues, or principles of moral conduct, related to end-of-life care and decision-making. For example, should a child request the withdrawal of nutrition and hydration from a parent in a persistent vegetative state, knowing that parent's respect for the sanctity of life? Does a physician honor a patient's do-not-resuscitate request when it goes against the physician's ethical convictions? Who should determine when medical care is futile and no longer benefits the dying patient?

The answers to questions about care at the end of life, as well as decisions made by persons who are dying and by their loved ones, vary in response to cultural influences, family issues, and spiritual beliefs. Historical, social, cultural, political, and religious convictions shape ethical beliefs about death and guide the actions of health care professionals and persons who are terminally ill. For people of faith, religious convictions are vitally important when making end-of-life decisions.

RELIGIOUS TEACHINGS

All major religions consider life sacred. When it comes to death and dying, they take seriously the fate of the soul, be it eternal salvation (as in Christian belief) or reincarnation (as in Buddhist philosophy).

Roman Catholicism

According to Catholic teachings, death is contrary to God's plan for humankind. When God created man and woman, He did not intend for them to die. But when they disobeyed God in the Garden of Eden, physical death was the consequence of their sin. Jesus Christ, the Son of God, out of love for humankind, was born into the world and died as a man. God raised His Son from the dead to live eternally with Him, and Jesus promised humankind the same opportunity. Thus Jesus "transformed the curse of death into a blessing" (*Catechism of the Catholic Church,* Ignatius Press, San Francisco, California, 1994).

HISTORY. Early Christians believed that God was the giver of life, and therefore He alone could take life away. They viewed euthanasia as usurping that divine right. St. Augustine (circa 354–430), the great philosopher of early Christianity, taught that man must accept suffering because it comes from God. Suffering not only helps one grow spiritually, but also prepares Christians for the eternal joy that God has in store for them. Moreover, the healthy were exhorted to minister to the sick, not for the purpose of helping to permanently end their suffering, but in order to ease their pain.

St. Thomas Aquinas (circa 1225–74), considered to be one of the greatest Catholic theologians, taught that ending one's suffering by ending one's life was sinful. To help another take his or her life was just as sinful. However, in 1516 Sir Thomas More (circa 1477–1535), an English statesman, humanist, and loyal defender of the Catholic Church, published *Utopia,* which described an ideal country governed by reason. More argued that if a disease is not only incurable but also causes intractable pain, it is permissible to free the sufferer from his or her painful existence. This was a major departure from the medieval acceptance of suffering and death as the earthly price to be paid for eternal life.

PRINCIPLE OF DOUBLE EFFECT. Catholic moral theologians were said to have developed the ethical principle known as the "Rule of Double Effect." According to this principle, "Effects that would be morally wrong if caused intentionally are permissible if foreseen but unintended." For example, a physician prescribes an increased dosage of morphine, a painkiller, to ease a patient's pain, not to bring about his or her death. However, it is foreseen that the potent dosage may depress the patient's respiration and hasten death. *Catechism of the Catholic Church* states:

> The use of painkillers to alleviate the sufferings of the dying, even at the risk of shortening their days, can be morally in conformity with human dignity if death is not willed as either an end or a means, but only foreseen and tolerated as inevitable.

ON EUTHANASIA. Over the years, Catholic theologians have debated balancing the preservation of God-given life with the moral issue of continuing medical treatments that are of no apparent value to patients. In 1957 Pope Pius XII stated that if a patient is hopelessly ill, physicians may discontinue heroic measures "to permit the patient, already virtually dead, to pass on in peace" ("The Prolongation of Life"). He added that if the patient is unconscious, relatives may request withdrawal of life support under certain conditions.

In *Nutrition and Hydration: Moral and Pastoral Reflections* (1992), the Committee for Pro-Life Activities of the National Conference of Catholic Bishops (NCCB, Washington, D.C.) states,

> In the final stage of dying, one is not obligated to prolong the life of a patient by every possible means: "When inevitable death is imminent in spite of the means used, it is permitted in conscience to make the decision to refuse forms of treatment that would only secure a precarious and burdensome prolongation of life, so long as the normal care due the sick person in similar cases is not interrupted."

Eastern Orthodox Church

The Eastern Orthodox Church resulted from the division between eastern and western Christianity during the eleventh century. Differences in doctrines and politics, among other things, caused the separation. The Eastern Orthodox Church does not have a single worldwide leader like the Roman Catholic Pope. Instead, national jurisdictions called "Sees" are each governed by a bishop.

Eastern Orthodoxy relies on the Scriptures, tradition, and the decrees of the first seven ecumenical councils to regulate its daily conduct. In matters of present-day morality, such as the debates on end-of-life issues, contemporary Orthodox ethicists explore possible courses of action that are in line with the "sense of the Church." The sense of the Church is deduced from Church laws and dissertations of the Fathers of the Church, as well as previous council decisions. Their recommendations are subject to further review. The Eastern Orthodox Church currently has no official position on euthanasia.

Protestantism

The different denominations of Protestantism have varying positions about euthanasia. While many hold that active euthanasia is morally wrong, they believe that pro-longing life by extraordinary measures is not necessary. In other words, though few would condone active euthanasia, many accept passive euthanasia. (Active euthanasia involves the hastening of death through the administration of lethal drugs. Passive euthanasia refers to withdrawing life support or medical interventions necessary to sustain life, such as removing a patient from a ventilator.) Among those religions that support the latter view are the Jehovah's Witnesses, the Church of Jesus Christ of Latter-Day Saints (Mormons), the Lutheran Churches, the Reformed Presbyterians, the Presbyterian Church in America, the Christian Life Commission of the Southern Baptist Convention, and the General Association of the General Baptists.

Some denominations have no official policy on active or passive euthanasia. However, many individual ethicists and representatives within these churches agree with other denominations that active euthanasia is morally wrong but that futile life supports serve no purpose. Among these churches are the Seventh Day Adventists, the Episcopal Church, and the United Methodist Church.

Christian Scientists believe that prayer heals all diseases. They claim that illnesses are mental in origin and therefore cannot be cured by outside intervention, such as medical help. Some also believe that seeking medical help while praying diminishes or even cancels the effectiveness of the prayers. Since God can heal even those diseases others see as incurable, euthanasia has no practical significance among Christian Scientists.

The Unitarian Universalist Association, a union of the Unitarian and Universalist Churches, is perhaps the most liberal when it comes to the right to die. The Association believes that "human life has inherent dignity, which may be compromised when life is extended beyond the will or ability of a person to sustain that dignity." Furthermore, "Unitarian Universalists advocate the right to self-determination in dying, and the release from civil or criminal penalties of those who, under proper safeguards, act to honor the right of terminally ill patients to select the time of their own deaths."

Judaism

In the United States, there are three main branches of Judaism. The Orthodox tradition strictly adheres to Jewish laws. Conservative Judaism advocates adapting Jewish precepts to a changing world, but all changes must be consistent with Jewish laws and tradition. Reform Judaism, while accepting the ethical laws as coming from God, generally considers the other laws of Judaism as "instructional but not binding."

Like the Roman Catholics, Jews believe that life is precious because it is a gift from God. No one has the right to extinguish life, because one's life is not his or hers in the first place. Generally, rabbis from all branches of

Judaism agree that active euthanasia is not morally justified. It is tantamount to murder, which is forbidden by the Torah (the Five Books of Moses). Moreover, Jewish teaching holds that men and women are stewards entrusted with the preservation of God's gift of life and therefore are obliged to hold on to that life as long as possible.

PROLONGING LIFE VERSUS HASTENING DEATH. While Jewish tradition maintains that a devout believer must do everything possible to prolong life, this admonition is subject to interpretation even among Orthodox Jews.

The Torah and the Talmud provide the principles and laws that guide Jews. The Talmud, the definitive rabbinical compilation of Jewish laws, lore, and commentary, has provided continuity to Jewish culture by interpreting the Torah and adapting it to the constantly changing situations of Jewish people.

On the subject of prolonging life versus hastening death, when that life is clearly nearing death, the Talmud narrates a number of situations involving persons who are considered "goses" (literally, the death rattle is in the patient's throat, or one whose death is imminent). Scholars often refer to the story of Rabbi Haninah ben Teradyon, who, during the second century, was condemned to be burned to death by the Romans. To prolong his agonizing death, the Romans wrapped him in some wet material. At first the rabbi refused to hasten his own death; however, he later agreed to have the wet material removed, thus bringing about a quicker death.

Some Jews interpret this Talmudic narration to mean that in the final stage of a person's life, it is permissible to remove any hindrance to the dying process. In this modern age of medicine, this may mean implementing a patient's wish, such as the do-not-resuscitate directive or the withdrawal of artificial life support.

Islam

Islam was founded by the prophet Muhammad in the seventh century. The Qur'an (also transliterated as Koran), which is God's revelations to Muhammad, and the Sunnah, Muhammad's teachings and deeds, are the sources of Islamic beliefs and practice. Although there are numerous sects and cultural diversities within the religion, all Muslims (followers of Islam) are bound by a total submission to the will of Allah, or God. The basic doctrines of Allah's revelations were systematized into definitive rules and regulations that now comprise the Shari'ah, or the religious law that governs the life of Muslims.

Muslims look to the Shari'ah for ethical guidance in all aspects of life, including medicine. Sickness and pain are part of life and must be accepted as Allah's will. They should be viewed as a means to atone for one's sins. Death, on the other hand, is simply a passage to another existence in the afterlife. Those who die after leading a righteous life will merit the true life on Judgment Day. The Qur'an (chapter 2, verse 28) states, "How do you disbelieve in God seeing you were dead and He gave you life and then He shall cause you to die, then He shall give you life, then unto Him you shall be returned?"

Islam teaches that life is a gift from Allah; therefore, no one can end it except Allah. The prophet Muhammad said, "Whosoever takes poison and thus kills himself, his poison will be in his hand; he will be tasting it in Hell, always abiding therein, and being accommodated therein forever." While an ailing person does not have the right to choose death, even if he or she is suffering, Muslims heed the following admonition (*Islamic Code of Medical Ethics,* Kuwait Document, Kuwait Rabi 1, 1401, First International Conference on Islamic Medicine, 1981):

> [The] doctor is well advised to realize his limit and not transgress it. If it is scientifically certain that life cannot be restored, then it is futile to diligently [maintain] the vegetative state of the patient by heroic means.... It is the process of life that the doctor aims to maintain and not the process of dying. In any case, the doctor shall not take a positive measure to terminate the patient's life.

Hinduism

The Eastern religious tradition of Hinduism is founded on the principle of reincarnation—the cycle of life, death, and physical rebirth. Hindus believe that death and dying are intricately interwoven with life, and that the individual soul undergoes a series of physical life cycles before uniting with Brahman, or God. "Karma" refers to the ethical consequences of a person's actions during a previous life, which determine the quality of his or her present life. A person cannot change nor escape his or her karma. By conforming to "dharma," the religious and moral law, an individual is able to fulfill obligations from the past life. Life is sacred because it offers one the chance to perform good acts toward the goal of ending the cycle of rebirths.

A believer in Hinduism, therefore, views pain and suffering as personal karma, and serious illness as a consequence of past misdeeds. Death is simply a passage to another rebirth, which brings one closer to God. Artificial medical treatments to sustain life are not recommended, and medical intervention to end life is discouraged. Active euthanasia simply interrupts one's karma and the soul's evolution toward final liberation from reincarnations.

Buddhism

Buddhism, like Hinduism, is based on a cycle of reincarnation. To Buddhists, the goals of every life are emancipation from "samsara," the compulsory cycle of rebirths, and attainment of "nirvana," enlightenment or bliss. Like the Hindus, Buddhists believe that sickness, death, and karma are interrelated. Followers of Siddhartha Gautama, also called Buddha (circa 563–483 B.C.E.), the founder of Buddhism, claim that Buddha advised against taking too strict a position when it comes to issues such as the right to die.

The fourteenth Dalai Lama, Tenzin Gyatso, spiritual leader of Tibetan Buddhism, has commented on the use of mechanical life support when the patient has no chance to recover. Rather than advocating or condemning passive euthanasia, he advised that each case be considered individually (Sogyal Rinpoche, *The Tibetan Book of Living and Dying,* Harper San Francisco, 1992):

> If there is no such chance for positive thoughts [Buddhists believe that a dying person's final thoughts determine the circumstances of his next life], and in addition a lot of money is being spent by relatives simply in order to keep someone alive, then there seems to be no point. But each case must be dealt with individually; it is very difficult to generalize.

BIOETHICS AND MEDICAL PRACTICE

Since ancient times, medical practice has been concerned with ethical issues. But only since the last half of the twentieth century have the rapid advances in medicine given rise to so many ethical dilemmas. In matters of death and dying, the debate continues on such issues as physicians' honoring a patient's do-not-resuscitate order, withholding food and fluids, and withdrawing artificial respiration.

There are four basic tenets of bioethics—autonomy, beneficence, nonmaleficence, and justice. Autonomy refers to self-rule and self-determination. Beneficence is action that is in the best interest of the patient. Nonmaleficence means to do no harm. Justice is the practice of treating patients in comparable circumstances the same way, and also refers to equitable distribution of resources, risks, and costs. Although bioethics is subject to change and reinterpretation, medical practice continues to rely on these principles to guide the actions of physicians and other health care providers.

The Hippocratic Oath

The earliest document on medical ethics is generally attributed to Hippocrates (circa 460–370 B.C.E.), known as the father of medicine. For more than 2,000 years, the Hippocratic Oath has been adopted by Western physicians as a code of ethics, defining their conduct in the discharge of their duties. In part, the oath states:

> I will follow that method of treatment, which, according to my ability and judgment, I consider for the benefit of my patients, and abstain from whatever is deleterious [harmful] and mischievous. I will give no deadly medicine to anyone if asked, nor suggest any such counsel.

Nonetheless, some scholars claim that the giving of "deadly medicine" did not refer to euthanasia. During the time of Hippocrates, helping a suffering person end his or her life was common practice. The oath might therefore have been more an admonition to the medical profession to avoid acting as an accomplice to murder, rather than to refrain from the practice of euthanasia.

Some physicians believe that literal interpretation of the oath is not necessary. It simply offers guidelines that allow for adaptation to modern-day situations. In fact, in 1948 the World Medical Association modified the Hippocratic Oath to call attention to the atrocities committed by Nazi physicians. The Declaration of Geneva reads, in part:

> I will practice medicine with conscience and dignity. The health and life of my patient will be my first consideration.... I will not permit consideration of race, religion, nationality, party politics, or social standing to intervene between my duty and my patient. I will maintain the utmost respect for human life from the time of its conception. Even under threat, I will not use my knowledge contrary to the laws of humanity.

The Physician's Role

Even in ancient times, as can be gleaned from the Hippocratic Oath, physicians believed they knew what was best for their patients. Patients relied on their doctors' ability and judgment, and usually did not question the treatments prescribed. Doctors were not even required to tell their patients the details of their illness, even if they were terminally ill.

Beginning in the 1960s many patients assumed a more active role in their medical care. The emphasis on preventive medicine encouraged people to take responsibility for their own health. Physicians were faced with a new breed of patients who wanted to be active participants in their health care. Patients also wanted to know more about modern technologies and procedures that were evolving in medicine. With this new health consciousness, physicians and hospitals assumed the responsibility for informing and educating patients, and increasingly were legally liable for failing to inform patients of the consequences of medical treatments and procedures.

To compound the complexity of the changing patient-physician relationship, modern technology, which could sometimes prolong life, was also prolonging death. Historically, physicians had been trained to prevent and combat death, rather than to deal with dying patients, to communicate with the patient and the family about a terminal illness, to prepare them for an imminent death, or to respond to a patient requesting assisted suicide.

Until the late 1990s, medical education programs offered very little in the area of end-of-life care. Drs. J. Andrew Billings and Susan Block reported that a 1991 survey of medical school deans revealed that only 11 percent of schools offered a full-term course on death and dying ("Palliative Care in Undergraduate Medical Education," *The Journal of the American Medical Association,* vol. 278, no. 9, September 3, 1997). About 52 percent offered death education as part of other required courses, while another 30 percent offered only one or two lectures as part of another course. In 1997, while some medical schools offered information on dealing with death as part of other required courses, only 5 of 126 medical schools in the country offered a separate required course on death and dying.

This situation is improving. The EPEC Project (Education for Physicians on End-of-Life Care), developed in 1998 by the American Medical Association (AMA), is an ambitious training program that aims to provide physicians with the knowledge they need to care for dying patients. The curriculum emphasizes development of skills and competence in the areas of communication, ethical decision-making, palliative care, psychosocial issues, and pain and symptom management. The program became fully operational in 1999 and provides curricula to all new AMA members, leaders of medical societies, medical school deans, and major medical organizations.

In addition to acquiring the training and skills to effectively respond to the needs of dying patients, end-of-life education programs encourage physicians and other health care providers to examine their own feelings, values, and beliefs about dying. By questioning and understanding deeply held beliefs, such as the perception of a patient's death as a professional failure, health care professionals are less likely to feel conflicted or uncomfortable when caring for dying patients and their families.

Recent Ethical Guidelines for Physicians

Physicians are trained to save lives, not to let people die. Advanced medical technology, with respirators and parenteral nutrition (artificial feeding devices that provide nutrition to an otherwise unconscious patient), can prolong the process of dying. Dr. Ira Byock, in *Dying Well: The Prospect for Growth at the End of Life* (G.P. Putnam's Sons, New York, 1997), admitted:

> A strong presumption throughout my medical education was that all seriously ill people required vigorous life-prolonging treatments, including those who were expected to die, even patients with advanced, chronic illness such as widespread cancer, end-stage congestive heart failure, and kidney or liver failure. It even extended to patients who saw death as a relief from the suffering caused by their illness.

The Council on Ethical and Judicial Affairs of the American Medical Association published guidelines for physicians dealing with patients in non-emergency situations ("Decisions Near the End of Life," *The Journal of the American Medical Association,* vol. 267, no. 16, April 22, 1992). A summary of these guidelines follows:

- Following the principle of patient autonomy, physicians must respect the decision of a competent patient to forego life-sustaining treatment (any treatment that prolongs life without curing the conditions of the ill-

ness). Examples of life-sustaining treatment are mechanical respiration, dialysis, chemotherapy, antibiotics, and artificial nutrition and hydration.

- Medical ethics allows for the likelihood that withholding or withdrawing life-sustaining treatment per patient's request might result in death. Neither one is a harmful treatment but a foregoing of a treatment.

- Physicians must ease a patient's pain and suffering even if to do so may possibly hasten death.

- Physicians must not perform euthanasia or assist in suicide.

Another prominent professional medical organization, the American College of Physicians (ACP), revised its recommendations about end-of-life care in the fourth edition of its code of ethics, *The American College of Physicians Ethics Manual* (ACP, Philadelphia, 1998). The manual's guidelines for decision-making near the end of life emphasize that capable and informed adults nearly always have the legal and ethical right to refuse treatment. They advise physicians to practice empathy, to compromise, and to negotiate with patients who wish to forego recommended treatment. The guidelines offer an approach to clinical ethical decision-making that not only involves defining the problems and reviewing facts and uncertainties, but also considers the patient's emotional state, ethnicity, culture, and religious traditions.

PATIENT AUTONOMY

According to the principle of patient autonomy, competent patients have the right to self-rule—to choose among medically-recommended treatments and refuse any treatment they do not want. To be truly autonomous, they have to be told about the nature of their illness, prospects for recovery, the course of the illness, alternative treatments, and treatment consequences. After thoughtful consideration, a patient makes an informed choice and grants "informed consent" to treatment. Decisions about medical treatment may be influenced by the patient's psychological state, family history, culture, values, and religious beliefs.

Once informed by their physicians about their illnesses and medical options, patients also have the right to forego treatment. Former first lady Jacqueline Kennedy Onassis, after a difficult battle to arrest her non-Hodgkin's lymphoma, refused further treatment. When doctors told Mrs. Onassis that the cancer had spread to her brain and liver and that there was nothing else they could do, she asked to go home. She signed a living will that forbade any heroic measures should the doctor diagnose her condition as hopeless. Once home, she received only palliative care (care to relieve symptoms rather than cure), lapsed into a coma, and died soon after, on May 19, 1994.

FIGURE 3.1

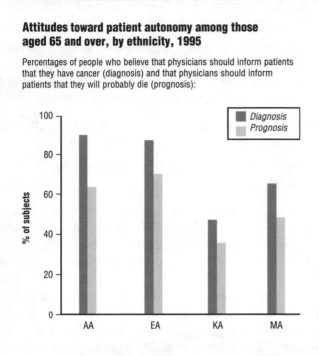

Attitudes toward patient autonomy among those aged 65 and over, by ethnicity, 1995

Percentages of people who believe that physicians should inform patients that they have cancer (diagnosis) and that physicians should inform patients that they will probably die (prognosis):

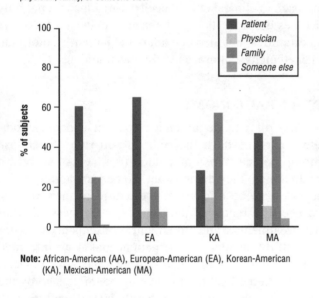

Percentages of people who believe that the decision about whether to put a patient on a life-support machine should be made by the patient, physician, family, or someone else:

Note: African-American (AA), European-American (EA), Korean-American (KA), Mexican-American (MA)

SOURCE: Leslie J. Blackhall, et al., "Ethnicity and Attitudes Toward Patient Autonomy," *JAMA: The Journal of the American Medical Association,* vol. 274, no. 10, September 13, 1995

Not All Patients Want to Know

While patient autonomy is a fundamental aspect of medical ethics, not all patients want to know about their illnesses or to be involved in decisions about their terminal care. A study published in *The Journal of the American Medical Association* (Leslie J. Blackhall, et al., "Ethnicity and Attitudes Toward Patient Autonomy," vol. 274, no. 10, September 13, 1995) found that the desire to know may not be equally shared by all ethnic groups in the United States.

The researchers surveyed 800 persons 65 years and older, self-identified as belonging to four ethnic groups. They found that Korean Americans (47 percent) and Mexican Americans (65 percent) were less likely than European Americans (87 percent) and African Americans (88 percent) to approve of telling a patient the truth about a diagnosis of metastatic cancer (cancer that has spread to sites distant from the primary tumor and that is usually incurable). (See Figure 3.1.)

Only about one-third of Korean Americans (35 percent) and about one-half of Mexican Americans (48 percent) thought the patient should be told a prognosis of terminal illness, compared with a larger percentage of African Americans (63 percent) and European Americans (69 percent). Korean Americans (28 percent) and Mexican Americans (41 percent) were also less likely to believe that a patient should make decisions concerning life support, compared with 60 percent of African Americans and 65 percent of European Americans. (See Figure 3.1.)

The Korean American and Mexican American subjects in the study were more family-centered, with the family, rather than the patient, acting as decision-maker. For these groups, patient autonomy was considered to be just another burden for patients already coping with serious illness. Surveys of Eastern European countries, as well as France, Spain, Greece, Japan, China, and Ethiopia, showed that doctors are more likely to inform families, rather than patients, about terminal illness.

The authors of the study believed it was important for physicians to realize that "the ideal of patient autonomy is far from universal." There are differences of opinion not only among ethnic groups but also within each ethnic group. For example, the subjects of this study were older adults. The authors speculated that younger people might have different feelings about these issues. They suggested that physicians keep in mind that, as with most issues, people bring their cultural values to bear on decisions about terminal care.

Health Care Proxies and Surrogate Decision-Makers

When a patient is incompetent to make informed decisions about his or her medical treatment, a proxy or a surrogate must make the decision for that patient. Some patients, in anticipation of being in a position of incompetence, will execute a durable power of attorney for health care, designating a proxy. Most people choose family members or close friends who will make all medical decisions, including the withholding or withdrawal of life-sustaining treatments.

When a proxy has not been named in advance, health care providers usually involve family members in medical decisions. Most states have laws that govern surrogate decision-making. Some states designate family members, by order of kinship, to assume the role of surrogates.

THE ETHICS OF AIDS

AIDS (acquired immunodeficiency syndrome) has directed societal attention to end-of-life decision-making because patients are faced with decisions about life-prolonging therapies for a disease that as yet has no cure. They know that a number of disorders await them as their immune system is progressively destroyed, including severe wasting, infections, intense pain, blindness, and dementia. Some AIDS patients who do not wish to undergo this protracted dying process or deplete family resources in prolonged care may ask for physicians' aid to hasten death.

Lee R. Slome, et al., surveyed all 228 physicians in the Community Consortium in the San Francisco Bay area in 1994–95 ("Physician-Assisted Suicide and Patients with Human Immunodeficiency Virus Disease," *The New England Journal of Medicine,* vol. 336, no. 6, February 6, 1997). The researchers wanted to find out "whether, and to what extent, physicians are participating—or would be willing to participate—in physician-assisted suicide." Physician-assisted suicide was defined as "a physician providing a sufficient dose of narcotics to enable a patient to kill himself."

The physicians who treated HIV patients were given an anonymous self-administered survey that described a fictitious patient, Tom, as a 30-year-old "mentally competent, severely ill individual facing imminent death." A similar survey was conducted in 1990. Compared with the 1990 respondents, the 118 physicians who responded to the 1995 survey were more racially diverse, more likely to be heterosexual, and more likely to have a large number of AIDS patients. (See Table 3.1.)

Of the 1995 respondents, 48 percent said they would be likely or very likely to grant Tom's initial request for physician-assisted suicide, compared with 28 percent of the 1990 respondents. (See Table 3.2.) When asked what they would do if Tom was adamant about his request, 51 percent of the 1995 respondents said they would grant an initial request by Tom, compared with 35 percent of the 1990 respondents. The 1995 physicians (11 percent) were also less likely than the 1990 physicians (23 percent) to talk the patient out of his request.

The researchers also asked the 1995 physicians to estimate the number of times they had helped an AIDS patient commit suicide. Of the 117 who responded, about half (53 percent) indicated that they had done so at least once by prescribing a fatal dose of medication. Figure 3.2 shows the distribution of the number of patients assisted in suicide. The researchers observed, "This is a surprisingly large proportion, given the possible legal and ethical repercussions of such an action."

TABLE 3.1

Characteristics of respondents to surveys of Community Consortium physicians, 1990 and 1995

Characteristic	1990 (n=69)	1995 (n=118)
	percent	
Sex		
Male	81	73
Female	19	27
Race or ethnic group		
White	97	80
Black	0	4
Hispanic	1	3
Asian or Pacific Islander	2	4
Sexual orientation		
Homosexual or bisexual	55	36
Heterosexual	45	64
Marital status		
Married	33	47
Unmarried but in a relationship	36	32
Unmarried and not in a relationship	30	21
Religion		
Protestant	26	17
Catholic	13	12
Jewish	36	30
Other	25	41
Total no. of patients with AIDS		
0	9	0
1-20	4	3
21-40	7	8
41-60	7	4
61-80	9	5
>80	63	78

Note: Because of rounding, percentages do not sum to 100.

SOURCE: Lee R. Slome, et al., "Table 1. Characteristics of Respondents to the 1990 and 1995 Surveys," in "Physician-Assisted Suicide and Patients with Human Immunodeficiency Virus Disease," *The New England Journal of Medicine,* vol. 336, no. 6, February 6, 1997

Finally, Slome, et al., drew the following conclusions:

• The survey suggests an increasing acceptance among physicians of assisted suicide.

• A physician's being gay, lesbian, or bisexual is positively related to his or her willingness to assist in suicide, although sexual orientation is only one of several factors affecting the doctor's decision. (See Table 3.1 for other characteristics of respondents.)

• Some doctors may consider their assistance as "a psychological intervention rather than a means of hastening death"—that is, the medication somehow gives the patients back some of the control that AIDS has taken away.

The AIDS epidemic and the struggles of AIDS patients have focused the attention of an entire generation on mortality. Since the disease affects mainly young adults, it has also served to increase awareness, among physicians and the public, that end-of-life issues concern persons of all ages, not only older adults.

TABLE 3.2

Survey responses from Community Consortium physicians, based on a case vignette, 1990 and 1995

Question and response	1990		1995	
	no. (%)			
How likely would you be to prescribe a lethal dose of medication for Tom?[1]				
Very unlikely	20	(29)	18	(16)
Unlikely	20	(29)	19	(17)
Neither likely nor unlikely	9	(13)	22	(19)
Likely	13	(19)	47	(41)
Very likely	6	(9)	8	(7)
If Tom was adamant about getting assistance in committing suicide, what course of action would you take?[2]				
Refuse his request	10	(14)	18	(16)
Talk him out of it	16	(23)	12	(11)
Hospitalize him as danger to himself	2	(3)	1	(1)
Refer him to a mental health professional	41	(59)	50	(45)
Refer him to a suicide-prevention program	4	(6)	5	(5)
Refer him to clergy	11	(16)	17	(15)
Refer him to another physician	1	(1)	8	(7)
Refer him to the Hemlock Society	32	(46)	42	(38)
Grant his request	24	(35)	56	(51)

[1] There were 68 respondents in 1990 and 114 in 1995.
[2] There were 69 respondents in 1990 and 110 in 1995. More than one response per physician was possible.

Note: Responses above based on the following vignette: "Tom is a 30-year-old gay male computer programmer diagnosed with AIDS two years ago. He has severe wasting syndrome and painful oral ulcers, and responded poorly to treatment for his third episode of *Pneumocystis carinii* pneumonia. There is no evidence of neurological impairment, and it is clear that Tom is mentally competent. His mood is mildly depressed, but the depression is not pronounced given the seriousness of his condition. Tom has been in a primary relationship for eight years and worked until several months ago. As his personal physician since his diagnosis, you consider Tom a thoughtful, intelligent patient who does not appear to have any significant psycho-pathology. During Tom's biweekly clinic visit, he asks you to prescribe a lethal dose of narcotics for possible use at some future date."

SOURCE: Lee R. Slome, et al., "Table 2. Responses to the Case Vignette in 1990 and 1995," in "Physician-Assisted Suicide and Patients with Human Immunodeficiency Virus Disease," *The New England Journal of Medicine,* vol. 336, no. 6, February 6, 1997

THE FUTURE OF MEDICAL ETHICS

Robert B. Mellert, a professor of philosophy and religious studies at Brookdale Community College in New Jersey, claims that "medical ethics is troubled today." In "Cure or Care? The Future of Medical Ethics" (*The Futurist,* vol. 31, no. 4, July–August 1997), Professor Mellert observes that the troubled state of medical ethics "is merely a reflection of the fact that we are all troubled today by the complexity of technology, by the innumerable options and choices, and by the larger questions about the purpose of being alive."

Professor Mellert claims that debates on medical ethics center on two theories about the nature of health care. These are:

• "Curing" approach—based on the traditional ethical principle that traces its roots to the Hippocratic Oath. The role of medicine, which is to heal, ties in with the traditional Western religious ethic of preserving life.

FIGURE 3.2

Survey responses from Community Consortium physicians on number of patients assisted in suicide, 1990 and 1995 surveys

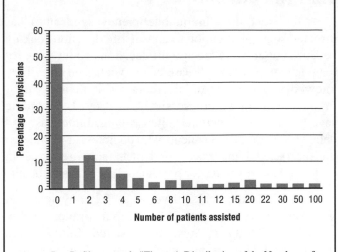

SOURCE: Lee R. Slome, et al., "Figure 1. Distribution of the Numbers of Patients Assisted in Suicide, as Reported by 117 Respondents to the 1995 Survey," in "Physician-Assisted Suicide and Patients with Human Immunodeficiency Virus Disease," *The New England Journal of Medicine,* vol. 336, no. 6, February 6, 1997

Patients must trust their doctors' judgment and decision to sustain life. Doctors must abstain from doing anything to shorten or end life even if the patient is suffering. The physician, therefore, acts as a "health care provider."

• "Caring" approach—based on the principle that the fundamental values of human existence are "the maximization of pleasure and the minimization of pain." The role of medicine, which is to minimize pain, stresses the importance of the quality of life. The physician, acting as a "medical consultant," discusses with the patient his or her options, possible treatments and their effects, complications, and costs. The patient weighs his or her options and decides on a course of action, which the physician carries out, whether the physician agrees with that decision or not.

Future Choices

Professor Mellert predicts that solutions to controversies in medical ethics will not be forthcoming any time soon. Autonomous patients will have to be prepared to learn enough about their illnesses to make their own decisions. This is a tremendous task for lay people, especially since medical science is advancing so rapidly. Professor Mellert believes that in the long run patients will have to trust their physicians.

Whichever approach patients choose, cure or care, they need to make their basic philosophical values known. Some questions patients may wish to consider are:

- How do I view my life at this stage and under these conditions?
- What do I see as the continuing purpose of my existence?
- Under what conditions do I wish to exercise my right to maintain my life?
- Are there conditions in which I would not wish to continue?

- What do I want my physician to do for me then?

Physicians also must make choices. Do they comply with a patient's wishes, perform the standard medical treatments to avoid lawsuits, or follow their own best medical judgment? Supporting patient autonomy requires physicians and other health care clinicians to provide the maximum benefit to patients without compromising their own moral convictions.

CHAPTER 4

THE END OF LIFE—MEDICAL CONSIDERATIONS

CAUSES OF DEATH

Over the course of the twentieth century, the primary causes of death in the United States changed. During the 1800s and early 1900s, infectious (communicable) diseases such as influenza, tuberculosis, and diphtheria were the leading causes of death. These have been replaced by chronic diseases, and heart disease, cancer (malignant neoplasms), and stroke (cerebrovascular diseases) were the three leading causes of death in 1999. (See Table 4.1.)

In 1999 the age-adjusted death rate (which accounts for changes in the age distribution of the population across time) for heart disease was 267.8 deaths per 100,000 persons, while that for cancer was 202.7 per

TABLE 4.1

Death rates for the 15 leading causes of death, 1999, and percent change, 1998–99

[Death rates on an annual basis per 100,000 population; age-adjusted rates per 100,000 U.S. standard population based on year 2000 standard]

					Age-adjusted death rate				
						Percent change[2]		Ratio	
Rank[1]	Cause of death	Number	Percent of total deaths	1999 crude death rate	1999	1998 to 1999	Male to female	Black to white	Hispanic to white non-Hispanic
...	All causes	2,391,399	100.0	877.0	881.9	0.7	1.4	1.3	0.7
1	Diseases of heart	725,192	30.3	265.9	267.8	−0.3	1.5	1.3	0.7
2	Malignant neoplasms	549,838	23.0	201.6	202.7	−0.5	1.5	1.3	0.6
3	Cerebrovascular diseases	167,366	7.0	61.4	61.8	−1.9	1.0	1.4	0.7
4	Chronic lower respiratory diseases	124,181	5.2	45.5	45.8	4.1	1.5	0.7	0.4
5	Accidents (unintentional injuries)	97,860	4.1	35.9	35.9	−0.6	2.2	1.1	0.9
6	Diabetes mellitus	68,399	2.9	25.1	25.2	3.3	1.2	2.2	1.5
7	Influenza and pneumonia	63,730	2.7	23.4	23.6	−2.5	1.3	1.1	0.7
8	Alzheimer's disease	44,536	1.9	16.3	16.5	[3]23.1	0.8	0.7	0.4
9	Nephritis, nephrotic syndrome and nephrosis	35,525	1.5	13.0	13.1	[3]8.3	1.4	2.5	0.9
10	Septicemia	30,680	1.3	11.3	11.3	6.6	1.2	2.5	0.8
11	Intentional self-harm (suicide)	29,199	1.2	10.7	10.7	−5.3	4.4	0.5	0.5
12	Chronic liver disease and cirrhosis	26,259	1.1	9.6	9.7	−1.0	2.2	1.1	1.7
13	Essential (primary) hypertension and hypertensive renal disease	16,968	0.7	6.2	6.3	5.0	1.0	3.0	1.0
14	Assault (homicide)	16,889	0.7	6.2	6.2	−4.6	3.2	5.4	2.9
15	Aortic aneurysm and dissection	15,807	0.7	5.8	5.8	−4.9	2.3	0.8	0.4
...	All other causes	378,970	15.8	139.0	...	...	...	...	...

− Quantity zero.
... Category not applicable.
[1]Rank based on number of deaths.
[2]Percent change is based on a comparison of the 1999 age-adjusted death rate with the 1998 comparability-modified, age-adjusted death rate.
[3]Percent change is not reliable because of problems in measuring comparability.

SOURCE: Donna L. Hoyert, et al.,"Table C. Percent of total deaths, death rates, age-adjusted death rates for 1999, percent change in age-adjusted death rates from 1998 to 1999 and ratio of age-adjusted death rates by race and sex for the 15 leading causes of death for the total population in 1999: United States," in *Deaths: Final Data for 1999, National Vital Statistics Reports,* National Center for Health Statistics, Hyattsville, MD, vol. 49, no. 8., September 21, 2001

100,000 persons. (See Table 4.1.) Together, these two diseases accounted for 53.3 percent of all deaths in the United States. Deaths from heart disease have been decreasing since 1950, while cancer mortality has been dropping only since 1990.

Not surprisingly, the leading causes of death vary by age. For those aged 1 to 44 years, accidents and their adverse effects were the leading causes of death. Cancer and heart disease account for most deaths among 45- to 64-year-olds. (See Table 4.2.) The Institute of Medicine of the National Academies reports that heart disease, cancer, and stroke "disproportionately affect older people"—those 65 years of age and over.

According to an HIV/AIDS Surveillance Report begun in 1993, 1996 marked the first year a decline occurred in U.S. deaths due to AIDS (acquired immunodeficiency syndrome), with reductions continuing through 2000. (See Table 4.3 and Table 4.4.) AIDS, the final stage of HIV (human immunodeficiency virus) infection, has had a tremendous effect on society. This epidemic has brought a painful, drawn-out process of dying to many, including young adults, an age group previously relatively untouched by death, particularly from infectious disease.

THE STUDY TO UNDERSTAND PROGNOSES AND PREFERENCES FOR OUTCOMES AND RISKS OF TREATMENTS (SUPPORT)

During the twentieth century in the United States, the process of dying shifted from the familiar surroundings of home to the hospital. While hospitalization ensures that the benefits of modern medicine are readily available, many patients dread leaving the comfort of their homes and losing, to some extent, control over their end-of-life decisions and wishes.

Between 1989 and 1994, in an effort to "improve end-of-life decision making and reduce the frequency of a mechanically supported, painful, and prolonged process of dying," a group of investigators from various disciplines undertook the largest study of death and dying ever conducted in the United States. The project, known as The Study to Understand Prognoses and Preferences for Outcomes and Risks of Treatments (SUPPORT), included more than 9,000 patients who suffered from life-threatening illnesses. Patients enrolled in the study had about a 50 percent chance of dying within six months.

The researchers published the results of their study in "A Controlled Trial to Improve Care for Seriously Ill Hospitalized Patients" (*The Journal of the American Medical Association,* vol. 274, no. 20, November 22/29, 1995). The SUPPORT investigators hypothesized that increased communication between patients and physicians, better understanding of patients' wishes, and the use of computer-based projections of patient survival would result in "earlier treat-

ment decisions, reductions in time spent in undesirable states before death, and reduced resource use."

Phase I of the study was observational. The researchers reviewed patients' medical records and interviewed patients, surrogates (persons who would make decisions if patients became incompetent), and patients' physicians. Discussions and decisions about life-sustaining measures were observed.

The researchers interviewed patients, families, and surrogates about the patients' thoughts on cardiopulmonary resuscitation (CPR), their perceptions of their quality of life, the frequency and severity of their pain, and their satisfaction with the care provided. The physicians who acknowledged responsibility for the patients' medical decisions were also interviewed to determine their understanding of patients' views on CPR and how patients' wishes influenced their medical care. The surrogates were again interviewed after the patients' deaths.

Problems with End-of-Life Care

Phase I of SUPPORT found a lack of communication between physicians and patients, showed aggressive treatment of dying patients, and revealed a disturbing picture of hospital death. Of the 4,301 patients, 31 percent expressed a desire that CPR be withheld. However, only 47 percent of physicians reported knowledge of their patients' wishes. About half (49 percent) of patients who requested not to be resuscitated did not have a DNR (do-not-resuscitate) order in their medical charts. Of the 79 percent who died with a DNR order, 46 percent of the orders were written within only two days of death.

The patients' final days in the hospital included an average of eight days in "generally undesirable states"—in an intensive care unit (ICU), receiving artificial respiration, or in a coma. More than a third (38 percent) stayed 10 days in the ICU, while almost half (46 percent) were mechanically ventilated within three days prior to death. Surrogates reported that 50 percent of conscious patients complained of moderate or severe pain at least half the time in their last three days.

Phase II: Intervention Fails to Improve Care

Phase II of SUPPORT, or the intervention phase, was implemented to address the shortcomings documented in Phase I. It lasted another two years, and involved patient participants with characteristics similar to those in Phase I. This time, however, the doctors were given printed reports about the patients and their wishes regarding life-sustaining treatments. SUPPORT nurses facilitated the flow of information among patients, families, and health care personnel, and helped manage patients' pain. The SUPPORT investigators were appalled that no improvement in the quality of hospital death occurred.

TABLE 4.2

Death rates by age and age-adjusted death rates for the 15 leading causes of death in 1999, 1998, and modified 1998

Cause of death and year	All ages[1]	Under 1 year[2]	1-4 years	5-14 years	15-24 years	25-34 years	35-44 years	45-54 years	55-64 years	65-74 years	75-84 years	85 years and over	Age-adjusted rate
All causes													
1999	877.0	731.4	34.7	19.2	81.2	108.3	199.2	427.3	1,021.8	2,484.3	5,751.3	15,476.1	881.9
1998 (modified)[3]	864.7	751.3	34.6	19.9	82.3	109.6	199.6	423.5	1,030.7	2,495.1	5,703.2	15,111.7	875.8
1998	864.7	751.3	34.6	19.9	82.3	109.6	199.6	423.5	1,030.7	2,495.1	5,703.2	15,111.7	875.8
Diseases of heart													
1999	265.9	13.7	1.2	0.7	2.8	8.1	30.3	97.7	274.3	709.5	1,861.8	6,032.5	267.8
1998 (modified)[3]	264.4	15.9	1.4	0.8	2.8	8.2	30.1	100.0	282.8	725.1	1,870.4	5,924.3	268.5
1998	268.2	16.1	1.4	0.8	2.8	8.3	30.5	101.4	286.9	735.5	1,897.3	6,009.6	272.4
Malignant neoplasms													
1999	201.6	1.8	2.8	2.6	4.6	10.6	37.3	130.4	380.8	836.2	1,340.0	1,796.7	202.7
1998 (modified)[3]	201.7	2.1	2.4	2.6	4.6	11.4	38.5	133.2	386.4	847.0	1,335.3	1,761.3	203.8
1998	200.3	2.1	2.4	2.6	4.6	11.3	38.2	132.3	383.8	841.3	1,326.3	1,749.4	202.4
Cerebrovascular diseases													
1999	61.4	2.7	0.3	0.2	0.5	1.5	5.7	15.5	41.3	132.2	472.8	1,606.7	61.8
1998 (modified)[3]	61.9	8.3	0.4	0.2	0.5	1.8	6.2	17.5	45.0	137.4	481.0	1,582.6	63.0
1998	58.5	7.8	0.4	0.2	0.5	1.7	5.9	16.5	42.5	129.8	454.3	1,494.7	59.5
Chronic lower respiratory diseases													
1999	45.5	0.9	0.4	0.4	0.6	0.9	2.0	8.7	48.3	179.2	400.4	642.7	45.8
1998 (modified)[3]	43.6	1.0	0.3	0.4	0.6	0.8	2.1	8.6	46.9	177.1	383.2	596.4	44.0
1998	41.6	1.0	0.3	0.4	0.6	0.8	2.0	8.2	44.8	169.0	365.7	569.2	42.0
Accidents (unintentional injuries)													
1999	35.9	22.1	12.6	7.8	36.2	31.3	34.0	32.5	31.1	45.1	101.1	280.9	35.9
1998 (modified)[3]	36.0	19.7	12.9	8.5	36.8	31.7	34.6	31.7	31.5	45.5	101.3	272.8	36.1
1998	34.9	19.1	12.5	8.2	35.7	30.8	33.6	30.8	30.6	44.2	98.3	264.7	35.0
Diabetes mellitus													
1999	25.1	*	*	0.1	0.4	1.5	4.3	13.2	38.9	92.8	179.1	315.6	25.2
1998 (modified)[3]	24.2	*	*	0.1	0.4	1.6	4.2	12.8	38.7	90.3	173.2	297.3	24.4
1998	24.0	*	*	0.1	0.4	1.6	4.2	12.7	38.4	89.6	171.8	294.9	24.2
Influenza and pneumonia													
1999	23.4	8.4	0.9	0.2	0.5	0.9	2.4	4.7	11.2	37.7	158.0	748.0	23.6
1998 (modified)[3]	23.7	8.2	0.7	0.2	0.4	1.0	2.2	4.4	11.9	41.8	168.5	742.8	24.2
1998	34.0	11.7	1.0	0.3	0.6	1.4	3.1	6.3	17.0	59.8	241.4	1,063.9	34.6
Alzheimer's disease													
1999	16.3	*	*	*	*	*	*	0.2	1.9	17.6	130.4	598.3	16.5
1998 (modified)[3]	13.1	*	*	*	*	*	*	0.2	1.7	16.2	108.8	465.3	13.4
1998	8.4	*	*	*	*	*	*	0.1	1.1	10.4	70.0	299.5	8.6
Nephritis, nephrotic syndrome and nephrosis													
1999	13.0	4.3	*	0.1	0.2	0.7	1.6	4.1	12.2	37.6	98.2	267.5	13.1
1998 (modified)[3]	12.0	4.6	*	0.1	0.1	0.5	1.2	3.3	9.9	32.0	93.4	267.6	12.1
1998	9.7	3.7	*	0.1	0.1	0.4	1.0	2.7	8.0	26.0	75.8	217.2	9.8
Septicemia													
1999	11.3	7.4	0.6	0.2	0.3	0.7	1.8	4.7	11.6	31.6	79.9	219.5	11.3
1998 (modified)[3]	10.5	6.8	0.7	0.1	0.4	0.8	1.8	4.3	11.0	29.0	74.3	209.5	10.6
1998	8.8	5.7	0.6	0.1	0.3	0.7	1.5	3.6	9.2	24.3	62.2	175.3	8.9
Intentional self-harm (suicide)													
1999	10.7	*	*	0.6	10.3	13.5	14.4	14.2	12.4	13.6	18.3	19.2	10.7
1998 (modified)[3]	11.3	*	*	0.8	11.1	13.7	15.3	14.7	13.1	14.0	19.6	20.9	11.3
1998	11.3	*	*	0.8	11.1	13.8	15.4	14.8	13.1	14.1	19.7	21.0	11.3

TABLE 4.2

Death rates by age and age-adjusted death rates for the 15 leading causes of death in 1999, 1998, and modified 1998 [CONTINUED]

Cause of death and year	All ages[1]	Under 1 year[2]	1-4 years	5-14 years	15-24 years	25-34 years	35-44 years	45-54 years	55-64 years	65-74 years	75-84 years	85 years and over	Age-adjusted rate
Chronic liver disease and cirrhosis													
1999	9.6	*	*	*	0.1	1.1	7.4	17.8	24.1	31.0	32.1	23.1	9.7
1998 (modified)[3]	9.6	*	*	*	0.1	1.3	7.9	17.2	24.2	31.8	32.1	22.7	9.8
1998	9.3	*	*	*	0.1	1.3	7.6	16.6	23.3	30.7	31.0	21.9	9.5
Essential (primary) hypertension and hypertensive renal disease													
1999	6.2	*	*	*	*	0.2	0.7	2.2	5.6	15.4	43.8	151.3	6.3
1998 (modified)[3]	5.9	*	*	*	*	0.1	0.6	1.9	5.6	15.2	42.9	143.7	6.0
1998	5.3	*	*	*	*	0.1	0.5	1.7	5.0	13.6	38.3	128.4	5.4
Assault (homicide)													
1999	6.2	8.7	2.5	1.1	13.2	11.2	7.2	4.7	3.1	2.6	2.5	2.4	6.2
1998 (modified)[3]	6.6	8.5	2.6	1.2	14.6	11.5	7.7	4.9	3.3	2.5	2.7	2.4	6.5
1998	6.6	8.5	2.6	1.2	14.6	11.5	7.7	4.9	3.3	2.5	2.7	2.4	6.5
Aortic aneurysm and dissection													
1999	5.8	*	*	*	0.1	0.2	0.7	1.8	6.1	22.0	48.9	79.9	5.8
1998 (modified)[3]	6.0	*	*	*	0.1	0.3	0.7	1.7	6.4	23.5	51.6	79.9	6.1
1998	6.0	*	*	*	0.1	0.3	0.7	1.7	6.4	23.5	51.5	79.8	6.1

Note: Rates on an annual basis per 100,000 population in specified group; age-adjusted rates per 100,000 U.S. standard population based on year 2000 standard.

*Figure does not meet standards of reliability or precision.

. . . Category not applicable.

[1] Figures for age not stated included in "All ages" but not distributed among age groups.

[2] Death rates for "Under 1 year" (based on population estimates) differ from infant mortality rates (based on live births).

[3] Age-specific and age-adjusted rates are modified.

SOURCE: Donna L. Hoyert, et al., "Table 8. Death rates by age and age-adjusted death rates by the 15 leading causes of death in 1999: United States, 1998, modified 1998, and 1999," in *Deaths: Final Data for 1999, National Vital Statistics Reports*, National Center for Health Statistics, Hyattsville, MD, vol. 49, no. 8, September 21, 2001

TABLE 4.3

Estimated number of deaths among persons with AIDS, by race/ethnicity and year of death, 1993–2000[1]

Race/ethnicity	Year of death							
	1993	1994	1995	1996	1997	1998	1999	2000
White, not Hispanic	21,803	22,828	22,189	14,665	7,310	6,016	5,234	4,532
Black, not Hispanic	15,543	18,024	19,115	15,936	10,316	8,803	8,576	7,781
Hispanic	7,780	8,976	9,215	6,992	4,116	3,368	3,166	2,780
Asian/Pacific Islander	307	410	366	293	154	124	114	90
American Indian/Alaska Native	134	154	195	132	93	76	73	57
Unknown	31	26	37	8	10	9	10	5
Total[2]	**45,598**	**50,418**	**51,117**	**38,025**	**21,999**	**18,397**	**17,172**	**15,245**

[1] These numbers do not represent the actual number of deaths among persons with AIDS. Rather, these numbers are point estimates adjusted for delays in the reporting of deaths, but not for incomplete reporting of deaths. The year 2000 is the most recent year for which reliable estimates are available.
[2] Because column totals were calculated independently of the values for the subpopulations, the values in each column may not sum to the column total.

SOURCE: "Table 29. Estimated number of deaths among persons with AIDS, by race/ethnicity, and year of death, 1993 through 2000, United States[1], " in *HIV/AIDS Surveillance Report,* Centers for Disease Control and Prevention, Atlanta, GA, vol. 13, no. 1, 2001

TABLE 4.4

Estimated number of deaths among persons with AIDS, by age group, sex, exposure category, and year of death, 1993–2000[1]

Male adult/adolescent exposure category	Year of death							
	1993	1994	1995	1996	1997	1998	1999	2000
Men who have sex with men	23,956	25,534	25,044	16,854	8,666	7,048	6,230	5,439
Injecting drug use	9,325	10,454	10,844	8,551	5,346	4,476	4,119	3,551
Men who have sex with men and inject drugs	3,188	3,528	3,467	2,591	1,447	1,262	1,182	1,120
Hemophilia/coagulation disorder[2]	357	346	330	246	136	117	100	*
Heterosexual contact	1,600	2,013	2,389	2,111	1,464	1,227	1,257	1,218
Receipt of blood transfusion, blood components, or tissue[2]	314	304	259	217	108	83	73	*
Other/risk not reported or identified[3]	168	143	102	66	44	28	29	187
Male subtotal	**38,908**	**42,322**	**42,434**	**30,636**	**17,212**	**14,241**	**12,991**	**11,514**
Female adult/adolescent exposure category								
Injecting drug use	3,152	3,713	3,824	3,289	2,137	1,900	1,920	1,662
Hemophilia/coagulation disorder[2]	17	28	31	30	20	14	17	*
Heterosexual contact	2,662	3,489	3,999	3,439	2,297	2,029	2,032	1,899
Receipt of blood transfusion, blood components, or tissue[2]	238	224	235	170	93	75	75	*
Other/risk not reported or identified[3]	77	56	56	32	20	15	19	95
Female subtotal	**6,146**	**7,510**	**8,144**	**6,960**	**4,567**	**4,033**	**4,063**	**3,656**
Pediatric (<13 years old) exposure category	544	586	539	429	221	123	118	74
Total[4]	**45,598**	**50,418**	**51,117**	**38,025**	**21,999**	**18,397**	**17,172**	**15,245**

[1] These numbers do not represent the actual number of deaths among persons with AIDS. Rather, these numbers are point estimates adjusted for delays in the reporting of deaths and for redistribution of cases initially reported with no identified risk, but not for incomplete reporting of deaths. The year 2000 is the most recent year for which reliable estimates are available.
[2] Statistical estimates for deaths in 2000 among persons with AIDS exposed to HIV through hemophilia/coagulation disorder or receipt of blood transfusion, blood components, or tissue are not presented, but are included in the exposure category "other." The relatively small number of AIDS cases in these categories in recent years does not provide information that results in reliable annual estimates of deaths (* = data not available); only cumulative estimates are presented. CDC is evaluating and revising the algorithm for estimating deaths among persons with AIDS infected in the early 1980's through these exposure categories.
[3] For 2000, estimates of "other" include cases exposed through hemophilia/coagulation disorder and receipt of blood transfusion, blood components, or tissue.
[4] Because column totals were calculated independently of the values for the subpopulations, the values in each column may not sum to the column total.

SOURCE: "Table 30. Estimated number of deaths among persons with AIDS, by age group, sex, exposure category, and year of death, 1993 through 2000, United States[1]," in *HIV/AIDS Surveillance Report,* Centers for Disease Control and Prevention, Atlanta, GA, vol. 13, no. 1, 2001

What Went Wrong?

Dr. Bernard Lo ("Improving Care Near the End of Life: Why Is It So Hard?," *The Journal of the American Medical Association,* vol. 274, no. 20, November 22/29, 1995) believes that the results reported in the SUPPORT study raise more questions than answers. Among other issues, Dr. Lo claims that while Phase I showed poor doctor-patient communication, Phase II, instead of directly addressing this shortcoming, added a third party, the SUPPORT nurses, to do the physicians' job. The issue of inadequate pain control was not resolved, in part, because the physicians were not routinely advised of the patients' pain.

Dr. Lo questions the physicians' apparent lack of interest in patients' preferences regarding CPR. Did the physicians think they knew what was best for the patients and, therefore, ignored information relayed by the nurses? Furthermore, no comparison was ever made between patients' perceived prognosis of their own condition and that made by their physicians. Patients who overestimated the likelihood of recovery might have requested life-sustaining measures, which their doctors might not have deemed appropriate.

Daniel Callahan, former president of The Hastings Center, a think tank for biomedical ethics, questions why the idea of patient empowerment, which includes issues that Americans love—self-determination, choice, patients' rights, the provision of timely scientific knowledge, a legal domestication of death—doesn't appear to work. Callahan believes Americans continue to be ambivalent in their attitude toward death ("Once Again, Reality: The Lessons of the SUPPORT Study," Special Supplement, *Hastings Center Report,* vol. 25, no. 6, 1995). Medical professionals and laypersons alike are often unsure whether to accept death as a part of life or see it as some kind of misplaced biological occurrence to be fought. In the SUPPORT study, this ambivalence was depicted in physicians' management of terminal care and even in the actions of some patients and their families.

Callahan points out that SUPPORT, while unsuccessful, illustrated the fact that a number of variables influence end-of-life decisions. Some of these are:

- Patients change their minds when it comes to life-sustaining treatments. Some do not really know what they want or what may happen in the course of their illness.

- Doctors may have differing opinions about prognosis, what specific treatments would accomplish, or how to balance their professional judgment and patient preferences.

- Families do not always know what should be done and can be uncertain in interpreting patients' preferences.

Callahan suggests that in order to resolve the continuing problems in terminal care, people have to revamp their attitudes about dying. Americans must decide if death is to be accepted as a part of life, or fought to the end.

LIFE-SUSTAINING TREATMENTS

Life-sustaining treatments, also called life support, can take over many functions of an ailing body. Under normal conditions, when a patient suffers from a treatable illness, life support is a temporary measure utilized only until the body can function on its own. The ongoing debate about prolonging life-sustaining treatments concerns the incurably ill and permanently unconscious.

Cardiopulmonary Resuscitation

Cardiopulmonary resuscitation (CPR) encompasses a group of procedures administered in the event of cardiac or respiratory arrest. Cardiac arrest may be caused by a heart attack, an interruption of blood flow to the heart muscle. A coronary artery clogged with an accumulation of cholesterol is a common cause of interrupted blood flow to the heart. Respiratory arrest, on the other hand, may be the result of an accident such as drowning, or the final stages of a pulmonary disease such as emphysema.

CPR consists of compressing the chest rhythmically to cause blood circulation to begin again, and delivering oxygen directly into the lungs through a tube inserted down the trachea (windpipe). Rarely, a tracheotomy is performed. In this procedure, an opening is made in the windpipe through which a breathing tube is inserted. Electrical shock and medication may also be used to "jump start" the heart.

CPR, initially intended for healthy individuals who unexpectedly suffered heart stoppage, is now widely used in a variety of circumstances. While CPR does not always work (it has a 20–50 percent success rate in healthy persons), it does help save lives. Generally, following CPR, healthy persons eventually resume normal lives. The outcome is quite different, however, for patients in the final stages of a terminal illness. Nancy Dubler and David Nimmons (*Ethics on Call,* Harmony Books, New York, 1992) observe that for people with a terminal disease, dying after being "successfully" resuscitated virtually ensures a slower, harder, more painful death.

REFUSAL OF CPR WITH A DO-NOT-RESUSCITATE ORDER. A person not wishing to be resuscitated in case of cardiac or respiratory arrest may request a physician to write a do-not-resuscitate (DNR) order on his or her chart. This written order instructs health care personnel not to initiate CPR, which can be very important since CPR is usually performed in an emergency. Even if a patient's living will includes refusal of CPR, emergency personnel rushing to a patient have no time to check the living will. A DNR order on a patient's chart is more accessible.

NONHOSPITAL DNR ORDERS. Most hospitals have policies governing DNR orders in the event a patient has no advance directives refusing CPR. Outside the hospital setting, such as at home, persons who do not want CPR

FIGURE 4.1

State laws and protocols governing nonhospital do-not-resuscitate (DNR) orders, September 2001

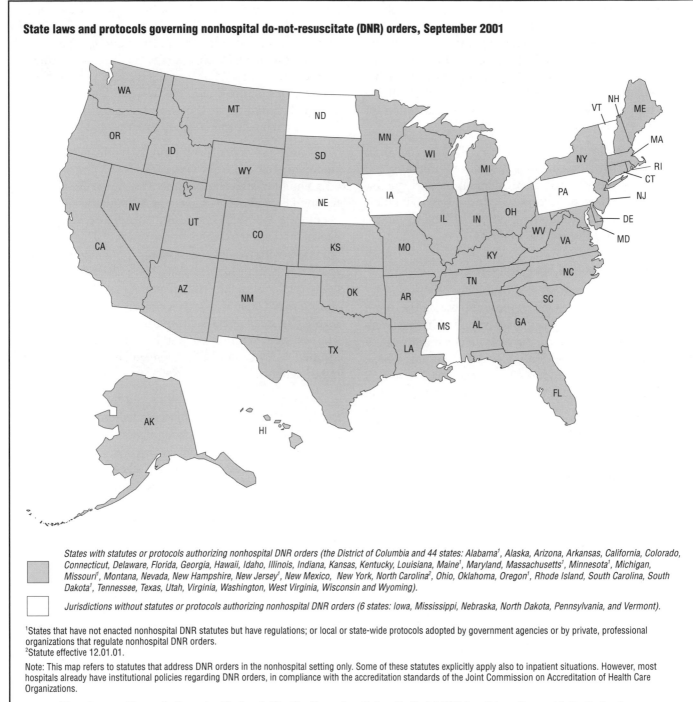

States with statutes or protocols authorizing nonhospital DNR orders (the District of Columbia and 44 states: Alabama[1], Alaska, Arizona, Arkansas, California, Colorado, Connecticut, Delaware, Florida, Georgia, Hawaii, Idaho, Illinois, Indiana, Kansas, Kentucky, Louisiana, Maine[1], Maryland, Massachusetts[1], Minnesota[1], Michigan, Missouri[1], Montana, Nevada, New Hampshire, New Jersey[1], New Mexico, New York, North Carolina[2], Ohio, Oklahoma, Oregon[1], Rhode Island, South Carolina, South Dakota[1], Tennessee, Texas, Utah, Virginia, Washington, West Virginia, Wisconsin and Wyoming).

Jurisdictions without statutes or protocols authorizing nonhospital DNR orders (6 states: Iowa, Mississippi, Nebraska, North Dakota, Pennsylvania, and Vermont).

[1]States that have not enacted nonhospital DNR statutes but have regulations; or local or state-wide protocols adopted by government agencies or by private, professional organizations that regulate nonhospital DNR orders.
[2]Statute effective 12.01.01.

Note: This map refers to statutes that address DNR orders in the nonhospital setting only. Some of these statutes explicitly apply also to inpatient situations. However, most hospitals already have institutional policies regarding DNR orders, in compliance with the accreditation standards of the Joint Commission on Accreditation of Health Care Organizations.

SOURCE: "State Laws and Protocols Governing Nonhospital Do-Not-Resuscitate Orders," in *End-Of-Life Law Digest,* Partnership for Caring, Inc., Washington, DC, 2001.

performed in case of an emergency can request a nonhospital DNR order from their physicians. (See Figure 4.1 for the list of states that had laws authorizing nonhospital DNR orders as of September 2001.) Also called a prehospital DNR order, it instructs emergency medical personnel to withhold CPR. The DNR order may be on a bracelet, necklace, or a wallet card. Laypersons performing CPR on an individual with a nonhospital DNR order cannot be prosecuted by the law.

Mechanical Ventilation

When a patient's lungs are not functioning properly, a ventilator, or respirator, breathes for the patient. Oxygen is supplied to the lungs through a tube inserted through the mouth or nose into the windpipe. Mechanical ventilation is generally used to temporarily maintain normal breathing in those who have been in serious accidents or who suffer from a serious illness, such as pneumonia.

Today, a person who suffers cardiac or respiratory arrest is attached to a respirator after CPR has restarted the heart. In some cases, if the patient needs ventilation indefinitely, the physician might perform a tracheotomy to open a hole in the neck for placement of the breathing tube in the windpipe. Even if a patient has irreversible brain damage, as long as the brain stem is functioning, the person is considered alive and the mechanical respirator cannot be withdrawn.

Ventilators are also used in terminally ill patients. In these cases, the machine keeps the patient breathing but does nothing to cure the disease. Persons preparing a living will are advised to give clear instructions about their desires regarding continued use of an artificial respirator that could prolong the process of dying.

Artificial Nutrition and Hydration

Artificial nutrition and hydration are other modern-day technologies that have further complicated the dying process. Today, nutrients and fluids supplied intravenously or through a stomach or intestinal tube can indefinitely sustain comatose and terminally ill patients. These processes have strong emotional impacts, relating as they do to basic sustenance. Partnership for Caring, Inc., an organization "dedicated to fostering communication about complex end-of-life decisions among individuals, their loved ones, and health-care professionals," explains in their September 2000 fact sheet "Artificial Nutrition and Hydration: Comfort Care or Medical Treatment?":

> Normally, feeding a helpless person—a baby, an invalid—is a lifesaving and deeply caring act. When someone is dying and there is "nothing more to be done," that urge may become even stronger. The desire to show our caring often reflects a sense of powerlessness in the face of death.
>
> It's one thing when a competent dying person refuses tube feeding and can explain her choice, while reassuring her loved ones that she's not in pain. It's another to make that decision for someone who is unconscious or incompetent.
>
> The symbolism of feeding can be so powerful that families who know that their loved one would not want to be kept alive may still feel that stopping feeding is taboo.

Robert M. McCann, et al., in "Comfort Care for Terminally Ill Patients: The Appropriate Use of Nutrition and Hydration" (*The Journal of the American Medical Association,* vol. 272, no. 16, October 26, 1994), observed that while there is a widespread assumption that artificial nutrition and hydration add to the well-being of patients—especially those who are mentally competent—there are no clinical data to support this assumption.

The researchers studied 32 terminally ill patients from their admission until their death in a comfort care unit. Most were diagnosed with cancer or stroke. The patients were offered food, and fed if necessary, but were never forced to eat. Pain was relieved with drugs, but not to the point of sedation. Several times each day, the health team assessed patients' discomfort from hunger or thirst by asking them and their families about pain, shortness of breath, nausea, fears, and anxiety. If the patient became unconscious before dying, the family and the health team assessed patient comfort by observing signs, such as grimacing, moaning, and constant tossing and turning.

Thirty-two patients were monitored from their admission until their death. Twenty patients (63 percent) reported no hunger. Eleven patients (34 percent) who initially reported being hungry during the first quarter of their stay eventually lost their appetites. Those who were hungry needed only a very small amount of food. Thirst was more common, with twenty-one patients (66 percent) reporting it. Nine experienced thirst initially, while twelve reported being thirsty until they died. Families and the health team administered sips of liquid, ice chips, and hard candy, as well as lip moisteners and mouth care to alleviate thirst. The researchers observed that the decreased liquid intake resulted in fewer cases of prolonged choking and suctioning of patients.

McCann, et al., further point out that artificial nutrition and hydration are usually initiated more to relieve the anxiety of caregivers and patients' families than to benefit the patient. Competent patients have been known to refuse artificial feeding during the final stages of their illness. In this study, nine of the patients who ate to please their families experienced nausea and stomach discomfort. Appetite loss is common in dying patients and is not a significant contributor to their suffering.

Kidney Dialysis

Kidney dialysis is a medical procedure by which a machine takes over the function of the kidneys in removing waste products from the blood. Dialysis can be used when an illness or injury temporarily impairs kidney function. It may also be used by patients with irreversibly damaged kidneys awaiting organ transplantation.

Kidney failure may also occur as an end-stage of a terminal illness. While dialysis may cleanse the body of waste products, it cannot cure the disease. Persons who wish to let their illness take its course may refuse dialysis. They will eventually lapse into a coma and die.

PERSISTENT VEGETATIVE STATE

Severe damage to the brain can cause a vegetative state. This state is characterized by waking and sleeping periods accompanied by a complete lack of cognition (learning, memory, self-awareness, and adaptive behavior). Patients have been known to recover from vegetative states after a few days or weeks; however, when loss of cognition lasts more than a few weeks, the patient is said to be in a persistent vegetative state (PVS).

The American Medical Association (AMA), in light of the continuing debate involving life-sustaining treatments and permanently unconscious patients, has discussed the so-called persistent vegetative state and outlined the criteria for diagnosis of this condition. In "Persistent Vegetative State and the Decision to Withdraw or Withhold Life Support" (*The Journal of the American Medical Association,* vol. 263, no. 3, January 19, 1990), the most recent estimates available on the topic, the Council on Scientific Affairs and the Council on Ethical and Judicial Affairs of the AMA estimated that there were 15,000 to 25,000 PVS patients in the United States.

The AMA clinical criteria for PVS are:

- Chronic unconscious wakefulness without awareness, though wakefulness may be accompanied by opening of eyes, unintelligible sounds, movements of facial muscles, and even smiles.

- Lack of intelligible speech and failure to comprehend others' words.

- Inability to make purposeful or voluntary movements—movements made are reflex responses to external or unpleasant stimuli.

- Lack of sustained visual and auditory responses to external stimuli. Some PVS patients may turn their heads or move their eyes toward sounds or moving objects, but these movements are brief reflex reactions that do not require upper-brain functioning.

- Lack of bowel and bladder control.

- Presence of non-neurological functions, such as the ability to swallow and digest food.

- Ability to breathe independently.

Chances of Recovery

Representatives from five neurological societies, along with medical, ethical, and legal consultants, joined forces to investigate the medical facts about PVS, and published the results of their study in 1994. The Multi-Society Task Force concluded that the clinical course and outcome of a persistent vegetative state depend on the initial cause of the condition. In "Medical Aspects of the Persistent Vegetative State" (*The New England Journal of Medicine,* vol. 330, nos. 21 and 22, May 26 and June 2, 1994), the task force reported the recovery rates from disorders that may cause PVS.

TRAUMATIC BRAIN INJURIES. The task force investigated a total of 434 adult PVS patients one month after their traumatic brain injuries. Three months after the injury, 33 percent had recovered consciousness, while 67 percent had either died or remained in a PVS. At six

TABLE 4.5

Incidence of recovery of consciousness and function in adults and children in a persistent vegetative state (PVS) after traumatic or nontraumatic brain injury

Outcome and functional recovery*	3 months	6 months	12 months
		% of patients	
Adults			
Traumatic injury (n = 434)			
Death	15	24	33
PVS	52	30	15
Recovery of consciousness	33	46	52
Severe disability			28
Mode rate disablity			17
Good recovery			7
Nontraumatic injury (n = 169)			
Death	24	40	53
PVS	65	45	32
Recovery of consciousness	11	15	15
Severe disability			11
Moderate disability			3
Good recovery			1
Children			
Traumatic injury (n = 106)			
Death	4	9	9
PVS	72	40	29
Recovery of consciousness	24	51	62
Severe disability			35
Moderate disability			16
Good recovery			11
Nontraumatic injury (n = 45)			
Death	20	22	22
PVS	69	67	65
Recovery of consciousness	11	11	13
Severe disability			7
Moderate disability			0
Good recovery			6

*Data on functional recovery are for patients who had recovered consciousness within 12 months after injury.

Note: Data were collected from series of patients in a PVS one month after injury and do not include individual case reports. Some patients who recovered consciousness died within 12 months after injury or were lost to follow-up. The data for nontraumatic injuries reflect all causes, not just postanoxic injury; for this category alone, the prognosis is poorer than that suggested by the data.

SOURCE: The Multi-Society Task Force on PVS, "Table 3. Incidence of Recovery of Consciousness and Function in Adults and Children in a Persistent Vegetative State (PVS) after Traumatic or Nontraumatic Brain Injury," in "Medical Aspects of the Persistent Vegetative State," *The New England Journal of Medicine,* vol. 330, nos. 1 and 2, May 26, 1994 and June 2, 1994

months, 46 percent had recovered consciousness, compared with 52 percent at one year. (See Figure 4.2 and Table 4.5.)

Recovery from PVS has another dimension: function recovery. After one year, 33 percent of the 434 patients had died, 15 percent remained in a PVS, 28 percent were severely disabled, and 17 percent were moderately disabled. Only 7 percent were diagnosed as having a good recovery, which meant they were able to resume normal social and job-related activities. (See Table 4.5.) The task force also found that PVS patients younger than 40 years of age had a better chance of improvement than those older than 40.

FIGURE 4.2

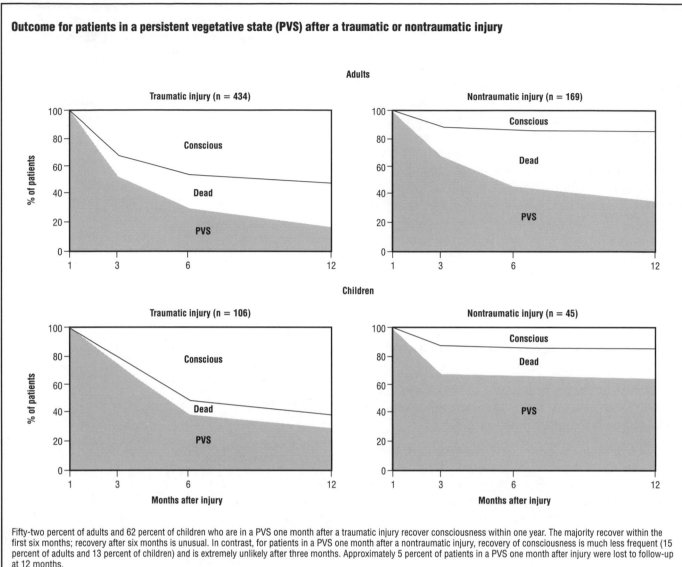

Outcome for patients in a persistent vegetative state (PVS) after a traumatic or nontraumatic injury

Fifty-two percent of adults and 62 percent of children who are in a PVS one month after a traumatic injury recover consciousness within one year. The majority recover within the first six months; recovery after six months is unusual. In contrast, for patients in a PVS one month after a nontraumatic injury, recovery of consciousness is much less frequent (15 percent of adults and 13 percent of children) and is extremely unlikely after three months. Approximately 5 percent of patients in a PVS one month after injury were lost to follow-up at 12 months.

SOURCE: The Multi-Society Task Force on PVS, "Figure 1. Outcome for Patients in a Persistent Vegetative State (PVS) after a Traumatic or Nontraumatic Injury," in "Medical Aspects of the Persistent Vegetative State," *The New England Journal of Medicine,* vol. 330, nos. 1 and 2, May 26, 1994 and June 2, 1994

Children who experienced traumatic injuries causing a PVS also showed a better recovery rate than adults. Of the 106 PVS children surveyed, one-quarter (24 percent) recovered consciousness within three months. At one year, almost two-thirds (62 percent) had recovered, while 9 percent had died. (See Figure 4.2 and Table 4.5.) Of the 29 percent who remained in a PVS after one year, none regained consciousness.

The prognosis of functional recovery among children, like that among adults, was better when consciousness was regained within six months. After one year, 35 percent of the children suffered severe disability, 16 percent had moderate disability, and 11 percent had a good recovery. The researchers found that while children had a good recovery after six months and exhibited moderate disabili-

ty after one year, adults who recovered after six months suffered serious disabilities.

NONTRAUMATIC BRAIN INJURIES. Nontraumatic brain injuries, which refer to oxygen deprivation caused by things such as stroke, are far more likely to result in death or PVS and much less likely to result in recovery of consciousness. Of the 169 adult PVS patients who experienced nontraumatic injuries after three months, about 89 percent stayed in a PVS or died, while only 11 percent had regained consciousness. After a year, half (53 percent) had died, one-third (32 percent) remained in a PVS, and 15 percent had recovered consciousness. (See Figure 4.2 and Table 4.5.) The 15 percent who regained consciousness showed little recovery of function, with only one patient having a good recovery.

Of 45 PVS children who had nontraumatic brain injuries, only 13 percent regained consciousness at one year. One-fifth (22 percent) died, and most of the children (65 percent) remained in PVS. As with traumatic head injuries, children fared better in recovery of function than adults. (See Figure 4.2 and Table 4.5.)

DEGENERATIVE AND METABOLIC BRAIN DISORDERS. The Multi-Society Task Force on PVS reported that persons who enter PVS resulting from degenerative and metabolic diseases do not regain consciousness. Degenerative brain disorders, such as Alzheimer's disease, produce irreversible unconsciousness at their terminal stages. Within a few weeks or months, the patient usually succumbs to the disease. Metabolic disorders, such as toxic kidney disease, are severe conditions that also result in irreversible coma.

SEVERE CONGENITAL MALFORMATIONS OF THE NERVOUS SYSTEM. Infants and children in a PVS due to severe brain malformations are unlikely to regain consciousness. Most who do recover consciousness exhibit serious disabilities. Anencephalic babies, missing a major part of the brain, skull, and scalp, have no capacity for consciousness.

LATE RECOVERY OF CONSCIOUSNESS. Only a handful of PVS patients have been known to regain consciousness after 12 months. All have been left with severe disabilities.

The Possibility of Locked-In Syndrome

Locked-in syndrome is a rare neurological disorder that has added to the controversy involving PVS patients and the withdrawal of life-sustaining treatments. Locked-in syndrome is characterized by the complete paralysis of all voluntary muscles except those controlling the eye muscles. According to the National Institute of Neurological Disorders and Stroke, persons with locked-in syndrome are conscious and have cognitive function. Paralysis, not coma, causes the patients' inability to respond. Patients with this syndrome have been known to communicate by blinking.

Those opposing withdrawing life supports from unconscious patients argue that a patient diagnosed to be in a PVS may actually be suffering from locked-in syndrome. However, a thorough neurological examination or an imaging technique known as positron emission tomography (PET) can distinguish between PVS and locked-in patients.

Treatment of PVS Patients

PATIENTS' INTERESTS. The President's Commission for the Study of Ethical Problems in Medicine and Biomedical and Behavioral Research published the report *Deciding to Forego Life-Sustaining Treatment* (U.S. Government Printing Office, Washington, D.C., 1983) as an offshoot of their study on the definition of death and other health care issues. These landmark reports continue to set the standards for many medical and bioethical decisions. The commission noted that medical treatment of PVS patients is based primarily on maintaining their well-being—"preserving life, relieving pain and suffering, protecting against disability, and returning maximally effective functioning."

However, if a patient is diagnosed as irreversibly unconscious, then continued treatment does not really benefit the patient. The only reason for continued treatment is the possibility that the prognosis of PVS might be incorrect. The commission observed that the few patients who did regain consciousness suffered severe disabilities. It concluded that most patients would not want to recover and find themselves in a severely disabled condition. The commission added that continuing treatment with the belief that the patient would have refused such a treatment would even be more harmful.

Finally, continued long-term care creates financial and emotional burdens for the patient's family. The commission concluded that most patients value their family's well-being and that it would not serve a patient's interests to let prolonged care exact such heavy tolls on the family.

OTHERS' INTERESTS. Society in general puts a high value on human life, and the continued care of permanently unconscious patients both reflects and reinforces that value. Further, society does not appear to want to see PVS patients abandoned, since such an attitude might carry over to less seriously ill patients.

The patient's family also has a vested interest in continued care, hoping that continued treatment might bring back their loved one. Many find comfort and meaning in taking care of the patient.

Health care personnel, trained to save lives, often feel that discontinuing treatment is at odds with their professional training. The traditional training of aggressive intervention can be hard to set aside in order to honor a patient's or family's request to forego life support. Health care professionals also lack training in moving from taking care of a dying patient to withdrawing his or her life support. Howard Brody, et al., in "Withdrawing Intensive Life-Sustaining Treatment—Recommendations for Compassionate Clinical Management" (*The New England Journal of Medicine,* vol. 336, no. 9, February 27, 1997), observe that "caring for dying patients and their families exacts a serious toll on physicians and nurses."

HOSPITAL SUES TO DISCONTINUE CARE: HELGA WANGLIE

In 1991 a hospital in Minneapolis, Minnesota, sued to discontinue treatment of a patient. This was the first time that a health care provider had gone to court to seek help in ending life-sustaining treatment for a patient.

Helga Wanglie, an 87-year-old woman, had been in a PVS for eight months. Physicians at Hennepin County Medical Center in Minneapolis suggested to her family that her respirator be turned off since the life support was simply prolonging her dying process. Her family refused to give consent. They argued that it was against Helga's and their religious beliefs to end her life, a life that belonged to God. Mr. Wanglie added that his wife had specifically told him that if she ever became incompetent, she did not want her life ended. The court ruled that Mr. Wanglie was in the best position to represent his wife's interests and she was sustained on life support until her death shortly afterward.

Ethics or Economics?

Helga Wanglie's physicians and the hospital ethics committee claimed that continuance of her treatment went against the ethical principle of nonmaleficence, or "do not harm." In other words, the continued life support was not in the patient's best interests. Advocates of this reasoning argue that most of us would not want our bodies indefinitely and artificially sustained with no hope of future recovery.

Others argue that the underlying reason for the suit was the enormous cost of caring for Helga Wanglie. By the time the lawsuit was filed, the patient's medical expenses were well over $800,000. Proponents of the restricted use of life support suggest that the money spent keeping PVS patients alive could be better used to provide treatment for those with more positive prognoses. Moreover, such unlimited health care could be disastrous to the whole health care system. Naturally, the question arises as to whether economics should enter into health care providers' and insurance companies' considerations about terminating life support.

PHYSICIAN IGNORES PATIENT'S REFUSAL OF TREATMENT

In July 1973 Dax Cowart suffered burns to most of his body in a gas explosion that killed his father. He also lost his eyesight and the use of his hands. Throughout the terribly painful treatments, which lasted 14 months in the hospital, Cowart asked to die by refusing consent to treatments. His pleas were ignored. In "Confronting Death: Who Chooses, Who Controls? A Dialogue between Dax Cowart and Robert Burt" (*Hastings Center Report,* vol. 28, no. 1, January-February 1998), Cowart, now a plaintiffs personal injury trial lawyer, and Burt, a Yale University law professor, probe the patient's right to refuse life-sustaining treatments.

Although Cowart's accident occurred three decades ago and patient autonomy today theoretically requires that competent patients have the right to refuse treatments, Cowart thinks doctors continue to believe that they know what is best for their patients. In fact, he believes that many patients are forced to endure medical treatments and procedures that they do not wish to go through. He feels the situation is further aggravated by physicians' failure to communicate.

According to Cowart, the excruciating pain he had to endure was by far the biggest reason he refused life-sustaining treatments. He naively thought that no doctor could possibly let a patient suffer so much, and that his doctors were doing everything possible to ease his suffering. Later on, he found out there were additional measures the doctors could have taken to alleviate his pain.

Pain in Modern Times

Despite medical advances, severe pain still often accompanies the dying process. Joanne Lynn, M.D., et al. ("Perceptions by Family Members of the Dying Experience of Older and Seriously Ill Patients," *Annals of Internal Medicine,* vol. 126, no. 2, January 15, 1997), analyzed the data from SUPPORT, the biggest research project ever done on death and dying in the United States. Dr. Lynn, et al., found that four in ten elderly and seriously ill patients who were conscious during the last three days prior to death suffered from severe pain most of the time. The authors claim that health care professionals continue to fail to manage patients' pain due to a lack of patient-doctor communication, misplaced concern about "drug addiction," and inadequate professional training in pain management.

Along with these concerns, many physicians who prescribe narcotics (a class of addictive, depressant drugs that can only be obtained with a physician's prescription) to relieve pain are concerned about legal and professional consequences. These include the possibility of legal prosecution for over-prescribing or under-prescribing narcotic pain relievers. Fear of scrutiny and disciplinary action by the federal Drug Enforcement Administration (DEA) may also contribute to physicians' reluctance to prescribe powerful pain medication.

ORGAN TRANSPLANTATION

Organ transplantation has come a long way since the first kidney was transplanted from one identical twin to another in 1954. The introduction in 1983 of cyclosporine, an immunosuppressant drug that helps prevent the body's immune system from rejecting a donated organ, made it possible to successfully transplant nearly a dozen different organs and tissues. (See Figure 4.3.) The demand for donor organs soon exceeded the supply. In 1984 Congress passed the National Organ Transplant Act (PL 98-507) in order to create "a centralized network to match scarce donated organs with critically ill patients." (See Figure 4.4 for the process of matching organ donors and recipients.) Today, organ transplant is an accepted medical treatment for end-stage illnesses.

The organs that may be transplanted from persons who have died include the heart, intestines, kidneys, liver, lungs, and pancreas. Tissues that may be harvested for transfer include bone, cartilage, corneas, heart valves, pancreas islet cells, skin, tendons, and veins. Living persons may donate a kidney or parts of a lung or liver. Typically, donated organs must be transplanted within 6 to 48 hours of harvest, while some tissue may be stored for future use.

The United Network for Organ Sharing (UNOS), a private company under contract with the Division of Transplantation of the Department of Health and Human Services (HHS), manages the national transplant waiting list. It maintains data on all clinical organ transplants and distributes organ donor cards. (See Figure 4.5.) UNOS reported that over 79,000 people were waiting for a transplant in the United States as of March 2002. (See Table 4.6.) Each month this list grows by an estimated 1,000 people. In the year ending June 30, 2001, more than 6,000 people died while awaiting a transplant because donor organs were not available.

In 2000, 58 percent of all organs retrieved were kidneys, 22 percent were livers, 10 percent hearts, 4 percent lungs, 2 percent pancreases, and .3 percent intestines. The remaining 4 percent were multi-organ procedures, for a total of 22,953 transplants. (See Table 4.7.)

The number of all donors rose 59 percent between 1990 and 1999, from 6,633 to 10,561. While the number of cadaveric donors (dead bodies from which organs are harvested) increased 30 percent, from 4,509 to 5,849, living donors showed a significant increase of 122 percent, from 2,124 to 4,712. (See Table 4.8.)

Organ Donation

The Uniform Anatomical Gift Act of 1968 gives a person the opportunity to sign a donor card indicating a desire to donate organs or tissue after death. Persons who wish to be donors should complete a donor card. (See Figure 4.5.) This card should be carried at all times. Alternatively, the wish to be a donor can be indicated on a driver's license or in a living will. Prospective donors should inform their family and physician of their decision. At the time of death, hospitals always ask for the family's consent, even if a donor has already indicated his or her wish to donate organs. Should the family refuse, the doctors will not take the organs, despite the deceased's wish. In 1999 most organ donors whose cause of death was known died of head trauma (42 percent) or cerebrovascular disease or stroke (43 percent). (See Table 4.9.)

In 1986 the Consolidated Omnibus Budget Reconciliation Act (PL 99-509) required all hospitals receiving federal funding to adopt procedures to identify potential organ donors and notify families of their option to donate. In June 1998, the government transferred this responsibil-

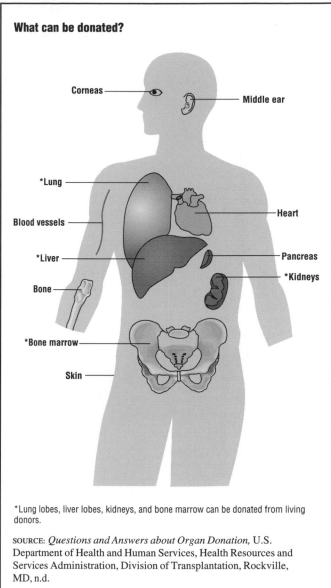

FIGURE 4.3

What can be donated?

Corneas

Middle ear

*Lung

Heart

Blood vessels

*Liver

Pancreas

*Kidneys

Bone

*Bone marrow

Skin

*Lung lobes, liver lobes, kidneys, and bone marrow can be donated from living donors.

SOURCE: *Questions and Answers about Organ Donation,* U.S. Department of Health and Human Services, Health Resources and Services Administration, Division of Transplantation, Rockville, MD, n.d.

ity from hospitals to local organ procurement organizations because the hospitals were not doing the job. The Department of Health and Human Services estimates that 12,000 to 15,000 potential organ donors die each year whose families are never asked to donate their loved ones' organs. Under the new procedure, hospitals are required to report every death to the procurement organizations.

In 1997, to promote awareness of organ and tissue donation, Congress authorized the Internal Revenue Service (IRS) to include organ and tissue donor information with federal tax refund checks. In another effort to increase public support for organ donation, the U.S. Postal Service introduced a new stamp in 1998 showing two intertwined figures, their hands reaching to touch each other's hearts.

By 2001 demand continued to outpace the supply of available organs and tissues for transplants. Governors of

FIGURE 4.4

Matching donors and recipients: The Organ Procurement & Transplantation Network (OPTN) and the Scientific Registry of Transplant Recipients

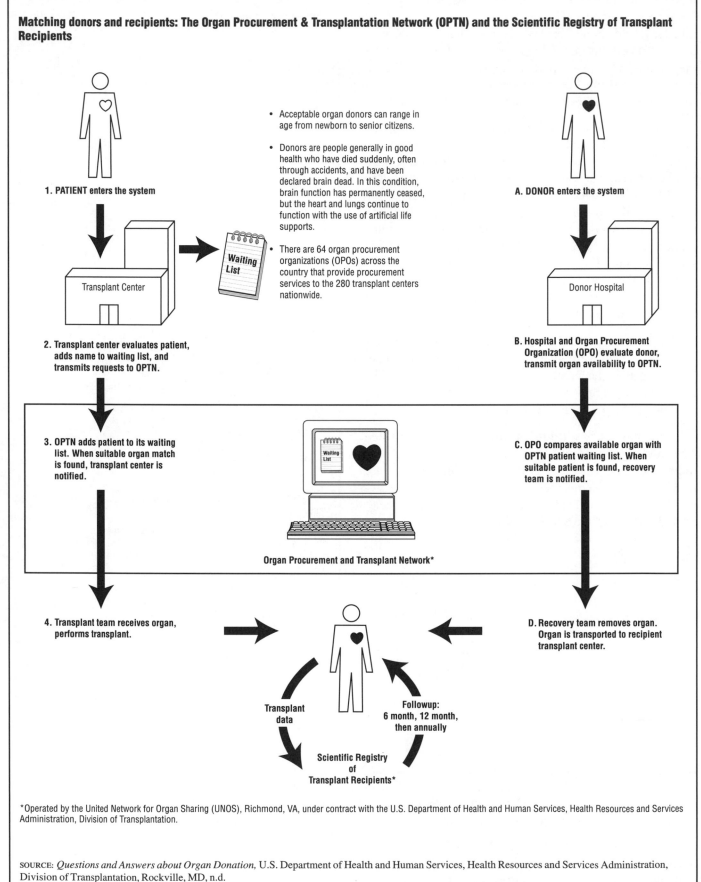

1. PATIENT enters the system

Transplant Center

Waiting List

- Acceptable organ donors can range in age from newborn to senior citizens.

- Donors are people generally in good health who have died suddenly, often through accidents, and have been declared brain dead. In this condition, brain function has permanently ceased, but the heart and lungs continue to function with the use of artificial life supports.

- There are 64 organ procurement organizations (OPOs) across the country that provide procurement services to the 280 transplant centers nationwide.

A. DONOR enters the system

Donor Hospital

2. Transplant center evaluates patient, adds name to waiting list, and transmits requests to OPTN.

B. Hospital and Organ Procurement Organization (OPO) evaluate donor, transmit organ availability to OPTN.

3. OPTN adds patient to its waiting list. When suitable organ match is found, transplant center is notified.

Waiting List

Organ Procurement and Transplant Network*

C. OPO compares available organ with OPTN patient waiting list. When suitable patient is found, recovery team is notified.

4. Transplant team receives organ, performs transplant.

D. Recovery team removes organ. Organ is transported to recipient transplant center.

Transplant data

Followup: 6 month, 12 month, then annually

Scientific Registry of Transplant Recipients*

*Operated by the United Network for Organ Sharing (UNOS), Richmond, VA, under contract with the U.S. Department of Health and Human Services, Health Resources and Services Administration, Division of Transplantation.

SOURCE: *Questions and Answers about Organ Donation,* U.S. Department of Health and Human Services, Health Resources and Services Administration, Division of Transplantation, Rockville, MD, n.d.

FIGURE 4.5

Organ/ Tissue Donor Card

I wish to donate my organs and tissues. I wish to give:

☐ any needed organs and tissues   ☐ only the following organs and tissues:

_____

Donor
Signature _____ Date _____
Witness _____
Witness _____

SOURCE: U.S. Department of Health and Human Services, Health Resources and Services Administration, Division of Transplantation, Rockville, MD [Online] http://www.organdonor.gov/newdonorcard.pdf [accessed April 25, 2002]

TABLE 4.6

United Network for Organ Sharing (UNOS) national patient waiting list for organ transplant, March 1, 2002

Type of transplant	Patients waiting for transplant
Kidney transplant	51,215
Liver transplant	17,886
Pancreas transplant	1,245
Pancreas islet cell transplant	270
Kidney-pancreas transplant	2,486
Intestine transplant	178
Heart transplant	4,143
Heart-lung transplant	209
Lung transplant	3,824
Total	**79,125**

Note: United Network for Organ Sharing/Organ Procurement and Transplantation Network (UNOS/OPTN) policies allow patients to be listed with more than one transplant center (multiple-listing), thus the number of registrations is greater than the actual number of patients. Some patients are waiting for more than one organ, therefore the total number of patients is less than the sum of patients waiting for each organ.

SOURCE: "On March 1, 2002 the UNOS national patient waiting list for organ transplant included the following:" in *Critical Data: U.S. Facts About Transplantation,* United Network for Organ Sharing, Richmond, VA [Online] http://www.unos.org/Newsroom/critdata_main.htm [accessed March 27, 2002]

TABLE 4.7

Number of organ transplants performed, 2000*

Type of transplant	Number
Kidney alone transplants (5,293 were living donors)	13,372
Liver transplants	4,954
Pancreas alone transplants	435
Kidney-pancreas transplants	911
Intestine transplants	79
Heart transplants	2,198
Heart-lung transplants	48
Lung transplants	956
Total	**22,953**

*Based on Organ Procurement and Transplantation Network (OPTN) data as of August 3, 2001. Double kidney, double lung, and heart-lung transplants are counted as one transplant.

SOURCE: "Number of Transplants Performed in 2000," in *Critical Data: U.S. Facts About Transplantation,* United Network for Organ Sharing, Richmond, VA [Online] http://www.unos.org/Newsroom/critdata_main.htm [accessed March 27, 2002]

many states began a variety of programs aimed at increasing public awareness of the lack of donor organs and honoring people who have chosen to become donors. For example, Alabama Governor Don Siegelman created an Alabama Donor Registry, Georgia Governor Roy Barnes designated March 2001 as Eye Donor Month, and Utah Governor Michael O. Leavitt and his state's legislature adopted a resolution to improve public awareness about organ and tissue donation. Governors of at least nine states forged partnerships with local advocacy, medical, religious, and business groups to strengthen support for transplant programs.

State programs were also reinforced by a national organ donation initiative announced by Health and Human Services Secretary Tommy G. Thompson in April 2001. Secretary Thompson vowed to create a national medal to honor families of organ donors and called upon powerful alliances between employers and unions to promote donation. Called the "Workplace Partnership for Life," this coalition includes some of the largest U.S. employers: Aetna, American Airlines, Bank of America, DaimlerChrysler Corporation UAW, Ford Motor Company, General Motors, 3M, MetLife, Verizon, and the United States Postal Service.

New Transplant Regulations Come and Go

In March 1998 the Clinton administration ordered UNOS to change its organ allocation policy. The network fought the new rules for two years in favor of the system already in place, which was based on geography. When an organ became available in a local area, that organ was offered to the sickest patient in that area. If no local patient needed the organ, it was then offered regionally, and last of all, nationally. The government, however, wanted organs to be given to the sickest patients first, regardless of geographic location. Then–Secretary of Health and Human Services Donna Shalala claimed, "People are dying unnecessarily, not because they don't have health insurance, not because they don't have access to care, but simply because of where they happen to live in the country. We need a level playing field for all patients."

The new system, based on need rather than location, took effect in March 2000, although the issue of precisely

TABLE 4.8

Donations by organ and donor type, 1990–99

	Organ donor type								
	Kidney			Liver			Pancreas		
Year	Cadaveric	Living	Total	Cadaveric	Living	Total	Cadaveric	Living	Total
1990	4,306	2,095	6,401	2,868	14	2,882	951	2	953
1991	4,268	2,393	6,661	3,165	22	3,187	1,066	1	1,067
1992	4,276	2,535	6,811	3,334	33	3,367	1,004	3	1,007
1993	4,609	2,851	7,460	3,764	36	3,800	1,243	2	1,245
1994	4,798	3,009	7,807	4,094	60	4,154	1,360	2	1,362
1995	4,998	3,364	8,362	4,324	46	4,370	1,277	7	1,284
1996	5,038	3,656	8,694	4,462	56	4,518	1,294	11	1,305
1997	5,082	3,909	8,991	4,600	76	4,676	1,319	6	1,325
1998	5,346	4,341	9,687	4,846	85	4,931	1,458	2	1,460
1999	5,396	4,466	9,862	4,954	218	5,172	1,627	5	1,632

	Organ/donor type											
	Heart			Lung			Intestine			Overall		
Year	Cadaveric	Living	Total	Cadaveric	Living	Total	Cadaveric	Living	Total	Cadaveric	Living	Total
1990	2,167	12	2,179	275	1	276	6	0	6	4,509	2,124	6,633
1991	2,198	4	2,202	395	4	399	11	0	11	4,526	2,424	6,950
1992	2,246	1	2,247	526	0	526	21	0	21	4,520	2,572	7,092
1993	2,442	2	2,444	790	14	804	34	0	34	4,861	2,905	7,766
1994	2,526	3	2,529	918	30	948	62	0	62	5,100	3,102	8,202
1995	2,495	0	2,495	880	45	925	121	1	122	5,358	3,457	8,815
1996	2,474	1	2,475	758	41	799	48	2	50	5,418	3,757	9,175
1997	2,425	0	2,425	836	34	870	71	2	73	5,477	4,022	9,499
1998	2,449	0	2,449	764	47	811	78	1	79	5,801	4,475	10,276
1999	2,316	2	2,318	781	26	807	97	0	97	5,849	4,712	10,561

SOURCE: "Table1: U.S. donors by organ and donor type—1990 to 1999," in *2000 Annual Report of the U.S. Scientific Registry for Transplant Recipients and the Organ Procurement and Transplantation Network: Transplant Data: 1990–1999,* U.S. Department of Health and Human Services, Health Resources and Services Administration, Division of Transplantation, Rockville, MD; and United Network for Organ Sharing (UNOS), Richmond, VA

who would decide the allocation of organs remained unresolved until April 2000, when the U.S. House of Representatives passed a proposal to restore decision-making to UNOS, where it has remained.

Anencephalic Newborns and Organ Transplantation

The scarcity of organs for infants and young children has led to a consideration of the possibility of harvesting organs from anencephalic newborns—babies born without a major part of the brain, skull, and scalp, and who usually die shortly after birth. Organs must be removed while these newborns are still alive to avoid compromising the viability of the organs. In 1995 the Council on Ethical and Judicial Affairs of the American Medical Association (AMA), in "The Use of Anencephalic Neonates as Organ Donors" (*The Journal of the American Medical Association,* vol. 273, no. 20, May 24/31, 1995), indicated its support for taking organs from anencephalic babies. This reversed the 1988 decision in which the council opposed taking organs from anencephalic babies.

While federal and state laws expressly forbid taking organs from live donors (except for special circumstances, such as a kidney or parts of the lung or liver, which donors are able to live without), the AMA claimed that this situation was unique because, unlike live adult donors, anencephalic neonates have never experienced consciousness and will never experience consciousness, and thus cannot have interests of any kind.

The AMA concluded that although an anencephalic neonate is still alive according to the current definition of death, it is ethically permissible to consider the baby as a potential organ donor under three conditions. First, the diagnosis of anencephaly must be certain and confirmed by two physicians who are not part of the transplant team. Second, the parents of the neonate must initiate any discussions about organ retrieval and indicate their desire in writing. Third, there must be compliance with the Council's Guidelines for the Transplantation of Organs.

Two-thirds of the ethicists and experts in anencephaly surveyed believed the use of organs from anencephalic newborns to be "intrinsically moral," and more than half would like to see the law changed to allow this procedure. Critics, however, charge that if organs can be removed from living anencephalic newborns, they could eventually also be removed from infants with other brain injuries, demented adults, and persons in PVS. Moreover, public confidence in the organ transplant system might be undermined in response to the fear that doctors would prematurely remove organs from dying patients.

TABLE 4.9

Causes of death for cadaveric donors, 1990–99

Year	Motor vehicle accident		Gunshot/stab		Cerebrovascular		Head trauma		Asphyxiation	
	N	%	N	%	N	%	N	%	N	%
1990	1,241	27.8	733	16.4	1,458	32.6	503	11.2	140	3.1
1991	1,164	25.9	804	17.9	1,529	34.0	463	10.3	144	3.2
1992	997	22.4	796	17.9	1,633	36.7	521	11.7	106	2.4
1993	1,100	23.1	807	17.0	1,786	37.5	558	11.7	132	2.8

Year	Drowning		Drug intoxication		Cardiovascular		Other		Un-known	Total
	N	%	N	%	N	%	N	%		
1990	50	1.1	31	0.7	75	1.7	241	5.4	37	4,509
1991	38	0.8	31	0.7	78	1.7	246	5.5	29	4,526
1992	45	1.0	37	0.8	82	1.8	229	5.2	74	4,520
1993	53	1.1	24	0.5	112	2.4	187	3.9	102	4,861

Year	Anoxia		Cerebro-vascular/stroke		Head trauma		CNS Tumor		Other		Un-known	Total
	N	%	N	%	N	%	N	%	N	%		
1994	424	8.3	1,948	38.2	2,360	46.3	47	0.9	316	6.2	5	5,100
1995	526	9.8	2,051	38.4	2,616	49.0	53	1.0	98	1.8	14	5,358
1996	527	9.8	2,270	42.1	2,455	45.6	50	0.9	86	1.6	30	5,418
1997	561	10.4	2,220	41.0	2,470	45.6	63	1.2	104	1.9	59	5,477
1998	637	11.1	2,465	43.0	2,488	43.4	55	1.0	88	1.5	68	5,801
1999	569	10.9	2,236	43.0	2,182	42.0	51	1.0	160	3.1	651	5,849

Note: Percentages are based on totals excluding unknown cases. Form changes on April 1, 1994 changed the way "Cause of Death" data were collected.

SOURCE: "Cadaveric Donor Characteristics—1990 to 1999," in *Critical Data: U.S. Facts About Transplantation,* United Network for Organ Sharing, Richmond, VA [Online] http://www.unos.org/Newsroom/critdata_main.htm [accessed March 26, 2002]

THE AMA RECONSIDERS ITS OPINION. In 1996 the Council on Ethical and Judicial Affairs of the AMA retracted its 1995 opinion supporting the retrieval of organs from anencephalic newborns (Letter to the Editor, *The Journal of the American Medical Association,* vol. 275, no. 6, February 14, 1996). Concerned about the understanding of consciousness and certain diagnoses of anencephaly in some newborns, the council reversed its opinion. As of April 2002 the AMA maintained the position that these infants should not be used for organ donation until such time as a determination of death can be made according to accepted medical standards, relevant law, and regional organ procurement organization policy.

Other Countries

Many European countries, including France and Belgium, procure organs under the "presumed consent" law, which presumes everyone is a potential organ donor unless he or she forbids it.

In the United States, selling organs is unlawful under the National Organ Transplant Act of 1984. Organ markets, where people sell their organs to the affluent or to organ "brokers," exist in some Third World countries, including Brazil and Turkey. In India, many hospitals and physicians deal in organ transactions, employing middlemen who buy organs from the poor.

In 1995 Chinese refugees testified before the U.S. Senate that condemned Chinese prisoners are shot and their organs sold for transplant. Kidneys and corneas are harvested annually from about 2,000 to 10,000 executed prisoners. The recipients are reportedly Chinese officials, as well as wealthy foreigners from Hong Kong, Britain, Japan, and the United States.

In June 1997 the Japanese parliament passed a bill defining brain death as death, thereby legalizing organ transplantation. Nonetheless, the issues of brain death and organ transplantation are so sensitive to the Japanese people that the law suggests that brain death may only be considered the end of life when donors have agreed with this definition and expressed their wishes in writing. The family's consent is needed to retrieve organs, and family members are allowed to dispute the diagnosis of brain death.

Although doctors in Japan have been performing procedures such as kidney transplants with organs from live donors, historically many Japanese patients traveled to other countries for heart or lung transplants when these organs were not readily available. The scarcity of donor organs was believed to reflect discomfort with the practice of harvesting donor organs from persons at the end of life.

The situation is slowly changing. By the end of 1999 more than 7 percent of Japan's population carried donor cards and more than half of the general population indicated a willingness to donate organs. Nonetheless, many observers of Japanese society believe that when the time comes to carry out a donor's wish, some families may be unable to comply and cultural tradition will prevail. Many Japanese find it unacceptable to "desecrate a body," especially one that is still breathing.

CHAPTER 5
SERIOUSLY ILL CHILDREN

What greater pain could mortals have than this;
To see their children dead before their eyes?
—Euripides

To a parent, the death of a child is an affront to the proper order of things. Children are supposed to outlive their parents, not the other way around. And when a child comes into the world irreparably ill, what is a parent to do—insist on continuous medical intervention, hoping against hope that a miracle happens, or let nature take its course and allow the newborn to die? When a five-year-old child has painful, life-threatening disabilities, the parent is faced with a similar agonizing decision. That decision, hopefully with advice from a sensitive physician, is still the parent's to make. But what if the ailing child is an adolescent who refuses further treatment for a terminal illness? Does a parent honor that wish?

INFANT MORTALITY

Since 1960 the infant mortality rate in the United States has declined 72 percent—from 26 deaths per 1,000 live births in 1960 to 6.9 deaths per 1,000 live births in 2000. (Table 5.1 shows the decline from 1983–98, while Table 5.2 shows figures for 1999 and preliminary figures for 2000.) Advances in neonatology (the medical subspecialty concerned with the care of newborns, especially those at risk), which date back to the 1960s, have contributed to the huge drop in infant death rates. Infants born prematurely or with low birthweights, who were once likely to die, now can survive life-threatening conditions because of the development of neonatal intensive care units (NICUs). However, despite the tremendous improvements in neonatal treatment, there is still a connection between race and infant mortality. Black infants are more than twice as likely as white and Hispanic infants to die before their first birthday. In 2000 the national death rate for black infants was 14 percent, compared with 5.7 percent for white infants and 5.6 percent for Hispanic infants. (See Table 5.2 and Table 5.3.)

As neonatology has progressed, it has enabled physicians to aggressively treat more babies, and those at greater risk. Margot C.J. Mabie, in *Bioethics and the New Medical Technology* (Atheneum, New York, 1993), points out that neonatologists have taken on infants with serious abnormalities that in the past would have caused the infant to die, as well as full-term normal babies who were injured in the birth process. However, although many infants have been saved, some survive with constant pain. Others require continuous medical care, which can exact heavy emotional and financial tolls on the family.

Leading Causes of Infant Mortality

Birth defects are the leading cause of infant mortality in the United States. Some of the more serious birth defects are anencephaly, spina bifida, and Down syndrome (babies born with an extra copy of chromosome 21 in their cells). The Centers for Disease Control and Prevention (CDC) estimate that about 120,000 babies will be born with serious birth defects during 2002, and of these, about 8,000 will die during their first year of life. Many of those who survive will suffer from lifelong disabilities.

In 2000 birth defects (identified as "congenital malformations, deformations and chromosomal abnormalities" by the *Tenth Revision, International Classification of Diseases 1992,*) accounted for 21 percent of all infant deaths (142.2 infant deaths per 100,000 live births). (See Table 5.4.)

Disorders related to short gestation (premature birth) and low birthweight accounted for the second leading cause of infant mortality (105.8 deaths per 100,000 live births). Among black infants, they were the leading cause of death (284.4 deaths per 100,000 live births). Other causes of infant deaths were sudden infant death syndrome (SIDS), maternal complications of pregnancy, and complications of the placenta, cord, and membranes. These five leading causes of infant mortality accounted for more than half the total infant deaths. (See Table 5.4.)

TABLE 5.1

Infant, neonatal, and postnatal mortality rates, according to detailed race and Hispanic origin of mother, selected years 1983–98

[DATA ARE BASED ON NATIONAL LINKED BIRTH/INFANT DEATH DATA SETS.]

Race and Hispanic origin of mother	1983[1]	1990[1]	1995[2]	1997[2]	1998[2]	1983–85[1]	1986–88[1]	1989–91[1]	1996–98[2]
	Infant[3] deaths per 1,000 live births								
All mothers	10.9	8.9	7.6	7.2	7.2	10.6	9.8	9.0	7.2
White	9.3	7.3	6.3	6.0	6.0	9.0	8.2	7.4	6.0
Black	19.2	16.9	14.6	13.7	13.8	18.7	17.9	17.1	13.9
American Indian or Alaska Native	15.2	13.1	9.0	8.7	9.3	13.9	13.2	12.6	9.3
Asian or Pacific Islander	8.3	6.6	5.3	5.0	5.5	8.3	7.3	6.6	5.2
Chinese	9.5	4.3	3.8	3.1	4.0	7.4	5.8	5.1	3.4
Japanese	*5.6	*5.5	*5.3	*5.3	*3.5	6.0	6.9	5.3	4.3
Filipino	8.4	6.0	5.6	5.8	6.2	8.2	6.9	6.4	5.9
Hawaiian and part Hawaiian	11.2	*8.0	*6.6	9.0	10.0	11.3	11.1	9.0	8.2
Other Asian or Pacific Islander	8.1	7.4	5.5	5.0	5.7	8.6	7.6	7.0	5.5
Hispanic origin[4,5]	9.5	7.5	6.3	6.0	5.8	9.2	8.3	7.5	5.9
Mexican	9.1	7.2	6.0	5.8	5.6	8.8	7.9	7.2	5.8
Puerto Rican	12.9	9.9	8.9	7.9	7.8	12.3	11.1	10.4	8.1
Cuban	7.5	7.2	5.3	5.5	*3.6	8.0	7.3	6.2	4.7
Central and South American	8.5	6.8	5.5	5.5	5.3	8.2	7.5	6.6	5.2
Other and unknown Hispanic	10.6	8.0	7.4	6.2	6.5	9.8	9.0	8.2	6.8
White, non-Hispanic [5]	9.2	7.2	6.3	6.0	6.0	8.8	8.1	7.3	6.0
Black, non-Hispanic [5]	19.1	16.9	14.7	13.7	13.9	18.5	17.9	17.2	13.9
	Neonatal [3] deaths per 1,000 live births								
All mothers	7.1	5.7	4.9	4.8	4.8	6.9	6.3	5.7	4.8
White	6.1	4.6	4.1	4.0	4.0	5.9	5.2	4.7	4.0
Black	12.5	11.1	9.6	9.2	9.4	12.2	11.7	11.1	9.3
American Indian or Alaska Native	7.5	6.1	3.9	4.5	5.0	6.7	5.9	5.9	4.7
Asian or Pacific Islander	5.2	3.9	3.4	3.2	3.9	5.2	4.5	3.9	3.5
Chinese	5.5	2.3	2.3	2.1	2.7	4.3	3.3	2.7	2.3
Japanese	*3.7	*3.5	*3.3	*3.0	*2.5	3.4	4.4	3.0	2.6
Filipino	5.6	3.5	3.4	3.6	4.6	5.3	4.5	4.0	4.1
Hawaiian and part Hawaiian	*7.0	*4.3	*4.0	*6.3	*7.3	7.4	7.1	4.8	5.6
Other Asian or Pacific Islander	5.0	4.4	3.7	3.3	3.9	5.5	4.7	4.2	3.6
Hispanic origin[4,5]	6.2	4.8	4.1	4.0	3.9	6.0	5.3	4.8	3.9
Mexican	5.9	4.5	3.9	3.8	3.7	5.7	5.0	4.5	3.8
Puerto Rican	8.7	6.9	6.1	5.4	5.2	8.3	7.2	7.0	5.4
Cuban	*5.0	5.3	*3.6	4.0	*2.7	5.9	5.3	4.6	3.5
Central and South American	5.8	4.4	3.7	3.9	3.6	5.7	4.9	4.4	3.6
Other and unknown Hispanic	6.4	5.0	4.8	3.7	4.5	6.1	5.8	5.2	4.5
White, non-Hispanic [5]	5.9	4.5	4.0	3.9	3.9	5.7	5.1	4.6	3.9
Black, non-Hispanic [5]	12.0	11.0	9.6	9.2	9.4	11.8	11.4	11.1	9.3
	Postneonatal [3] deaths per 1,000 live births								
All mothers	3.8	3.2	2.6	2.4	2.4	3.7	3.5	3.3	2.5
White	3.2	2.7	2.2	2.1	2.0	3.1	3.0	2.7	2.1
Black	6.7	5.9	5.0	4.5	4.4	6.4	6.2	6.0	4.6
American Indian or Alaska Native	7.7	7.0	5.1	4.2	4.3	7.2	7.3	6.7	4.6
Asian or Pacific Islander	3.1	2.7	1.9	1.8	1.7	3.1	2.8	2.6	1.8
Chinese	4.0	*2.0	*1.5	*1.0	*1.3	3.1	2.5	2.4	1.2
Japanese	*	*	*	*2.2	*	2.6	2.5	2.2	*1.7
Filipino	*2.8	2.5	2.2	2.3	1.6	2.9	2.4	2.3	1.9
Hawaiian and part Hawaiian	*4.2	*3.8	*	*	*	3.9	4.0	4.1	*2.6
Other Asian or Pacific Islander	3.0	3.0	1.9	1.7	1.8	3.1	2.9	2.8	1.8
Hispanic origin[4,5]	3.3	2.7	2.1	2.0	1.9	3.2	3.0	2.7	2.0
Mexican	3.2	2.7	2.1	2.0	1.9	3.2	2.9	2.7	2.0
Puerto Rican	4.2	3.0	2.8	2.5	2.6	4.0	3.9	3.4	2.7
Cuban	*2.5	*1.9	*1.7	*	*	2.2	2.0	1.6	*1.3
Central and South American	2.6	2.4	1.9	1.5	1.7	2.5	2.6	2.2	1.6
Other and unknown Hispanic	4.2	3.0	2.6	2.5	2.0	3.7	3.2	3.0	2.3
White, non-Hispanic [5]	3.2	2.7	2.2	2.1	2.0	3.1	3.0	2.7	2.1
Black, non-Hispanic [5]	7.0	5.9	5.0	4.5	4.5	6.7	6.5	6.1	4.6

*Rates preceded by an asterisk are based on fewer than 50 events. Rates not shown are based on fewer than 20 events.
[1] Rates based on unweighted birth cohort data.
[2] Rates based on a period file using weighted data.
[3] Infant (under 1 year of age), neonatal (under 28 days), and postneonatal (28 days–11 months).
[4] Persons of Hispanic origin may be of any race.
[5] Data shown only for states with an Hispanic-origin item on their birth certificates. The number of states reporting the item increased from 23 and the District of Columbia (DC) in 1983–87, to 30 and DC in 1988, 47 and DC in 1989, 48 and DC in 1990, 49 and DC in 1991, and 50 and DC starting in 1995.

Note: The race groups white, black, American Indian or Alaska Native, and Asian or Pacific Islander include persons of Hispanic and non-Hispanic origin.

SOURCE: "Table 20. Infant, neonatal, and postneonatal mortality rates, according to detailed race and Hispanic origin of mother: United States, selected years 1983–98," in *Health, United States, 2001,* Centers for Disease Control and Prevention, National Center for Health Statistics, Hyattsville, MD, 2001

BIRTH DEFECTS

The March of Dimes Birth Defects Foundation, a national voluntary organization that seeks to improve infant health by preventing birth defects and mortality, reports that every three and one-half minutes, a baby is born with a birth defect, and one in five infant deaths is caused by birth defects. In March 1998 the Birth Defects Prevention Act (PL105-168) was passed, "expressing the sense of Congress that birth defects are a major public health problem and need to be addressed." The March of Dimes observed in 2002 that despite research and many medical advances, birth defects have persisted as the leading cause of infant death for more than 20 years.

A birth defect may be a structural defect, a deficiency of function, or a disease that an infant has at birth. Some birth defects are genetic—inherited abnormalities such as Tay-Sachs disease (a fatal disease that generally affects children of eastern European Jewish ancestry), or chromosomal irregularities such as Down syndrome. Other birth defects result from environmental factors—infections during pregnancy, such as rubella (German measles), or drugs used by the pregnant woman. Although the specific causes of many birth defects are unknown, scientists believe many result from a combination of genetic and environmental factors. Though many birth defects are impossible to prevent, those caused by maternal alcohol and drug consumption during pregnancy can be prevented.

Two birth defects that have been the subject of considerable ethical debate are neural tube defects (NTDs) and permanent disabilities coupled with operable but life-threatening factors. An example of the latter is Down syndrome, a genetic abnormality that causes mental retardation and, frequently, malformations of the heart or kidneys.

Neural Tube Defects

Neural tube defects (NTDs) are abnormalities of the brain and spinal cord resulting from the failure of the neural tube to develop properly during early pregnancy. The neural tube is the embryonic nerve tissue that eventually develops into the brain and the spinal cord. Every year about 4,000 unborn children are affected with NTDs. Of these, approximately 2,500 involve infants born with the two most common NTDs—anencephaly and spina bifida.

ANENCEPHALY. Anencephalic infants die before birth (in utero or stillborn) or shortly thereafter. The incidence of anencephaly (absence of a major part of the brain, skull, and scalp) dropped significantly from 1991 to 2000 in the states where data were reported. (See Figure 5.1.)

In 1992 a Florida couple discovered through prenatal testing that their baby would be born without a fully-developed brain. They decided to carry their baby to term and donate her organs for transplantation. When their baby, Theresa Ann Campo, was born, her parents wanted her

TABLE 5.2

Infant deaths and infant mortality rates, by age and race and Hispanic origin, final 1999 and preliminary 2000

Age and race/Hispanic origin	2000 Number	2000 Rate	1999 Number	1999 Rate
All races[1]				
Under 1 year	27,987	6.9	27,937	7.1
Under 28 days	18,737	4.6	18,728	4.7
28 days-11 months	9,250	2.3	9,209	2.3
White, total[2]				
Under 1 year	18,216	5.7	18,067	5.8
Under 28 days	12,263	3.8	12,164	3.9
28 days-11 months	5,954	1.9	5,903	1.9
White, non-Hispanic				
Under 1 year	13,579	5.7	13,553	5.8
Under 28 days	9,127	3.8	9,054	3.9
28 days-11 months	4,452	1.9	4,499	1.9
Black, total[2]				
Under 1 year	8,665	14.0	8,822	14.6
Under 28 days	5,750	9.3	5,920	9.8
28 days-11 months	2,915	4.7	2,902	4.8
Hispanic[3]				
Under 1 year	4,572	5.6	4,412	5.8
Under 28 days	3,034	3.7	2,986	3.9
28 days-11 months	1,538	1.9	1,426	1.9

[1] Includes races other than white and black.
[2] Race and Hispanic origin are reported separately on both the birth and death certificates. Data for persons of Hispanic origin are included in the data for each race group, according to the decedent's reported race.
[3] Includes all persons of Hispanic origin of any race.

Note: Data are based on a continuous file of records received from the states. Rates per 1,000 live births. Figures for 2000 are based on weighted data rounded to the nearest individual, so categories may not add to totals. Rates for Hispanic origin should be interpreted with caution because of inconsistencies between reporting Hispanic origin on birth and death certificates. Data are subject to sampling and/or random variation.

SOURCE: Arialdi M. Minino and Betty L. Smith, "Table 4. Infant deaths and infant mortality rates, by age and race and Hispanic origin: United States, final 1999 and preliminary 2000," in *Deaths: Preliminary Data for 2000, National Vital Statistics Reports,* National Center for Health Statistics, Hyattsville, MD, vol. 49, no. 12, October 9, 2001

declared brain dead. But because Theresa was not legally dead (her brain stem was still functioning), the court ruled against the parents' decision. Baby Theresa died ten days later and her organs were not usable for transplant, having deteriorated as a result of oxygen deprivation.

Some physicians and ethicists agree that even if anencephalic babies have a brain stem, they should be considered brain dead. Lacking a functioning higher brain, these babies can feel nothing; they have no consciousness. Others fear that declaring anencephalic babies dead could be the start of a "slippery slope" which might eventually include babies with other birth defects, such as spina bifida, in the same category. Spina bifida defects run the gamut of mild to severe. Still others are concerned that anencephalic babies may be kept alive for the purpose of harvesting their organs for transplant at a later date.

SPINA BIFIDA. Spina bifida, which literally means "divided spine," is caused by the failure of the vertebrae

TABLE 5.3

Deaths, age-adjusted death rates, and life expectancy at birth, by race and sex; and infant deaths and mortality rates, by race, final 1999 and preliminary 2000

Measure and sex	All races[1]		White		Black	
	2000	1999	2000	1999	2000	1999
All deaths	2,404,598	2,391,399	2,074,157	2,061,348	284,561	285,064
Age-adjusted death rate[2]	872.4	881.9	853.2	860.7	1,124.8	1,147.1
Male	1,042.7	1,061.8	1,019.3	1,035.8	1,371.3	1,412.5
Female	739.8	743.6	723.4	725.7	943.9	955.0
Life expectancy at birth[3]	76.9	76.7	77.4	77.3	71.8	71.4
Male	74.1	73.9	74.8	74.6	68.3	67.8
Female	79.5	79.4	80.0	79.9	75.0	74.7
Infant deaths	27,987	27,937	18,216	18,067	8,665	8,822
Infant mortality rate[4]	6.9	7.1	5.7	5.8	14.0	14.6

[1] Includes races other than white and black.
[2] Age-adjusted death rates are per 100,000 U.S. standard population, based on the year 2000 standard.
[3] Life expectancy at birth stated in years.
[4] Infant mortality rates are deaths under 1 year per 1,000 live births in specified group.

SOURCE: Arialdi M. Minino and Betty L. Smith, "Table A. Deaths, age-adjusted death rates, and life expectancy at birth, by race and sex; and infant deaths and mortality rates, by race: United States, final 1999 and preliminary 2000," in *Deaths: Preliminary Data for 2000, National Vital Statistics Reports,* National Center for Health Statistics, Hyattsville, MD, vol. 49, no. 12, October 9, 2001

(backbone) to completely cover the spinal cord early in fetal development, leaving the spinal cord exposed. Depending upon the amount of nerve tissue exposed, spina bifida defects range from minor developmental disabilities to paralysis.

Before the advent of antibiotics in the 1950s, most babies with severe spina bifida died soon after birth. With antibiotics and numerous medical advances, some of these newborns can be saved.

The treatment of newborns with spina bifida can pose serious ethical problems. Should an infant with a milder form of the disease be treated actively while another with severe defects is left untreated? In severe cases, should the newborn be sedated and allowed to starve to death? Or should this seriously disabled infant be cared for while suffering from bladder and bowel malfunctions, infections, and paralysis? What if infants who have been left to die unexpectedly survive? They would surely be more disabled than if they had been treated right away.

The development of fetal surgery to correct spina bifida before birth added another dimension to the debate. Physicians realized that by covering the exposed spinal cord during pregnancy, they could prevent some of the damage caused by amniotic fluid and an increasingly crowded environment in the womb. In 1994 several doctors attempted the surgery by making a tiny incision in the mother's uterus and performing the procedure with the help of an endoscope (viewing instrument). After several unsuccessful attempts, in 1997 they opened an entire uterus and performed the corrective surgery. This surgery is extremely risky and, after it is over, the mother must stay in bed and take medication to postpone labor to as close to the due date as possible. Four U.S. hospitals perform the procedure, and as of March 30, 2002, approximately 215 fetuses had undergone the operation.

So far the results have been promising: most of the babies have shown few physical or mental symptoms of spina bifida. Further tests will be necessary when these children reach school age, in order to help assess their progress. The surgery does, however, raise ethical questions—it is not performed to save the infant's life, as in most other fetal surgeries, but to improve quality of life. Parents must weigh the potential failure of the operation and death of the child against the possible benefits. On the other hand, at least 2,000 women annually choose to terminate their pregnancies after prenatal testing reveals this birth defect. (This figure is an estimate, as many states do not track or record these cases.)

Scientists now know that daily consumption of 0.4 mg of the B vitamin folic acid by women before and during the first trimester (three months) of pregnancy greatly reduces the risk of spina bifida and other birth defects. To comply with a mandate from the U.S. Food and Drug Administration (FDA), as of January 1998 all enriched cereal grain products must be fortified with folic acid.

In the United States the rates of spina bifida have been declining since 1960 and decreased from nearly .025 percent in 1991 to .021 percent in 2000 (note that not all states participated in reporting spina bifida cases). Figure 5.2 shows case rates per 100,000 births. The decline is an early indicator of successful efforts to prevent this defect by increasing folate consumption among women of childbearing age.

TABLE 5.4

Infant deaths and infant mortality rates for the 10 leading causes of infant death, by race and Hispanic origin, preliminary 2000

Rank [1]	Cause of death and race	Number	Rate
	All races [2]		
...	All causes	27,983	688.4
1	Congenital malformations, deformations and chromosomal abnormalities (Q00-Q99)	5,779	142.2
2	Disorders related to short gestation and low birth weight, not elsewhere classified (P07)	4,299	105.8
3	Sudden infant death syndrome (R95)	2,151	52.9
4	Newborn affected by maternal complications of pregnancy (P01)	1,372	33.8
5	Newborn affected by complications of placenta, cord and membranes (P02)	1,028	25.3
6	Respiratory distress of newborn (P22)	1,018	25.0
7	Accidents (unintentional injuries) (V01-X59)	826	20.3
8	Bacterial sepsis of newborn (P36)	723	17.8
9	Intrauterine hypoxia and birth asphyxia (P20-P21)	642	15.8
10	Diseases of the circulatory system (I00-I99)	632	15.5
...	All other causes (Residual)	9,513	234.0
	White, total [3]		
...	All causes	18,340	572.6
1	Congenital malformations, deformations and chromosomal abnormalities (Q00-Q99)	4,458	139.2
2	Disorders related to short gestation and low birth weight, not elsewhere classified (P07)	2,396	74.8
3	Sudden infant death syndrome (R95)	1,374	42.9
4	Newborn affected by maternal complications of pregnancy (P01)	851	26.6
5	Newborn affected by complications of placenta, cord and membranes (P02)	706	22.0
6	Respiratory distress of newborn (P22)	642	20.0
7	Accidents (unintentional injuries) (V01-X59)	537	16.8
8	Bacterial sepsis of newborn (P36)	450	14.0
9	Intrauterine hypoxia and birth asphyxia (P20-P21)	443	13.8
10	Diseases of the circulatory system (I00-I99)	442	13.8
...	All other causes (Residual)	6,041	188.6
	White, non-Hispanic		
...	All causes	13,647	575.6
1	Congenital malformations, deformations and chromosomal abnormalities (Q00-Q99)	3,281	138.4
2	Disorders related to short gestation and low birth weight, not elsewhere classified (P07)	1,700	71.7
3	Sudden infant death syndrome (R95)	1,154	48.7
4	Newborn affected by maternal complications of pregnancy (P01)	672	28.3
5	Newborn affected by complications of placenta, cord and membranes (P02)	558	23.5
6	Respiratory distress of newborn (P22)	462	19.5
7	Accidents (unintentional injuries) (V01-X59)	432	18.2
8	Intrauterine hypoxia and birth asphyxia (P20-P21)	344	14.5
9	Diseases of the circulatory system (I00-I99)	329	13.9
10	Bacterial sepsis of newborn (P36)	323	13.6
...	All other causes (Residual)	4,392	185.3
	Black, total [3]		
...	All causes	8,529	1,375.7
1	Disorders related to short gestation and low birth weight, not elsewhere classified (P07)	1,763	284.4
2	Congenital malformations, deformations and chromosomal abnormalities (Q00-Q99)	1,065	171.8
3	Sudden infant death syndrome (R95)	700	112.9
4	Newborn affected by maternal complications of pregnancy (P01)	477	76.9
5	Respiratory distress of newborn (P22)	348	56.1
6	Newborn affected by complications of placenta, cord and membranes (P02)	291	46.9
7	Bacterial sepsis of newborn (P36)	253	40.8
8	Accidents (unintentional injuries) (V01-X59)	252	40.6
9	Intrauterine hypoxia and birth asphyxia (P20-P21)	165	26.6
10	Diseases of the circulatory system (I00-I99)	160	25.8
...	All other causes (Residual)	3,055	492.8

Down Syndrome

Down syndrome (also called Down's syndrome) is a birth defect caused by chromosomal irregularities. Instead of the normal 46 chromosomes, Down syndrome newborns have an extra copy of chromosome 21, giving them a total of 47 chromosomes. These children have varying degrees of mental retardation, and approximately 40 percent have congenital heart diseases.

The CDC estimate prevalence of Down syndrome at birth as approximately 10 cases per 10,000 live births.

The occurrence of this birth defect rises with increasing maternal age, with a marked increase seen in children of women over 35 years of age at the time of delivery.

In the past, babies born with Down syndrome were usually institutionalized. Many died in infancy. Today, with the help of modern medical care, children with Down syndrome are typically raised at home and attain adulthood, although their life expectancy is shorter than average (approximately 55 years). Except for the most severe heart defects, many other malformations accompanying Down

TABLE 5.4

Infant deaths and infant mortality rates for the 10 leading causes of infant death, by race and Hispanic origin, preliminary 2000 [CONTINUED]

Rank [1]	Cause of death and race	Number	Rate
	Hispanic [4]		
...	All causes	4,601	564.0
1	Congenital malformations, deformations and chromosomal abnormalities (Q00-Q99)	1,170	143.4
2	Disorders related to short gestation and low birth weight, not elsewhere classified (P07)	634	77.7
3	Sudden infant death syndrome (R95)	234	28.7
4	Newborn affected by maternal complications of pregnancy (P01)	175	21.5
4	Respiratory distress of newborn (P22)	175	21.5
6	Newborn affected by complications of placenta, cord and membranes (P02)	138	16.9
7	Bacterial sepsis of newborn (P36)	127	15.6
8	Diseases of the circulatory system (I00-I99)	112	13.7
9	Accidents (unintentional injuries) (V01-X59)	111	13.6
10	Neonatal hemorrhage (P50-P52,P54)	106	13.0
...	All other causes (Residual)	1,619	198.5

... Category not applicable.
[1] Rank based on number of deaths.
[2] Includes races other than white and black.
[3] Race and Hispanic origin are reported separately on both the birth and death certificate. Data for persons of Hispanic origin are included in the data for each race group, according to the decedent's reported race.
[4] Includes all persons of Hispanic origin of any race.

Note: Data are based on a continuous file of records received from the states. Rates per 100,000 live births. Figures are based on weighted data rounded to the nearest individual, so categories may not add to totals. Rates for Hispanic origin should be interpreted with caution because of inconsistencies between reporting Hispanic origin on birth and death certificates. Data are subject to sampling and/or random variation.

SOURCE: Arialdi M. Minino and Betty L. Smith, "Table 8. Infant deaths and infant mortality rates for the 10 leading causes of infant death, by race and Hispanic origin: United States, preliminary 2000," in *Deaths: Preliminary Data for 2000, National Vital Statistics Reports,* National Center for Health Statistics, Hyattsville, MD, vol. 49, no. 12, October 9, 2001

syndrome may be corrected by surgery. Depending on the degree of mental retardation, many persons with Down syndrome are able to hold jobs and live independently.

Birth Defects Prevention Act of 1998

On April 21, 1998, then-President Bill Clinton signed into law the Birth Defects Prevention Act (PL105-168), which authorized a nationwide network of birth defects research and prevention programs and called for a nationwide information clearinghouse on birth defects. The law initially appropriated $70 million for fiscal years (FY) 1998 and 1999. Congress appropriated $90 million for FY 2002. Dr. Jennifer L. Howse, president of the March of Dimes Birth Defects Foundation, noted, "This legislation will help us find the causes of major birth defects, devise new ways to help prevent them, and better apply what we already know."

The bill was first introduced in 1992 by Representatives Solomon Ortiz (D-TX) and Henry Bonilla (R-TX) and Senator Christopher "Kit" Bond (R-MO) in response to the clusters of anencephalic newborns in Cameron County, Texas. The Texas Department of Health reported an anencephaly rate of 13 per 10,000 live births in Cameron County from 1986 to 1991, a rate four times greater than the national rate. During 1990 to 1991 the rate climbed to 19.7 per 10,000 births. The cause of the outbreak was never determined.

The Cost of Continued Care

The CDC reported that in 1992 (the most recent information available), the estimated cost of cerebral palsy and 17 other birth defects was $8 billion ("Economic Costs of Birth Defects and Cerebral Palsy—United States, 1992," *Morbidity and Mortality Weekly Report,* vol. 44, no. 37, September 22, 1995). Costs ranged from $75,000 to $503,000 per child and covered medical, developmental, and special education services, as well as lost productivity resulting from the child's death or disability. However, these estimated amounts do not include the costs to the family of wages lost for caring for the children. Birth defects characterized by long-term disabilities, such as cerebral palsy, Down syndrome, and spina bifida, cost the most. Moreover, these conditions accounted for the highest total lifetime costs.

Research examining selected developmental disabilities (conditions that impair day-to-day functioning, such as difficulties with communication, learning, behavior, and motor skills) associated with major birth defects was reported by Pierre Decoufle, et al. ("Increased Risk for Developmental Disabilities in Children Who Have Major Birth Defects: A Population-Based Study," *Pediatrics,* vol. 108, no. 3, September 2001). The investigators linked data from two independent population-based surveillance systems to find out if major birth defects were associated with serious developmental disabilities.

When compared with children who had no major birth defects, the prevalence of developmental disabilities among children with major birth defects was extremely high. The researchers observed that conditions such as mental retardation, cerebral palsy, epilepsy, autism, profound hearing loss, and legal blindness "prove costly in terms of special education services, medical and supportive care, demands on caregivers, and economic loss to society." They concluded, "Our data suggest that birth defects pose a greater burden on society than previously recognized."

LOW BIRTHWEIGHT AND PREMATURITY

Low Birthweight

Infants who weigh less than 2,500 grams (or 5 pounds, 8 ounces) at birth are considered to be of low birthweight. Those born weighing less than 1,500 grams (3 pounds, 4 ounces) have very low birthweight. Low birthweight may result from premature birth, poor maternal nutrition, teen pregnancy, drug and alcohol use, smoking, or sexually transmitted diseases.

In 2000, 7.6 percent of the approximately 4 million live births were low birthweight infants, the highest level reported in more than two decades. About 1.4 percent were very low birthweight infants. Black mothers were nearly twice as likely as white mothers and Hispanic mothers to have low-birthweight babies (13 percent of children born to black birth mothers had low birthweight, compared to 6.5 and 6.4 percent, respectively, born to white and Hispanic mothers). (See Table 5.5 and Table 5.6.) Like the proportion of low birthweight babies, the proportion of very low birthweight babies has also been increasing since 1980. (See Table 5.7.) The increase in low and very low birthweight babies during the 1990s is attributed to the increase in the multiple birth rate. Multiple births are at much greater risk of low birthweight than single births.

Prematurity

The usual length of pregnancy is 40 weeks. Infants born before 37 weeks of pregnancy are considered premature. A premature infant does not have fully formed organ systems. If the premature infant is born with a birthweight comparable to a full-term baby and has organ systems only slightly undeveloped, the chances of survival are great. Premature infants of very low birthweight are susceptible to numerous risks and are less likely to survive than full-term infants. If they survive, they may suffer from mental retardation and other abnormalities of the nervous system.

A severe medical condition called hyaline membrane disease, or respiratory distress syndrome (RDS), commonly affects premature infants. It is caused by the inability of the immature lungs to function properly. Occurring right after birth, it may cause infant death within hours. Intensive care includes the use of a mechanical ventilator to facilitate breathing. Also, premature infants' immature gastrointestinal systems preclude them from taking in nourishment properly. Unable to suck and swallow, they must be fed through a stomach tube.

FIGURE 5.1

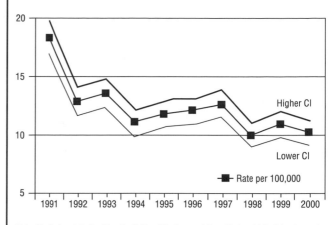

Anencephalus rates and number of live births and anencephalus cases, 1991–2000

ANENCEPHALUS RATES, 1991–2000

Note: Excludes data for Maryland, New Mexico, and New York, which did not require reporting for anencephalus for some years. Data for 2000 are preliminary. CI is 95% confidence interval.

NUMBER OF LIVE BIRTHS AND ANENCEPHALUS CASES AND RATES PER 100,000 LIVE BIRTHS, 1991–2000

	Anencephalus cases	Total live births	Rate
2000	367	3,647,367	10.08
1999	382	3,533,565	10.81
1998	349	3,519,240	9.92
1997	434	3,469,667	12.51
1996	416	3,478,723	11.96
1995	408	3,484,539	11.71
1994	387	3,527,482	10.97
1993	481	3,562,723	13.50
1992	457	3,572,890	12.79
1991	655	3,564,453	18.38

Note: Excludes data for Maryland, New Mexico, and New York, which did not require reporting for anencephalus for some years.

SOURCE: Adapted from "Figure 2. Anencephalus rates, 1991-2000," and "Table 2. Number of live births and anencephalus cases and rates per 100,000 live births for the United States, 1991–2000," in *Trends in Spina Bifida and Anencephalus in the United States, 1991–2000,* Centers for Disease Control and Prevention, National Center for Health Statistics, Hyattsville, MD, 2002 [Online] http://www.cdc.gov/nchs/products/pubs/pubd/hestats/spine_anen.htm [accessed April 25, 2002]

WHO MAKES MEDICAL DECISIONS FOR INFANTS?

Court Cases Attempt to Define Parental Roles

THE "BABY DOE" RULES. In April 1982 an infant with Down syndrome was born in Bloomington Hospital, Indiana. The infant also had esophageal atresia, an obstruction in the esophagus that prevents the passage of food from the mouth to the stomach. Following their obstetrician's recommendation, the parents decided to forego surgery to repair the baby's esophagus. The baby would be kept pain-free with medication and allowed to die.

Disagreeing with the parents' decision, the hospital took them to the county court. The judge ruled that the

FIGURE 5.2

Spina bifida rates and number of live births and spina bifida cases, 1991–2000

SPINA BIFIDA RATES, 1991–2000

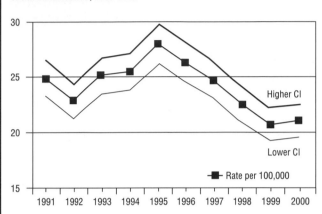

Note: Excludes data for Maryland, New Mexico, and New York, which did not require reporting for spina bifida for some years. Data for 2000 are preliminary. CI is 95% confidence interval.

NUMBER OF LIVE BIRTHS AND SPINA BIFIDA CASES AND RATES PER 100,000 LIVE BIRTHS, 1991–2000

	Spina bifida cases	Total live births	Rate
2000	759	3,647,367	20.85
1999	732	3,533,565	20.72
1998	790	3,519,240	22.45
1997	857	3,469,667	24.70
1996	917	3,478,723	26.36
1995	975	3,484,539	27.98
1994	900	3,527,482	25.51
1993	896	3,562,723	25.15
1992	816	3,572,890	22.84
1991	887	3,564,453	24.88

Note: Excludes data for Maryland, New Mexico, and New York, which did not require reporting for spina bifida for some years.

SOURCE: Adapted from "Figure 1. Spina bifida rates, 1991-2000," and "Table 1. Number of live births and spina bifida cases and rates per 100,000 live births for the United States, 1991-2000," in *Trends in Spina Bifida and Anencephalus in the United States, 1991–2000,* Centers for Disease Control and Prevention, National Center for Health Statistics, Hyattsville, MD, 2002 [Online] http://www.cdc.gov/nchs/products/pubs/pubd/hestats/spine_anen.htm [accessed April 25, 2002]

112). This section (nondiscrimination under federal grants and programs) states:

> No otherwise qualified individual with a disability in the United States ... shall, solely by reason of her or his disability, be excluded from the participation in, be denied the benefits of, or be subjected to discrimination under any program or activity receiving Federal financial assistance.

Furthermore, all hospital delivery rooms and nurseries were ordered to have posters warning that "DISCRIMINATORY FAILURE TO FEED AND CARE FOR HANDICAPPED INFANTS IN THIS FACILITY IS PROHIBITED BY FEDERAL LAW." The posters listed a toll-free hotline for anonymous reports of wrongdoing.

Although government investigators were summoned to many hospitals to verify claims of mistreatment (the hotline had 500 calls in its first three weeks alone), no violation of the law could be found. On the contrary, the investigators found doctors resuscitating babies who were beyond treatment because they feared legal actions. Finally, a group led by the American Academy of Pediatrics filed suit in March 1983 to have the Baby Doe rules overturned. Judge Gerhard Gesell agreed, saying in part that the Reagan administration could not prove that these rules would improve the care of handicapped infants.

BABY JANE DOE. The debates about handicapped babies and their right to medical treatment became focused upon another handicapped baby born in October 1983. "Baby Jane Doe" had severe spina bifida. Her deformities were so serious that even if she were to undergo painful surgeries (which might not fix her problems), she would suffer from great mental retardation and physical disability. The Reagan administration and pro-life advocates entered discussions about the care of this infant; however, the court ruled that the government and strangers had no business interfering with decisions made by Baby Jane Doe's family.

The Baby Doe and Baby Jane Doe cases resulted in an agreement among government officials, physicians, and pro-lifers about the medical and ethical treatment of newborns with life-threatening conditions, and Congress passed a law based on the language of this agreement. On October 9, 1984, President Reagan signed an amendment to the Child Abuse Prevention and Treatment Act (PL 98-457). It specified that "medically indicated treatment" was not required (1) if the infant was irreversibly comatose, (2) if the treatment would "merely prolong dying," or (3) if the treatment would be "virtually futile in terms of the survival of the infant and the treatment itself under such circumstances would be inhumane."

In January 1984 the Department of Health and Human Services (HHS) issued regulations promoting establishment of Infant Care Review Committees to help

parents had the legal right to their decision, which was based on a valid medical recommendation. The Indiana Supreme Court refused to hear the appeal. Before the county prosecutor could present the case to the United States Supreme Court, the six-day-old baby died.

The public outcry following the death of "Baby Doe" (the infant's court-designated name) brought immediate reaction from President Ronald Reagan's administration. The Department of Health and Human Services (HHS) informed all hospitals receiving federal funding that discrimination against handicapped newborns would violate Section 504 of the Rehabilitation Act of 1973 (PL 93-

TABLE 5.5

Percent of births with selected medical or health characteristics, by race, Hispanic origin, and birth place of mother, 2000

| Characteristic | All origins[1] | Origin of mother | | | | | | | | |
| | | Hispanic | | | | | | Non-Hispanic | | |
		Total	Mexican	Puerto Rican	Cuban	Central and South American	Other and unknown Hispanic	Total[2]	White	Black
All births										
Mother										
Prenatal care beginning in the first trimester	83.2	74.4	72.9	78.5	91.7	77.6	75.8	85.4	88.5	74.3
Late or no prenatal care	3.9	6.3	6.9	4.5	1.4	5.4	5.9	3.2	2.3	6.7
Smoker[3]	12.2	3.5	2.4	10.3	3.3	1.5	7.4	13.8	15.6	9.2
Drinker[4]	0.9	0.5	0.4	0.8	0.3	0.3	1.0	1.0	1.0	1.1
Weight gain of less than 16 lbs[5]	11.6	13.9	15.1	12.5	8.1	11.9	12.1	11.1	9.7	16.8
Median weight gain[5]	30.5	29.6	28.3	30.6	32.2	30.3	30.4	30.7	30.9	30.1
Cesarean delivery rate	22.9	22.1	21.4	23.0	33.7	23.9	21.9	23.1	23.1	24.3
Infant										
Preterm births[6]	11.6	11.2	11.0	13.5	10.6	11.0	12.2	11.7	10.4	17.4
Birthweight										
Very low birthweight[7]	1.4	1.1	1.0	1.9	1.2	1.2	1.4	1.5	1.1	3.1
Low birthweight[8]	7.6	6.4	6.0	9.3	6.5	6.3	7.8	7.9	6.6	13.1
4,000 grams or more[9]	9.9	9.0	9.3	7.3	9.5	9.0	7.4	10.1	11.7	5.3
5-minute Apgar score of less than 7[10]	1.4	1.1	1.2	1.4	0.8	1.0	1.2	1.4	1.2	2.4
Births to mothers born in the 50 states and DC										
Mother										
Prenatal care beginning in the first trimester	84.9	77.8	77.3	78.3	91.9	82.5	76.4	85.7	88.7	74.1
Late or no prenatal care	3.3	4.8	4.9	4.6	1.5	3.6	5.7	3.1	2.2	6.6
Smoker[3]	14.3	6.8	5.1	11.6	4.4	5.2	9.2	14.9	16.1	10.1
Drinker[4]	1.0	0.9	0.8	0.9	0.4	0.7	1.3	1.0	1.0	1.1
Weight gain of less than 16 lbs[5]	11.3	12.5	13.1	11.8	8.8	9.3	12.3	11.2	9.8	17.1
Median weight gain[5]	30.7	29.6	28.3	30.6	32.2	30.3	30.4	30.7	30.9	30.1
Cesarean delivery rate	23.1	22.2	22.2	22.6	28.8	22.0	21.4	23.2	23.1	24.0
Infant										
Preterm births[6]	11.9	12.1	11.9	13.5	10.5	10.9	12.7	11.9	10.5	17.8
Birthweight										
Very low birthweight[7]	1.5	1.3	1.2	2.0	1.1	1.2	1.4	1.5	1.1	3.1
Low birthweight[8]	7.9	7.3	6.8	9.2	6.5	7.1	8.3	7.9	6.6	13.5
4,000 grams or more[9]	10.2	8.2	8.6	7.4	8.4	8.6	7.1	10.4	11.7	5.0
5-minute Apgar score of less than 7[10]	1.4	1.3	1.3	1.4	0.8	1.0	1.3	1.5	1.2	2.4

hospital personnel make decisions about the care of severely disabled infants. On April 15, 1985, HHS published regulations that required examination of medical records and independent medical examinations of disabled newborns. However, in June 1986, the U.S. Supreme Court invalidated the HHS regulations, and has since barred the federal government from intervening in these cases.

Treating Critically Ill Infants and Children

The American Academy of Pediatrics (AAP) contends that many physicians and laypersons agree that some critically ill infants who were previously denied treatment may benefit from, and should receive, medical and surgical care. Examples of these are Down syndrome babies with gastrointestinal blockage and babies with less severe forms of spina bifida. However, in cases involving extreme prematurity, complex birth defects, and life-limiting chronic disorders, there is less agreement on the extent of treatment.

In "Ethics and the Care of Critically Ill Infants and Children" (*Pediatrics,* vol. 98, no. 1, 1996), the AAP Committee on Bioethics points out that the federal legislation, the Child Abuse Prevention and Treatment Act, has brought about two unintended consequences. The law, with its three exceptions, might have inadvertently given physicians more leeway in making judgments about seriously ill infants. On the other hand, fear of lawsuits might predispose some physicians to overtreat irreparably ill infants.

Because the outcomes of neonatal intensive care are often unpredictable, physicians and parents have to rely on their best judgment. Nonetheless, according to the AAP, evidence shows that decreased mortality resulting from neonatal intensive care has been accompanied by increased mental and physical limitations among survivors that impose burdens on affected children and their families.

With the escalating cost of critical care, some observers believe that resources would be better used to

TABLE 5.5

Percent of births with selected medical or health characteristics, by race, Hispanic origin, and birth place of mother, 2000 [CONTINUED]

| | | Origin of mother | | | | | | | | |
| | | Hispanic | | | | | | Non-Hispanic | | |
Characteristic	All origins[1]	Total	Mexican	Puerto Rican	Cuban	Central and South American	Other and unknown Hispanic	Total[2]	White	Black
Births to mothers *born outside the 50 states and DC*										
Mother										
Prenatal care beginning in the first trimester	76.8	72.4	70.2	78.7	91.5	77.0	74.5	83.1	85.3	75.7
Late or no prenatal care	5.9	7.2	8.0	4.4	1.3	5.6	6.1	4.0	3.5	6.9
Smoker[3]	2.2	1.3	0.8	7.9	2.5	1.0	1.9	3.2	6.0	1.3
Drinker[4]	0.4	0.3	0.2	0.8	*	0.3	0.3	0.5	0.9	0.3
Weight gain of less than 16 lbs[5]	12.6	14.8	16.4	13.7	7.6	12.3	11.4	10.2	8.7	14.4
Median weight gain[5]	29.1	28.1	26.5	30.4	32.3	30.1	30.3	30.3	30.7	29.5
Cesarean delivery rate	22.3	22.0	20.9	23.9	37.3	24.1	23.5	22.6	21.6	26.9
Infant										
Preterm births[6]	10.5	10.7	10.5	13.5	10.8	11.0	10.5	10.2	9.1	14.0
Birthweight										
Very low birthweight[7]	1.1	1.0	0.9	1.9	1.3	1.2	1.1	1.2	0.9	2.6
Low birthweight[8]	6.4	5.8	5.5	9.4	6.5	6.3	6.0	7.1	5.8	9.8
4,000 grams or more[9]	8.9	9.5	9.8	7.0	10.3	9.1	8.5	8.1	11.3	8.3
5-minute Apgar score of less than 7[10]	1.1	1.1	1.1	1.5	0.8	1.0	0.8	1.2	0.9	2.0

*Figure does not meet standards of reliability or precision; based on fewer than 20 births in the numerator.
[1] Includes origin not stated.
[2] Includes races other than white and black.
[3] Excludes data for California, which did not report tobacco use on the birth certificate.
[4] Excludes data for California, which did not report alcohol use on the birth certificate.
[5] Excludes data for California, which did not report weight gain on the birth certificate. Median weight gain shown in pounds.
[6] Born prior to 37 completed weeks of gestation.
[7] Birthweight of less than 1,500 grams (3 lb 4 oz).
[8] Birthweight of less than 2,500 grams (5 lb 8 oz).
[9] Equivalent to 8 lb 14 oz.
[10] Excludes data for California and Texas, which did not report 5-minute Apgar score on the birth certificate.
NOTE: Race and Hispanic origin are reported separately on birth certificates. Persons of Hispanic origin may be of any race. In this table Hispanic women are classified only by place of origin; non-Hispanic women are classified by race.

SOURCE: Joyce A. Martin, et al.,"Table 25. Percent of births with selected medical or health characteristics, by Hispanic origin of mother and by race for mothers of non-Hispanic origin and by place of birth of mother: United States, 2000," in *Births: Final Data for 2000, National Vital Statistics Reports*, vol. 50, no. 5, February 12, 2002

treat infants who have less severe disabilities. Others feel that this would discriminate against persons least able to advocate for themselves—the disabled, the poor, and the dying. The AAP believes these decisions should be made at the public policy level, not at the bedside, where parents and doctors may be in intense emotional distress.

OLDER CHILDREN

The American Academy of Pediatrics reports that not much has been written about life-sustaining treatments as they apply to older children. Generally the courts have been lenient in allowing parents to act in the best interest of their children. The courts have been known to let the parents' decisions stand, even when court-appointed guardians disagreed with those decisions.

Religious Beliefs and Medical Treatment

During the 1970s, 1980s, and 1990s, there were documented cases of children who died because their parents chose, on the basis of their religious beliefs, not to seek or accept medical care. Several of these highly publicized childhood deaths occurred among children of Christian Scientists, who chose to receive care from religious rather than medical practitioners.

The courts have been inconsistent in their rulings about these cases. For example, two 1984 California cases involving Christian Scientists returned decidedly different verdicts. In the first, 17-month-old Seth Ian Glazer died of bacterial meningitis after he was treated by a Christian Scientist healer. The child's mother was charged with manslaughter and child endangerment, but the court ruled in favor of the defendant. The same year, eight-month-old Natalie Rippberger also died of meningitis after her parents sought Christian Science care, which relied on prayer and Bible reading rather than medical treatment. Natalie's parents were charged with felony child endangerment and involuntary manslaughter, but were only convicted of felony child endangerment.

TABLE 5.6

Number and percent of low birthweight and number of live births by selected characteristics, 2000

Age and race and Hispanic origin of mother	Low birthweight Number	Low birthweight Percent	Total	Less than 500 grams	500-999 grams	1,000-1,499 grams	1,500-1,999 grams	2,000-2,499 grams	2,500-2,999 grams	3,000-3,499 grams	3,500-3,999 grams	4,000-4,499 grams	4,500-4,999 grams	5,000 grams or more	Not stated
All races[2]															
All ages	307,030	7.6	4,058,814	5,952	22,797	29,218	60,793	188,270	670,849	1,510,314	1,164,440	340,384	54,748	6,208	4,841
Under 15 years	1,199	14.1	8,519	36	109	134	229	691	2,101	3,372	1,538	261	29	3	16
15-19 years	44,598	9.5	468,990	849	3,472	4,109	8,364	27,804	101,145	188,544	108,500	22,715	2,775	270	443
15 years	2,463	11.3	21,845	49	230	242	474	1,468	5,194	8,860	4,420	803	76	13	16
16 years	5,116	10.5	48,581	114	444	495	982	3,081	11,217	19,668	10,416	1,898	204	25	37
17 years	8,516	9.8	86,783	167	711	816	1,584	5,238	19,101	35,021	19,603	3,981	442	34	85
18 years	12,640	9.5	132,786	213	967	1,167	2,342	7,951	28,686	53,244	30,654	6,528	837	71	126
19 years	15,863	8.9	178,995	306	1,120	1,389	2,982	10,066	36,947	71,751	43,407	9,505	1,216	127	179
20-24 years	77,324	7.6	1,017,806	1,483	5,613	6,877	14,494	48,857	187,016	398,663	272,830	69,979	10,067	1,007	920
25-29 years	72,736	6.7	1,087,547	1,505	5,465	6,762	14,207	44,797	167,531	403,959	327,259	97,462	15,591	1,740	1,269
30-34 years	63,949	6.9	929,278	1,254	4,775	6,478	13,196	38,246	131,673	329,497	290,589	94,397	15,988	1,836	1,349
35-39 years	37,363	8.3	452,057	688	2,643	3,816	8,058	22,158	66,156	154,916	137,051	46,360	8,440	1,106	665
40-44 years	9,025	10.0	90,013	128	672	942	2,032	5,251	14,336	30,032	25,559	8,868	1,787	238	168
45-54 years	836	18.2	4,604	9	48	100	213	466	891	1,331	1,114	342	71	8	11
White, total															
All ages	208,818	6.5	3,194,005	3,265	13,700	19,344	41,848	130,661	478,863	1,174,494	976,947	297,496	48,330	5,357	3,700
Under 15 years	531	12.0	4,439	10	54	46	114	307	977	1,787	935	178	21	2	8
15-19 years	26,730	8.0	333,013	435	1,888	2,433	4,944	17,030	65,554	135,039	84,346	18,553	2,289	218	284
15 years	1,252	9.3	13,487	22	121	118	240	751	2,871	5,583	3,105	599	58	7	12
16 years	2,914	9.0	32,499	54	223	301	565	1,771	6,841	13,320	7,722	1,488	165	23	26
17 years	5,058	8.3	60,800	93	403	468	929	3,165	12,179	24,877	15,061	3,205	339	26	55
18 years	7,735	8.1	95,390	110	527	693	1,418	4,987	18,882	38,530	24,049	5,387	675	59	73
19 years	9,771	7.5	130,837	156	614	853	1,792	6,356	24,781	52,729	34,409	7,874	1,052	103	118
20-24 years	49,539	6.4	772,811	731	3,200	4,237	9,287	32,084	129,625	301,489	222,559	59,412	8,678	852	657
25-29 years	51,059	5.8	874,180	830	3,335	4,640	10,102	32,152	122,581	320,079	278,446	85,767	13,802	1,497	949
30-34 years	46,745	6.1	764,708	750	3,059	4,593	9,859	28,484	99,013	266,505	250,900	84,494	14,344	1,608	1,099
35-39 years	27,077	7.4	368,711	419	1,692	2,685	5,912	16,369	49,740	124,558	117,260	41,002	7,554	968	552
40-44 years	6,482	9.0	72,414	83	435	631	1,474	3,859	10,669	23,974	21,573	7,793	1,577	204	142
45-54 years	655	17.6	3,729	7	37	79	156	376	704	1,063	928	297	65	8	9
White, non-Hispanic															
All ages	155,648	6.6	2,362,968	2,349	9,951	14,486	31,649	97,213	342,874	847,967	738,192	232,986	38,308	4,023	2,970
Under 15 years	223	12.1	1,840	3	22	15	50	133	382	699	434	87	9	2	4
15-19 years	16,784	8.2	204,056	279	1,213	1,549	3,185	10,558	38,919	80,056	53,574	12,763	1,628	148	184
15 years	610	9.6	6,387	10	64	65	126	345	1,326	2,459	1,593	350	41	3	5
16 years	1,590	9.3	17,086	36	132	174	317	931	3,411	6,755	4,298	896	104	15	17
17 years	2,982	8.5	35,286	59	255	276	548	1,844	6,777	14,038	9,088	2,119	232	17	33
18 years	4,947	8.3	59,491	68	350	461	954	3,114	11,513	23,286	15,382	3,793	475	44	51
19 years	6,655	7.8	85,806	106	412	573	1,240	4,324	15,892	33,518	23,213	5,605	776	69	78
20-24 years	34,629	6.6	523,971	509	2,228	3,054	6,481	22,357	86,216	199,492	153,422	42,759	6,382	596	475
25-29 years	38,594	5.9	651,445	603	2,453	3,536	7,739	24,263	89,687	233,871	210,330	66,356	10,773	1,075	759
30-34 years	37,681	6.1	617,371	573	2,357	3,664	8,031	23,056	78,292	212,523	204,968	69,857	11,845	1,255	950
35-39 years	21,973	7.3	302,576	315	1,321	2,104	4,843	13,390	40,228	101,242	97,082	34,490	6,296	784	481
40-44 years	5,207	8.9	58,631	60	329	506	1,187	3,125	8,561	19,211	17,636	6,431	1,318	157	110
45-54 years	557	18.1	3,078	7	28	58	133	331	589	873	746	243	57	6	7

TABLE 5.6

Number and percent of low birthweight and number of live births by selected characteristics, 2000 [CONTINUED]

Age and race and Hispanic origin of mother	Low birthweight [1]		Total	Birthweight											
	Number	Percent		Less than 500 grams	500-999 grams	1,000-1,499 grams	1,500-1,999 grams	2,000-2,499 grams	2,500-2,999 grams	3,000-3,499 grams	3,500-3,999 grams	4,000-4,499 grams	4,500-4,999 grams	5,000 grams or more	Not stated
Black, total															
All ages	80,778	13.0	622,598	2,442	8,129	8,507	15,745	45,955	142,881	236,467	128,173	28,749	4,308	543	699
Under 15 years	636	16.7	3,808	25	52	84	110	365	1,057	1,467	560	72	8	1	7
15-19 years	16,326	13.7	118,954	382	1,488	1,555	3,147	9,754	31,874	46,660	20,296	3,303	345	35	115
15 years	1,132	14.9	7,577	26	99	119	229	659	2,143	2,962	1,154	165	13	5	3
16 years	2,003	14.1	14,243	55	203	176	381	1,188	3,943	5,659	2,279	320	30	1	8
17 years	3,163	13.9	22,798	70	295	315	610	1,873	6,186	8,930	3,820	603	72	4	20
18 years	4,454	13.7	32,581	93	416	442	840	2,663	8,786	12,731	5,534	912	115	10	39
19 years	5,574	13.4	41,755	138	475	503	1,087	3,371	10,816	16,378	7,509	1,303	115	15	45
20-24 years	24,730	12.2	202,596	712	2,265	2,415	4,667	14,671	48,438	79,828	40,073	8,175	1,041	111	200
25-29 years	16,968	12.0	141,968	614	1,888	1,808	3,282	9,376	30,051	53,891	31,802	7,691	1,217	158	190
30-34 years	12,527	13.2	94,808	442	1,442	1,509	2,493	6,641	19,004	34,026	22,142	5,803	1,050	135	121
35-39 years	7,591	15.4	49,295	226	792	889	1,596	4,088	10,021	17,004	10,949	3,078	518	80	54
40-44 years	1,896	17.7	10,699	39	195	236	417	1,009	2,326	3,452	2,270	596	125	23	11
45-54 years	104	22.2	470	2	7	11	33	51	110	139	81	31	4	-	1
Black, non-Hispanic															
All ages	79,243	13.1	604,346	2,394	7,976	8,363	15,457	45,053	139,478	229,400	123,436	27,503	4,102	522	662
Under 15 years	625	16.8	3,736	25	52	83	107	358	1,035	1,441	549	70	8	1	7
15-19 years	16,055	13.9	116,019	372	1,467	1,531	3,090	9,595	31,181	45,458	19,669	3,176	337	35	108
15 years	1,110	15.0	7,397	26	97	117	224	646	2,092	2,900	1,116	159	13	5	2
16 years	1,969	14.2	13,895	52	199	176	374	1,168	3,854	5,516	2,208	309	30	1	8
17 years	3,109	14.0	22,228	70	294	310	601	1,834	6,053	8,697	3,702	575	69	4	19
18 years	4,378	13.8	31,737	91	406	432	826	2,623	8,581	12,395	5,350	875	113	10	35
19 years	5,489	13.5	40,762	133	471	496	1,065	3,324	10,601	15,950	7,293	1,258	112	15	44
20-24 years	24,305	12.3	197,190	699	2,228	2,375	4,603	14,400	47,338	77,679	38,713	7,866	994	107	188
25-29 years	16,639	12.1	137,545	605	1,857	1,778	3,219	9,180	29,337	52,169	30,570	7,334	1,162	149	185
30-34 years	12,263	13.4	91,477	436	1,410	1,481	2,444	6,492	18,471	32,799	21,192	5,520	988	132	112
35-39 years	7,409	15.6	47,577	218	768	873	1,551	3,999	9,733	16,406	10,477	2,934	491	76	51
40-44 years	1,845	17.8	10,347	37	187	231	411	979	2,278	3,313	2,189	572	118	22	10
45-54 years	102	22.5	455	2	7	11	32	50	105	135	77	31	4	-	1

TABLE 5.6

Number and percent low birthweight and number of live births by birthweight, by age and race and Hispanic origin of mother: United States, 2000 [continued]

Age and race and Hispanic origin of mother	Low birthweight[1]		Total	Birthweight											
	Number	Percent		Less than 500 grams	500-999 grams	1,000-1,499 grams	1,500-1,999 grams	2,000-2,499 grams	2,500-2,999 grams	3,000-3,499 grams	3,500-3,999 grams	4,000-4,499 grams	4,500-4,999 grams	5,000-grams or more	Not stated
Hispanic[3]															
All ages	52,247	6.4	815,868	847	3,707	4,779	9,993	32,921	134,672	321,881	233,127	62,537	9,650	1,294	460
Under 15 years	314	11.9	2,638	8	30	30	67	179	606	1,109	505	88	12	-	4
15-19 years	9,974	7.7	129,469	158	665	871	1,776	6,504	26,878	55,326	30,734	5,763	652	68	74
15 years	656	9.1	7,187	12	60	54	116	414	1,577	3,157	1,525	245	17	4	6
16 years	1,339	8.5	15,588	20	91	126	253	849	3,471	6,666	3,443	596	59	8	6
17 years	2,089	8.2	25,648	34	143	193	384	1,335	5,463	10,888	5,983	1,092	107	9	17
18 years	2,802	7.3	36,064	44	181	229	470	1,878	7,437	15,354	8,661	1,579	197	14	20
19 years	3,088	6.9	44,982	48	190	269	553	2,028	8,930	19,261	11,122	2,251	272	33	25
20-24 years	14,808	6.0	247,552	214	970	1,189	2,776	9,659	43,456	101,659	68,550	16,446	2,255	251	127
25-29 years	12,210	5.3	218,167	210	870	1,083	2,303	7,744	32,373	84,753	66,509	18,849	2,925	420	128
30-34 years	8,756	6.2	141,493	144	693	904	1,775	5,240	20,084	52,031	43,900	13,915	2,381	344	82
35-39 years	4,908	7.3	62,993	93	364	571	1,016	2,864	9,167	22,289	19,111	6,144	1,175	170	29
40-44 years	1,197	9.2	12,987	20	105	116	261	695	2,002	4,538	3,669	1,284	243	39	15
45-54 years	80	14.1	569	-	10	15	19	36	106	176	149	48	7	2	1

- Quantity zero.
[1] Less than 2,500 grams (5 lb 8 oz).
[2] Includes races other than white and black and origin not stated.
[3] Includes all persons of Hispanic origin of any race.

SOURCE: Joyce A. Martin, et al., "Table 45. Number and percent low birthweight and number of live births by birthweight, by age and race and Hispanic origin of mother: United States, 2000," in *Births: Final Data for 2000, National Vital Statistics Reports*, vol., 50. no.5, February 12, 2002

TABLE 5.7

Low-birthweight live births, according to mother's detailed race, Hispanic origin, and smoking status, selected years, 1970–99

[DATA ARE BASED ON THE NATIONAL VITAL STATISTICS SYSTEM.]

Birthweight, race, Hispanic origin of mother, and smoking status of mother	1970	1975	1980	1985	1990	1993	1994	1995	1996	1997	1998	1999
Low birthweight (less than 2,500 grams)					Percent of live births[1]							
All races	7.93	7.38	6.84	6.75	6.97	7.22	7.28	7.32	7.39	7.51	7.57	7.62
White	6.85	6.27	5.72	5.65	5.70	5.98	6.11	6.22	6.34	6.46	6.52	6.57
Black	13.90	13.19	12.69	12.65	13.25	13.34	13.24	13.13	13.01	13.01	13.05	13.11
American Indian or Alaska Native	7.97	6.41	6.44	5.86	6.11	6.42	6.45	6.61	6.49	6.75	6.81	7.15
Asian or Pacific Islander	---	---	6.68	6.16	6.45	6.55	6.81	6.90	7.07	7.23	7.42	7.45
Chinese	6.67	5.29	5.21	4.98	4.69	4.91	4.76	5.29	5.03	5.06	5.34	5.19
Japanese	9.03	7.47	6.60	6.21	6.16	6.53	6.91	7.26	7.27	6.82	7.50	7.95
Filipino	10.02	8.08	7.40	6.95	7.30	6.99	7.77	7.83	7.92	8.33	8.23	8.30
Hawaiian and part Hawaiian	---	---	7.23	6.49	7.24	6.76	7.20	6.84	6.77	7.20	7.15	7.69
Other Asian or Pacific Islander	---	---	6.83	6.19	6.65	6.89	7.06	7.05	7.42	7.54	7.76	7.76
Hispanic origin[2,3]	---	---	6.12	6.16	6.06	6.24	6.25	6.29	6.28	6.42	6.44	6.38
Mexican	---	---	5.62	5.77	5.55	5.77	5.80	5.81	5.86	5.97	5.97	5.94
Puerto Rican	---	---	8.95	8.69	8.99	9.23	9.13	9.41	9.24	9.39	9.68	9.30
Cuban	---	---	5.62	6.02	5.67	6.18	6.27	6.50	6.46	6.78	6.50	6.80
Central and South American	---	---	5.76	5.68	5.84	5.94	6.02	6.20	6.03	6.26	6.47	6.38
Other and unknown Hispanic	---	---	6.96	6.83	6.87	7.51	7.54	7.55	7.68	7.93	7.59	7.63
White, non-Hispanic[2]	---	---	5.67	5.60	5.61	5.92	6.06	6.20	6.36	6.47	6.55	6.64
Black, non-Hispanic[2]	---	---	12.71	12.61	13.32	13.43	13.34	13.21	13.12	13.11	13.17	13.23
Cigarette smoker[4]	---	---	---	---	11.25	11.84	12.28	12.18	12.13	12.06	12.01	12.06
Nonsmoker[4]	---	---	---	---	6.14	6.56	6.71	6.79	6.91	7.07	7.18	7.21
Very low birthweight (less than 1,500 grams)												
All races	1.17	1.16	1.15	1.21	1.27	1.33	1.33	1.35	1.37	1.42	1.45	1.45
White	0.95	0.92	0.90	0.94	0.95	1.01	1.02	1.06	1.09	1.13	1.15	1.15
Black	2.40	2.40	2.48	2.71	2.92	2.96	2.96	2.97	2.99	3.04	3.08	3.14
American Indian or Alaska Native	0.98	0.95	0.92	1.01	1.01	1.05	1.10	1.10	1.21	1.19	1.24	1.26
Asian or Pacific Islander	---	---	0.92	0.85	0.87	0.86	0.93	0.91	0.99	1.05	1.10	1.08
Chinese	0.80	0.52	0.66	0.57	0.51	0.63	0.58	0.67	0.64	0.74	0.75	0.68
Japanese	1.48	0.89	0.94	0.84	0.73	0.74	0.92	0.87	0.81	0.78	0.84	0.86
Filipino	1.08	0.93	0.99	0.86	1.05	0.95	1.19	1.13	1.20	1.29	1.35	1.41
Hawaiian and part Hawaiian	---	---	1.05	1.03	0.97	1.14	1.20	0.94	0.97	1.41	1.53	1.41
Other Asian or Pacific Islander	---	---	0.96	0.91	0.92	0.89	0.93	0.91	1.04	1.07	1.12	1.09
Hispanic origin[2,3]	---	---	0.98	1.01	1.03	1.06	1.08	1.11	1.12	1.13	1.15	1.14
Mexican	---	---	0.92	0.97	0.92	0.97	0.99	1.01	1.01	1.02	1.02	1.04
Puerto Rican	---	---	1.29	1.30	1.62	1.66	1.63	1.79	1.70	1.85	1.86	1.86
Cuban	---	---	1.02	1.18	1.20	1.23	1.31	1.19	1.35	1.36	1.33	1.49
Central and South American	---	---	0.99	1.01	1.05	1.02	1.06	1.13	1.14	1.17	1.23	1.15
Other and unknown Hispanic	---	---	1.01	0.96	1.09	1.23	1.29	1.28	1.48	1.35	1.38	1.32
White, non-Hispanic[2]	---	---	0.86	0.90	0.93	1.00	1.01	1.04	1.08	1.12	1.15	1.15
Black, non-Hispanic[2]	---	---	2.46	2.66	2.93	2.99	2.99	2.98	3.02	3.05	3.11	3.18
Cigarette smoker[4]	---	---	---	---	1.73	1.77	1.81	1.85	1.85	1.83	1.87	1.91
Nonsmoker[4]	---	---	---	---	1.18	1.28	1.30	1.31	1.35	1.40	1.44	1.43

--- Data not available.

[1] Excludes live births with unknown birthweight. Percent based on live births with known birthweight.

[2] Trend data for Hispanics and non-Hispanics are affected by expansion of the reporting area for an Hispanic-origin item on the birth certificate and by immigration. These two factors affect numbers of events, composition of the Hispanic population, and maternal and infant health characteristics. The number of states in the reporting area increased from 22 in 1980, to 23 and the District of Columbia (DC) in 1983–87, 30 and DC in 1988, 47 and DC in 1989, 48 and DC in 1990, 49 and DC in 1991–92, and 50 and DC in 1993 and later years.

[3] Includes mothers of all races.

[4] Percent based on live births with known smoking status of mother and known birthweight. Includes data for 43 states and the District of Columbia (DC) in 1989, 45 states and DC in 1990, 46 states and DC in 1991–93, 46 states, DC, and New York City (NYC) in 1994–98, and 48 states, DC, and NYC in 1999. Excludes data for California and South Dakota (1989–99), Indiana and New York (1989–98), New York City (1989–93), Oklahoma (1989–90), and Louisiana and Nebraska (1989), which did not require the reporting of mother's tobacco use during pregnancy on the birth certificate.

Note: The race groups, white, black, American Indian or Alaska Native, and Asian or Pacific Islander, include persons of Hispanic and non-Hispanic origin. Conversely, persons of Hispanic origin may be of any race.

SOURCE: "Table 12. Low-birthweight live births, according to mother's detailed race, Hispanic origin, and smoking status: United States, selected years 1970–99" in *Health, United States, 2001*, Centers for Disease Control and Prevention, National Center for Health Statistics, Hyattsville, MD, 2001

Adolescents

Historically, physicians deferred to parents' wishes when it came to decisions about an adolescent's health care treatment, but this is no longer the case. Robert F. Weir and Charles Peters, in "Affirming the Decisions Adolescents Make about Life and Death" (*Hastings Center Report,* vol. 27, no. 6, 1997), report that doctors and parents have been known to abide by decisions made by critically, chronically, and terminally ill adolescents, rather than imposing their wishes on these adolescents.

Over the past 20 years, a number of studies have concluded that, by age 14, many adolescents are capable of making decisions about their own health care. In 1995 the AAP recommended that minors should have more say about their health care as they mature.

While many laws concerning minors have changed, such as the lowering of the legal age, and allowing minors to seek medical treatments such as reproductive health and birth control services without parental consent, most states have no laws for end-of-life decisions by legal minors.

Weir and Peters observe that because of their condition, chronically ill adolescents are frequently mature beyond their years. They have suffered physically and psychologically, have seen other patients die, and have considered the choices they would make should their conditions worsen. The authors suggest that adolescents may want to provide directions about their care should it develop that they are no longer able to communicate their decisions. Such an advance directive would help guide parents and physicians in carrying out adolescents' wishes.

AGONIZING DECISIONS

While the government, ethicists, and pro-life advocates debate life-and-death decisions, parents and physicians of ailing children are the ones faced with immediate, difficult, real-life choices. Many factors influence decision-making, and each situation is unique.

Saying No to Treatment

In 1993 Francisca Rodriguez died of AIDS, which she had contracted from her former husband. Prior to her death, she had requested that her family not subject her to futile, life-prolonging treatments. She signed a living will and appointed a health proxy. Rodriguez died at home peacefully, comforted by her family.

Rodriguez left behind a three-year-old daughter, Gabriella. Gabriella was also dying of AIDS, contracted from her mother at birth. Rodriguez had not only made arrangements for her own final days, but also did the same for her daughter—no experimental drugs or invasive procedures. Gabriella was to live the rest of her short life like any child her age.

Rodriguez's family and the child's doctor honored the mother's wishes. At a time when many physicians were reluctant to give up on dying patients, in part because they feared litigation, and when families usually did not discuss end-of-life care and impending death, Gabriella's family openly discussed her condition with the child and her caregivers. Like her mother, Gabriella died surrounded by her loved ones.

Against All Odds

In October 1994 Ryan Nguyen was born six weeks premature. Diagnosing irreversible brain damage, kidney failure, and intestinal obstruction, hospital doctors recommended that life support be withdrawn. The Nguyens refused to allow their son to die. In response to the parents' petition, the court ordered the hospital to "take whatever immediate steps [are] necessary to stabilize and maintain the life of Ryan Nguyen, including dialysis of the kidney functions."

Approximately two months later, another hospital offered to operate on Ryan's blocked intestine. Following this surgery, the infant required no additional dialysis for his kidney problem and, moreover, a brain scan showed no brain damage. Ryan lived for four years, and though he was a sickly child, his cheerful disposition filled his parents' lives with joy.

CHAPTER 6
EUTHANASIA AND ASSISTED SUICIDE

BACKGROUND

The dictionary defines euthanasia, which derives from the Greek for "good death," as "the act or practice of killing or permitting the death of hopelessly sick or injured individuals in a relatively painless way for reasons of mercy." This present-day definition of euthanasia differs from that of the classical Greeks, who considered euthanasia simply "one mode of dying." The ancient Greeks considered euthanasia a rational act by persons who deemed their lives no longer useful. That these individuals sought the help of others to end their lives was considered morally acceptable.

The movement to legalize euthanasia in England began in 1935 with the founding of the Voluntary Euthanasia Society by such well-known figures as George Bernard Shaw, Bertrand Russell, and H.G. Wells. In 1936 the House of Lords (one of the houses in the English Parliament) defeated a bill that would have permitted euthanasia in cases of terminal illness. Nonetheless, it was common knowledge that physicians practiced euthanasia. The same year, it was rumored that King George V, who had been seriously ill for several years, was "relieved of his sufferings" by his physician, with the approval of his wife, Queen Mary.

In the United States, the Euthanasia Society of America was established in 1938. In 1967 this group prepared the first living will. Renamed the Society for the Right to Die in 1974, it merged in 1991 with another organization called Concern for Dying to become Choice in Dying (CID). While CID took no position on physician-assisted suicide, it "advocated for the rights of dying patients." It also educated the public about the importance of advance directives and end-of-life issues. In early 2000, CID dissolved, taking many of its programs and staff to become Partnership for Caring, Inc. The new organization's goal is to "ensure that everyone in this country soon has access to quality end-of-life care."

Euthanasia and the Nazis

The Nazis' version of euthanasia was a bizarre interpretation of an idea espoused by two German professors, Alfred Hoche and Karl Binding, in their 1920 book, *The Permission to Destroy Life Unworthy of Life*. While initially advocating that it was ethical for physicians to assist in the death of those who requested an end to their suffering, the authors later argued that it was also permissible to end the lives of the mentally retarded and the mentally ill.

Some present-day opponents of euthanasia fear that a society that allows physician-assisted suicide may eventually follow the path of Nazi dictator Adolf Hitler's euthanasia program, which began with the killing of physically and mentally imperfect individuals and culminated with the annihilation of entire religious and ethnic groups considered by the Nazis to be unworthy of life. However, those supporting euthanasia argue that unlike the murderous Nazi euthanasia program practiced by a dictator, modern-day proposals are based upon voluntary requests by individuals in situations of physical suffering and would be sanctioned by laws passed by democratic governments.

The Debate

In the United States, the debate on euthanasia distinguishes between active and passive euthanasia. Active euthanasia, also called voluntary active euthanasia by those who distinguish it from Nazi euthanasia, involves the hastening of death through the administration of lethal drugs, as requested by the patient or other competent individual.

Passive euthanasia, on the other hand, involves foregoing medical treatment, knowing that such a decision will result in death. This action is not considered illegal because the underlying illness, permitted to run its natural course, will ultimately cause death. It is generally accepted in the United States that terminally ill individuals have a right to refuse medical treatment, as do persons who are not terminally ill. However, some people feel that allowing patients to forego medical treatment is a practice tantamount to enabling suicide and is therefore morally reprehensible.

The debate about euthanasia in the United States has been expanded to include the question of whether a competent, terminally ill patient has the right to physician-assisted suicide, in which a physician provides the means (such as lethal drugs) for the patient to self-administer and commit suicide. The distinction between the two actions, euthanasia and physician-assisted suicide, is at times difficult to define: a patient in the latter stages of Lou Gehrig's disease (ALS), for example, is physically unable to kill him or herself; therefore, a physician who aids in such a person's suicide would technically be committing euthanasia.

SUICIDE

Different Cultures and Religions

Different religions and cultures have viewed suicide in different ways. Ancient Romans who dishonored themselves or their families were expected to commit suicide in order to maintain their dignity and, frequently, the family property. Early Christians were quick to embrace martyrdom as a guarantee of eternal salvation, but during the fourth century, St. Augustine discouraged the practice. He and later theologians were concerned that many Christians who were suffering in the world would see suicide as a reasonable and legitimate way to depart to a better place in the hereafter. The view of the Christian theologian St. Thomas Aquinas (circa 1225–74) is reflected in the present-day Roman Catholic teaching that "suicide contradicts the natural inclination of the human being to preserve and perpetuate his life ... and is contrary to love for the living God."

While Islam and Judaism also condemn the taking of one's own life, Buddhist monks and nuns have been known to commit suicide by self-immolation (burning themselves alive) as a form of social protest. In a ritual called suttee (now outlawed), widows in India showed devotion to their deceased husbands by being cremated with them, sometimes throwing themselves on the funeral pyres of their husbands, although it was not always voluntary. Widowers (men whose wives had died), however, did not follow this custom.

Quasi-religious reasons sometimes motivate mass suicide. In 1978 more than 900 members of a group known as The People's Temple killed themselves in Jonestown, Guyana. In 1997 a group called Heaven's Gate also committed mass suicide in California. The devastating terrorist attacks of September 11, 2001, and the rash of suicide bombers in the Middle East have been attributed to religious extremist groups that have twisted or misinterpreted the fundamental tenets of Islam to further their political objectives.

The Japanese people have traditionally associated a certain idealism with suicide. During the twelfth century, samurai warriors practiced voluntary *seppuku* (more commonly known as *hara-kiri*,) or ritual self-disembowelment, to avoid dishonor at the hands of their enemies. Some samurais committed this slow suicide to atone for wrongdoing or to express devotion to a superior who had died. Even as late as 1970, famed author Yukio Mishima publicly committed *seppuku*. During World War II, Japanese kamikaze pilots inflicted serious casualties with suicidal assaults in which they would purposely crash their planes into enemy ships, killing themselves.

Suicide is still commonly practiced in modern Japan. In early 1998 several government officials and businessmen hanged themselves in separate incidents involving scandals that attracted public attention. The reasons given for the suicides ranged from proclaiming innocence to assuming responsibility for wrongdoing.

Suicide in America

With the exception of certain desperate medical situations, suicide in the United States is generally considered an unacceptable act, the product of irrationality or severe depression. It is often referred to as a "permanent solution to a short-term problem."

In spite of this generally held philosophy, in 1999 suicide was the eleventh leading cause of death in America. In fact there were more suicides (1.2 percent) than homicides (.7 percent). Since 1950, the national suicide rate has dropped from 13.2 suicides per 100,000 people to 10.6 per 100,000 in 1999. (See Table 6.1.)

The Centers for Disease Control and Prevention (CDC) did a five-year study of suicide patterns in different geographic regions across the country ("Regional Variations in Suicide Rates—United States, 1990–1994," *Morbidity and Mortality Weekly Report,* vol. 46, no. 34, August 29, 1997). The CDC found that the suicide rate was the highest in the West, at 14.7 suicides per 100,000 people. (See Table 6.2 and Figure 6.1.) No reason for this finding has yet been determined.

Suicide Among Young People

According to the American Association of Suicidology, the rate of suicide among young people increased 200 percent between the 1950s and 1990s. During the 1990s death rates for suicide declined, but in some age groups the rate of suicide attempts actually rose. In 1999 suicide was the third leading cause of death among people ages 15 to 24 years, and more teens and young adults died from suicide than from AIDS, birth defects, cancer, chronic lung disease, heart disease, pneumonia and influenza, and stroke combined. While females are more likely to attempt suicides, males are more likely to die from their attempts.

In recent years, clusters of suicides among young people have occurred in different areas of the country—

TABLE 6.1

Death rates for suicide, according to sex, race, Hispanic origin, and age, selected years 1950–99

[DATA ARE BASED ON THE NATIONAL VITAL STATISTICS SYSTEM.]

Sex, race, Hispanic origin, and age	1950[1]	1960[1]	1970	1980	1985	1990	1995	1996	1997	1998	Preliminary 1999
All persons					Deaths per 100,000 resident population						
All ages, age adjusted	13.2	12.5	13.1	12.2	12.5	12.5	12.0	11.7	11.4	11.3	10.6
All ages, crude	11.4	10.6	11.6	11.9	12.4	12.4	11.9	11.6	11.4	11.3	10.6
Under 1 year	...	...	...	...	...	...	...	...	...	...	...
1–4 years	...	...	...	...	...	...	...	...	...	...	...
5–14 years	0.2	0.3	0.3	0.4	0.8	0.8	0.9	0.8	0.8	0.8	0.6
15–24 years	4.5	5.2	8.8	12.3	12.8	13.2	13.3	12.0	11.4	11.1	10.3
25–44 years	11.6	12.2	15.4	15.6	15.0	15.2	15.3	15.0	14.8	14.6	13.9
25–34 years	9.1	10.0	14.1	16.0	15.3	15.2	15.4	14.5	14.3	13.8	13.4
35–44 years	14.3	14.2	16.9	15.4	14.6	15.3	15.2	15.5	15.3	15.4	14.3
45–64 years	23.5	22.0	20.6	15.9	16.3	15.3	14.1	14.4	14.2	14.1	13.4
45–54 years	20.9	20.7	20.0	15.9	15.7	14.8	14.6	14.9	14.7	14.8	14.1
55–64 years	26.8	23.7	21.4	15.9	16.8	16.0	13.3	13.7	13.5	13.1	12.3
65 years and over	30.0	24.5	20.8	17.6	20.4	20.5	18.1	17.3	16.8	16.9	15.8
65–74 years	29.6	23.0	20.8	16.9	18.7	17.9	15.8	15.0	14.4	14.1	13.5
75–84 years	31.1	27.9	21.2	19.1	23.9	24.9	20.7	20.0	19.3	19.7	18.2
85 years and over	28.8	26.0	19.0	19.2	19.4	22.2	21.6	20.2	20.8	21.0	19.2
Male											
All ages, age adjusted	21.2	20.0	19.8	19.9	21.1	21.5	20.6	20.0	19.4	19.2	18.1
All ages, crude	17.8	16.5	16.8	18.6	20.0	20.4	19.8	19.3	18.7	18.6	17.5
Under 1 year	...	...	...	...	...	...	...	...	...	...	...
1–4 years	...	...	...	...	...	...	...	...	...	...	...
5–14 years	0.3	0.4	0.5	0.6	1.2	1.1	1.3	1.1	1.2	1.2	1.0
15–24 years	6.5	8.2	13.5	20.2	21.0	22.0	22.5	20.0	18.9	18.5	17.1
25–44 years	17.2	17.9	20.9	24.0	23.7	24.4	24.9	24.3	23.8	23.5	22.3
25–34 years	13.4	14.7	19.8	25.0	24.7	24.8	25.6	24.0	23.6	22.9	22.2
35–44 years	21.3	21.0	22.1	22.5	22.3	23.9	24.1	24.6	23.9	24.0	22.4
45–64 years	37.1	34.4	30.0	23.7	25.3	24.3	22.5	23.0	22.5	22.4	21.2
45–54 years	32.0	31.6	27.9	22.9	23.6	23.2	22.8	23.3	22.5	23.1	21.9
55–64 years	43.6	38.1	32.7	24.5	27.1	25.7	22.0	22.7	22.4	21.3	20.1
65 years and over	52.8	44.0	38.4	35.0	40.9	41.6	36.3	35.2	33.9	34.1	32.1
65–74 years	50.5	39.6	36.0	30.4	33.9	32.2	28.7	27.7	26.4	26.2	25.0
75–84 years	58.3	52.5	42.8	42.3	53.1	56.1	44.8	43.4	40.9	42.0	38.3
85 years and over	58.3	57.4	42.4	50.6	56.2	65.9	63.1	59.9	60.3	57.8	55.0
Female											
All ages, age adjusted	5.6	5.6	7.4	5.7	5.2	4.8	4.4	4.3	4.4	4.3	4.0
All ages, crude	5.1	4.9	6.6	5.5	5.2	4.8	4.4	4.4	4.4	4.4	4.1
Under 1 year	...	...	...	...	...	...	...	...	...	...	...
1–4 years	...	...	...	...	...	...	...	...	...	...	...
5–14 years	0.1	0.1	0.2	0.2	0.4	0.4	0.4	0.4	0.4	0.4	0.3
15–24 years	2.6	2.2	4.2	4.3	4.3	3.9	3.7	3.6	3.5	3.3	3.1
25–44 years	6.2	6.6	10.2	7.7	6.5	6.2	5.8	5.8	6.0	6.0	5.6
25–34 years	4.9	5.5	8.6	7.1	5.9	5.6	5.2	5.0	5.0	4.9	4.7
35–44 years	7.5	7.7	11.9	8.5	7.1	6.8	6.5	6.6	6.8	6.9	6.3
45–64 years	9.9	10.2	12.0	8.9	8.0	7.1	6.1	6.4	6.5	6.4	6.0
45–54 years	9.9	10.2	12.6	9.4	8.3	6.9	6.7	7.0	7.3	7.0	6.6
55–64 years	9.9	10.2	11.4	8.4	7.8	7.3	5.3	5.5	5.4	5.5	5.2
65 years and over	9.4	8.4	8.1	6.1	6.6	6.4	5.5	4.8	4.9	4.7	4.3
65–74 years	10.1	8.4	9.0	6.5	6.9	6.7	5.4	4.8	4.7	4.3	4.2
75–84 years	8.1	8.9	7.0	5.5	6.7	6.3	5.5	5.0	5.2	4.9	4.7
85 years and over	8.2	6.0	5.9	5.5	4.7	5.4	5.5	4.4	4.9	5.8	4.1
White male											
All ages, age adjusted	22.3	21.1	20.8	20.9	22.4	22.8	21.9	21.3	20.6	20.6	19.3
All ages, crude	19.0	17.6	18.0	19.9	21.6	22.0	21.4	20.9	20.2	20.3	19.1
15–24 years	6.6	8.6	13.9	21.4	22.3	23.2	23.5	20.9	19.5	19.3	17.8
25–44 years	17.9	18.5	21.5	24.6	24.8	25.4	26.3	25.7	25.3	25.2	23.8
45–64 years	39.3	36.5	31.9	25.0	27.0	26.0	24.2	24.9	24.2	24.2	22.9
65 years and over	55.8	46.7	41.1	37.2	43.7	44.2	38.7	37.8	36.1	36.6	34.5
65–74 years	53.2	42.0	38.7	32.5	35.8	34.2	30.3	29.6	28.0	27.9	26.7
75–84 years	61.9	55.7	45.5	45.5	57.0	60.2	47.5	46.1	43.4	44.7	40.8
85 years and over	61.9	61.3	45.8	52.8	60.9	70.3	68.2	65.4	65.0	62.7	59.7

TABLE 6.1

Death rates for suicide, according to sex, race, Hispanic origin, and age, selected years 1950–99 [CONTINUED]

[DATA ARE BASED ON THE NATIONAL VITAL STATISTICS SYSTEM.]

Sex, race, Hispanic origin, and age	1950[1]	1960[1]	1970	1980	1985	1990	1995	1996	1997	1998	Preliminary 1999
Black male					Deaths per 100,000 resident population						
All ages, age adjusted	7.5	8.4	10.0	11.4	11.8	12.8	12.5	11.9	11.4	10.6	10.5
All ages, crude	6.3	6.4	8.0	10.3	11.0	12.0	11.9	11.4	10.9	10.2	10.0
15–24 years	4.9	4.1	10.5	12.3	13.3	15.1	18.0	16.7	16.0	15.0	14.3
25–44 years	9.8	12.6	16.1	19.2	17.8	19.6	18.6	17.8	17.0	15.2	15.3
45–64 years	12.7	13.0	12.4	11.8	12.9	13.1	11.8	11.8	10.5	11.1	10.1
65 years and over	9.0	9.9	8.7	11.4	15.8	14.9	14.3	12.6	13.6	11.6	12.2
65–74 years	10.0	11.3	8.7	11.1	16.7	14.7	13.5	12.7	12.9	11.4	11.5
75–84 years[2]	*	*	*	10.5	15.6	14.4	16.6	12.5	14.1	12.5	13.7
85 years and over	- - -	*	*	*	*	*	*	*	*	*	*
American Indian or Alaska Native male[3]											
All ages, age adjusted	- - -	- - -	- - -	19.3	17.9	20.1	18.9	19.2	20.5	20.1	19.1
All ages, crude	- - -	- - -	- - -	20.9	20.3	20.9	19.6	19.9	20.9	21.1	19.6
15–24 years	- - -	- - -	- - -	45.3	42.0	49.1	34.2	32.1	38.4	41.8	36.6
25–44 years	- - -	- - -	- - -	31.2	30.2	27.8	31.8	34.8	32.6	33.3	29.5
45–64 years	- - -	- - -	- - -	*	*	*	15.0	11.5	15.5	11.3	16.0
65 years and over	- - -	- - -	- - -	*	*	*	*	*	*	*	*
Asian or Pacific Islander male[4]											
All ages, age adjusted	- - -	- - -	- - -	10.7	9.3	9.6	10.4	9.3	10.5	10.2	9.7
All ages, crude	- - -	- - -	- - -	8.8	8.4	8.7	9.4	8.6	9.2	9.1	9.0
15–24 years	- - -	- - -	- - -	10.8	14.2	13.5	16.0	11.9	12.2	10.9	10.3
25–44 years	- - -	- - -	- - -	11.0	9.3	10.6	11.5	11.5	10.6	11.9	12.0
45–64 years	- - -	- - -	- - -	13.0	10.4	9.7	9.1	8.6	12.3	10.2	12.4
65 years and over	- - -	- - -	- - -	18.6	16.7	16.8	20.3	16.0	21.0	21.0	13.9
Hispanic male[5]											
All ages, age adjusted	- - -	- - -	- - -	- - -	11.0	13.7	13.1	12.0	11.2	11.0	10.7
All ages, crude	- - -	- - -	- - -	- - -	9.8	11.4	11.5	10.6	9.8	9.4	9.1
15–24 years	- - -	- - -	- - -	- - -	13.8	14.7	18.3	15.5	14.4	13.4	11.9
25–44 years	- - -	- - -	- - -	- - -	14.8	16.2	15.5	14.6	13.9	13.0	13.1
45–64 years	- - -	- - -	- - -	- - -	12.3	16.1	14.2	13.3	11.6	11.5	11.9
65 years and over	- - -	- - -	- - -	- - -	14.7	23.4	19.9	17.7	17.7	20.0	17.4
White, non-Hispanic male[5]											
All ages, age adjusted	- - -	- - -	- - -	- - -	22.9	23.5	22.4	22.0	21.5	21.5	20.2
All ages, crude	- - -	- - -	- - -	- - -	22.3	23.1	22.3	22.0	21.5	21.6	20.4
15–24 years	- - -	- - -	- - -	- - -	22.6	24.4	23.8	21.4	20.2	20.2	18.7
25–44 years	- - -	- - -	- - -	- - -	25.1	26.4	27.3	27.1	26.8	26.7	25.3
45–64 years	- - -	- - -	- - -	- - -	27.3	26.8	24.8	25.6	25.1	25.1	23.7
65 years and over	- - -	- - -	- - -	- - -	46.4	45.4	39.2	38.6	36.8	37.3	35.3
White female											
All ages, age adjusted	6.0	5.9	7.9	6.1	5.7	5.2	4.7	4.7	4.8	4.7	4.4
All ages, crude	5.5	5.3	7.1	5.9	5.6	5.3	4.8	4.8	4.9	4.8	4.5
15–24 years	2.7	2.3	4.2	4.6	4.7	4.2	3.9	3.8	3.7	3.5	3.2
25–44 years	6.6	7.0	11.0	8.1	7.0	6.6	6.3	6.4	6.6	6.6	6.2
45–64 years	10.6	10.9	13.0	9.6	8.7	7.7	6.7	7.0	7.2	7.1	6.7
65 years and over	9.9	8.8	8.5	6.4	6.9	6.8	5.7	5.0	5.1	5.0	4.6
Black female											
All ages, age adjusted	1.8	2.0	2.9	2.4	2.3	2.4	2.1	2.0	2.0	1.8	1.7
All ages, crude	1.5	1.6	2.6	2.2	2.1	2.3	2.0	2.0	1.9	1.8	1.6
15–24 years	1.8	*	3.8	2.3	2.0	2.3	2.2	2.3	2.4	2.2	2.0
25–44 years	2.3	3.0	4.8	4.3	3.2	3.8	3.4	2.9	2.7	2.7	2.5
45–64 years	2.7	3.1	2.9	2.5	2.8	2.9	2.0	2.3	2.4	2.2	1.8
65 years and over	*	*	2.6	*	2.7	1.9	2.2	2.1	1.6	1.2	1.5

Westchester County, New York; Bergenfield, New Jersey; Pierre, South Dakota; and Plano, Texas. Experts have found no significant pattern in any of these strings of suicides. They happened in rich and poor communities, and in urban, suburban, and rural areas.

While the suicide rate among black youths has been historically low, between 1980 and 1995 the rate rose among black males ("Suicide Among Black Youths—United States, 1980–1995," *Morbidity and Mortality Weekly Report,* vol. 47, no. 10, March 20, 1998). By 1995

TABLE 6.1

Death rates for suicide, according to sex, race, Hispanic origin, and age, selected years 1950–99 [CONTINUED]

[DATA ARE BASED ON THE NATIONAL VITAL STATISTICS SYSTEM.]

Sex, race, Hispanic origin, and age	1950[1]	1960[1]	1970	1980	1985	1990	1995	1996	1997	1998	Preliminary 1999
American Indian or Alaska Native female[3]					Deaths per 100,000 resident population						
All ages, age adjusted	- - -	- - -	- - -	4.7	4.1	3.6	4.2	5.7	4.5	5.3	4.7
All ages, crude	- - -	- - -	- - -	4.7	4.4	3.7	4.2	5.6	4.2	5.4	4.8
15–24 years	- - -	- - -	- - -	*	*	*	*	10.2	*	*	*
25–44 years	- - -	- - -	- - -	10.7	*	*	7.1	9.0	6.4	8.0	8.3
45–64 years	- - -	- - -	- - -	*	*	*	*	*	*	*	*
65 years and over	- - -	- - -	- - -	*	*	*	*	*	*	*	*
Asian or Pacific Islander female[4]											
All ages, age adjusted	- - -	- - -	- - -	5.5	5.0	4.1	4.3	4.0	4.0	3.6	3.6
All ages, crude	- - -	- - -	- - -	4.7	4.3	3.4	3.8	3.7	3.6	3.3	3.4
15–24 years	- - -	- - -	- - -	*	5.8	3.9	5.2	3.0	4.7	2.7	4.4
25–44 years	- - -	- - -	- - -	5.4	4.2	3.8	3.8	4.5	3.7	4.0	4.0
45–64 years	- - -	- - -	- - -	7.9	5.4	5.0	4.9	5.2	4.4	4.3	4.1
65 years and over	- - -	- - -	- - -	*	13.6	8.5	9.0	8.4	8.9	7.2	6.5
Hispanic female[5]											
All ages, age adjusted	- - -	- - -	- - -	- - -	1.9	2.3	2.1	2.2	1.8	2.0	1.9
All ages, crude	- - -	- - -	- - -	- - -	1.6	2.2	1.9	2.1	1.6	1.8	1.7
15–24 years	- - -	- - -	- - -	- - -	2.1	3.1	2.6	3.3	2.4	2.8	2.0
25–44 years	- - -	- - -	- - -	- - -	2.1	3.1	2.7	2.8	2.2	2.2	2.5
45–64 years	- - -	- - -	- - -	- - -	3.2	2.5	2.7	2.6	2.3	2.7	2.5
65 years and over	- - -	- - -	- - -	- - -	*	*	*	2.5	*	2.5	2.2
White, non-Hispanic female[5]											
All ages, age adjusted	- - -	- - -	- - -	- - -	6.1	5.4	4.9	4.9	5.1	5.0	4.7
All ages, crude	- - -	- - -	- - -	- - -	6.2	5.6	5.1	5.0	5.3	5.2	4.8
15–24 years	- - -	- - -	- - -	- - -	4.7	4.3	4.0	3.8	3.9	3.6	3.4
25–44 years	- - -	- - -	- - -	- - -	7.7	7.0	6.7	6.7	7.2	7.2	6.7
45–64 years	- - -	- - -	- - -	- - -	9.2	8.0	7.0	7.3	7.6	7.4	7.0
65 years and over	- - -	- - -	- - -	- - -	7.5	7.0	5.8	5.1	5.2	5.2	4.7

. . . Category not applicable.

- - - Data not available.

* Based on fewer than 20 deaths.

[1] Includes deaths of persons who were not residents of the 50 states and the District of Columbia.

[2] In 1950 rate is for the age group 75 years and over.

[3] Interpretation of trends should take into account that population estimates for American Indians increased by 45 percent between 1980 and 1990, partly due to better enumeration techniques in the 1990 decennial census and to the increased tendency for people to identify themselves as American Indian in 1990.

[4] Interpretation of trends should take into account that the Asian population in the United States more than doubled between 1980 and 1990, primarily due to immigration.

[5] Excludes data from states lacking an Hispanic-origin item on their death certificates.

Notes: Age-adjusted rates are calculated using the year 2000 standard population. Age groups were selected to minimize the presentation of unstable age-specific death rates based on small numbers of deaths and for consistency among comparison groups. The race groups, white, black, Asian or Pacific Islander, and American Indian or Alaska Native, include persons of Hispanic and non-Hispanic origin. Conversely, persons of Hispanic origin may be of any race. Bias in death rates results from inconsistent race identification between the death certificate (source of data for numerator of death rates) and data from the Census Bureau (denominator); and from undercounts of some population groups in the census. The net effects of misclassification and under coverage result in death rates estimated to be overstated by 1 percent for the white population and 5 percent for the black population; and death rates estimated to be understated by 21 percent for American Indians, 11 percent for Asians, and 2 percent for Hispanics.

SOURCE: "Table 47. Death rates for suicide, according to sex, race, Hispanic origin, and age; United States, selected years 1950–99," in *Health, United States, 2001*, Centers for Disease Control and Prevention, National Center for Health Statistics, Hyattsville, MD, 2001

the death rate for suicide among black males aged 15–24 had risen to a high of 18 suicides per 100,000 population and suicide was the third leading cause of death among blacks aged 15 to 19 years. Since 1995 the death rate for young black males has steadily declined and in 1999 it dropped to 14.3 per 100,000, the lowest reported rate since 1985. (See Table 6.1.)

Death rates for suicide have declined for white males aged 15 to 24 years from a 1995 high of 23.5 suicides per 100,000 population to 17.8 per 100,000 in 1999. In 1999 the highest suicide death rate among youth—36.6 suicides per 100,000 population—was among young male American Indian or Alaska Natives. (See Table 6.1.) While death rates have declined among young adults, the percentage of high school students who attempted suicide increased from 7.3 percent in 1991 to 8.3 percent in 1999, and the percentage of students injured during a suicide attempt also rose (from 1.7 percent to 2.6 percent). (See Table 6.3.) These statistics underscore the urgent need for prevention, education, and support programs to help teens and young adults at risk.

TABLE 6.2

Number of suicides and rate of suicides per 100,000 population, by region and state, 1990–94

Region/State	No. deaths	Crude rate	Adjusted rate*
Northeast			
Connecticut	1,553	9.5	8.3
Maine	838	13.6	11.3
Massachusetts	2,530	8.4	7.7
New Hampshire	697	12.5	NC**
New Jersey	2,729	7.0	6.8
New York	7,551	8.4	7.6
Pennsylvania	6,976	11.6	11.0
Rhode Island	454	9.1	8.9
Vermont	406	14.2	11.4
Total	**23,734**	**9.3**	**8.6**
Midwest			
Illinois	5,717	9.9	9.8
Indiana	3,575	12.7	12.0
Iowa	1,598	11.4	10.8
Kansas	1,546	12.3	11.4
Michigan	5,403	11.5	11.0
Minnesota	2,562	11.5	11.1
Missouri	3,448	13.3	12.6
Nebraska	958	12.0	11.4
North Dakota	371	11.7	10.2
Ohio	5,875	10.7	10.1
South Dakota	479	13.5	12.2
Wisconsin	2,960	11.9	11.3
Total	**34,492**	**11.4**	**10.9**
South			
Alabama	2,659	12.9	13.0
Arkansas	1,550	12.9	12.3
Delaware	421	12.2	11.7
District of Columbia	177	6.0	6.7
Florida	10,413	15.4	14.3
Georgia	4,275	12.6	13.2
Kentucky	2,572	13.7	12.5
Louisiana	2,727	12.8	NC
Maryland	2,433	9.9	9.9
Mississippi	1,589	12.1	13.4
North Carolina	4,319	12.6	12.4
Oklahoma	2,248	14.0	NC
South Carolina	2,278	12.7	13.4
Tennessee	3,298	13.1	12.5
Texas	11,316	12.8	14.2
Virginia	4,008	12.6	12.3
West Virginia	1,226	13.6	12.3
Total	**57,509**	**13.1**	**13.1**
West			
Alaska	451	15.5	11.6
Arizona	3,495	18.1	18.0
California	18,734	12.2	13.8
Colorado	2,936	16.9	16.3
Hawaii	619	10.8	11.3
Idaho	915	17.1	16.6
Montana	794	19.2	18.6
Nevada	1,606	24.1	22.2
New Mexico	1,459	18.4	18.5
Oregon	2,367	15.9	14.8
Utah	1,357	15.0	15.7
Washington	3,512	13.7	12.7
Wyoming	464	20.0	19.8
Total	**38,709**	**14.1**	**14.7**
Total	**154,444**	**12.0**	**11.8**

* Adjusted to the age, sex, and race/Hispanic ethnicity of the 1980 U.S. population.
**Not calculated because of incomplete reporting.

SOURCE: Adapted from "Table 1. Number and rate of suicides, by region and rate—United States, 1990–1994," in "Regional Variations in Suicide Rates—United States, 1990–1994," *Morbidity and Mortality Weekly Report,* vol. 46, no. 34, August 29, 1997

The National Center for Injury Prevention and Control (NCIPC) sponsors initiatives to raise public awareness of suicide and institutes strategies to reduce suicide deaths. Along with support for research about risk factors for suicide in the general population, NCIPC also addresses high-risk populations with programs such as the American Indian/Alaska Native Community Suicide Prevention and Network Conference held in San Diego, California, in November 1998.

GAY AND LESBIAN ADOLESCENTS. Gay and lesbian adolescents are two to three times more likely than heterosexual adolescents to attempt suicide, making suicide the leading cause of death among this group of young people. Adolescence (the transition to adulthood) is often a difficult period. For gay and lesbian adolescents, this transition is compounded by having to come to terms with their sexuality in a society generally unaccepting of homosexuality.

At this period in their lives, when the need to confide in and gain acceptance from friends and family may be very crucial, they are often torn between choices that do not necessarily meet either of these needs. Those who are open about their sexual orientation risk disappointing or even alienating their families and facing the hostility of their peers. Teens who choose not to disclose their secrets may suffer emotional distress because they have nowhere to turn for emotional support. In either scenario, despair, isolation, anger, guilt, and overwhelming depression may promote suicidal thoughts or actual suicide attempts.

THE RIGHT TO DIE

The American Constitution does not guarantee the right to choose to die. The U.S. Supreme Court, however, currently recognizes that Americans have a fundamental right to privacy, or what is sometimes called the "right to be left alone." While the right to privacy is not explicitly mentioned in the Constitution, the Supreme Court has interpreted several amendments as encompassing this right. In *Roe v. Wade* (410 US 113, 1973), the High Court ruled that the Fourteenth Amendment protects the right to privacy against state action, specifically a woman's right to abortion. In the landmark Karen Ann Quinlan case, the Court held that the right to privacy included the right to refuse unwanted medical treatment and, as a consequence, the right to die.

THE RIGHT TO LIFE

The National Right to Life Committee (NRLC) opposes euthanasia of any kind. This group opposes the belief that persons who do not have a good quality of life should have the right to choose to die. In "What's Wrong with Making Assisted Suicide Legal?" (NRLC, 1998), David N. O'Steen, executive director of NRLC, and Burke J. Balch, director of the NRLC medical ethics

FIGURE 6.1

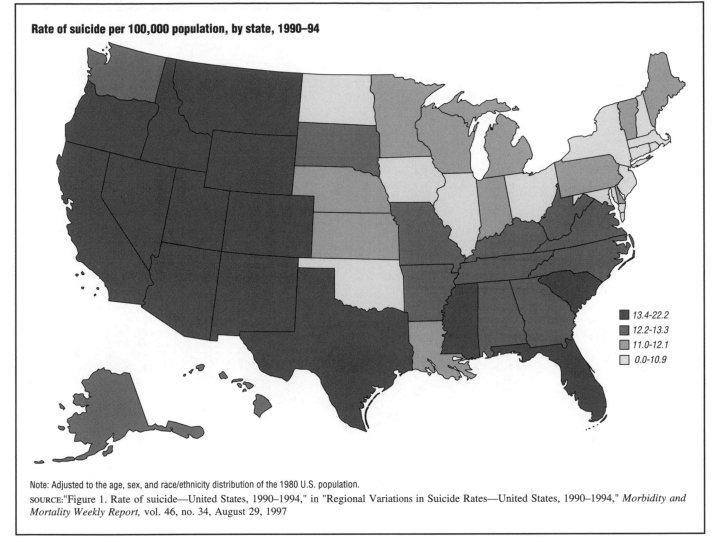

Rate of suicide per 100,000 population, by state, 1990–94

13.4-22.2
12.2-13.3
11.0-12.1
0.0-10.9

Note: Adjusted to the age, sex, and race/ethnicity distribution of the 1980 U.S. population.

SOURCE:"Figure 1. Rate of suicide—United States, 1990–1994," in "Regional Variations in Suicide Rates—United States, 1990–1994," *Morbidity and Mortality Weekly Report,* vol. 46, no. 34, August 29, 1997

department, propose that people who are feeling suicidal should be helped with their problems, not helped to die.

O'Steen and Balch believe that the assumption that suicidal people are competent and are simply exercising their right to make a rational decision to die is false. They contend that suicidal people are usually depressed or mentally ill, and their attempts to end their lives do not necessarily stem from specific wishes to die. On the contrary, O'Steen and Balch feel these attempts are cries for help that should be answered.

They point to a number of studies showing that most terminally ill patients are suicidal not because they are sick but because they are depressed. Their solution is to treat the depression, not end it by euthanasia. In the case of the severely disabled who might be contemplating suicide, O'Steen and Balch report that most people with disabilities feel that it is the conduct of the able-bodied majority toward them, rather than their own physical or mental impairment, which makes their lives even more difficult. Persons with disabilities face many obstacles

that are the result of social problems such as denial of access, discrimination in employment, and attitudes of aversion or pity instead of respect. The authors feel that true respect for the rights of people with disabilities would prompt actions to remove those obstacles; instead, "help" is given to commit suicide.

Assisted Suicide Funding Restriction Act of 1997

In April 1997 President Bill Clinton signed into law the Assisted Suicide Funding Restriction Act of 1997 (PL 105-12). (See Figure 6.2 for the statement President Clinton made on signing the bill.) The law bans federal funding of "active means of causing death, such as by lethal injection or the provision of a lethal oral drug overdose." It does not, however, prohibit the use of federal funds for actions some consider passive euthanasia—withholding or withdrawing medical treatment or artificial nutrition and hydration, which may eventually lead to death. Neither does it prohibit "the use of items, goods, benefits, or services" to relieve pain or discomfort, even if they hasten death, so long as they are not intended to do so.

TABLE 6.3

Suicidal ideation, suicide attempts, and injurious suicide attempts among students in grades 9–12, by sex, grade level, race, and Hispanic origin, selected years 1991–99

[DATA ARE BASED ON A NATIONAL SAMPLE OF HIGH SCHOOL STUDENTS, GRADES 9–12.]

Sex, grade level, race, and Hispanic origin	1991	1993	1995	1997	1999
			Percent of students who seriously considered suicide[1]		
Total	**29.0**	**24.1**	**24.1**	**20.5**	**19.3**
Male					
Total	20.8	18.8	18.3	15.1	13.7
9th grade	17.6	17.7	18.2	16.1	11.9
10th grade	19.5	18.0	16.7	14.5	13.7
11th grade	25.3	20.6	21.7	16.6	13.7
12th grade	20.7	18.3	16.3	13.5	15.6
White, non-Hispanic	21.7	19.1	19.1	14.4	12.5
Black, non-Hispanic	13.3	15.4	16.7	10.6	11.7
Hispanic	18.0	17.9	15.7	17.1	13.6
Female					
Total	37.2	29.6	30.4	27.1	24.9
9th grade	40.3	30.9	34.4	28.9	24.4
10th grade	39.7	31.6	32.8	30.0	30.1
11th grade	38.4	28.9	31.1	26.2	23.0
12th grade	30.7	27.3	23.9	23.6	21.2
White, non-Hispanic	38.6	29.7	31.6	26.1	23.2
Black, non-Hispanic	29.4	24.5	22.2	22.0	18.8
Hispanic	34.6	34.1	34.1	30.3	26.1
			Percent of students who attempted suicide[1]		
Total	**7.3**	**8.6**	**8.7**	**7.7**	**8.3**
Male					
Total	3.9	5.0	5.6	4.5	5.7
9th grade	4.5	5.8	6.8	6.3	6.1
10th grade	3.3	5.9	5.4	3.8	6.2
11th grade	4.1	3.4	5.8	4.4	4.8
12th grade	3.8	4.5	4.7	3.7	5.4
White, non-Hispanic	3.3	4.4	5.2	3.2	4.5
Black, non-Hispanic	3.3	5.4	7.0	5.6	7.1
Hispanic	3.7	7.4	5.8	7.2	6.6
Female					
Total	10.7	12.5	11.9	11.6	10.9
9th grade	13.8	14.4	14.9	15.1	14.0
10th grade	12.2	13.1	15.1	14.3	14.8
11th grade	8.7	13.6	11.4	11.3	7.5
12th grade	7.8	9.1	6.6	6.2	5.8
White, non-Hispanic	10.4	11.3	10.4	10.3	9.0
Black, non-Hispanic	9.4	11.2	10.8	9.0	7.5
Hispanic	11.6	19.7	21.0	14.9	18.9

PHYSICIAN-ASSISTED SUICIDE

The Dr. Quill Case—A Model Case...

A well-publicized case of physician-assisted suicide in 1991 continues to be a major topic of discussion among those in the medical, bioethical, and legal professions. Dr. Timothy Quill, in "Death and Dignity—A Case of Individualized Decision-Making" (*The New England Journal of Medicine,* vol. 324, no. 10, March 7, 1991), wrote about helping a patient identified as Diane commit suicide. Dr. Quill, who had known Diane for eight years, had seen her battle and overcome alcoholism and depression. Eventually Diane was diagnosed with an acute form of leukemia. She was very sure not only that she would die

during treatment, but also that she would suffer unbearably while undergoing chemotherapy (drug treatment to fight cancer). Diane decided that she would rather end her life than lose control over her body. Dr. Quill prescribed barbiturates that Diane subsequently used to kill herself.

Through an anonymous tip, authorities identified the real "Diane" whom Dr. Quill had helped to commit suicide. As a result, the case was brought to a grand jury. Asked to decide whether Dr. Quill's action constituted a crime, the grand jury declined to recommend an indictment. Meanwhile, the New York State Department of Health's Board for Professional Misconduct considered his actions "legal and ethically appropriate."

TABLE 6.3

Suicidal ideation, suicide attempts, and injurious suicide attempts among students in grades 9–12, by sex, grade level, race, and Hispanic origin, selected years 1991–99 [CONTINUED]

[DATA ARE BASED ON A NATIONAL SAMPLE OF HIGH SCHOOL STUDENTS, GRADES 9–12.]

Sex, grade level, race, and Hispanic origin	1991	1993	1995	1997	1999
			Percent of students with an injurious suicide attempt[1,2]		
Total	**1.7**	**2.7**	**2.8**	**2.6**	**2.6**
Male					
Total	1.0	1.6	2.2	2.0	2.1
9th grade	1.0	2.1	2.3	3.2	2.6
10th grade	0.5	1.3	2.4	1.4	1.8
11th grade	1.5	1.1	2.0	2.6	2.1
12th grade	0.9	1.5	2.2	1.0	1.7
White, non-Hispanic	1.0	1.4	2.1	1.5	1.6
Black, non-Hispanic	0.4	2.0	2.8	1.8	3.4
Hispanic	0.5	2.0	2.9	2.1	1.4
Female					
Total	2.5	3.8	3.4	3.3	3.1
9th grade	2.8	3.5	6.3	5.0	3.8
10th grade	2.6	5.1	3.8	3.7	4.0
11th grade	2.1	3.9	2.9	2.8	2.8
12th grade	2.4	2.9	1.3	2.0	1.3
White, non-Hispanic	2.3	3.6	2.9	2.6	2.3
Black, non-Hispanic	2.9	4.0	3.6	3.0	2.4
Hispanic	2.7	5.5	6.6	3.8	4.6

[1] Response is for the 12 months preceding the survey.
[2] A suicide attempt that required medical attention.
Note: Only youth attending school participated in the survey.

SOURCE: "Table 59 Suicidal ideation, suicide attempts, and injurious suicide attemps among students in grades 9–12, by sex, grade level, race, and Hispanic origin: United States selected years 1991–99," *Health, United States, 2001,* Centers for Disease Control and Prevention, National Center for Health Statistics, Hyattsville, MD, 2001

Many observers were not surprised at the outcome of the grand jury proceedings. They cited growing public concern about how easily patients could lose control over end-of-life decisions. Some bioethicists thought that Dr. Quill's handling of Diane's case would make a suitable model for how physician-assisted suicides should be practiced. Many of Dr. Quill's colleagues lauded his act, some claiming that it was generally known some doctors do assist in suicides. They were glad that, because of Dr. Quill's confession, the practice was now in the open.

...Or a Case of Misguided Judgment?

Dr. Herbert Hendin, a psychiatrist and psychologist as well as a world-renowned authority on suicide, claimed that "the doctor assisting a suicide is not simply a dispassionate observer responding to the patient's needs and wishes." In *Seduced by Death: Doctors, Patients, and the Dutch Cure* (W. W. Norton and Company, New York, 1997), Dr. Hendin noted that Dr. Quill's account of Diane's suicide belied his supposedly disinterested, albeit compassionate, response to his patient's request. Dr. Hendin believed "emotional involvement" on Dr. Quill's part "[had] clouded his judgment."

When Diane decided to refuse the treatment recommended by her oncologist (cancer specialist), Dr. Quill,

instead of exploring with the patient the reason for her seemingly hasty decision, told his readers, "Together we lamented her tragedy and the unfairness of life." Dr. Hendin believed Diane must have been suffering from depression. Once she had told Dr. Quill of her decision to end her life, she calmed down. Dr. Hendin explained that suicidal persons become less depressed after their decision: "Coping with the uncertainties of life and death is what agitates and depresses them."

Dr. Hendin believed that Dr. Quill's failure to challenge Diane's presumption that the cancer treatment would fail opened the door to her next decision—to commit suicide with Dr. Quill's help. Although Dr. Quill told Diane that he could not assist in her suicide, Dr. Hendin claimed in his article that Dr. Quill "appears to have conveyed to her ... that her request 'made perfect sense'," and he subsequently referred her to the Hemlock Society. Founded in 1980, the Hemlock Society advocates for choice and dignity at the end of life and the legal availability of the means to hasten death. Dr. Hendin felt it probably confused the patient that while Dr. Quill was saying that he was "leav[ing] the door open for her to change her mind," he pointed her to a place that could help her fulfill her wish. "Quill once again powerfully shaped the clinical interaction between himself and his patient," wrote Dr. Hendin.

FIGURE 6.2

ASSISTED SUICIDE FUNDING RESTRICTION ACT OF 1997

PUBLIC LAW 105-12

STATEMENT BY PRESIDENT OF THE UNITED STATES

STATEMENT BY PRESIDENT WILLIAM J. CLINTON UPON SIGNING H.R. 1003

Today I am signing into law H.R. 1003, the "Assisted Suicide Funding Restriction Act of 1997," which reaffirms current Federal policy banning the use of Federal funds to pay for assisted suicide, euthanasia, or mercy killing.

This is appropriate legislation. Over the years, I have clearly expressed my personal opposition to assisted suicide, and I continue to believe that assisted suicide is wrong. While I have deep sympathy for those who suffer greatly from incurable illness, I believe that to endorse assisted suicide would set us on a disturbing and perhaps dangerous path. This legislation will ensure that tax-payer dollars will not be used to subsidize or promote assisted suicide. The Act will, among other things, ban the funding of assisted suicide, euthanasia, or mercy killing through Medicaid, Medicare, military and Federal employee health plans, the veterans health care system, and other Federally funded programs.

Section 5(a)(3) of the Act also assures that taxpayer funds will not be used to subsidize legal assistance or other forms of advocacy in support of legal protection for assisted suicide, euthanasia, or mercy killing. The restrictions on the use of funds contained in this section, properly construed, will allow the Federal Government to speak with a clear voice in opposing these practices. The Department of Justice has advised, however, that a broad construction of this section would raise serious First Amendment concerns. I am therefore instructing the Federal agencies that they should construe section 5(a)(3) only to prohibit Federal funding for activities and services that provide legal assistance for the purpose of advocating a right to assisted suicide, or that have as their purpose the advocacy of assisted suicide, and not to restrict Federal funding for other activities, such as those that provide forums for the free exchange of ideas. In addition, I emphasize that section 5(a)(3) imposes no restriction on the use of nonfederal funds.

WILLIAM J. CLINTON

THE WHITE HOUSE,
April 30, 1997

SOURCE: William J. Clinton, "Statement on Signing the Assisted Suicide Funding Restriction Act of 1997," *Weekly Compilation of Presidential Documents,* vol. 33, no. 18, May 5, 1997

Dr. Hendin pointed out that, at her last meeting with Dr. Quill, Diane promised she would reunite with the doctor "in the future at her favorite spot on the edge of Lake Geneva, with dragons swimming in the sunset." According to Dr. Hendin, "death as a metaphor for reunion in a magical netherworld is a common fantasy among suicidal

TABLE 6.4

Physician willingness to provide assistance with suicides, number of such requests from patients, and physician compliance with requests, by speciality, 1996 physician survey results

Variable	Specialty										
	All respondents	Family practice	Cardiology	Geriatrics	Infectious disease	Nephrology	Neurology	Hematology-oncology	Pulmonary disease	Internal medicine	Other
	percentage of respondents*										
Would write prescription for a lethal dose of medication if it were legal to do so	36	39	49	40	43	32	46	44	40	33	44
Would write prescription under current legal constraints	11	10	9	13	11	4	11	8	15	11	9
Have received request for assistance with suicide	18	15	12	26	21	9	9	25	18	21	12
Have written prescription for for a lethal dose of medication	3.3	2	1	1	4	0	1	3	5	4	2
Would give lethal injection if it were legal to do so	24	28	28	25	31	21	32	27	31	23	28
Would give lethal injection under current legal constraints	7	7	2	4	5	3	7	2	9	8	5
Have received a request for a lethal injection	11	8	9	14	11	7	5	13	19	13	6
Have given a lethal injection	4.7	4	2	2	4	2	3	2	6	6	3

*Unweighted (raw) percentages are given for each specialty, with weighted percentages for all respondents.

SOURCE: Diane E. Meier et al., "Table 6. Willingness to Provide Assistance, Requests for Assistance, and Compliance with Requests, According to Specialty," in "A National Survey of Physician-Assisted Suicide and Euthanasia in the United States," *The New England Journal of Medicine,* vol. 338, no. 17, April 23, 1998

people. That both doctor and patient shared it suggests that neither really came to grips with the fact of death."

Dr. Quill, an active advocate of the legalization of physician-assisted suicide, joined two other physicians and three patients in 1994 to sue the New York State Attorney General for violating the Fourteenth Amendment by banning physician-assisted suicide. The Supreme Court ruled on this case in June 1997, reversing an earlier ruling made by the Court of Appeals for the Second Circuit. The Supreme Court distinguished between withdrawing life-sustaining treatment and physician-assisted suicide, and differentiated between physician actions taken to relieve pain and suffering and those intended to hasten death.

REQUEST TO DIE AND PHYSICIAN COMPLIANCE

As various states enacted right-to-die legislation, researchers sought to determine physicians' attitudes toward assisting in patient death. Earlier surveys of physician attitudes about assisted suicide and euthanasia concentrated on specific medical specialties or particular states. In "A National Survey of Physician-Assisted Suicide and Euthanasia in the United States" (*The New England Journal of Medicine,* vol. 338, no. 17, April 23, 1998), Diane E. Meier, et al., surveyed physicians across medical specialties and throughout the country "to assess the prevalence of requests for assistance with suicide or euthanasia and of compliance with such requests."

The 1,902 respondents were drawn from the 10 medical specialties in which physicians are most likely to get requests for such assistance. Given the laws in effect at the time of the survey, 11 percent of the physicians said that they would write a lethal prescription, knowing that the patient would use the prescription to commit suicide. If assisted suicide and euthanasia were legalized, 36 percent of the respondents would do so. Under contemporary laws, 7 percent would give a lethal injection to help end a patient's life, and this percentage would rise to 24 percent if it were legal. (See Table 6.4.)

Since starting practice, 18 percent of the physicians surveyed had received at least one request for assisted suicide; one in nine (11 percent) had received a request for a lethal injection. Of the 320 physicians who had received a request for a lethal prescription, 16 percent (3.3 percent of the total respondents) granted the patients' requests. Fifty-nine percent of the patients used the lethal prescription to commit suicide. All the physicians were asked if they had ever given a patient a lethal injection. Almost 5 percent reported that they had administered a lethal injection to help end a patient's life. (See Table 6.4.)

Patients Receiving Assisted Suicide and Euthanasia

The survey found that while almost all (95 percent) of the requests for a lethal prescription were made by the patients themselves, more than half (54 percent) of the requests for a lethal injection were made by a partner or a family member. In cases where lethal injection was requested,

TABLE 6.5

Characteristics of 81 patients who received a prescription for a lethal dose of medication or a lethal injection, 1996 physician survey results

CHARACTERISTIC	PRESCRIPTION	INJECTION	CHARACTERISTIC	PRESCRIPTION	INJECTION
	weighted percent			weighted percent	
Person who made request[1][2]			Patient hospitalized at time of request	5[3]	99
Patient	95	39	Family member or friends closely involved	83	95
Family member or partner	5	54	Request reflected patient's wishes[2]	100	100
Not specified	0	7	Length of time physician had known patient		
Request explicit	75	21	<1 wks.	0	8
Request somewhat indirect	25	79	1-4wks.	0	4
Patient's clinical status[2]			2-11 mos.	12	26
Experiencing severe discomfort	75	73	≥12 mos.	88	62
Dependent on others for personal care	68	55	Request repeated[2]	51	53
Bedridden 50% or more of the time	57	55	Immediate assistance requested	33	94
Experiencing severe pain	54	24	Second opinion obtained by physician[3]	<1	32
Depressed	19	39	Patient's primary diagnosis		
Confused 50% or more of the time	5	7	Cancer	70	23
None of the above	2	15	Neurologic disease	6	17
Patient's sex			Acquired immunodeficiency syndrome	6	16
Male	97	57	Other[4]	18	44
Female	3	43	Someone else present at patient's death	98	65
Patient's age[2]			Physician tried to dissuade patient from hastening death	34	11
<18 yr.	<1	<1	Physician's comfort with role in assisting patient		
19 - 45 yr.	28	17	Very comfortable	58	83
46 - 75 yr.	43	38	Somewhat comfortable	24	5
>75 yr.	29	45	Somewhat uncomfortable	18	6
Patient's education			Very uncomfortable	<1	6
<12 yrs.	<1	17	Physician's willingness to comply with future requests of the same type		
12-15 yrs.	29	60	Would definitely comply	39	28
>16 yrs.	64	21	Would probably comply	42	60
Don't know or don't remember	7	2	Unsure	18	5
Life expectancy[2]			Would probably not comply	1	1
<24 hrs.	<1	59	Would definitely not comply	0	6
1- 6 days	26	37			
1 - 3 wks.	22	2			
1- 5 mos.	50	2			
6 - 12 mos.	1	0			
>12 mos.	1	1			

Note: The Oregon Death with Dignity Act specifies criteria for complying with requests from patients for assistance with suicide. The patient must be an adult with a terminal illness and a life expectancy of less than six months. The request must be made by the patient and must be voluntary. Procedural guidelines require that the initial request be repeated after 15 days, with an opportunity to rescind it, and that the physician obtain a second opinion, with a psychiatric evaluation if the disorder is causing impaired judgment. The survey did not query physicians about all these criteria and did not determine whether all were met.

[1] If someone other than the patient made the request, the survey did not ask whether the patient later made the same request.
[2] This involves one of the criteria specified in the Oregon Death with Dignity Act.
[3] Ninety percent of lethal prescriptions were given to patients who were at home, and 5 percent were given to patients in nursing homes.
[4] Other diagnoses included end-stage heart or lung disease and multiorgan-system failure.

SOURCE: Diane E. Meier et al., "Table 4. Characteristics of 81 Patients Who Received a Prescription for a Lethal Dose of Medication or a Lethal Injection," in "A National Survey of Physician-Assisted Suicide and Euthanasia in the United States," *The New England Journal of Medicine,* vol. 338, no. 17, April 23, 1998.

the patient was usually in the hospital (99 percent). Fifty-nine percent of those requesting an injection were estimated to have less than 24 hours to live, and 96 percent were estimated to have less than a week. (See Table 6.5.)

A majority of those who received a lethal prescription (75 percent) or a lethal injection (73 percent) were experiencing severe discomfort. Half (54 percent) of the lethal-prescription recipients and one-fourth (24 percent) of the lethal-injection recipients had severe pain. There were twice as many depressed patients (39 percent) who received a lethal injection as those who had a lethal prescription (19 percent). (See Table 6.5.)

Five percent of patients who received a lethal prescription, and 7 percent of those given a lethal injection, were "confused" 50 percent or more of the time. (See

Table 6.5.) However, the researchers did not ask the physicians whether the patients were incompetent when the decision for assisted suicide or euthanasia was made.

The physicians were also asked how comfortable they were in assisting with patient suicide. A great majority responded they were somewhat comfortable or very comfortable with prescribing lethal medication (82 percent) or giving a lethal injection (88 percent). Similar percentages said they would probably or definitely comply with future requests for a lethal prescription (81 percent) or injection (88 percent). (See Table 6.5.)

Reasons for Assisted Suicide Requests

The physicians were asked to describe the reasons why patients were requesting assistance to die. The patients' reasons, as perceived by the physicians, were:

- Discomfort other than pain (reported by 79 percent of the physicians)

- Loss of dignity (53 percent)

- Fear of uncontrollable symptoms (52 percent)

- Actual pain (50 percent)

- Loss of meaning in life (47 percent)

- Being a burden (34 percent)

- Dependency (30 percent)

Interestingly, the patients' primary concerns were not physical (pain and suffering), but were more likely to be focused on loss of control, being a burden or dependent on others, and loss of dignity.

PAIN NOT THE MAJOR REASON FOR REQUEST TO DIE. Ezekiel Emanuel, an associate professor at Harvard Medical School and a member of the National Bioethics Advisory Commission, claimed that contrary to popular belief, pain is not the major motivation behind a patient's request to die. In "Whose Right to Die?" (*Atlantic Monthly,* March 1997), Dr. Emanuel reported that empirical studies support this fact. Washington State physicians who received requests to assist in death or to perform euthanasia indicated that severe pain played a role in patient decisions in only about one-third of the requests. Dr. Emanuel's own study of cancer patients in Boston revealed that patients in pain were more likely to oppose euthanasia and physician-assisted suicide.

According to Dr. Emanuel, studies in the Netherlands, where assisted suicide and euthanasia have been practiced for many years, provide more evidence that pain is a minor factor in requests to end one's life. (The Netherlands, Belgium, and the state of Oregon in the United States are the only places in the world where physician-assisted suicide is legal.) A 1996 update of the Dutch government's landmark *Remmelink Report* illustrated that, while pain played some role in 32 percent of the requests, there was not a single case in which pain was the only reason for requesting assistance to die.

The findings of Dr. Emanuel's study are remarkably similar to those reported by researchers Diane E. Meier, et al., from the national physician survey discussed above. Dr. Emanuel found that the major reasons for assisted suicide and euthanasia requests ranged from depression to hopelessness, to fear of loss of dignity and being a burden. His Boston study also showed that depressed patients were more likely to discuss euthanasia, to stockpile drugs for future suicide, and to have read the suicide manual *Final Exit* by the Hemlock Society.

NURSES AND PATIENT REQUESTS FOR ASSISTED SUICIDE

According to a national survey, one in five nurses who worked in adult critical care units hastened a patient's death. In this survey, "The Role of Critical Care Nurses in Euthanasia and Assisted Suicide" (*The New England Journal of Medicine,* vol. 334, no. 21, May 23, 1996), David A. Asch, M.D., defined euthanasia and assisted suicide as circumstances in which a person performs an act with the specific intent of causing or hastening a patient's death. In this category, Dr. Asch included intentional overdose of narcotics or other substances, or providing explicit advice to patients about how to commit suicide. Withholding and withdrawing life-sustaining treatment, such as removing a mechanical ventilator, were not included.

A total of 852 nurses responded to the survey. Sixteen percent (129 nurses) reported that they had participated in active euthanasia and assisted suicide at least once in their careers. Sixty-five percent had done so three or fewer times, while five percent reported doing so more than 20 times.

Based on the responses, Dr. Asch estimated that at least 7 percent (58 nurses) had engaged in euthanasia or assisted suicide at least once without a request from either the patient or a surrogate. Eight percent (62 nurses) indicated having done so at least once without a request from the attending physician. These 62 nurses further indicated some instances in which they practiced euthanasia or assisted suicide following an attending physician's explicit request, or with the physician's advance knowledge.

Reasons given by the nurses for practicing euthanasia or assisted suicide included concern about the overuse of life-sustaining technology; a sense of responsibility for the patient's welfare; a desire to relieve suffering; and a desire to overcome the perceived unresponsiveness of physicians toward that suffering.

Some experts questioned the accuracy of the survey's results, and considered the survey questions ambiguous. Others claimed that the interpretation of euthanasia and assisted suicide was questionable in cases in which the dispensing of pain-relieving medicine resulted in death. Many nurses expressed concern that publicizing the results of the study would undermine the patients' and families' trust in nurses who work in intensive care units.

Individually and as members of professional associations, nurses continue to grapple with questions about end-of-life care and patient requests for assisted suicide. To assist all nurses to provide competent and compassionate care for the dying, the Oncology Nursing Society (ONS) published a position paper and practice guidelines, "The Nurse's Responsibility to the Patient Requesting Assisted Suicide," in January 2001. (Oncology is the specialty devoted to care of cancer patients, and oncology nurses care for terminally ill patients more often than nurses in other clinical settings.)

The ONS guidelines encourage nurses to engage in frank discussions with patients requesting assisted suicide, while actively seeking to identify and address patients' previously unmet needs. Although ONS guidelines definitively prohibit nurse involvement in assisted suicide, the professional society also cautions nurses to "resist the inclination to abandon terminally ill patients who request assisted suicide." The guidelines advise that, "In state(s) where assisted suicide is legal, the nurse may choose to continue to provide care or may withdraw from the situation after transferring responsibility for care to a nursing colleague."

SUPPORTERS OF ASSISTED SUICIDE

The Hemlock Society USA

The Hemlock Society USA (formerly the Hemlock Society) was founded in 1980 by Derek Humphry, a journalist from England. The society aims to "maximize the options for a good death, including aid in dying for mentally competent, terminally ill adults who request it from physicians willing to provide it." Members of the society euphemistically refer to suicide as "self-deliverance."

In 1975 Humphry helped his wife take her own life, to end the pain and suffering caused by her terminal bone cancer. Humphry recounted this incident in *Jean's Way: A Love Story* (Harper and Row, New York, 1978). The book launched his career in the voluntary euthanasia movement two years later.

In 1991 Humphry published *Final Exit: The Practicalities of Self-Deliverance and Assisted Suicide for the Dying* (The Hemlock Society, Eugene, Oregon). The suicide manual, which was on the *New York Times* best-seller list for 18 weeks, gave explicit instructions on how to commit suicide. While Humphry insisted that his how-to book was addressed only to those who are terminally ill, and not those suffering from depression, some physicians were concerned about how the book would affect those suffering from depression. Dr. Sherwin B. Nuland felt that depression is not a strong enough justification for teaching people how to kill themselves, to help them do it, or to bestow blessing on it (*How We Die,* Alfred A. Knopf, New York, 1994). In his opinion, no one with judgement impaired by depression is in a position to make a critical decision about ending his or her life.

In October 1991, while *Final Exit* was selling out at bookstores, Humphry's second wife, Ann Wickett, whom he had divorced the year before, committed suicide. She had been diagnosed with cancer and was reportedly depressed.

Humphry retired from the Hemlock Society in 1992, but his more recent activities have also sparked controversy. In 1999 he recorded a video depicting a variety of methods for committing suicide. Though it had been available from the Hemlock Society USA for several months, the video drew even more criticism when it aired on public television in Oregon a number of times in 2000. Critics asserted that this airing provided dangerous information, particularly to people who were depressed or mentally ill, and to children.

Dr. Jack Kevorkian

Dr. Jack Kevorkian first earned the nickname "Dr. Death" when, as a medical resident, he would photograph patients at the time of death to gather data that would help him differentiate death from coma, shock, and fainting. During his study and residency, he suggested unconventional ideas, such as the harvesting of organs from death row inmates. His career as a doctor was also "checkered" (Dr. Kevorkian's own word) and notable for controversy.

In the late 1980s, Dr. Kevorkian retired from pathology work, and pursued an interest in the idea of physician-assisted suicide, becoming one of its most well-known and passionate advocates. He constructed a machine that would allow a patient to press a red button and self-administer a lethal dose of poisonous potassium chloride, along with thiopental, a pain killer. With the use of this device, Kevorkian claims to have assisted in more than 130 suicides.

The first patient to commit suicide with Dr. Kevorkian's assistance and his suicide device, called Mercitron, was Janet Adkins. Adkins, a Hemlock Society member, sought Dr. Kevorkian's aid because she did not want to wait until she lost her mind to Alzheimer's disease. In June 1990 Adkins committed suicide in Dr. Kevorkian's van in a public campground.

In 1991 Dr. Kevorkian assisted in the deaths of two Michigan women on the same day. Sherry Miller, 43, had multiple sclerosis; Marjorie Wantz, 58, complained of a painful pelvic disease. Neither one was terminally ill, but court findings showed that they both suffered from depression. In 1996 Dr. Kevorkian was tried for the assisted deaths of Miller and Wantz under the common law that considers assisted suicide illegal. He was acquitted.

Dr. Kevorkian continued to draw media attention with increasingly controversial actions. In February 1998, 21-year-old Roosevelt Dawson, a paralyzed university student, became the youngest person to commit suicide with Dr. Kevorkian's help. In June 1998 Dr. Kevorkian announced that he was donating kidneys from Joseph Tushkowski, a quadriplegic whose death he had assisted. His actions were denounced by transplant program leaders, medical ethicists, and most of the public. The organs were refused by all medical centers and transplant teams.

In October 1998 Dr. Kevorkian euthanized 52-year-old Thomas Youk, a man afflicted with Lou Gehrig's disease (amyotrophic lateral sclerosis, also known as ALS), at the patient's request. Dr. Kevorkian videotaped the death and gave the video to the CBS television show *60 Minutes* for broadcast. The death was televised nationwide in November 1998 during primetime and included an interview with Dr. Kevorkian. He taunted Oakland County, Michigan, prosecutors to file charges against him. They did, and Dr. Kevorkian was convicted of second-degree murder in March 1999. On April 13, 1999, the 70-year-old retired pathologist was sentenced to 10–25 years in prison. While in prison, Dr. Kevorkian has staged three hunger strikes and has been subjected to force feeding by prison officials. As of April 2002, Dr. Kevorkian remained in prison pending appeal to higher courts. He will not be eligible for parole until May 2007.

THE BATTLE OVER LEGALIZING PHYSICIAN-ASSISTED SUICIDE

By the year 2002, Oregon remained the only state in the United States with a law allowing physician-assisted suicide, and then only in limited circumstances. At that time, 38 states had explicit laws against assisted suicide, and of these 38, 10 had provisions for additional civil penalties. Six states plus the District of Columbia had "common law" provisions against assisted suicide. This means there was a precedent of customs, usage, and court decisions that would support prosecution of an individual assisting in a suicide. The remaining five states had no laws regarding assisted suicide.

California

Two Los Angeles lawyers, Michael White and Robert Risley, wrote the first proposed euthanasia legislation, known as the Humane and Dignified Death Act. However, the initiative failed to get enough signatures to get on the California ballot in 1988. In 1992 California voters returned to the polls to vote on another effort to legalize euthanasia. Proposition 161 was rejected by a narrow margin of 54 to 46 percent.

Washington

In November 1991 voters in the state of Washington rejected Initiative 119, which would have legalized voluntary euthanasia for the terminally ill. It was also defeated by a margin of 54 to 46 percent.

Michigan

In 1997 a group called Merian's Friends, named after one of the women who committed suicide with Dr. Kevorkian's assistance, began collecting enough signatures to put the issue of assisted suicide on Michigan's ballot in 1998.

TABLE 6.6

Provisions of Oregon's Death with Dignity Act

- The request must be voluntary
- No doctor is forced to comply
- The patient must be an adult who is terminally ill and mentally competent
- The request must be an enduring one; a 15-day waiting period is required
- An examination by a mental health professional may be required
- The request must be made orally and in writing and witnessed
- All alternatives will be explained to the patient
- The patient will receive a prescription for a lethal dose of medication, which must be self-administered
- The patient may change his or her mind at any time

SOURCE: "The Oregon Victory: Its Significance and What Happens Next?" The Hemlock Society, Denver, CO [Online] http://www.hemlock.org/changing_laws.htm#oregon [accessed April 9, 2002].

Because Michigan is Dr. Kevorkian's home state, many expected the proposal to pass by a slight margin. However, a coalition of groups organized in opposition to the proposal, calling themselves Citizens for Compassionate Care. Disability rights groups, hospice and medical professionals, advocates for the poor, pro-life groups, and religious organizations banded together to form a united front. They emphasized several key messages, mainly focusing on the potential abuses if assisted suicide were legal and the possible side effects of legalization (such as less concern for end-of-life care and insurance cost-cutting).

The messages reached a wide audience through a well-financed campaign, with most money going toward television commercials. Voters responded by defeating the proposal 71 to 29 percent.

Oregon

In November 1994 Oregon voters approved Measure 16 by a vote of 51 to 49 percent, making Oregon the first jurisdiction in the world to legalize physician-assisted suicide. Under the Death with Dignity Act, a mentally competent adult resident of Oregon who is terminally ill (likely to die within six months) may request a prescription for a lethal dose of medication to end his or her life. (See Table 6.6 for the provisions of the Act.) Critics charge that assisted death is now "state-subsidized" because Medicaid money may be used to pay for physician-assisted suicide for the poor.

Between 1994 and 1997 the Death with Dignity Act was kept on hold due to legal challenges. In November 1997, 60 percent of Oregonians voted to defeat a measure to repeal the 1994 law (40 percent of voters voted in favor of repealing the Act). Immediately after this voter reaffirmation of the Death with Dignity Act, the Drug Enforcement Administration (DEA) warned Oregon doctors that they could be arrested or have their medical licenses revoked for prescribing lethal doses of drugs. DEA administrator Thomas Constantine, under pressure from some members of Congress, stated that prescribing a drug for suicide would be a violation of the Controlled Substances Act (PL 91-513) because assisted suicide was not a "legitimate medical purpose." Janet Reno, who was then the U.S. Attorney General, overruled Constantine and decided that that portion of the Controlled Substances Act would not apply in states that legalize assisted suicide. Those opposed to the practice observed that it was inconsistent, citing the government's opposite ruling in states that have legalized marijuana for medical use. (Reno maintained that the prescription of marijuana is still illegal, regardless of its medicinal value.)

In response to the DEA decision, Congress moved toward passage of the Pain Relief Promotion Act. This law would prevent the use of federally-controlled drugs for the purpose of assisted suicide and euthanasia. It would also strengthen protections for doctors who use narcotics to manage patients' pain, provide research grants, and establish a program for palliative care. As of June 2000, the House had passed the measure (HR 2260) by 271 to 156. In April 2000, it was favorably reported out of the Senate Judiciary Committee; however, a scheduled vote was stalled in the Senate, and as of April 2002 the Act had not been passed.

On November 6, 2001, John Ashcroft, who succeeded Janet Reno as U.S. Attorney General, overturned Reno's 1998 ruling that prohibited the DEA from acting against physicians who use drugs under Oregon's physician-assisted suicide law. Attorney General Ashcroft said that taking the life of terminally ill patients is not a "legitimate medical purpose" for federally-controlled drugs. The Oregon Medical Association and Washington State Medical Association opposed Attorney General Ashcroft's ruling, and even physicians opposed to assisted suicide expressed concern that the ruling might compromise patient care and that any DEA investigation might discourage physicians from prescribing pain medication to patients in need.

The State of Oregon disagreed so vehemently with Attorney General Ashcroft's interpretation of the Controlled Substances Act that on November 7, 2001, Oregon's Attorney General filed suit, claiming that Ashcroft was acting unconstitutionally. A November 8 restraining order allowed the Death with Dignity Act to remain in effect while the case was tried.

On April 17, 2002, U.S. District Judge Robert E. Jones ruled in favor of the Death with Dignity Act. His decision read, in part:

> State statutes, state medical boards, and state regulations control the practice of medicine. The [Controlled Substances Act] was never intended, and the [U.S. Department of Justice] and [Drug Enforcement Administration] were never authorized, to establish a national medical practice or act as a national medical board. To allow an attorney general—an appointed executive

whose tenure depends entirely on whatever administration occupies the White House—to determine the legitimacy of a particular medical practice without a specific congressional grant of such authority would be unprecedented and extraordinary.... Without doubt, there is tremendous disagreement among highly respected medical practitioners as to whether assisted suicide or hastened death is a legitimate medical practice, but opponents have been heard and, absent a specific prohibitive federal statute, the Oregon voters have made the legal, albeit controversial, decision that such a practice is legitimate in this sovereign state.

As of May 2002, the Justice Department was expected to appeal the ruling to the Ninth Circuit Court of Appeals.

ANALYSIS OF THE EFFECTS OF THE DEATH WITH DIGNITY ACT. In March 1998 an Oregon woman in her mid-80s who had terminal breast cancer ended her life with a lethal dose of barbiturates. Hers was the first known death under Oregon's assisted-suicide law. By 2002, a total of 70 people had reportedly committed suicide with the help of a doctor under the Death with Dignity Act. According to the *Fourth Annual Report on Oregon's Death with Dignity Act* (Oregon Department of Human Services, Office of Disease Prevention and Epidemiology, Portland, Oregon, February 6, 2002), in 1998, 16 assisted suicides were reported; 27 in 1999; 27 in 2000; and 21 in 2001. The number of lethal prescriptions written was higher each year than the number of completed suicides: the number of lethal prescriptions written was 24 in 1998; 33 in 1999; 39 in 2000; and 44 in 2001.

The median age of persons who took lethal medication in 2001 was 68 years, and 18 of the 21 suffered from end-stage cancer. Of the 21 people who committed physician-assisted suicide under the Death with Dignity Act in 2001, 17 provided information about what contributed to their request. Of these, more than half expressed concerns about loss of control of bodily functions, three-quarters mentioned "decreased ability to participate in activities that make life enjoyable," and 94 percent cited "loss of autonomy." Inadequate pain control was not a pressing concern in most of the cases.

Based on the Oregon Health Division's annual reports, groups in favor of assisted suicide conclude that the law is working as intended and without abuse. Opponents of the law continue to charge that the law discriminates against the elderly and seriously ill and express concern about reporting requirements. The Oregon Health Division admits that "Underreporting cannot be assessed, and noncompliance is difficult to assess because of the possible repercussions for noncompliant physicians reporting data to the division."

OREGON PHYSICIANS' ATTITUDES. Bioethicists, physicians, legislators, and patient advocacy groups have watched with interest to learn whether the attitudes and practices of Oregon physicians would change in response to passage of the 1994 Oregon Death with Dignity Act. In early 1999 researchers mailed questionnaires to 3,981 Oregon physicians to find out about their experiences with the Act. The responses of the 2,641 physicians who returned the survey by August 1999 were reported by Linda Ganzini, M.D., et al., in "Oregon Physicians' Attitudes About and Experiences with End-of-Life Care Since Passage of the Oregon Death with Dignity Act" (*Journal of the American Medical Association,* vol. 285, no. 18, May 9, 2001).

Dr. Ganzini, et al., found that 51 percent of responding physicians supported the Act, 32 percent opposed it, and 17 percent neither supported nor opposed it. Four out of five respondents said their attitude about the law was unchanged since it passed; however, among those whose feelings changed, nearly twice as many supported the Act as opposed it. Thirty percent considered prescribing lethal medication under the Act immoral or unethical, and 46 percent were unwilling to prescribe lethal medication. Despite their reluctance to assist patients to die, more than half of the respondents (53 percent) reported that if terminally ill, they would consider seeking physician assistance to end their own lives.

The researchers found that more than three-quarters of physicians who had cared for a terminally ill patient in the prior year had sought to improve their knowledge by recognizing and treating depression as well as prescribing pain medication. Nearly all respondents (91 percent) indicated some degree of comfort discussing the Act with patients and 36 percent said patients had asked them whether they would be willing to prescribe lethal medication. Nearly 60 percent of physicians who were not morally opposed to prescribing lethal medication expressed concerns about adhering to federal Drug Enforcement Agency law and feared public scrutiny and hospital sanction.

OPPOSITION TO PHYSICIAN-ASSISTED SUICIDE

Devaluing the Life of the Terminally Ill

In 1996 the Second and Ninth Circuit Courts of Appeals lifted the bans on assisted suicide in New York and Washington State, respectively, and both cases eventually went to the U.S. Supreme Court, which ruled on them in June 1997 (*Washington et al. v. Harold Glucksberg et al. and Dennis C. Vacco, Attorney General of New York et al. v. Timothy E. Quill et al.*). Kathleen M. Foley, M.D., co-chief of the Pain and Palliative Care Service of the Memorial Sloan-Kettering Cancer Center in New York, was appalled at these rulings. In "Competent Care for the Dying Instead of Physician-Assisted Suicide" (*The New England Journal of Medicine,* vol. 336, no. 1, January 2, 1997), Dr. Foley commented that the courts' response was a dangerous form of affirmative action that ran the risk of further devaluing the lives of terminally ill patients and providing an excuse for society to end its responsibility for their care.

Dr. Foley claimed that physicians are not adequately trained to deal with the dying, much less to determine the many symptoms associated with patients' requests to die. She feared that if physician-assisted suicide were legalized, it would take the place of a variety of interventions—therapeutic, psychological, and social—that might very well improve the life of dying patients. She was also concerned that patients, especially minorities who may already be distrustful of the health care system, might not seek medical or psychological treatment for fear that physicians might hasten their deaths.

Oppression of the Disabled

An attorney for the Anti-Euthanasia Task Force, Wesley J. Smith is a staunch defender of the sanctity of human life and an articulate, outspoken opponent of assisted suicide. In his books *Forced Exit: The Slippery Slope From Assisted Suicide to Legalized Murder* (Times Books, New York, 1997) and *Culture of Death: The Assault on Medical Ethics in America* (Encounter Books, San Francisco, California, 2001) Smith warns that legalized euthanasia could become a form of oppression. Citing the Jim Crow laws (1880s–1960s), which discriminated against blacks, Smith raises the concern that a person's state of health might soon become a basis for the oppression of specific groups of people. He speaks specifically of the disabled as being further oppressed if physician-assisted suicide were legalized.

Disabled people tell of incidents where able-bodied persons have told them that they would rather be dead than disabled, or that if they were disabled, they'd as soon give up and kill themselves. Such attitudes are also reportedly found in the health care system. Further, some observers feel that the financial pressures exerted by private and government payers might lead to hastening the death of disabled patients.

EUTHANASIA IN THE NETHERLANDS

The Netherlands is currently the only country in which active euthanasia is practiced openly, even though technically it was illegal until April 10, 2001. Prior to that date, active euthanasia was a criminal offense under Article 293 of the Dutch Penal Code, which read, "He who takes the life of another person on this person's explicit and serious request will be punished with imprisonment of up to 12 years or a fine of the fifth category." At the same time, however, Section 40 of the same penal code stated that an individual was not punishable if he or she was driven by "an irresistible force" (legally known as force majeure) to put another person's welfare above the law. This might include a circumstance in which a physician is confronted with the conflict between the legal duty of not taking a life, and the humane duty to end a patient's intolerable suffering.

Origin of Open Practice

In 1971 Dr. Geertruida Postma granted an elderly nursing-home patient's request to die by injecting the patient with morphine and ending her life. The patient was her 78-year-old mother, who was partially paralyzed and had to be tied to a chair to keep her from falling. Dr. Postma was found guilty of murder, but her penalty consisted of a one-week suspended jail sentence and a one-year probation. This "slap on the wrist" encouraged other physicians to come forward, admitting they had also assisted in patients' suicides.

Two years later, the Royal Dutch Medical Association announced that, should a physician assist in the death of a terminally ill patient, it was up to the court to decide if the physician's action could be justified by "a conflict of duties." In Alkmaar, Netherlands, Dr. Schoonheim helped Marie Barendregt to die in 1982, using a lethal injection. The 95-year-old, severely disabled Barendregt had initially signed an advance directive refusing artificial (life-prolonging) treatment. Dr. Schoonheim assisted in Barendregt's death with the knowledge of the patient's son and after consultation with two independent physicians. In 1984 the Dutch Supreme Court, ruling on this well-known Alkmaar case (the court case is referred to by the name of the city where the trial took place), found Dr. Schoonheim not guilty of murder.

Since then, each euthanasia case brought under prosecution has been judged on its individual circumstances. The force majeure defense has ensured acquittal, while compliance with the following guidelines for performing euthanasia laid down by the Royal Dutch Medical Association and the Dutch courts in 1984 has protected physicians from prosecution:

- The patient's wish to die must be expressed clearly and repeatedly.

- The patient's decision must be well-informed and voluntary.

- The patient must be suffering intolerably, with no hope of relief; however, the patient does not have to be terminally ill.

- The physician must consult with at least one other physician.

- The physician must notify the local coroner that death resulting from unnatural causes has occurred.

However, several events led the Royal Dutch Medical Association to refine the 1984 guidelines. In 1994 a film showing a doctor putting a patient to death produced negative reactions worldwide. The practice of the so-called "angels of death," traveling physicians who performed euthanasia where family doctors refused to assist in suicide, also generated unwelcome publicity. Finally, a star-tling announcement by the chief inspector of public health that doctors who refused to refer patients to another doctor would be found guilty of malpractice and disciplined led to the following changes in the guidelines:

- Physician-assisted euthanasia is preferable to active euthanasia. Physicians should let a patient self-administer lethal medication instead of giving the patient a lethal injection.

- The consulting physician must not have a personal or professional relationship to either the primary physician or patient.

- No doctor is required to perform euthanasia, but must refer the patient to one who will do it.

- Physicians must report all euthanasia performed.

On April 10, 2001, the Dutch Parliament voted 46-28 to legalize physician-assisted suicide by passing the Termination of Life on Request and Assisted Suicide (Review Procedures) Act. Arguments in favor of the bill included public approval ratings of 90 percent. In May 2001 the results of a Dutch public opinion poll revealed that nearly half of respondents favored making lethal drugs available to older adults who no longer wanted to live.

The Remmelink Commission

In 1990 the Dutch government commissioned a landmark study to investigate the actual medical practice of euthanasia and physician-assisted suicide. The Commission of Inquiry into the Medical Practice Concerning Euthanasia is commonly known as the Remmelink Commission, named after the committee chairman Jan Remmelink, who was then the Attorney General of the Dutch Supreme Court.

According to the *Remmelink Report* (English version, Paul J. van der Maas, M.D., et al., "Euthanasia and Other Medical Decisions Concerning the End of Life," *The Lancet,* 1991), 54 percent of the surveyed physicians had performed euthanasia or assisted suicide. Another 34 percent indicated that they might perform euthanasia or assisted suicide, although some might do it only in extreme situations. While 12 percent reported that they would never participate in euthanasia or assisted suicide, two-thirds of these physicians (8 percent of the total) would refer patients to another physician. Four percent would never have anything to do with such requests. Of the nearly 129,000 deaths in the Netherlands in 1990, 2,300 (1.8 percent) were the result of euthanasia, and 400 (0.3 percent) were assisted suicides.

INVOLUNTARY EUTHANASIA. The Remmelink Commission uncovered 1,040 deaths (0.8 percent of all deaths) from involuntary euthanasia. The Dutch do not refer to this practice as euthanasia, but call it "termination of life without patient's explicit request." Fourteen percent of these patients were fully competent, and 72 percent had

TABLE 6.7

Estimated incidence of medical decisions related to the end of life in the Netherlands, 1990–95

Variable	Interview Study				Death-certificate study			
	1995		1990		1995		1990	
No. of requests for euthanasia or assisted suicide later in disease	34,500	(3l,800-37,100)	25,100	(23,400-27,000)	ND		ND	
No. of explicit requests for euthanasia or assisted suicide at a particular time	9700	(8800-10,600)	8900	(8200-9700)	ND		ND	
End-of-life practices–% of deaths†								
Euthanasia	2.3	(1.9-2.7)	1.9	(1.6-2.2)	2.4	(2.1-2.6)	1.7	(1.4-2.1)
Physician-assisted suicide	0.4	(0.2-0.5)	0.3	(0.2-0.4)	0.2	(0-1-0.3)	0.2	(0.1-0.3)
Ending of life without patient's explicit request	0.7	(0.5-0.8)		ND	0.7	(0.5-0.9)	0.8	(0.6-1.1)
Opioids in large doses	14.7	(13.5-15.7)	16.3	(15.3-17.4)	19.1	(18.1-20.1)	18.8	(17.9-19.9)
Decision to forgo treatment	ND		ND		20.2	(19.1-21.3)	17.9	(17.0-18.9)
All of these	–		–		42.6	(41.3-43.9)	39.4	(38.1-40.7)

*Numbers in parentheses are 95 percent confidence intervals. ND denotes not determined, because the study data did not permit these estimates to be calculated.

†Percentages are based on the total number of deaths in the Netherlands: 135,546 in 1995 and 125,756 in 1990.

SOURCE: Paul J. van der Maas et al., "Euthanasia, Physician-Assisted Suicide, and Other Medical Practices Involving the End of Life in the Netherlands, 1990–95," *The New England Journal of Medicine,* vol. 335, no. 22, pp. 1699–1705.

not given any indication that they wanted to be euthanized. In 59 percent of the deaths, the physicians claimed that they had had discussions with the patients, who had expressed an interest in euthanasia before they became incompetent or unconscious. Nonetheless, these patients had never made an explicit request. (In the Netherlands, it is accepted practice for physicians to offer euthanasia as an option to patients.) Another 8,100 patients died from a deliberate overdose of pain medication given by doctors, not to control pain but to hasten death. Sixty-one percent had not consented to the overdose.

An Update of the *Remmelink Report*

In 1995 another nationwide investigation was conducted in the Netherlands as a follow-up study of physician-assisted suicide and euthanasia. In "Euthanasia, Physician-Assisted Suicide, and Other Medical Practices Involving the End of Life in the Netherlands" (*The New England Journal of Medicine,* vol. 335, no. 22, November 28, 1996), Paul J. van der Maas, et al., reported on an update of the *Remmelink Report.*

The study consisted of two parts—interviews with 405 physicians and a study of death certificates through questionnaires returned by about 5,000 physicians. The results of the 1995 two-part study, as compared with the 1990 results, show that the incidence of euthanasia among total deaths in the Netherlands increased from about 1.9 percent in 1990 to about 2.3 percent in 1995, and assisted suicides increased somewhat during the same period. (See Table 6.7.) The increases are attributed to an aging population, increased deaths from cancer as a result of decreased deaths from heart disease, rising availability of life-prolonging techniques, and changes in patients' attitudes toward euthanasia and physician-assisted suicide.

The update of the *Remmelink Report* also shows that the frequency with which patients' lives were terminated without their explicit requests (what Americans call involuntary euthanasia) decreased somewhat—from 0.8 percent in 1990 to 0.7 percent in 1995. (See Table 6.7.)

A New Update Underway

In 2001 a new study began, to gather data to compare with data from the 1991 and 1995 studies. As of May 2002, no data were yet available from the new study.

Journal of Medical Ethics Report

The *Journal of Medical Ethics,* a British publication, released a report in February 1999 based on its own research in the Netherlands. According to this report, studies conducted in 1996 revealed that the safeguards established by the Royal Dutch Medical Association were not being followed. Almost two-thirds of euthanasia and physician-assisted suicide cases went unreported. In 20 percent of euthanasia cases, the patient did not make a request; for 17 percent of these, there were other available treatment options.

Despite the law's "unbearable suffering" requirement, more than half of doctors listed the patient's primary concern as "loss of dignity." Taking into account all situations with explicit intention to end life, the number of deaths increased from 3,200 to 24,500 ("Euthanasia does not seem to be under effective control in the Netherlands," *Journal of Medical Ethics,* February 16, 1999).

Mental Suffering Acceptable As Reason for Performing Assisted Suicide and Euthanasia

In 1994 the Dutch Supreme Court ruled that euthanasia may be performed in cases of mental suffering. In the landmark Assen case, which used the defense of force majeure, the court exonerated a Dutch psychiatrist who had helped a patient commit suicide. The patient, Hilly Bosscher, although severely mentally distressed, was physically healthy. After a disastrous marriage that ended in divorce, and the deaths of her sons (one to suicide and the second to cancer), Bosscher wanted to die. She refused treatment for her depression, claiming that her mental suffering was such that nothing would help. Dr. Boudewijn Chabot was acquitted of assisted suicide because the patient was rational and had not been diagnosed with any psychiatric illness. Thereafter, the Dutch guidelines included assisting depressed people to commit suicide.

Belgium to Follow the Dutch

In October 2001 Belgium became the second country to legalize euthanasia. The legislation passed by 44 to 23 votes in the Belgian senate, with two abstentions and two senators failing to vote. The law will apply to competent adults who have an incurable illness causing unbearable, constant suffering and patients in a persistent vegetative state who made their wishes known within the prior five years in front of two witnesses.

SHOULD THE U.S. FOLLOW THE DUTCH?

Advocates of assisted suicide point to the Dutch system as a model for the United States, claiming that the U.S. could establish guidelines not unlike those in the Netherlands. However, Richard M. Doerflinger, in *Life at Risk* (National Conference of Catholic Bishops, Washington, D.C., April 1998), reported that the 1994 Dutch law that regulates euthanasia now allows the killing of handicapped newborns. Doerflinger felt that the Dutch court's reasoning invalidly equates euthanasia with discontinuing the use of life support and providing relief for pain.

The New York State Task Force on Life and the Law, a commission composed of persons from various disciplines, studied the feasibility of legalizing physician-assisted suicide. In their comprehensive 1994 report, *When Death Is Sought: Assisted Suicide and Euthanasia in the Medical Context,* the Task Force concluded that legalizing or legitimizing euthanasia would carry the substantial risk that patients might be assisted in suicide without adequate counseling and exploration of other avenues. They feared that for some people, the system might even work to encourage euthanasia. And they further felt that the risk was unacceptably high that vulnerable individuals with limited control over their lives, such as persons with disabilities, the elderly, and the poor, might be discriminated against.

Unlike the Netherlands, which provides medical care to all, in the United States medical care is not automatical-

ly available to every individual. The number of uninsured persons continues to increase, rising from 30.5 million in 1979 to 44 million in 2000. Job losses in 2001 produced an estimated 2 million additional uninsured Americans. Uninsured persons are already at risk because they are often unable to obtain needed medical care. Legalized assisted suicide could make them even more vulnerable to potential abuses of resource allocations. Might a hospital be more likely to recommend euthanasia for a non-paying patient who is draining the hospital resources than for one who is covered by insurance?

Physician-Patient Relationship

Current American medical practice does not differ much from the 1980s, when the President's Commission for the Study of Ethical Problems in Medicine and Biomedical and Behavioral Research investigated the relationship between patients and doctors. In *Making Health Care Decisions: The Ethical and Legal Implications of Informed Consent in the Patient-Practitioner Relationship* (U.S. Government Printing Office, Washington, D.C., 1982), the President's Commission observed:

> In addition to making a recommendation, the doctor's self-perceived role is to get the patient to go along with this recommendation if there is any hesitancy on the patient's part. This is done by some explanation about the need for the recommended treatment and the consequences of not heeding the recommendation. But in the doctor's view there is no decision for the patient to make, except whether or not to get proper medical care.

If assisted suicide is legalized, it becomes a treatment option that may be recommended by physicians. As the President's Commission noted, physicians often believe that they know what is the best treatment for their patients. Yet, as the New York State Task Force pointed out, physicians' judgments may not always be impartial. Their professional judgment is shaped by their own attitudes toward illness and euthanasia in general, and toward each patient in particular.

In April 1997 the New York Task Force issued a supplement to *When Death Is Sought: Assisted Suicide and Euthanasia in the Medical Context*. The Task Force reiterated its initial 1994 finding that physician-assisted suicide would be seriously harmful to a large number of people. The Task Force claimed that the widespread interest in physician-assisted suicide is a symptom of a bigger problem—our failure as a nation to alleviate the pain and suffering of terminally ill patients. The Task Force recommended that even if physician-assisted suicide were legalized, the national priority should be the improvement of end-of-life medical care for everyone.

CHAPTER 7
ADVANCE DIRECTIVES

Every human being of adult years and sound mind has a right to determine what shall be done with his own body.

—Supreme Court Justice Benjamin Cardoza

The movement toward participation in health care that began during the 1960s and escalated in the 1970s focused increasing attention on the desire for control over nearly all aspects of medical care, even critical care. Dramatic medical and technological advances further underscored the importance of planning ahead for end-of-life care. Baby boomers (persons born between 1946 and 1964), on the threshold of aging and faced with caring for elderly parents, have become increasingly aware of the need to make provisions for their own future medical treatment. Some hope that executing advance directives will help protect their rights to self-determination (the right to make one's own medical decisions, including the right to accept or refuse treatments).

A BRIEF HISTORY OF ADVANCE DIRECTIVES

Advance directive is the general term that refers to a wish (oral and/or written) a person expresses concerning health care, should he or she become incompetent. There are two categories of advance directives—living wills and durable power of attorney for health care. Many states have special forms or specific procedures for creating an advance directive. Some people think it is sufficient to tell a loved one or a physician what they desire. However, the National Health Lawyers Association stresses that although courts have enforced oral instructions, and physicians often consider the information that family members offer about a patient's requests, the wishes of the terminally ill are more likely to be honored if they are written.

In 1967 the Euthanasia Society of America and attorney Luis Kutner, co-founder of Amnesty International, devised the first living will (later called an advance directive). The Euthanasia Society of America, renamed Society for the Right to Die in 1974, merged in 1991 with Concern for Dying to become Choice in Dying (CID). CID had no official position on physician-assisted suicide; it advocated the right of individuals to make their own decisions about medical care at the end of life. Between 1967 and 1999, CID distributed more than 10 million living wills.

(In January 2000 the board of CID disbanded and transferred its programs and personnel to a new organization dedicated to creating partnerships between health consumers and professionals to improve end-of-life care. The new organization is aptly named Partnership for Caring: America's Voices for the Dying, and like the organizations that preceded it, the national, nonprofit Partnership for Caring aims to educate consumers and professionals and change attitudes to improve how dying people are treated.)

California was the first state to legally recognize living wills (1976) and the durable power of attorney for health care (1984). The California Natural Death Act of 1976 states that to preserve "dignity and privacy ... any adult person may execute a directive directing the withholding or withdrawal of life-sustaining procedures in a terminal condition."

All states and the District of Columbia passed laws recognizing the use of living wills and durable power of attorney for health care, although the provisions of these laws vary from state to state. As of March 2001, 46 states and the District of Columbia had laws authorizing both living wills and the appointment of a health care proxy or agent. Alaska's law permits living wills only; even if a patient has a health care agent, that agent is not permitted to order the termination of life-sustaining treatment. While Massachusetts, Michigan, and New York laws only authorize the appointment of a health care agent, their laws do permit the inclusion of specific instructions about medical care at the end of life within the appointment of the agent. (See Figure 7.1.)

FIGURE 7.1

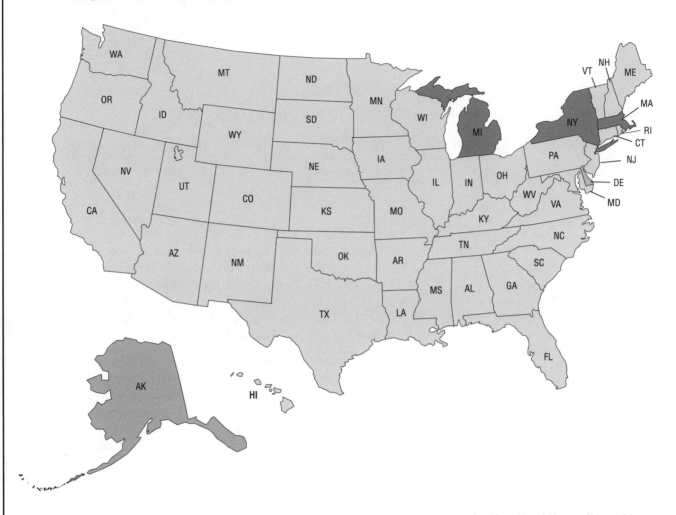

State statutes governing living wills and appointment of health care agents, March 2001

Jurisdictions with legislation that authorizes both living wills and the appointment of a health care agent (the District of Columbia and 46 states: Alabama, Arizona, Arkansas, California, Colorado, Connecticut, Delaware, Florida, Georgia, Hawaii, Idaho, Illinois, Indiana, Iowa, Kansas, Kentucky, Louisiana, Maine, Maryland, Minnesota, Mississippi, Missouri, Montana, Nebraska, Nevada, New Hampshire, New Jersey, New Mexico, North Carolina, North Dakota, Ohio, Oklahoma, Oregon, Pennsylvania, Rhode Island, South Carolina, South Dakota, Tennessee, Texas, Utah, Vermont, Virginia, Washington, West Virginia, Wisconsin and Wyoming).

Alaska's Power of Attorney Act precludes health care agent authority to terminate life-sustaining medical procedures. The Act does provide that the health care agent may enforce a Declaration.

States with legislation that authorizes only the appointment of a health care agent (3 states: Massachusetts, Michigan and New York).

Note: The specifics of living will and health care agent legislation vary greatly from state to state. In addition, many states also have court-made law that affects residents' rights.

SOURCE: "State Statutes Governing Living Wills and Appointment of Health Care Agents," in *End-Of-Life Law Digest*, Partnership for Caring, Inc., Washington, DC, 2001.

LIVING WILLS

A living will is a written advance directive that outlines a patient's preferences about end-of-life medical treatments in the event that he or she is unable to communicate or make his or her own decisions. It is sometimes called a directive or a declaration. Laws regulating living wills vary from state to state. For example, in 31 states, a pregnant woman's living will cannot be honored due to restrictions in that state's statutes. (See Figure 7.2.)

Living wills enable people to list the types of medical treatments they want or do not want. It is therefore important for an individual contemplating a living will to know what these treatments involve. Some examples of life-

FIGURE 7.2

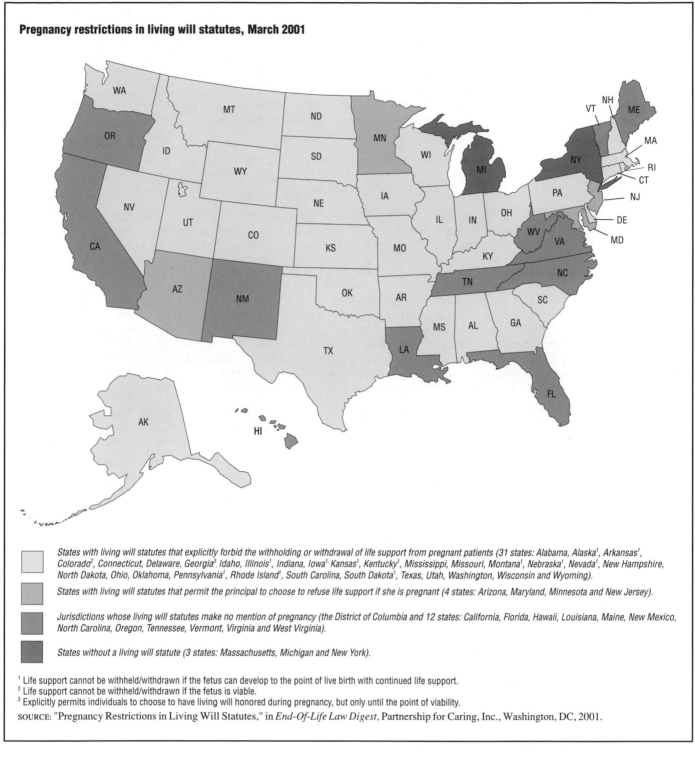

Pregnancy restrictions in living will statutes, March 2001

States with living will statutes that explicitly forbid the withholding or withdrawal of life support from pregnant patients (31 states: Alabama, Alaska[1], Arkansas[1], Colorado[2], Connecticut, Delaware, Georgia[3], Idaho, Illinois[1], Indiana, Iowa[1], Kansas[1], Kentucky[1], Mississippi, Missouri, Montana[1], Nebraska[1], Nevada[1], New Hampshire, North Dakota, Ohio, Oklahoma, Pennsylvania[1], Rhode Island[1], South Carolina, South Dakota[1], Texas, Utah, Washington, Wisconsin and Wyoming).

States with living will statutes that permit the principal to choose to refuse life support if she is pregnant (4 states: Arizona, Maryland, Minnesota and New Jersey).

Jurisdictions whose living will statutes make no mention of pregnancy (the District of Columbia and 12 states: California, Florida, Hawaii, Louisiana, Maine, New Mexico, North Carolina, Oregon, Tennessee, Vermont, Virginia and West Virginia).

States without a living will statute (3 states: Massachusetts, Michigan and New York).

[1] Life support cannot be withheld/withdrawn if the fetus can develop to the point of live birth with continued life support.
[2] Life support cannot be withheld/withdrawn if the fetus is viable.
[3] Explicitly permits individuals to choose to have living will honored during pregnancy, but only until the point of viability.

SOURCE: "Pregnancy Restrictions in Living Will Statutes," in *End-Of-Life Law Digest,* Partnership for Caring, Inc., Washington, DC, 2001.

prolonging treatments patients should consider when preparing a living will include cardiopulmonary resuscitation (CPR), mechanical ventilation, artificial nutrition and hydration, and kidney dialysis.

Some Are Opposed to Non-Treatment Directives

Some people point out that discussions about advance directives focus on discontinuing or withholding life-sustaining treatments. Wesley J. Smith, in *Forced Exit:*

The Slippery Slope from Assisted Suicide to Legalized Murder (Times Books, New York, 1997), notes that some advance directives only list one choice: non-treatment. According to Smith, if a person chooses to fight for his or her life, that person may be faced with the daunting task of writing out detailed treatment instructions.

This need not be the case. An advance directive form included in the model Uniform Health Care Decisions Act

FIGURE 7.3

Advance health-care directive

Optional Form.

The following form may, but need not, be used to create an advance health-care directive. The other sections of this [Act] govern the effect of this or any other writing used to create an advance health-care directive. An individual may complete or modify all or any part of the following form:

ADVANCE HEALTH-CARE DIRECTIVE

Explanation

You have the right to give instructions about your own health care. You also have the right to name someone else to make health-care decisions for you. This form lets you do either or both of these things. It also lets you express your wishes regarding donation of organs and the designation of your primary physician. If you use this form, you may complete or modify all or any part of it. You are free to use a different form.

Part 1 of this form is a power of attorney for health care. Part 1 lets you name another individual as agent to make health-care decisions for you if you become incapable of making your own decisions or if you want someone else to make those decisions for you now even though you are still capable. You may also name an alternate agent to act for you if your first choice is not willing, able, or reasonably available to make decisions for you. Unless related to you, your agent may not be an owner, operator, or employee of [a residential long-term health-care institution] at which you are receiving care.

Unless the form you sign limits the authority of your agent, your agent may make all health-care decisions for you. This form has a place for you to limit the authority of your agent. You need not limit the authority of your agent if you wish to rely on your agent for all health-care decisions that may have to be made. If you choose not to limit the authority of your agent, your agent will have the right to:
  a) consent or refuse consent to any care, treatment, service, or procedure to maintain, diagnose, or otherwise affect a physical or mental condition;
  b) select or discharge health-care providers and institution;
  c) approve or disapprove diagnostic tests, surgical procedures, programs of medication, and orders not to resuscitate; and
  d) direct the provision, withholding, or withdrawal of artificial nutrition and hydration and all other forms of health care.

(UHCDA) offers several options that include treatments to prolong life. (See Figure 7.3, Part 2: Instructions for Health Care.) This model law was approved by the National Conference of Commissioners on Uniform State Laws in 1993 to provide some consistency among state advance directives.

Another form, called "Five Wishes," was developed in Florida by a nonprofit organization called Aging with Dignity, and is now distributed nationwide. The document probes legal and medical issues as well as spiritual and emotional ones. It even outlines small details, such as requests for favorite music to be played and poems read, and provides space for individuals to record their wishes for funeral arrangements. The document is relatively easy to complete since it uses simplified language rather than legal or medical jargon. As of April 2002, "Five Wishes" met living will or advance directive criteria in 33 states; in the other 17, specif-ic forms were necessary, although the "Five Wishes" document can still serve as a guide for family and physicians.

Pro-Life Alternative to Living Wills

The National Right to Life Committee (NRLC) opposes active and passive euthanasia, and offers an alternative to the standard living will. Called the "Will to Live," it does not consider artificial nutrition and hydration as forms of medical treatment but as basic necessities needed for the preservation of life. (See Figure 7.4.)

DURABLE POWER OF ATTORNEY FOR HEALTH CARE

A durable power of attorney for health care, also called a medical power of attorney, designates a health care agent or proxy authorized to make medical treatment decisions on behalf of a patient who can no longer make these

FIGURE 7.3

Advance health-care directive [CONTINUED]

Part 2 of this form lets you give specific instructions about any aspect of your health care. Choices are provided for you to express your wishes regarding the provision, withholding, or withdrawal of treatment to keep you alive, including the provision of artificial nutrition and hydration, as well as the provision of pain relief. Space is also provided for you to add to the choices you have made or for you to write out any additional wishes.

Part 3 of this form lets you express an intention to donate your bodily organs and tissues following your death.

Part 4 of this form lets you designate a physician to have primary responsibility for your health care.

After completing this form, sign and date the form at the end. It is recommended but not required that you request two other individuals to sign as witnesses. Give a copy of the signed and completed form to your physician, to any other health-care providers you may have, to any health-care institution at which you are receiving care, and to any health-care agents you have named. You should talk to the person you have named as agent to make sure that he or she understands your wishes and is willing to take the responsibility.

You have the right to revoke this advance health-care directive or replace this form at any time.

* * * * * * * * *

PART 1
POWER OF ATTORNEY FOR HEALTH CARE

1) DESIGNATION OF AGENT: I designate the following individual as my agent to make health-care decisions for me:

_____
(name of individual you choose as agent)

_____
(address)   (city)   (state)   (zip code)

_____
(home phone)   (work phone)

---

decisions for him or herself. (See Figure 7.3, Part 1: Power of Attorney for Health Care.) The role of this agent or proxy begins as soon as the physician certifies that a patient is incompetent to make his or her own decisions. The agent's role may or may not be limited to end-of-life care.

Is a Durable Power of Attorney the Same as a Living Will?

While a living will provides specific directions about medical treatment, it cannot address every possible future medical situation. Most standard living wills apply only to limited circumstances, such as terminal illness or permanent coma. There are, however, many medical treatments that require decision-making. Examples of these are surgical procedures, diagnostic tests, blood transfusion, the use of antibiotics, radiation therapy, and chemotherapy.

A durable power of attorney for health care is generally more flexible than a living will. It allows proxies to use their judgment to respond to unforeseen situations based on their knowledge of the patient and the patient's values and beliefs. Since there is no uniform advance directive statute nationally, the rights of health care proxies vary in different states.

In California, a proxy may make all decisions for the patient, even if specific instructions have not been included in the document. Nevada and Rhode Island, on the other hand, not only require the use of state-specific forms, but the grantor (person granting the power of attorney) has to check off treatment options on the form. The grantor then discusses with the proxy when to accept or refuse medical treatments. Under New York law, the

FIGURE 7.3

Advance health-care directive [CONTINUED]

OPTIONAL: If I revoke my agent's authority or if my agent is not willing, able, or reasonably available to make a health-care decision for me, I designate as my first alternate agent:

_____
(name of individual you choose as first alternate agent)

_____
(address)   (city)   (state)   (zip code)

_____
(home phone)   (work phone)

OPTIONAL: If I revoke the authority of my agent and first alternate agent or if neither is willing, able, or reasonably available to make a health-care decision for me, I designate as my second alternate agent:

_____
(name of individual you choose as second alternate agent)

_____
(address)   (city)   (state)   (zip code)

_____
(home phone)   (work phone)

2) AGENT'S AUTHORITY: My agent is authorized to make all health-care decisions for me, including decisions to provide, withhold, or withdraw artificial nutrition and hydration and other forms of health care to keep me alive, except as I state here:

_____

_____

_____
(Add additional sheets if needed.)

3) WHEN AGENT'S AUTHORITY BECOMES EFFECTIVE: My agent's authority becomes effective when my primary physician determines that I am unable to make my own health-care decisions unless I mark the following box. If I mark this box [], my agent's authority to make health-care decisions for me takes effect immediately.

4) AGENT'S OBLIGATION: My agent shall make health-care decisions for me in accordance with this power of attorney for health care, any instructions I give in Part 2 of this form, and my other wishes to the extent known to my agent. To the extent my wishes are unknown, my agent shall make health-care decisions for me in accordance with what my agent determines to be in my best interest. In determining my best interest, my agent shall consider my personal values to the extent known to my agent.

power of the proxy is strictly limited to relaying the instructions of the grantor.

IMPORTANCE OF COMMUNICATION

The consideration of an advance directive should be the start of an ongoing discussion among the individual, family members, and the family doctor about end-of-life health care. Discussions about one's advance directive need not be limited to treatment preferences and medical circumstances. Sometimes knowing things such as the patient's religious beliefs and values can be important for the proxy when speaking for the patient's interests. The Center for Health Law and Ethics of the University of New

FIGURE 7.3

NOMINATION OF GUARDIAN: If a guardian of my person needs to be appointed for me by a court, I nominate the agent designated in this form. If that agent is not willing, able, or reasonably available to act as guardian, I nominate the alternate agents whom I have named, in the order designated.

PART 2
INSTRUCTIONS FOR HEALTH CARE

If you are satisfied to allow your agent to determine what is best for you in making end-of-life decisions, you need not fill out this part of the form. If you do fill out this part of the form, you may strike any wording you do not want.

6) END-OF-LIFE DECISIONS: I direct that my health-care providers and others involved in my care provide, withhold, or withdraw treatment in accordance with the choice I have marked below:

[ ] a) Choice Not To Prolong Life

I do not want my life to be prolonged if (i) I have an incurable and irreversible condition that will result in my death within a relatively short time, (ii) I become unconscious and, to a reasonable degree of medical certainty, I will not regain consciousness, or (iii) the likely risks and burdens of treatment would outweigh the expected benefits, OR

[ ] b) Choice To Prolong Life

I want my life to be prolonged as long as possible within the limits of generally accepted health-care standards.

7) ARTIFICIAL NUTRITION AND HYDRATION: Artificial nutrition and hydration must be provided, withheld, or withdrawn in accordance with the choice I have made in paragraph (6) unless I mark the following box. If I mark this box [ ], artificial nutrition and hydration must be provided regardless of my condition and regardless of the choice I have made in paragraph (6).

8) RELIEF FROM PAIN: Except as I state in the following space, I direct that treatment for alleviation of pain or discomfort be provided at all times, even if it hastens my death:

_____

_____

9) OTHER WISHES: (If you do not agree with any of the optional choices above and wish to write your own, or if you wish to add to the instructions you have given above, you may do so here.) I direct that:

_____

_____

(Add additional sheets if needed.)

Mexico has devised a values questionnaire to help people examine their attitudes about issues related to illness, health care, and dying. It may serve as a valuable tool to guide discussions between the patient and the proxy, as well as among family members. (See Figure 7.5.)

When preparing an advance directive, it is vitally important for the family and proxy to fully understand the care and measures that are wanted. Even when a patient has a living will calling for no "heroic measures," if the family demands such medical intervention, it is likely that the hospital or doctor will comply with the family's wishes rather than risk a lawsuit.

Highlighting the need for communication, a 1998 study of 250 terminally ill patients and their families showed that only 66 percent of the families surveyed accurately predicted the level of treatment their dying family member would want. Researchers from the Georgetown University Center for Clinical Bioethics

FIGURE 7.3

Advance health-care directive [CONTINUED]

```
                                PART 3
                    DONATION OF ORGANS AT DEATH
                            (OPTIONAL)

10) Upon my death (mark applicable box)
[  ] a) I give any needed organs, tissues, or parts, OR
[  ] b) I give the following organs, tissues, or parts only

    _____

[  ] c) My gift is for the following purposes (strike any of the following you do not want)
    (i)   Transplant
    (ii)  Therapy
    (iii) Research
    (iv)  Education

                                PART 4
                        PRIMARY PHYSICIAN
                            (OPTIONAL)

11) I designate the following physician as my primary physician:

    _____
                        (name of physician)

    _____
    (address)           (city)           (state)        (zip code)

    _____
                            (phone)

    OPTIONAL: If the physician I have designated above is not willing, able, or reasonably
available to act as my primary physician, I designate the following physician as my primary
physician:

    _____
                        (name of physician)

    _____
    (address)           (city)           (state)        (zip code)

    _____
                            (phone)
                    * * * * * * * *
```

separately questioned the patient and the patient's likely surrogate about the treatment the patient would desire in three different end-of-life scenarios. One-third of the surrogates chose differently than the patient, evenly divided between picking too much and too little treatment.

In the Absence of Advance Directives

Physicians usually involve family members in medical decisions when the patient has not designated a health care proxy in advance. Most states have family consent or surrogate consent laws for this purpose. (See Figure 7.6.) Some states have laws that designate the order in which family members may assume the role of surrogates or decision-makers. For example the spouse may be the prime surrogate, followed by an adult child, then the patient's parent, etc. Twelve states allow close friends to act as surrogates. By April 2002 Arizona was the only state that included a patient's domestic partner in the list of surrogates.

ADDITIONAL INSTRUCTIONS IN ADVANCE DIRECTIVES

Artificial Nutrition and Hydration

Some living wills contain a provision for the withdrawing of nutrition and hydration. (See Figure 7.3, Part 2: Instructions for Health Care.) Artificial nutrition and

FIGURE 7.3

Advance health-care directive [CONTINUED]

```
     EFFECT OF COPY: A copy of this form has the same effect as
the original.

13) SIGNATURES: Sign and date the form here:
```

_____	_____
(date)	(sign your name)
_____	_____
(address)	(print your name)
_____	
(city) (state)	

Optional SIGNATURES OF WITNESSES:

First witness	Second Witness
_____	_____
(print name)	(print name)
_____	_____
(address)	(address)
_____	_____
(city) (state)	(city) (state)
_____	_____
(signature of witness)	(signature of witness)
_____	_____
(date)	(date)

SOURCE: "Advance Health-Care Directive," in *Patient Self-Determination Act: Providers Offer Information on Advance Directives but Effectiveness Uncertain,* U.S. General Accounting Office, Washington, DC, 1995

hydration are legally considered medical treatments and may, therefore, be refused. However, artificial nutrition and hydration remain controversial in the right-to-die issue because food and drink are the most basic forms of life sustenance. The unresolved problem is mirrored in the fact that not all states' advance directive statutes address this issue. (See Figure 7.7 and Figure 7.8.)

Relief from Pain

Some living wills also enable an individual to give instructions about the management of pain. While a number of studies have shown that pain is not the primary motivation for assisted suicide requests, many people have seen family and friends suffer painful deaths, and they fear the same fate. Experts advise that advance directives should expressly indicate desires for pain control and comfort care, even when individuals have chosen to forego life-sustaining treatments.

In the past, patients' pain may not have been adequately treated by medical professionals because they lacked training or feared over-prescribing pain medications. A variety of legislative and education initiatives by states and medical professional societies have dramatically improved pain management. During 2000 the National Cancer Policy Board issued a report recommending additional funding for research for palliative care and encouraging physicians to redouble their efforts to relieve the pain and other symptoms of dying cancer patients. The Federation of State Medical Boards has developed guidelines to help physicians use medication to safely and effectively manage pain. Special instruction in pain management for patients with life-limiting illnesses is now offered in many medical and nursing schools.

Further pressure to improve pain management is coming from patients and their families. In December 2000, a

FIGURE 7.4

Will to live

GENERAL PRESUMPTION FOR LIFE

I direct my health care provider(s) and health care agent to make health care decisions consistent with my general desire for the use of medical treatment that would preserve my life, as well as for the use of medical treatment that can cure, improve, or reduce or prevent deterioration in, any physical or mental condition.

Food and water are not medical treatment, but basic necessities. I direct my health care provider(s) and health care agent to provide me with food and fluids orally, intravenously, by tube, or by other means to the full extent necessary both to preserve my life and to assure me the optimal health possible.

I direct that medication to alleviate my pain be provided, as long as the medication is not used in order to cause my death.

I direct that the following be provided:
• the administration of medication
• cardiopulmonary resuscitation (CPR); and
• the performance of all other medical procedures, techniques, and technologies, including surgery — all to the full extent necessary to correct, reverse, or alleviate life-threatening or health-impairing conditions, or complications arising from those conditions.

I also direct that I be provided basic nursing care and procedures to provide comfort care.

I reject, however, any treatments that use an unborn or newborn child, or any tissue or organ of an unborn or newborn child, who has been subject to an induced abortion. This rejection does not apply to the use of tissues or organs obtained in the course of the removal of an ectopic pregnancy.

I also reject any treatments that use an organ or tissue of another person obtained in a manner that causes, contributes to, or hastens that person's death.

The instructions in this document are intended to be followed even if suicide is alleged to be attempted at some point after it is signed.

I request and direct that medical treatment and care be provided to me to preserve my life without discrimination based on my age or physical or mental disability or the "quality" of my life. I reject any action or omission that is intended to cause or hasten my death.

I direct my health care provider(s) and health care agent to follow the above policy, even if I am judged to be incompetent.

During the time I am incompetent, my agent, as named below, is authorized to make medical decisions on my behalf, consistent with the above policy, after consultation with my health care provider(s), utilizing the most current diagnoses and/or prognosis of my medical condition, in the following situations with the written special conditions.

WHEN MY DEATH IS IMMINENT

A. If I have an incurable terminal illness or injury, and I will die imminently — meaning that a reasonably prudent physician, knowledgeable about the case and the treatment possibilities with respect to the medical conditions involved, would judge that I will live only a week or less even if lifesaving treatment or care is provided to me — the following may be withheld or withdrawn:

California jury held a physician liable for prescribing too little pain medication for a patient dying from lung cancer. The children of 85-year-old William Bergman sued his physician for elder abuse on the grounds that the doctor failed to prescribe strong enough medication to control their father's pain before, during, and after his hospitalization in 1998. The jury awarded the family $1.5 million, but to comply with the state limit on such awards, it was reduced to $250,000. Advocates for improved end-of-life care hoped the verdict would remind physicians about the importance of pain management.

ARE ADVANCE DIRECTIVES EFFECTIVE?

It is time for legislators around the nation to recognize that individuals have the right to die with dignity. As public policymakers, we must not take away that right with restrictive legislation.

—John Maitland, Jr., Illinois state senator and co-chair of the Illinois Task Force on Comfort Care for the Terminally Ill, 1998

Some people are skeptical about the effectiveness of living wills. They claim that many living wills say very little about real life clinical situations. Others feel that the

FIGURE 7.4

Will to live [CONTINUED]

WHEN I AM TERMINALLY ILL

B. Final Stage of Terminal Condition. If I have an incurable terminal illness or injury and even though death is not imminent I am in the final stage of that terminal condition — meaning that a reasonably prudent physician, knowledgeable about the case and the treatment possibilities with respect to the medical conditions involved, would judge that I will live only three months or less, even if lifesaving treatment or care is provided to me — the following may be withheld or withdrawn:

IF I AM PREGNANT

D. Special Instructions for Pregnancy. If I am pregnant, I direct my health care provider(s) and health care agent to use all lifesaving procedures for myself with none of the above special conditions applying if there is a chance that prolonging my life might allow my child to be born alive. I also direct that lifesaving procedures be used even if I am legally determined to be brain dead if there is a chance that doing so might allow my child to be born alive. Except as I specify by writing my signature in the box below, no one is authorized to consent to any procedure for me that would result in the death of my unborn child.

If I am pregnant, and I am not in the final stage of a terminal condition as defined above, medical proedures required to prevent my death are authorized even if they may result in the death of my unborn child provided every possible effort is made to preserve both my life and the life of my unborn child.

Notice: *Although this is the content of the Will to Live, it is not itself a legal document. Different forms exist for each state. Do not attempt to sign this version. Instead, to obtain the Will to Live valid in your state, send a self-addressed, stamped business (9 1/2" wide) envelope to Will to Live Project, Suite 500, 419 Seventh St, N.W. Washington, DC 20004.*

SOURCE: "Will to Live," National Right to Life Committee [Online] http://www.nrlc.org [Accessed April 24, 2002]

average person cannot be expected to know the ramifications of different medical treatments, much less name them. The National Conference of State Legislatures (NCSL) and The Center to Improve Care of the Dying (CICD) agree. In *State Initiatives in End of Life Care: Policy Guide for State Legislators* (Washington, D.C., June 1998) these groups reported that the standard forms used by most states do not encompass the wide range of scenarios that a patient may face, nor would it be realistic to try to do so. Many states use living will forms that contain vague language requiring a subjective interpretation.

The NCSL and the CICD believe that a written advance directive should ideally include both a living will and a durable power of attorney. They suggest that, instead of having separate laws for these two documents, states should combine different right-to-die laws into a single statute. By the year 2002, 13 states had done just that. (See Table 7.1. The data in the table were originally compiled in 1997, but were still accurate as of April 2002.) Of these states, Alabama, Delaware, Maine, and New Mexico had adopted the Uniform Health-Care Decisions Act (UHCDA) as a model.

The UHCDA has been recommended by the NCSL and the CICD as a model law because it is simple and

TABLE 7.1

States with combined advance directive statutes, 1997

Alabama	Maryland
Arizona	New Jersey*
Connecticut	New Mexico
Delaware	Oklahoma*
Florida	Oregon
Kentucky	Virginia
Maine	

*Does not include surrogate consent.

SOURCE: Dick Merritt, et al., "Figure 13. States with Combined Advance Directive Statutes," in *State Initiatives in End-of-Life Care: Policy Guide for State Legislators*, National Conference of State Legislatures and The Center to Improve Care of the Dying, The George Washington University, Washington, DC, June 1998. Data from ABA Commission on Legal Problems of the Elderly.

comprehensive. It contains provisions governing living wills and durable power of attorney, as well as surrogate consent. The law permits instructions regarding one's future health care to be either written or oral. States using the law as a model may adopt the optional combined directive, which does not require witnesses to the document. It further enables individuals to express their preferences about organ donation and to designate a primary physician. (See Figure 7.3: Parts 3 and 4.)

Little Impact on End-of-Life Decision-Making

According to the Alliance for Aging Research, in *Seven Deadly Myths: Uncovering the Facts About the High Cost of the Last Year of Life* (Washington, D.C., 1997), even when patients have completed advance directives they often have little influence on end-of-life decision-making. The Alliance observed that physicians often cannot predict with certainty that a given patient is at the end of his or her life. "Most advance directives embody the concept of not using life-sustaining measures when they would be futile. When physicians cannot predict futility, however, such instructions offer little guidance."

Advance Directives Lack Specificity

Joan M. Teno, et al., in "Do Advance Directives Provide Instructions That Direct Care?" (*Journal of the American Geriatrics Society,* vol. 45, no. 4, April 1997), investigated whether the content of advance directives contributes to their ineffectiveness. The researchers analyzed 688 advance directives collected from five hospitals.

Teno, et al., found that only 13 percent (90 advance directives) contained additional instructions beyond the general statement—not wanting treatments that would prolong death—found in standard living wills. Just 5 percent (36) gave specific instructions about the use of life-sustaining treatments, while 3 percent (22) mentioned foregoing life-sustaining treatments in the patient's current situation. The researchers pointed out that what is ordinarily at stake for very seriously or terminally ill patients is not whether efforts to prolong life should cease, but exactly which efforts, and when.

The NCSL and CICD have recommended to state legislators that any advance directive form adopted be modifiable. As the health care environment continues to evolve, standard advance directives may not be applicable to specific medical conditions. Not only should advance directives be flexible enough to allow for changes in a patient's medical condition, but states should also educate the public, as was initially intended in the Patient Self-Determination Act of 1990.

THE PATIENT SELF-DETERMINATION ACT

In 1990 Congress enacted the Patient Self-Determination Act (PSDA) as part of the Omnibus Budget Reconciliation Act of 1990 (PL 101-508). This legislation was intended to "reinforce individuals' constitutional right to determine their final health care."

The PSDA took effect on December 1, 1991. It requires all health care providers participating in Medicare (an entitlement program of the federal government through which persons aged 65 and older receive health insurance) and Medicaid (an entitlement program run by the federal and state governments to provide health insurance to persons younger than 65 years of age who cannot afford to pay for private health insurance) to provide all patients over the age 18 years with the following written information:

- The patient's rights under the law to participate in decisions about his or her medical care, including the right to accept or refuse treatments.

- The patient's right under state law to complete advance directives, which will be documented in his or her medical records.

- The health care provider's policies honoring these rights.

Providers include hospitals, nursing homes, home health care providers, hospices, and health maintenance organizations (HMOs), but not outpatient-service providers and emergency medical personnel. The PSDA requires health care providers to educate their staff and the community about advance directives. It also prohibits hospital personnel from discriminating against patients based on whether or not they have an advance directive. (Patients are informed that having an advance directive is not a prerequisite to receiving medical care.)

PSDA: The Right Idea at the Wrong Time?

The Institute of Medicine's Committee on Care at the End of Life believes that admission to a hospital or long-term facility is not the appropriate time to question or advise patients about their end-of-life preferences. In *Approaching Death* (National Academy Press, Washington, D.C., 1997), the Committee noted that the advance directive information required by the PSDA would be just one of many pieces of information given to patients during stressful situations. Patients may not only be seriously ill, but also frightened and confused. Family members who receive the information may be too distraught or traumatized to fully understand the information imparted. Others may not respond well or favorably to discussions of death when they are feeling vulnerable.

The Committee believes that advance directives are best discussed before a medical crisis—when individuals, their families, and physicians can have a series of in-depth discussions. Since health status changes and perspectives often change, the topics of discussion should be revisited. Health care providers must fulfill their responsibility to educate the community as required by the PSDA.

PSDA Has No Impact on Terminal Care

Despite the promise of greater patient participation in health care decisions through advance directives, the PSDA has not changed the way seriously ill patients die. Joan M.

FIGURE 7.5

Values questionnaire from the University of New Mexico's Center for Health Law and Ethics "Values History Form"

The University of New Mexico

Center for Health Law and Ethics
Institute of Public Law
School of Law
1117 Stanford NE
Albuquerque, NM 87131-1446
Telephone (505) 277-5006
FAX (505) 277-7064

VALUES HISTORY FORM

NAME: _____

DATE: _____

If someone assisted you in completing this form, please fill in his or her name, address, and relationship to you.

Name: _____
Address: _____
_____
Relationship: _____

It is important that your medical treatment be **your choice**.

The purpose of this form is to assist you in thinking about and writing down what is important to you about your health. If you should at some time become unable to make health care decisions, this form may help others make a decision for you in accordance with your values.

The first section of this form provides an opportunity for you to discuss your values, wishes, and preferences in a number of different areas such as your personal relationships, your overall attitude toward life, and your thoughts about illness.

The second section of this form provides a space for indicating whether you have completed an Advance Directive, e.g., a Living Will, Durable Power of Attorney for Health Care Decisions or Health Care Proxy, and where such documents may be found.

This form is not copyrighted; you may make as many copies as you wish.

FIGURE 7.5

Values questionnaire from the University of New Mexico's Center for Health Law and Ethics "Values History Form" [CONTINUED]

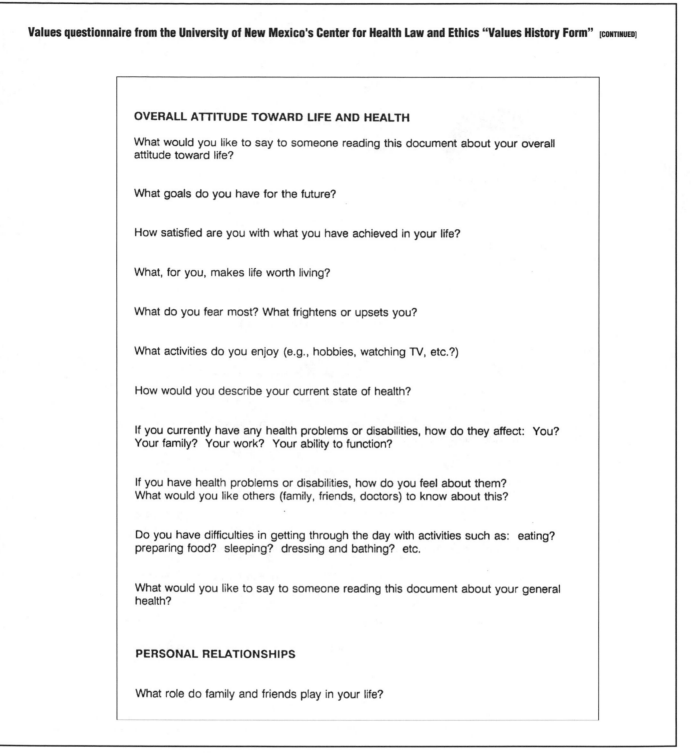

OVERALL ATTITUDE TOWARD LIFE AND HEALTH

What would you like to say to someone reading this document about your overall attitude toward life?

What goals do you have for the future?

How satisfied are you with what you have achieved in your life?

What, for you, makes life worth living?

What do you fear most? What frightens or upsets you?

What activities do you enjoy (e.g., hobbies, watching TV, etc.?)

How would you describe your current state of health?

If you currently have any health problems or disabilities, how do they affect: You? Your family? Your work? Your ability to function?

If you have health problems or disabilities, how do you feel about them? What would you like others (family, friends, doctors) to know about this?

Do you have difficulties in getting through the day with activities such as: eating? preparing food? sleeping? dressing and bathing? etc.

What would you like to say to someone reading this document about your general health?

PERSONAL RELATIONSHIPS

What role do family and friends play in your life?

Teno, et al., in "Advance Directives for Seriously Ill Hospitalized Patients: Effectiveness with the Patient Self-Determination Act and the SUPPORT Intervention" (*Journal of the American Geriatrics Society,* vol. 45, no. 4, April 1997), found that having an advance directive did not always result in physician action honoring patients' treatment requests.

Although documentation in patients' charts of the existence of an advance directive increased from 6 to 35 percent, physicians did not seem to pay much attention to patients' written instructions. Almost half the patients who indicated refusal of CPR did not have a do-not-resuscitate (DNR) notation in their medical charts. Moreover, despite increased efforts to foster communication among patients, families, and doctors, there was no improvement in following through with patients' directives.

FIGURE 7.5

Values questionnaire from the University of New Mexico's Center for Health Law and Ethics "Values History Form" [CONTINUED]

How do you expect friends, family and others to support your decisions regarding medical treatment you may need now or in the future?

Have you made any arrangements for family or friends to make medical treatment decisions on your behalf? If so, who has agreed to make decisions for you and in what circumstances?

What general comments would you like to make about the personal relationships in your life?

THOUGHTS ABOUT INDEPENDENCE AND SELF-SUFFICIENCY

How does independence or dependence affect your life?

If you were to experience decreased physical and mental abilities, how would that affect your attitude toward independence and self-sufficiency?

If your current physical or mental health gets worse, how would you feel?

LIVING ENVIRONMENT

Have you lived alone or with others over the last 10 years?

How comfortable have you been in your surroundings? How might illness, disability or age affect this?

What general comments would you like to make about your surroundings.

RELIGIOUS BACKGROUND AND BELIEFS

What is your spiritual/religious background?

FIGURE 7.5

Values questionnaire from the University of New Mexico's Center for Health Law and Ethics "Values History Form" [CONTINUED]

How do your beliefs affect your feelings toward serious, chronic or terminal illness?

How does your faith community, church or synagogue support you?

What general comments would you like to make about your beliefs?

RELATIONSHIPS WITH DOCTORS AND OTHER HEALTH CAREGIVERS

How do you relate to your doctors? Please comment on: trust; decision making; time for satisfactory communication; respectful treatment.

How do you feel about other caregivers, including nurses, therapists, chaplains, social workers, etc.?

What else would you like to say about doctors and other caregivers?

THOUGHTS ABOUT ILLNESS, DYING AND DEATH

What general comments would you like to make about illness, dying and death?

What will be important to you when you are dying (e.g., physical comfort, no pain, family members present, etc.)?

Where would you prefer to die?

How do you feel about the use of life-sustaining measures if you were: suffering from an irreversible chronic illness (e.g., Alzheimer's disease)? terminally ill? in a permanent coma?

What general comments would you like to make about medical treatment?

FIGURE 7.5

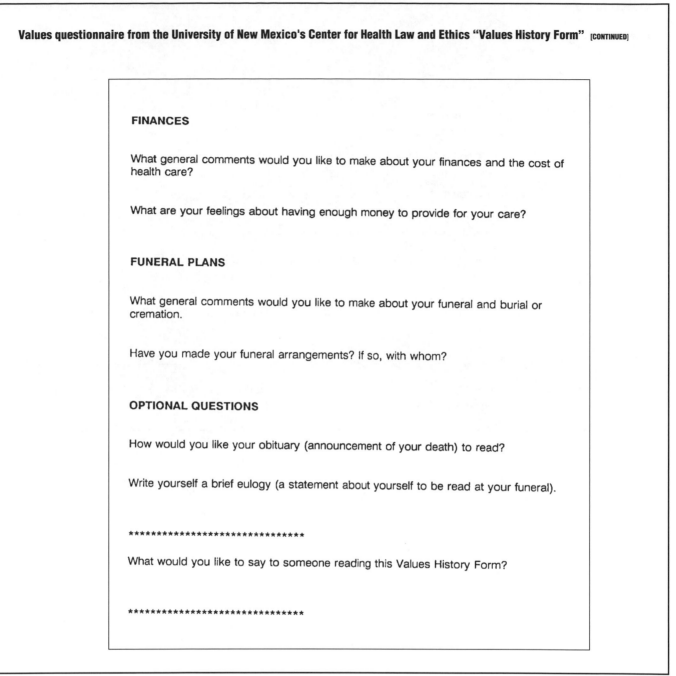

Values questionnaire from the University of New Mexico's Center for Health Law and Ethics "Values History Form" [CONTINUED]

FINANCES

What general comments would you like to make about your finances and the cost of health care?

What are your feelings about having enough money to provide for your care?

FUNERAL PLANS

What general comments would you like to make about your funeral and burial or cremation.

Have you made your funeral arrangements? If so, with whom?

OPTIONAL QUESTIONS

How would you like your obituary (announcement of your death) to read?

Write yourself a brief eulogy (a statement about yourself to be read at your funeral).

****

What would you like to say to someone reading this Values History Form?

****

FIGURE 7.5

Values questionnaire from the University of New Mexico's Center for Health Law and Ethics "Values History Form" [CONTINUED]

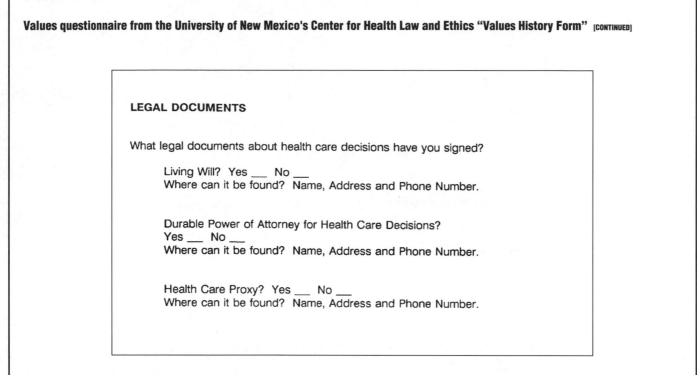

LEGAL DOCUMENTS

What legal documents about health care decisions have you signed?

Living Will? Yes ___ No ___
Where can it be found? Name, Address and Phone Number.

Durable Power of Attorney for Health Care Decisions?
Yes ___ No ___
Where can it be found? Name, Address and Phone Number.

Health Care Proxy? Yes ___ No ___
Where can it be found? Name, Address and Phone Number.

SOURCE: "Figure I.3: Values History Form Developed at the University of New Mexico," in *Patient Self-Determination Act: Providers Offer Information on Advance Directives but Effectiveness Uncertain*, U.S. General Accounting Office, Washington, DC, August 1995.

FIGURE 7.6

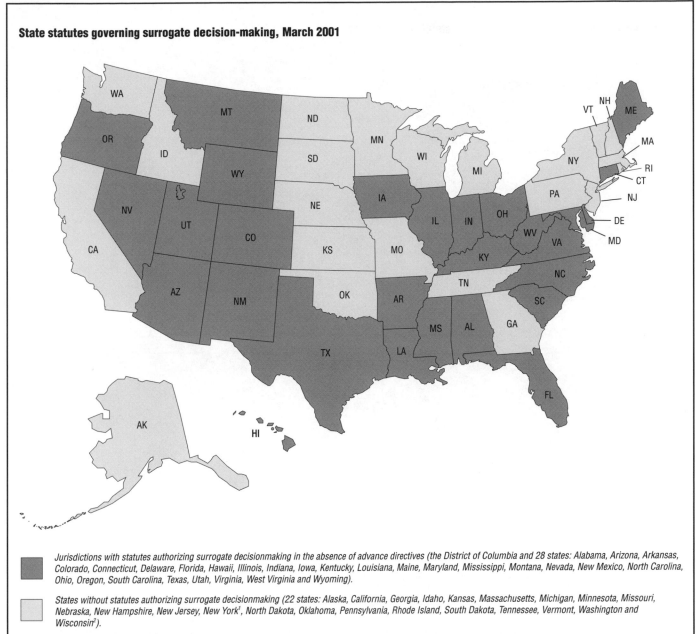

State statutes governing surrogate decision-making, March 2001

Jurisdictions with statutes authorizing surrogate decisionmaking in the absence of advance directives (the District of Columbia and 28 states: Alabama, Arizona, Arkansas, Colorado, Connecticut, Delaware, Florida, Hawaii, Illinois, Indiana, Iowa, Kentucky, Louisiana, Maine, Maryland, Mississippi, Montana, Nevada, New Mexico, North Carolina, Ohio, Oregon, South Carolina, Texas, Utah, Virginia, West Virginia and Wyoming).

States without statutes authorizing surrogate decisionmaking (22 states: Alaska, California, Georgia, Idaho, Kansas, Massachusetts, Michigan, Minnesota, Missouri, Nebraska, New Hampshire, New Jersey, New York[1], North Dakota, Oklahoma, Pennsylvania, Rhode Island, South Dakota, Tennessee, Vermont, Washington and Wisconsin[2]).

[1] New York does authorize surrogate decisionmaking for do-not-resuscitate order decisions.
[2] Wisconsin does authorize surrogate decisionmaking for the sole purpose of admittance of a terminally ill incapacitated patient to hospice.

SOURCE: "State Statutes Governing Surrogate Decisionmaking," in *End-Of-Life Law Digest*, Partnership for Caring, Inc., Washington, DC, 2001

FIGURE 7.7

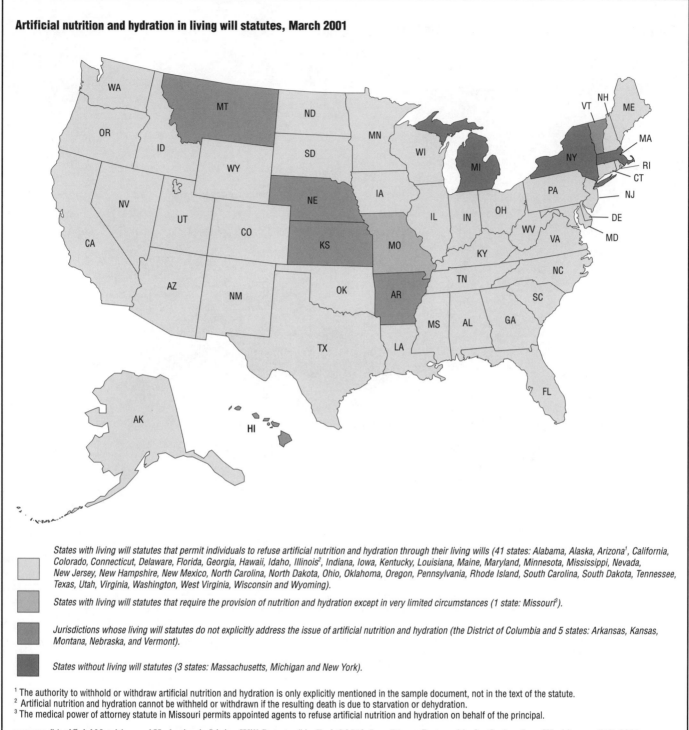

Artificial nutrition and hydration in living will statutes, March 2001

States with living will statutes that permit individuals to refuse artificial nutrition and hydration through their living wills (41 states: Alabama, Alaska, Arizona[1], California, Colorado, Connecticut, Delaware, Florida, Georgia, Hawaii, Idaho, Illinois[2], Indiana, Iowa, Kentucky, Louisiana, Maine, Maryland, Minnesota, Mississippi, Nevada, New Jersey, New Hampshire, New Mexico, North Carolina, North Dakota, Ohio, Oklahoma, Oregon, Pennsylvania, Rhode Island, South Carolina, South Dakota, Tennessee, Texas, Utah, Virginia, Washington, West Virginia, Wisconsin and Wyoming).

States with living will statutes that require the provision of nutrition and hydration except in very limited circumstances (1 state: Missouri[3]).

Jurisdictions whose living will statutes do not explicitly address the issue of artificial nutrition and hydration (the District of Columbia and 5 states: Arkansas, Kansas, Montana, Nebraska, and Vermont).

States without living will statutes (3 states: Massachusetts, Michigan and New York).

[1] The authority to withhold or withdraw artificial nutrition and hydration is only explicitly mentioned in the sample document, not in the text of the statute.
[2] Artificial nutrition and hydration cannot be withheld or withdrawn if the resulting death is due to starvation or dehydration.
[3] The medical power of attorney statute in Missouri permits appointed agents to refuse artificial nutrition and hydration on behalf of the principal.

SOURCE: "Artificial Nutrition and Hydration in Living Will Statutes," in *End-Of-Life Law Digest*, Partnership for Caring, Inc., Washington, DC, 2001.

FIGURE 7.8

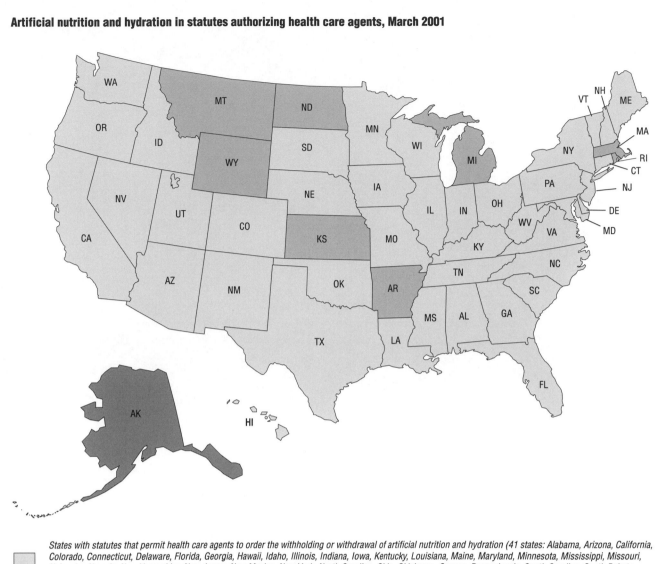

Artificial nutrition and hydration in statutes authorizing health care agents, March 2001

States with statutes that permit health care agents to order the withholding or withdrawal of artificial nutrition and hydration (41 states: Alabama, Arizona, California, Colorado, Connecticut, Delaware, Florida, Georgia, Hawaii, Idaho, Illinois, Indiana, Iowa, Kentucky, Louisiana, Maine, Maryland, Minnesota, Mississippi, Missouri, Nebraska, Nevada, New Hampshire, New Jersey, New Mexico, New York, North Carolina, Ohio, Oklahoma, Oregon, Pennsylvania, South Carolina, South Dakota, Tennessee, Texas, Utah, Virginia, Vermont, Washington, West Virginia, and Wisconsin).

Jurisdictions whose medical power of attorney statutes do not explicitly address the issue of artificial nutrition and hydration (the District of Columbia and 9 states: Arkansas, California, Kansas, Massachusetts, Michigan, Montana, North Dakota, Rhode Island, and Wyoming).

Alaska's Power of Attorney Act precludes health care agent authority to terminate life-sustaining medical procedures. The Act does provide that the agent may enforce a Declaration.

SOURCE: "Artificial Nutrition and Hydration in Statutes Authorizing Health Care Agents," in *End-Of-Life Law Digest*, Partnership for Caring, Inc., Washington, DC, 2001.

CHAPTER 8
COURTS AND THE END OF LIFE

Traditionally, death was defined as the total cessation of circulatory and respiratory functions. In 1968 the Ad Hoc Committee of the Harvard Medical School defined irreversible coma, or brain death, as a new criterion for death. As medical technology has become increasingly able to maintain patients who would otherwise die from severe injuries and/or illnesses, the debate about defining death, and whether patients have the right to choose to die, has intensified.

THE RIGHT TO PRIVACY—KAREN ANN QUINLAN

The landmark case of Karen Ann Quinlan was the first to deal with the dilemma of withdrawing life-sustaining treatment from a patient who was not terminally ill but who was not really "alive." The decision to terminate life support, which was once a private matter between the patient's family and doctor, became an issue to be decided by the courts. The New Jersey Supreme Court ruling on this case became the precedent for nearly all right-to-die cases nationwide.

In 1975, 21-year-old Karen Ann Quinlan suffered cardiopulmonary arrest after ingesting a combination of alcohol and drugs. She subsequently went into a persistent vegetative state (PVS). Dr. Fred Plum, a neurological expert, described her as no longer having any cognitive function but retaining the capacity to maintain the vegetative parts of neurological function. She grimaced, made chewing movements, uttered sounds, and maintained a normal blood pressure, but was entirely unaware of anyone or anything. The medical opinion was that Quinlan had some brain-stem function, but that in her case it could not support breathing. She had been on a respirator since her admission to the hospital.

Quinlan's parents asked that her respirator be removed and that she be allowed to die. Quinlan's doctor refused, claiming that his patient did not meet the Harvard Criteria

for brain death. Based on the existing medical standards and practices, a doctor could not terminate a patient's life support if that patient did not meet the legal definitions for brain death. According to the Harvard Criteria, Quinlan could not be declared legally dead, and medical experts believed she would die if the respirator were removed.

Quinlan's father, Joseph Quinlan, went to court to seek appointment as his daughter's guardian and to gain the power to authorize "the discontinuance of all extraordinary procedures for sustaining Quinlan's vital processes." The court denied his petition to have Quinlan's respirator turned off and also refused to grant him guardianship over his daughter.

First and Eighth Amendments Are Irrelevant to Case

Joseph Quinlan subsequently appealed to the Supreme Court of New Jersey (*In re Quinlan,* 70 N.J. 10, 355 A.2d 647, 1976). He requested, as a parent, to have Quinlan's life support removed based on the U.S. Constitution's First Amendment—the right to religious freedom. The court rejected his request. It also considered the Eighth Amendment—protection against cruel and unusual punishment—inapplicable in Quinlan's case, stating that this amendment applied to protection from excessive criminal punishment. The court considered Quinlan's cruel and unusual circumstances not punishment inflicted by the law or state, but the result of "an accident of fate and nature."

The Right to Privacy

The New Jersey Supreme Court stated, however, that an individual's right to privacy was most relevant to the case. Although the U.S. Constitution does not expressly indicate a right to privacy, U.S. Supreme Court (often called the High Court) rulings in past cases had not only recognized this right but had also determined that some areas of the right to privacy are guaranteed by the

Constitution. For example, the High Court had upheld the right to privacy in *Griswold v. Connecticut* (the right to marital privacy, or the right to use contraception, 381 US 479, 1965) and in *Roe v. Wade* (the right to abortion, 410 US 113, 1973). The U.S. Supreme Court had further presumed that the right to privacy included a patient's right to refuse medical treatment in some situations.

Based on these U.S. Supreme Court rulings, the New Jersey Supreme Court ruled that "Karen's right of privacy may be asserted on her behalf by her guardian under the peculiar circumstances here present," and further noted:

> We have no doubt ... that if Karen were herself miraculously lucid for an interval (not altering the existing prognosis of the condition to which she would soon return) and perceptive of her irreversible condition, she could effectively decide upon discontinuance of the life-support apparatus, even if it meant the prospect of natural death.

The State's Interest

Balanced against Quinlan's constitutional right to privacy was the state's interest in preserving life. Judge Hughes of the New Jersey Supreme Court noted that in many cases, the court had ordered medical treatment continued because the minimal bodily invasion (usually blood transfusion) resulted in recovery. He indicated that, in Quinlan's case, bodily invasion was far greater than minimal, consisting of 24-hour nursing care, antibiotics, respirator, catheter, and feeding tube. Judge Hughes further noted:

> We think that the State's interest ... weakens and the individual's right to privacy grows as the degree of bodily invasion increases and the prognosis dims. Ultimately there comes a point at which the individual's rights overcome the State's interest.

Prevailing Medical Standards and Practices

Quinlan's physicians had refused to remove the respirator because they did not wish to violate the prevailing medical standards and practices. Even though Quinlan's physicians assured the court that the possibility of lawsuits and criminal sanctions did not influence their decision in this specific case, the court believed that the threat of legal ramifications strongly influenced the existing medical standards and practices of health care providers.

The court also observed that life-prolongation advances had rendered the existing medical standards ambiguous (unclear), leaving doctors in a quandary. Moreover, modern devices used for prolonging life, such as respirators, had confused the issue of "ordinary" and "extraordinary" measures. Therefore, the court suggested that respirators could be considered "ordinary" care for a curable patient, but "extraordinary" care for irreversibly unconscious patients.

The court also suggested that hospitals form ethics committees to assist physicians with difficult cases like Quinlan's. These committees would be similar to a multijudge panel exploring different solutions to an appeal. The committees would not only diffuse professional responsibility, but also eliminate any possibly unscrupulous motives of physicians or families. The justices considered the court's intervention on medical decisions an infringement on the physicians' field of competence.

Is It Homicide?

The state had promised to prosecute anyone who terminated Quinlan's life support because such an act would constitute homicide. The New Jersey Supreme Court, however, rejected this consequence because the resulting death would be from natural causes. The court stated:

> The exercise of a constitutional right, such as we have here found, is protected from criminal prosecution.... The constitutional protection extends to third parties whose action is necessary to effectuate the exercise of that right....

After the Respirator Was Removed

In March 1976 the New Jersey Supreme Court ruled that, if the hospital ethics committee agreed that Quinlan would not recover from irreversible coma, her respirator could be removed. Furthermore, all parties involved would be legally immune from criminal and civil prosecution. However, after Quinlan's respirator was removed, she continued to breathe on her own and remained in a PVS until she died of multiple infections in 1985.

Some people wondered why the Quinlans did not request permission to discontinue Karen's artificial nutrition and hydration. In *Karen Ann: The Quinlans Tell Their Story* (Joseph and Julia Quinlan with Phyllis Battelle, Doubleday & Company, New York, 1977) the Quinlans stated that they would have had moral problems with depriving their daughter of food and antibiotics.

SUBSTITUTED JUDGMENT

Superintendent of Belchertown State School et al. v. Joseph Saikewicz

Joseph Saikewicz was a mentally incompetent resident of the Belchertown State School of the Massachusetts Department of Mental Health. In April 1976 Saikewicz was diagnosed with acute myeloblastic monocytic leukemia. He was 67 years old but had the mental age of about two years and eight months. The superintendent of the mental institution petitioned the court for a guardian *ad litem* (a temporary guardian for the duration of the trial), who recommended that it would be in the patient's best interests that he not undergo chemotherapy.

In May 1976 the probate judge ordered non-treatment of the disease based in part on findings of medical experts who indicated that chemotherapy might produce remission of leukemia in 30 to 50 percent of the cases. If remission occurred, it would last between 2 and 13 months. Chemotherapy, however, would make Saikewicz suffer adverse side effects that he would not understand. Without chemotherapy, the patient might live for several weeks or months, but would die without the pain or discomfort associated with chemotherapy.

In fact, Saikewicz died on September 4, 1976, from pneumonia, a complication of the leukemia. Nevertheless, his case was heard by the Supreme Court of Massachusetts in order to establish a precedent on the question of substituted judgment (*Superintendent of Belchertown State School et al. v. Joseph Saikewicz,* Mass., 370 N.E.2d 417, 1977).

The court agreed that extraordinary measures should not be used if the patient would not recover from the disease. The court also ruled that a person has a right to the preservation of his or her bodily integrity and can refuse medical invasion. The Massachusetts Supreme Court turned to *Quinlan* in support of the right of privacy.

THE RIGHTS OF AN INCOMPETENT PATIENT. Once the right to refuse treatment had been established, the court declared that everyone, including an incompetent person, has the right of choice:

> To presume that the incompetent person must always be subjected to what many rational and intelligent persons may decline is to downgrade the status of the incompetent person by placing a lesser value on his intrinsic human worth and vitality.

Referring to *Quinlan,* the *Saikewicz* court recommended that the patient not receive the treatment most people with leukemia would choose. (Unlike some later courts, the *Quinlan* court accepted the premise that a vegetative patient would not want to remain "alive.") The *Saikewicz* court believed that the "substituted judgment" standard would best preserve respect for the integrity and autonomy of the patient. In other words, the decision-maker—in this case, the court—would put itself in Saikewicz's position and make the treatment decision the patient would make were he competent. The court believed Saikewicz would have refused treatment.

In evaluating the role of the hospital and the guardian in the decision-making process, the *Saikewicz* court rejected the *Quinlan* court's recommendation that an ethics committee should be the source of the decision. The court instead concluded:

> We do not view the judicial resolution of this most difficult and awesome question—whether potentially life-prolonging treatment should be withheld from a person incapable of making his own decision—as constituting a "gratuitous encroachment" on the domain of medical expertise. Rather, such questions of life and death seem to us to require the process of detached but passionate investigation and decision that forms the ideal on which the judicial branch of government was created.

The Case of John Storar

John Storar, a 52-year-old mentally retarded man with a mental age of about 18 months, was diagnosed with terminal cancer. His mother petitioned the court to discontinue blood transfusions that were delaying her son's death, which would probably occur within three to six months.

At the time of the hearing, Storar required two units of blood every week or two. He found the transfusions disagreeable and had to be given a sedative before the procedure. He also had to be restrained during the transfusions. Without the blood transfusions, however, there would be insufficient oxygen in his blood, causing his heart to beat faster and his respiratory rate to increase. After transfusions, the doctor reported, Storar had more energy and was able to resume most of his normal activities.

The probate court granted Mrs. Storar the right to terminate the treatments, but the order was stayed and treatment continued pending the appeal to the New York Appellate Division (or appellate court) (*Charles S. Soper, as Director of Newark Developmental Center et al. v. Dorothy Storar,* N.Y., 420 N.E.2d 64, 1981). Storar died before the case could be heard, rendering the decision moot, but since the issue was considered to be of public importance, the appellate court proceeded to hear the case.

The appellate court agreed with the probate court that a guardian can make medical decisions for an incompetent patient. However, the parent/guardian "may not deprive a child of life-saving treatment." In this case, however, there were two threats to Storar's life—the incurable cancer, and the loss of blood that could be remedied with transfusions. Because the transfusions did not, in the eyes of the majority opinion written by Judge Wachtler, cause much pain, the appellate court overturned the probate court's ruling.

Judge Jones, dissenting from the determination, believed the treatments did not serve Storar's best interests. They did not relieve his pain and, in fact, caused him additional pain. Since the blood transfusions would not cure his cancer, they could be considered extraordinary treatments. Finally, the judge reasoned that John's mother had cared for him for a long time and knew best how he felt, and therefore the court should respect her decision.

COMPETENT PATIENTS' WISHES

Satz v. Perlmutter

Not all the cases of patients seeking to terminate life support concern incompetent persons. Abe Perlmutter, 73 years old, was suffering from amyotrophic lateral sclerosis (ALS, sometimes called Lou Gehrig's disease). ALS is always fatal after prolonged physical degeneration, but does not affect mental functions.

Perlmutter's request to have his respirator removed was approved by the Circuit Court of Broward County,

Florida. At a bedside hearing, the court questioned whether the patient truly understood the consequences of his request. Perlmutter told the judge that, if the respirator were removed, "It can't be worse than what I'm going through now."

The state appealed the case before the Florida District Court of Appeal (appellate court), citing the state's duty to preserve life and to prevent the unlawful killing of a human being. The state also noted the hospital's and the doctors' fear of criminal prosecution and civil liability. In *Michael J. Satz, State Attorney for Broward County, Florida v. Abe Perlmutter* (Fla. App., 362 So.2d, 160, 1978) the appellate court concluded that Perlmutter's right to refuse treatment overrode the state's interests, and found in Perlmutter's favor.

THE STATE'S INTERESTS. An individual's right to refuse medical treatment is generally honored as long as it is consistent with the state's interests, which include:

- Interest in the preservation of life.
- Need to protect innocent third parties.
- Duty to prevent suicide.
- Requirement that it help maintain the ethical integrity of medical practice.

In the Perlmutter case, the Florida District Court of Appeal found that the preservation of life is an important goal, but not when the disease is incurable and causes the patient suffering. The need to protect innocent third parties refers to cases in which a parent refuses treatment and a third party dies, such as the abandonment of a minor child. Perlmutter's children were all adults and Perlmutter was not committing suicide. Were it not for the respirator, he would be dead; therefore, disconnecting it would not cause his death but would result in the disease running its natural course. Finally, the court turned to *Quinlan* and *Saikewicz* to support its finding that there are times when medical ethics dictates that a dying person needs comfort more than treatment. The court concluded:

> Abe Perlmutter should be allowed to make his choice to die with dignity.... It is all very convenient to insist on continuing Mr. Perlmutter's life so that there can be no question of foul play, no resulting civil liability and no possible trespass on medical ethics. However, it is quite another matter to do so at the patient's sole expense and against his competent will, thus inflicting never-ending physical torture on his body until the inevitable, but artificially suspended, moment of death. Such a course of conduct invades the patient's constitutional right of privacy, removes his freedom of choice and invades his right to self-determine.

The state again appealed the case, this time to the Supreme Court of Florida, which, in *Michael J. Satz, etc. v. Abe Perlmutter* (Fla., 379 So.2d 359, 1980), supported the decision by the Florida District Court of Appeals.

THE SUBJECTIVE, LIMITED-OBJECTIVE, AND PURE-OBJECTIVE TESTS

In the Matter of Claire C. Conroy

Claire Conroy was an 84-year-old nursing-home patient suffering from "serious and irreversible mental and physical impairments with a limited life expectancy." Her nephew (her only living relative and her guardian) petitioned the Superior Court of Essex County, New Jersey, for removal of her nasogastric feeding tube. Conroy's guardian *ad litem* appointed by the court opposed the petition. The Superior Court approved the nephew's request, and the guardian *ad litem* appealed. Claire Conroy died with the nasogastric tube in place while the appeal was pending. Nonetheless, the appellate court chose to hear the case (*In the Matter of Claire C. Conroy*, 486 A.2d 1209, [NJ 1985]). The court reasoned that this was an important case and that its ruling could influence future cases with comparable circumstances.

Conroy suffered from heart disease, hypertension, and diabetes. She also had a gangrenous leg, bedsores, and an eye problem that required irrigation. She lacked bowel control, could not speak, and had a limited swallowing ability. In the appeals trial, one medical expert testified that Conroy, although awake, was seriously demented. Another doctor testified that "although she was confused and unaware, 'she responds somehow.'"

Both experts were not sure if the patient could feel pain, although she had moaned when subjected to painful stimuli. They agreed, though, that if the nasogastric tube were removed, Conroy would die a painful death.

Conroy's nephew testified that his aunt would never have wanted to be maintained in this manner. She feared doctors and had avoided them all her life. Because she was Roman Catholic, a priest was brought in to testify. In his judgment, the removal of the tube would be ethical and moral even though her death might be painful.

The appeals court held that:

> The right to terminate life-sustaining treatment based on a guardian's judgment was limited to incurable and terminally ill patients who are brain dead, irreversibly comatose, or vegetative, and who would gain no medical benefit from continued treatment.

Furthermore, a guardian's decision did not apply to food withdrawal, which hastens death. The court considered this active euthanasia, which is not ethically permissible.

THE THREE TESTS. The court proposed three tests to determine if Conroy's feeding tube should have been removed. The subjective test served to clarify what Conroy would have decided about her tube feeding if she were able to do so. The court listed acceptable expressions of intent that should be considered by surrogates or the court—spoken expressions, living wills, durable power of attorney, oral directives, prior behavior, and religious beliefs.

If the court determines that patients in Conroy's circumstance have not explicitly expressed their wishes, two other "best interests" tests may be used—the limited-objective and the pure-objective tests. The limited-objective test permits discontinuing life-sustaining treatment if medical evidence shows that the patient would reject treatment that would only prolong suffering and that medication would not alleviate pain. Under this test, the court requires the additional evidence from the subjective test.

The pure-objective test applies when there is no trustworthy evidence, or any evidence at all, to help guide a decision. The burden imposed on the patient's life by the treatment should outweigh whatever benefit would result from the treatment. "Further, the recurring, unavoidable and severe pain of the patient's life with the treatment should be such that the effect of administering life-sustaining treatment would be inhumane."

Conroy, the court concluded, failed the tests. Her intentions, while perhaps clear enough to help support a limited-objective test (she had shown some evidence of a desire to reject treatment) were not strong enough for the subjective test (clear expressions of her intent). In addition, the information on her possible pain versus benefits of remaining alive was not sufficient for either the limited-objective test (her pain might outweigh her pleasure in life) or the pure-objective test (her pain would be so great it would be inhumane to continue treatment). Had Conroy survived the appellate court's decision, the court would have required her guardian to investigate these matters further before reaching a decision.

Judge Handler, dissenting in part, disagreed with the majority's decision to measure Conroy's "best interests" in terms of the possible pain she could have been experiencing. First, in many cases, pain can be controlled through medication. Second, pain levels cannot always be determined, as was shown in Conroy's case. Finally, not all patients make a decision based on pain. Some individuals fear being dependent on others, especially when their bodily functions deteriorate; others value personal privacy and dignity. Bodily integrity may be more important than simply prolonging life. Judge Handler supported reliance on knowledgeable, responsible surrogates as opposed to standards set in a series of tests.

CAN DOCTORS BE HELD LIABLE?

Barber v. Superior Court of the State of California

Historically, physicians have been free from prosecution for terminating life support. A precedent was set in 1983, however, when two doctors were charged with murder and conspiracy to commit murder after agreeing to requests from a patient's family to discontinue life support (Barber v. Superior Court of the State of California, 195 Cal.Rptr. 484 [Cal.App. 2 Dist. 1983]). The two physicians were Drs. Neil Barber and Robert Nejdl.

Clarence Herbert suffered cardio-respiratory arrest following surgery. He was revived and placed on a respirator. Three days later his doctors diagnosed him as deeply comatose. The prognosis was that he would likely never recover. The family requested in writing that Herbert's respirator and other life-sustaining equipment be removed. The doctors complied, but Herbert continued to breathe on his own. After two days the family asked the doctors to remove the intravenous tubes that provided nutrition and hydration. The request was honored. From that point until his death, Mr. Herbert received care that provided a clean and hygienic environment and allowed for preservation of his dignity.

A superior court judge ruled that because the doctors' behavior intentionally shortened the patient's life, they had committed murder. The Court of Appeals, however, found that a patient's right to refuse treatment, and a surrogate's right to refuse treatment for an incompetent, superseded any liability that could be attributed to the physicians.

In ruling that the physicians' compliance with the request of Herbert's family did not constitute murder, the Court of Appeals stated that "cessation of 'heroic' life support measures is not an affirmative act but rather a withdrawal or omission of further treatment." In addition, artificial nutrition and hydration also constituted a medical treatment.

WHAT ARE THE HOSPITAL'S RIGHTS?

Patricia E. Brophy v. New England Sinai Hospital, Inc.

In 1983 Paul E. Brophy, Sr., suffered an aneurysm (a blood-filled sac formed by dilation of a blood vessel with a weak wall, which makes the vessel more prone to burst) that left him in a PVS. He was not brain dead, nor was he terminal. He had been a fireman and emergency medical technician and often expressed the opinion that he never wanted to be kept alive artificially.

Patricia Brophy brought suit when physicians refused to remove or clamp a gastrostomy tube (g-tube) that supplied nutrition and hydration to her husband. The Massachusetts Appeals Court ruled against Mrs. Brophy, but the Massachusetts Supreme Court allowed substituted judgment for a comatose patient who had previously made his intentions clear.

The Massachusetts Supreme Court, however, did agree with the Massachusetts Appeals Court ruling that the hospital could not be forced to withhold food and water, which went against the hospital's ethical beliefs. Consequently, the Massachusetts Supreme Court ordered New England Sinai Hospital to facilitate Brophy's transfer to another facility or to his home where his wife could carry out his wishes (Patricia E. Brophy v. New England Sinai Hospital, Inc., 497 N.E.2d 626, [Mass. 1986]).

VITALIST DISSENSIONS. Justices Nolan and Lynch of the Massachusetts Supreme Court strongly disagreed with the majority opinion to allow removal of the gastrostomy tube. Justice Nolan argued that food and water were not medical treatments that could be refused. In his view, food and water are basic human needs, and by permitting removal of the g-tube, the court gave its stamp of approval to euthanasia and suicide.

Justice Lynch believed the Massachusetts Supreme Court majority had ignored what he considered valid findings by the Massachusetts Appeals Court which found that Brophy's wishes, as expressed in his wife's substituted-judgment decision of withholding food and water, did not concern intrusive medical treatment. Rather, Brophy's decision, if he were competent to make it, was to knowingly terminate his life by declining food and water. This was suicide and the state was, therefore, condoning suicide. Justice Lynch concluded:

> This case raises for the first time in this Commonwealth the question whether an individual has a legal right to choose to die, and to enlist the assistance of others to effectuate that choice on the ground that, irrespective of the nature of available life-prolonging treatment, life in any event is not worth living and its continuation is intolerable.

In the Matter of Beverly Requena

Beverly Requena was a competent 55-year-old woman with ALS (Lou Gehrig's disease). She informed St. Clare's/Riverside Medical Center—a Roman Catholic hospital—that when she lost the ability to swallow, she would refuse artificial feeding. The hospital filed a suit to force Requena to leave the hospital, citing its policy against withholding food or fluids from a patient.

Time was running out for Requena. She was paralyzed from the neck down, and unable to make sounds, although she could form words with her lips. At the time of the hearing, she could not eat but could suck some nutrient liquids through a straw. Soon she would not even be able to do that. Judge Stanton described the patient:

> Requena seems to have significant pain.... Her body is now almost totally useless. She is trapped within it. Most understandably, she feels enormous frustration and experiences a pervasive sense of helplessness and hopelessness. Her situation is desperately sad.

The court did not question Requena's right to refuse nutrition, nor did the hospital question that right. That was a right that had been upheld in many prior cases. But reasserting its policy of refusing to participate in the withholding or withdrawal of artificial nutrition and hydration, the hospital offered to help transfer Requena to another facility that was willing to fulfill her wishes.

Requena did not want to transfer to another hospital. In the last 17 months, she had formed a relationship of trust in, and affection for, the staff. She also liked the familiar surroundings. The court found that being forced to leave would upset her emotionally and psychologically. The hospital staff was feeling stress as well. They were fond of Requena and did not want to see her die a presumably painful death from dehydration.

SHE DOES NOT HAVE TO LEAVE. Judge Stanton ruled that Requena could not be removed from the hospital without her consent, and that the hospital would have to accede to her wishes (*In the Matter of Beverly Requena* 517 A.2d 869 [N.J.Super.A.D. 1986]). He stressed the importance of preserving the personal worth, dignity, and integrity of the patient. The hospital may provide her information about her prognosis and treatment options, but Requena alone had the right to decide what was best for her.

While Judge Stanton noted that Requena's desire to stay at St. Clare's spoke for the compassionate and excellent care she received, he felt the hospital policy to be "coercive." He stated:

> There has been a tendency on the part of the Hospital to find a "pro-life" versus "anti-life" issue where one does not exist.... This poor woman is not anti-life and her decision is not anti-life. She would dearly like to be well and to have a decent life.... It is simply not wrong in any sense for this good woman to want relief from her suffering.

> As manifested by the evidence in this case, the Hospital rejoices in its specifically Christian heritage. Perhaps it would not be amiss to ask the health care workers ... as they turn with loving compassion to the work of helping Beverly Requena, to recall the beautiful words of Jesus: "Come to me, all you who are weary and find life burdensome, and I will refresh you" (Matthew 11:28).

WHAT ARE THE NURSING HOME'S RIGHTS?

In the Matter of Nancy Ellen Jobes

In 1980, 24-year-old Nancy Ellen Jobes was in a car accident. At the time, she was four and one-half months pregnant. Doctors who treated her determined that her fetus was dead. During the surgery to remove the fetus, Jobes suffered loss of oxygen and blood flow to the brain. Never regaining consciousness, the patient was moved to the Lincoln Park Nursing Home several months later.

The nursing home provided nourishment to Jobes through a jejunostomy tube (j-tube) inserted into the jejunum of her small intestine. Five years later, Jobes' husband, John H. Jobes, requested the nursing home to stop his wife's artificial feeding. The nursing home refused, citing moral considerations.

The trial court appointed a guardian *ad litem*, who, after reviewing the case, filed in favor of Mr. Jobes. The nursing home moved to appoint a "life advocate" (a person who would support retaining the feeding tube), which was turned down by the trial court. The Supreme Court of

New Jersey heard the case (*In the Matter of Nancy Ellen Jobes,* 529 A.2d 434 [N.J. 1987]).

DIFFERING INTERPRETATIONS OF PERSISTENT VEGETATIVE STATE. Whether Jobes was in a PVS was hotly debated, revealing how different medical interpretations of the same patient's condition can produce different conclusions. After Mr. Jobes initiated the suit, his wife was transferred to Cornell Medical Center for four days of observation and testing. Dr. Fred Plum, a world-renowned expert who coined the term "persistent vegetative state," and his associate Dr. David Levy, concluded, after extensive examination and testing, that Jobes was indeed in a PVS and would never recover.

On the other hand, Drs. Maurice Victor and Allan Ropper testified for the nursing home. Having examined Jobes for about one and one-half hours, Dr. Victor reported that, although the patient was severely brain-damaged, he did not believe she was in a PVS. She had responded to his commands, such as to pick up her head or to stick out her tongue. However, he could not back up his testimony with any written record of his examination.

Dr. Ropper had also examined Jobes for about one and one-half hours. He testified that some of the patient's motions, such as lifting an arm off the bed, excluded her from his definition of PVS. (His definition of PVS differed from Dr. Plum's, in that it excluded patients who made reflexive responses to outside stimuli—a definition that would have also excluded Karen Quinlan.) Testimony from the nurses who had cared for Jobes over the past years was also contradictory, with some asserting she smiled or responded to their care and others saying they saw no cognitive responses.

The New Jersey Supreme Court concluded that the neurological experts, especially Drs. Plum and Levy, "offered sufficiently clear and convincing evidence to support the trial court's finding that Jobes is in an irreversibly vegetative state." However, the court could find no "clear and convincing" evidence that Jobes, if she were competent, would want the j-tube removed. Jobes's family and friends, including her minister, had testified that in general conversation, the patient had mentioned that she would not want to be kept alive with artificial life supports. The court did not accept these past remarks as clear evidence of the patient's intent.

With no clear and convincing evidence of Jobes's attitude toward artificial feeding, the New Jersey Supreme Court turned to *In re Quinlan* for guidance. The court stated:

> Our review of these cases and medical authorities confirms our conclusion that we should continue to defer, as we did in *Quinlan,* to family members' substituted judgments about medical treatment for irreversibly vegetative patients who did not clearly express their medical preferences while they were competent. Those

decisions are best made because the family is best able to decide what the patient would want.

THE NURSING HOME'S RESPONSIBILITY. The New Jersey Supreme Court reversed the trial court decision that had allowed the nursing home to refuse to participate in the withdrawal of the feeding tube. "Mrs. Jobes's family had no reason to believe that they were surrendering the right to choose among medical alternatives when they placed her in the nursing home." The court pointed out that it was not until 1985, five years after Jobes's admission to the Lincoln Park Nursing Home, and only after her family requested the removal of her feeding tube, that her family learned of the policy. The court ordered the nursing home to comply with the family's request.

Justice O'Hern dissented on both issues. He claimed that not all families may be as loving as Jobes's. He was concerned for other individuals whose family might not be so caring, but who would still have the authority to order the withdrawal of life-sustaining treatments. He also disagreed with the order given the nursing home to comply with the family's request to discontinue the patient's feeding. "I believe a proper balance could be obtained by adhering to the procedure adopted [in] *In re Quinlan,* that would have allowed the nonconsenting physician not to participate in the life-terminating process."

CLEAR AND CONVINCING EVIDENCE

Throughout the history of right-to-die cases, there has been considerable debate about how to determine a patient's wishes. How clearly must a patient have expressed his or her wishes before becoming incompetent? Does a parent or other family member best represent the patient? Are casual conversations sufficient to reveal intentions, or must they be written?

In the Matter of Philip K. Eichner, on Behalf of Joseph C. Fox

Eighty-three-year-old Joseph Fox went into a PVS after a hernia operation. He was a member of a religious order, the Society of Mary. The local director of the society, Philip Eichner, filed suit, asking for permission to have Fox's respirator removed.

The court reasoned that "the highest burden of proof beyond a reasonable doubt should be required when granting the relief that may result in the patient's death." The need for high standards "forbids relief whenever the evidence is loose, equivocal or contradictory." Fox, however, had discussed his feelings in the context of formal religious discussions. Only two months before his final hospitalization, he had stated he would not want his life prolonged if his condition were hopeless. "These were obviously solemn pronouncements and not casual remarks made at some social gathering, nor can it be said that he was too young to realize or feel the consequences of his statements" (*In the Matter of Philip K. Eichner, on Behalf of Joseph C. Fox v. Denis Dillon, as District Attorney of Nassau County,* N.Y., 420 N.E.2d 64, 1981).

The case of Joseph Fox was the first where the reported attitudes of an incompetent patient were accepted as "clear and convincing."

In the Matter of Westchester County Medical Center, on Behalf of Mary O'Connor

Not all patients express their attitudes about the use of life-sustaining treatments in serious religious discussions as did Joseph Fox. Nonetheless, courts have accepted evidence of "best interests" or "substituted judgments" in allowing the termination of life-sustaining treatments.

In 1985 Mary O'Connor had a stroke that rendered her mentally and physically incompetent. More than two years later, she suffered a second major stroke, after which she had additional disabilities and difficulty swallowing. O'Connor's two daughters moved her to a long-term geriatric facility associated with the Westchester County Medical Center. During her hospital admission, her daughters submitted a signed statement to be added to their mother's medical record. The document stated that O'Connor had indicated in many conversations that "no artificial life support be started or maintained in order to continue to sustain her life."

In June 1988, when Mary O'Connor's condition deteriorated, she was admitted to Westchester County Medical Center. Since she was unable to swallow, her physician prescribed a nasogastric tube. The daughters objected to the procedure, citing their mother's expressed wish. The hospital petitioned the court for permission to provide artificial feeding, without which O'Connor would starve to death within 7 to 10 days. The lower court found in favor of O'Connor's daughters. The hospital subsequently brought the case of the 77-year-old woman before the Court of Appeals of New York (*In the Matter of Westchester County Medical Center, on Behalf of Mary O'Connor,* 531 N.E.2d 607 [N.Y. 1988]).

O'Connor's physician testified that she was not in a coma. While he anticipated O'Connor's awareness might improve in the future, he believed she would never regain the mental ability to understand complex matters. This included the issue of her medical condition and treatment. The physician further indicated that, if his patient were allowed to starve to death, she would experience pain and "extreme, intense discomfort."

A neurologist testifying for the daughters reported that O'Connor's brain damage would keep her from experiencing pain. If she did have pain in the process of starving to death, she could be given medication. However, the doctor admitted he could not be "medically certain" because he had never had a patient die in the same circumstance.

The New York Court of Appeals majority concluded that, although family and friends testified that Mary O'Connor "felt that nature should take its course and not use artificial means" and that it is "monstrous" to keep someone alive by "machinery," these expressions did not constitute clear and convincing evidence of her present desire to die. Also, she had never specifically discussed the issue of artificial nutrition and hydration. Nor had she ever expressed her wish to refuse artificial medical treatment should such refusal result in a painful death.

The court further noted that O'Connor's statements about refusing artificial treatments had generally been made in situations involving terminal illness, specifically cancer—her husband had died of cancer and so did two of her brothers, her stepmother, and a close friend. Judge Wachtler, speaking for the Court of Appeals majority, stressed that O'Connor was not terminally ill, was conscious, and could interact with others, albeit minimally. Her main problem was that she could not eat on her own, and her physician could help her with that. Writing for the majority, Judge Wachtler stated:

> Every person has a right to life, and no one should be denied essential medical care unless the evidence clearly and convincingly shows that the patient intended to decline the treatment under some particular circumstances.... This is a demanding standard, the most rigorous burden of proof in civil cases. It is appropriate here because if an error occurs it should be made on the side of life.

THIS IS TOO RESTRICTIVE. New York Court of Appeals' Judge Simons differed from the majority in his opinion of O'Connor's condition. Her "conversations" were actually limited to saying her name and the words okay, all right, and yes. Neither the hospital doctor nor the neurologist who testified for her daughters could say for sure that she understood their questions. The court majority mentioned the patient's squeezing her doctor's hand in response to some questions, but failed to add that she did not respond to most questions.

While it was true the patient was not terminally ill, her severe mental and physical injuries—should nature take its course—would result in her death. Judge Simons believed the artificial feeding would not cure or improve her deteriorating condition.

The Court of Appeals' Judge Wachtler had noted that O'Connor talked about refusing artificial treatment in the aftermath of the deaths of loved ones from cancer. He claimed this had no bearing on her present condition, which was not terminal. Judge Simons pointed out that O'Connor worked 20 years in a hospital emergency room and pathology laboratory. She was no casual observer of death, and her "remarks" about not wanting artificial treatment for herself carried a lot of weight. Her expressed wishes to her daughters, who were nurses and co-workers in the same hospital, could not be considered "casual," as the majority observed. Judge Simons stated:

> Until today, under New York law, decisions concerning medical treatment remained the right of the patient. Today's opinion narrowly circumscribes our rule to a degree that makes it all but useless. Few, if any, patients can meet the demanding standard the majority has adopted....
>
> The majority, disguising its action as an application of the rule on self-determination, has made its own substituted judgment by improperly finding facts and drawing inferences contrary to the facts found by the courts below. Judges, the persons least qualified by training, experience, or affinity to reject the patient's instructions, have overridden Mrs. O'Connor's wishes, negated her long-held values on life and death, and imposed on her and her family their ideas of what her best interests require.

THE CASE OF NANCY CRUZAN

While *O'Connor* set a rigorous standard of proof for the state of New York, *Cruzan* was the first right-to-die case heard by the U.S. Supreme Court. It confirmed the legality of such strict standards for the entire country.

Cruzan, by Cruzan v. Harmon

In January 1983, 25-year-old Nancy Beth Cruzan lost control of her car. A state trooper found her lying face down in a ditch. She was in cardiac and respiratory arrest. Paramedics were able to revive her, but a neurosurgeon diagnosed "a probable cerebral contusion compounded by significant anoxia." The final diagnosis estimated she suffered anoxia (deprivation of oxygen) for 12 to 14 minutes. At the trial, the judge stated that after 6 minutes of oxygen deprivation, the brain generally suffers permanent damage.

At the time of the U.S. Supreme Court hearing in 1990, Cruzan was able to breathe on her own but was being nourished with a gastrostomy feeding tube. Doctors had surgically implanted the feeding tube about a month after the accident, following the consent of her then-husband. Medical experts diagnosed the 33-year-old patient to be in a PVS, capable of living another 30 years. Cruzan had been a ward of the state of Missouri since January 1986.

Cruzan's case was first heard by a Missouri trial court, which gave her parents, Joyce and Lester Cruzan, Jr., the right to terminate artificial nutrition and hydration. The state and the court-appointed guardian *ad litem* appealed to the Missouri Supreme Court (*Nancy Beth Cruzan, By co-guardians, Lester L. Cruzan, Jr., and Joyce Cruzan v. Robert Harmon*, 760 S.W.2d 408 [Mo.banc 1988]). The guardian *ad litem* believed it was in Cruzan's best interests to have the artificial feeding tube removed. However, he felt it was his duty as her attorney to take the case to the state supreme court because "this is a case of first impression in the state of Missouri." (A case of first impression is one without a precedent.)

THE RIGHT TO PRIVACY. The Missouri Supreme Court stressed that the state Constitution did not expressly provide for the right of privacy, which would support an individual's right to refuse medical treatment. While the U.S. Supreme Court had recognized the right of privacy in such cases as *Roe v. Wade* and *Griswold v. Connecticut,* this right did not extend to the withdrawal of food and water. In fact, the High Court, in *Roe v. Wade,* stressed that it "has refused to recognize an unlimited right of this kind in the past."

THE STATE'S INTEREST IN LIFE. In Cruzan's case, the Missouri Supreme Court majority confirmed that the state's interest in life encompassed the sanctity of life and the prolongation of life. The state's interest in the prolongation of life was especially valid in Cruzan's case. She was not terminally ill and, based on medical evidence, would "continue a life of relatively normal duration if allowed basic sustenance." Furthermore, the state was not interested in the quality of life. The court was mindful that its decision would apply not only to Cruzan and feared treading a slippery slope. "Were the quality of life at issue, persons with all manner of handicaps might find the state seeking to terminate their lives. Instead, the state's interest is in life; that interest is unqualified."

THE GUARDIANS' RIGHTS. The Missouri Supreme Court ruled that Cruzan had no constitutional right to die and that there was no clear and convincing evidence that she would not wish to continue her vegetative existence. The majority further found that her parents, or guardians, had no right to exercise substituted judgment on their daughter's behalf. The court concluded:

> We find no principled legal basis which permits the co-guardians in this case to choose the death of their ward. In the absence of such a legal basis for that decision and in the face of this State's strongly stated policy in favor of life, we choose to err on the side of life, respecting the rights of incompetent persons who may wish to live despite a severely diminished quality of life.

The Missouri Supreme Court, therefore, reversed the judgment of the Missouri trial court which had allowed discontinuance of Cruzan's artificial feeding.

THE STATE DOES NOT HAVE AN OVERRIDING INTEREST. In his dissent, Missouri Supreme Court's Judge Blackmar indicated that the state should not be involved in cases such as Cruzan's. He was not convinced that the state had spoken better for Cruzan's interests than did her parents. The judge also questioned the state's interest in life in the context of espousing capital punishment, which clearly establishes "the proposition that some lives are not worth preserving."

Judge Blackmar did not share the majority's opinion that acceding to the guardians' request would lead to the mass euthanasia of handicapped people whose conditions did not come close to Cruzan's. He stressed that a court ruling is precedent only for the facts of that specific case. Besides, one of the very purposes of courts is to protect incompetent people against abuse. He claimed:

> The principal opinion attempts to establish absolutes, but does so at the expense of human factors. In so doing, it unnecessarily subjects Nancy and those close to her to continuous torture, which no family should be forced to endure.

"ERRONEOUS DECLARATION OF LAW." Missouri Supreme Court's Judge Higgins, also dissenting, mainly disagreed with the majority's basic premise that the more than 50 precedent-setting cases from 16 other states were based on an "erroneous declaration of law." And yet, Judge Higgins noted, all cases cited by the majority upheld an individual's right to refuse life-sustaining treatment, either personally or through the substituted judgment of a guardian. The judge could not understand the majority's contradiction of its own argument.

Cruzan v. Director, Missouri Department of Health

Cruzan's father appealed the Missouri Supreme Court's decision and, in December 1989, the U.S. Supreme Court heard arguments in the case (*Nancy Beth Cruzan, by her Parents and Co-Guardians, Lester L. Cruzan et ux. v. Director, Missouri Department of Health et al.*, 497 US 261, 1990). This was the first time the right-to-die issue had been brought before the High Court, which chose not to rule on whether Cruzan's parents could have her feeding tube removed. Instead, it considered whether the U.S. Constitution prohibited the state of Missouri from requiring clear and convincing evidence that an incompetent person desires withdrawal of life-sustaining treatment. In a 5-4 decision, the Supreme Court held that the U.S. Constitution did not prohibit the state of Missouri from requiring convincing evidence that an incompetent person wants life-sustaining treatment withdrawn.

Chief Justice William Rehnquist wrote the opinion, with Justices White, O'Connor, Scalia, and Kennedy joining. (Justices Brennan, Marshall, Blackmun, and Stevens dissented.) The court majority believed that its rigorous requirement of clear and convincing evidence that Cruzan had refused termination of life-sustaining treatment was justified. An erroneous decision not to withdraw the patient's feeding tube meant that the patient would continue to be sustained artificially. Possible medical advances or new evidence of the patient's intent could correct the error. An erroneous decision to terminate the artificial feeding could not be corrected, because the result of that decision—death—is irrevocable. The chief justice concluded:

No doubt is engendered by anything in this record but that Nancy Cruzan's mother and father are loving and caring parents. If the State were required by the United States Constitution to repose a right of "substituted judgment" with anyone, the Cruzans would surely qualify. But we do not think the Due Process Clause requires the State to repose judgment on these matters with anyone but the patient herself. [The Due Process clause of the Fourteenth Amendment provides that no state shall "deprive any person of life, liberty, or property, without due process of law."]

STATE INTEREST DOES NOT OUTWEIGH THE FREEDOM OF CHOICE. Justice Brennan, dissenting, pointed out that the state of Missouri's general interest in the preservation of Cruzan's life in no way outweighed her freedom of choice—in this case, the choice to refuse medical treatment. "[T]he regulation of constitutionally protected decisions ... must be predicated on legitimate state concerns *other than* disagreement with the choice the individual has made.... Otherwise, the interest in liberty protected by the Due Process Clause would be a nullity."

Justice Brennan believed the state of Missouri had imposed an uneven burden of proof. The state would only accept clear and convincing evidence that the patient had made explicit statements refusing artificial nutrition and hydration. However, it did not require any proof that she had made specific statements desiring continuance of such treatment. Hence, it could not be said that the state had accurately determined Cruzan's wishes.

Justice Brennan disagreed that it is better to err on the side of life than death. He argued that to the patient, erring from either side is "irrevocable." He explained:

> An erroneous decision to terminate artificial nutrition and hydration, to be sure, will lead to failure of that last remnant of physiological life, the brain stem, and result in complete brain death. An erroneous decision not to terminate life support, however, robs a patient of the very qualities protected by the right to avoid unwanted medical treatment. His own degraded existence is perpetuated; his family's suffering is protracted; the memory he leaves behind becomes more and more distorted.

STATE USES NANCY CRUZAN FOR "SYMBOLIC EFFECT." Justice Stevens, in a separate dissenting opinion, believed the state of Missouri was using Cruzan for the "symbolic effect" of defining life. The state sought to equate Nancy's physical existence with life. But Justice Stevens pointed out that life is more than physiological functions. In fact, life connotes a person's experiences that make up his or her whole history, as well as "the practical manifestation of the human spirit."

Justice Stevens viewed the state's refusal to let Cruzan's guardians terminate her artificial feeding as ignoring their daughter's interests, and therefore, "unconscionable":

Insofar as Nancy Cruzan has an interest in being remembered for how she lived rather than how she died, the damage done to those memories by the prolongation of her death is irreversible. Insofar as Nancy Cruzan has an interest in the cessation of any pain, the continuation of her pain is irreversible. Insofar as Nancy Cruzan has an interest in a closure to her life consistent with her own beliefs rather than those of the Missouri legislature, the State's imposition of its contrary view is irreversible. To deny the importance of these consequences is in effect to deny that Nancy Cruzan has interests at all, and thereby to deny her personhood in the name of preserving the sanctity of her life.

CRUZAN IS FINALLY RESOLVED. On December 14, 1990, nearly eight years after Cruzan's car accident, a Missouri circuit court ruled that new evidence presented by three more friends constituted "clear and convincing" evidence that she would not want to continue existing in a persistent vegetative state. The court allowed the removal of her artificial feeding. Within two hours of the ruling, Cruzan's doctor removed the feeding tube. Cruzan's family kept a 24-hour vigil with her, until she died on December 26, 1990. Cruzan's family, however, believed she had left them many years earlier.

THE CONSTITUTIONALITY OF ASSISTED SUICIDE

At the heart of liberty is the right to define one's own concept of existence, of meaning, of the universe, and of the mystery of human life. Beliefs about these matters could not define the attributes of personhood were they formed under compulsion of the State.

—*Planned Parenthood of Southeastern Pennsylvania v. Casey,* 505 US 833, 1992

The right-to-die debates center on whether it should be legal for physicians to prescribe lethal drugs, which a terminally ill patient can self-administer to hasten his or her death. In June 1997 the U.S. Supreme Court held that "the 'liberty' specially protected by the Due Process Clause does not include a right to commit suicide, which itself includes a right to assistance in doing so." The High Court further relegated discussions and experiments in assisted suicide to the states. In November 1997 the state of Oregon legalized physician-assisted suicide. As of 2002, no other states have approved similar legislation.

Washington v. Glucksberg

FOURTH AMENDMENT PROTECTION. In January 1994 four Washington State doctors, three terminally ill patients, and Compassion in Dying (CID—a non-profit organization that provides counseling and education about end-of-life issues and was dissolved in January 2000 and reorganized as Partnership for Caring) filed a suit in the U.S. District Court. The plaintiffs sought to have the Washington Revised Code 9A.36.060(1) (1994) declared unconstitutional. This Washington law states: "A person is guilty of promoting a suicide attempt when he knowingly causes or aids another person to attempt suicide."

According to the plaintiffs, mentally competent terminally ill adults have the right, under the Equal Protection Clause of the Fourteenth Amendment, to a physician's assistance in determining the time and manner of their death. In *Compassion in Dying v. Washington* (850 F. Supp. 1454, 1459, [WD Wash. 1994]), the U.S. District Court agreed, stating that the Washington Revised Code violated the Equal Protection Clause's provision that "all persons similarly situated ... be treated alike."

In its decision, the District Court relied on *Planned Parenthood of Southeastern Pennsylvania v. Casey* (a reaffirmation of *Roe v. Wade*'s holding of the right to abortion, 505 US 833, 1992) and *Cruzan v. Director, Missouri Department of Health* (the right to refuse unwanted life-sustaining treatment, 497 US 261, 1990). The court found Washington's statute against assisted suicide unconstitutional because the law "places an undue burden on the exercise of [that] constitutionally protected liberty interest."

In 1995 a panel (three or more judges but not the full court) of the Court of Appeals for the Ninth Circuit Court reversed the District Court's decision, stressing that in the 205 years of United States' history, no court had ever recognized the right to assisted suicide (*Compassion in Dying v. Washington,* 49 F. 3d 586, 591, 1995). In 1996 the Ninth Circuit Court reheard the case en banc (by the full court), reversed the panel's decision, and affirmed the U.S. District Court's ruling (*Compassion in Dying v. Washington,* 79 F. 3d 790, 798, 1996).

The en banc Court of Appeals for the Ninth Circuit Court did not mention the Equal Protection Clause violation as indicated by the District Court; however, it referred to *Casey* and *Cruzan*, adding that the U.S. Constitution recognizes the right to die. Quoting from *Casey*, Judge Stephen Reinhardt wrote:

Like the decision of whether or not to have an abortion, the decision how and when to die is one of "the most intimate and personal choices a person may make in a lifetime," a choice "central to personal dignity and autonomy."

THE U.S. SUPREME COURT DECIDES. The state of Washington and its attorney general appealed to the U.S. Supreme Court (*Washington et al. v. Harold Glucksberg et al.,* 117 S.Ct 2258, 1997). U.S. Supreme Court Chief Justice William Rehnquist, instead of addressing the plaintiffs' initial question of whether mentally competent terminally ill adults have the right to physician-assisted suicide, reframed the issue, focusing on "whether Washington's prohibition against 'caus[ing]' or 'aid[ing]' a suicide offends the Fourteenth Amendment to the United States Constitution."

Chief Justice Rehnquist recalled the more than 700 years of Anglo-American common-law tradition disapproving suicide and assisted suicide. He added that assisted suicide is considered a crime in almost every state, with no exceptions granted to mentally competent terminally ill adults.

PRIOR SUBSTANTIVE DUE-PROCESS CASES. The plaintiffs argued that in prior substantive due-process cases, such as *Cruzan,* the U.S. Supreme Court had acknowledged the principle of self-autonomy by ruling "that competent dying persons have the right to direct the removal of life-sustaining medical treatment and thus hasten death." Chief Justice Rehnquist claimed that, although committing suicide with another's help is just as personal as refusing life-sustaining treatment, it is not similar to refusing unwanted medical treatment. In fact, according to the chief justice, in *Cruzan,* the court specifically stressed that most states ban assisted suicide.

STATE'S INTEREST. The High Court pointed out that Washington's interest in preserving human life includes the entire spectrum of that life, from birth to death, regardless of a person's physical or mental condition. The court agreed with the state that allowing assisted suicide might imperil the lives of vulnerable populations such as the poor, the elderly, and the disabled. The state included the terminally ill in this group.

The U.S. Supreme Court justices agreed with the state of Washington that legalizing physician-assisted suicide would eventually lead to voluntary and involuntary euthanasia. Since a health care proxy's decision is legally accepted as an incompetent patient's decision, what if the patient cannot self-administer the lethal medication? In such a case, a physician or a family member would have to administer the drug, thus committing euthanasia. The court gave as an example the current Dutch practice of assisted suicide, voluntary euthanasia, and involuntary euthanasia.

The U.S. Supreme Court unanimously ruled that:

[The Washington Revised] Code ... does not violate the Fourteenth Amendment, either on its face (in all or most cases in which it might be applied) or "as applied to competent terminally ill adults who wish to hasten their deaths by obtaining medication prescribed by their doctors." Our holding permits this debate to continue, as it should in a democratic society. The decision of the en banc Court of Appeals is reversed, and the case is remanded (sent back) for further proceedings consistent with this opinion.

PROVISION OF PALLIATIVE CARE. U.S. Supreme Court Justices Sandra O'Connor and Stephen Breyer, concurring, wrote that "terminally ill patients in New York and Washington ... can obtain palliative care (care that relieves pain but does not cure the illness), even potentially lethal doses of drugs that are foreseen to result in death." Hence, the justices did not see the need to address a dying person's constitutional right to obtain relief from pain. Justice O'Connor believed the court was justified in banning assisted suicide for two reasons: "The difficulty of defining terminal illness and the risk that a dying patient's request for assistance in ending his or her life might not be truly voluntary."

Vacco v. Quill

"ESSENTIALLY THE SAME THING." In 1994 three New York physicians and three terminally ill patients sued the State Attorney General. They claimed, before the U.S. District Court, that New York violated the Equal Protection Clause by prohibiting physician-assisted suicide. The state permits a competent patient to refuse life-sustaining treatment, but not to obtain physician-assisted suicide. Both, claimed the plaintiffs, are "essentially the same thing" (*Quill v. Koppell,* 870 F. Supp. 78, 84–85 [SDNY 1994]). The court disagreed, stating that withdrawing life support to let nature run its course differs from intentionally using lethal drugs to cause death.

The plaintiffs brought their case to the Court of Appeals for the Second Circuit (appellate court), which reversed the District Court's ruling (*Quill v. Vacco,* 80 F. 3d 716, 1996). The appellate court found that the New York statute does not treat equally all competent terminally ill patients wishing to hasten their deaths. The court stated:

The ending of life by [the withdrawal of life-support systems] is *nothing more or less* than assisted suicide.... To the extent that [New York's statutes] prohibit a physician from prescribing medications to be self-administered by a mentally competent, terminally ill person in the final stages of his terminal illness, they are not rationally related to any legitimate state interest.

REFUSING LIFE-SUSTAINING TREATMENT DIFFERS FROM ASSISTED SUICIDE. New York's Attorney General appealed the case to the U.S. Supreme Court (*Dennis C. Vacco, Attorney General of New York et al. v. Timothy E. Quill et al.,* 117 S.Ct 2293, 1997). The Supreme Court distinguished between withdrawing life-sustaining medical treatment and assisted suicide. The court contended that when a patient refuses life support, he or she dies because the disease has run its natural course. On the other hand, if a patient self-administers lethal drugs, death results from that medication.

The court also distinguished between the physician's role in both scenarios. A physician who complies with a patient's request to withdraw life support does so to honor a patient's wish because the treatment no longer benefits the patient. Likewise, when a physician prescribes pain-killing drugs, the needed drug dosage might hasten death, although the physician's only intent is to ease pain. However, when a physician assists in suicide, his or her prime intention is to hasten death. The U.S. Supreme Court, therefore, reversed the ruling made by the Court of Appeals for the Second Circuit.

STATE LEGISLATURES REJECT PHYSICIAN-ASSISTED SUICIDE

U.S. Supreme Court justices John Paul Stevens and David Souter issued opinions encouraging individual states to enact legislation to permit physician-assisted suicide in selected cases. At the state level, more than 30 bills to legalize physician-assisted suicide have been introduced. As of April 2002, Oregon remains the only state with a law that legalizes the practice. The Oregon legislation was approved in 1994 and reaffirmed by voters in 1997.

Five state ballot initiatives failed to garner enough votes to legalize physician-assisted suicide. Voters in California in 1988 and again in 1992 rejected the initiative along with Washington State in 1991, Michigan in 1998, and Maine in 2000.

CHAPTER 9
THE COST OF HEALTH CARE

INCREASING COSTS

Americans want quality medical care despite the increasingly high cost of that care. In 1970 the United States spent a little more than 7 percent of its gross domestic product (GDP—the total value of all the goods and services produced by the nation) on health care. In 1995 health care expenditures peaked at 13.4 percent ($990.3 billion) of the GDP. By 2000 that percentage dropped slightly to 13.2 percent, although actual dollars continued to rise, hitting nearly $1.3 trillion. Table 9.1 compares the growth in national health care expenditures and in GDP, and presents the national health expenditures as a percent of the GDP (1980–2000).

The Consumer Price Index (CPI) is a measure of the average change in prices paid by consumers. For many years, the medical component of the CPI increased at a greater rate than any other component, even food and housing. Between 1960 and 2000 the average annual percent change in the overall CPI was about 4.7 percent, compared with 6.6 percent for health care CPI. Between 1999 and 2000, the overall CPI increased by 3.4 percent, while medical care increased by 4.1 percent. (See Table 9.2.)

In 2000, 55 cents of every dollar spent for health care came from private funds, including private health insurance (34 cents), out-of-pocket expenses (15 cents), and other private sources (6 cents). The remaining 45 cents came from federal or state government sources. In 2000 there was also a continued shift in where health care dollars were spent. Hospital and physician expenditures, traditionally composing the greater part of spending, declined to 32 percent and 22 percent respectively, while prescription drug costs increased to 9 percent of all money spent on health care. (See Figure 9.1.) This shift was attributed to the availability of new high-priced drugs, increased consumer demand for drugs due to direct consumer advertising, and greater coverage of prescriptions by health insurers.

GOVERNMENT HEALTH CARE PROGRAMS

Unlike most developed countries, the United States does not have a universal health care program. Two government entitlement programs that provide health care coverage for older adults (age 65 years and older), the poor, and the disabled are Medicare and Medicaid. Enacted in 1965 as amendments to the Social Security Act of 1935 (PL 89-97), these programs went into effect in 1966. In 1972 amendments to Medicare extended medical insurance coverage to those disabled long-term and those with chronic kidney disease or end stage renal disease (ESRD). In 1999, 39.2 million older adults and persons with disabilities were enrolled in Medicare, with total expenditures of nearly $213 billion. (See Table 9.3.)

Medicare

The Medicare program, enacted under Title XVIII ("Health Insurance for the Aged") of the Social Security Act, comprises two health-related insurance plans:

- Part A, the hospital insurance plan, is funded by Social Security payroll taxes. It pays for inpatient hospital care, which includes physicians' fees, nursing services, meals, a semi-private room, special care units, operating room costs, laboratory tests, and some drugs and supplies. It also pays for skilled nursing facility care after hospitalization, home health care visits by nurses or medical technicians, and hospice care for the terminally ill.

- Part B, the supplemental medical insurance plan, also called Medigap, is an elective medical insurance. Since Part A does not pay all health care costs and other expenses associated with hospitalization, many beneficiaries enroll in the Part B plan. Members pay a premium for this coverage. Member payments and general federal revenues finance Part B. Coverage includes physicians' and surgeons' services, diagnostic and laboratory tests, outpatient hospital services,

TABLE 9.1

National health expenditures aggregate and per capita amounts, percent distribution, and average annual percent growth by source of funds, selected calendar years 1980–2000

Item	1980	1988	1990	1993	1994	1995	1996	1997	1998	1999	2000
						Amount in Billions					
National Health Expenditures	$245.8	$558.1	$696.0	$888.1	$937.2	$990.3	$1,040.0	$1,091.2	$1,149.8	$1,215.6	$1,299.5
Private	140.9	331.7	413.5	497.7	510.3	534.1	558.2	588.8	628.8	666.5	712.3
Public	104.8	226.4	282.5	390.4	427.0	456.2	481.8	502.4	520.9	549.0	587.2
Federal	71.3	154.1	192.7	274.4	298.5	322.0	343.9	358.8	367.7	384.8	411.5
State and Local	33.5	72.3	89.8	116.0	128.5	134.2	137.8	143.6	153.3	164.2	175.7
						Number in Millions					
U.S. Population[1]	230	249	254	263	265	268	270	273	275	278	$280.2
						Amount in Billions					
Gross Domestic Product[2]	$2,796	$5,108	$5,803	$6,642	$7,054	$7,400	$7,813	$8,318	$8,782	$9,269	$9,873
						Per Capita Amount					
National Health Expenditures	$1,067	$2,243	$2,738	$3,381	$3,534	$3,698	$3,849	$4,001	$4,177	$4,377	$4,637
Private	612	1,333	1,627	1,895	1,924	1,994	2,066	2,159	2,285	2,400	2,542
Public	455	910	1,111	1,486	1,610	1,704	1,783	1,842	1,893	1,977	2,096
Federal	310	619	758	1,045	1,125	1,202	1,273	1,316	1,336	1,385	1,468
State and Local	146	290	353	442	485	501	510	526	557	591	627
						Percent Distribution					
National Health Expenditures	100.0	100.0	100.0	100.0	100.0	100.0	100.0	100.0	100.0	100.0	100.0
Private	57.3	59.4	59.4	56.0	54.4	53.9	53.7	54.0	54.7	54.8	54.8
Public	42.7	40.6	40.6	44.0	45.6	46.1	46.3	46.0	45.3	45.2	45.2
Federal	29.0	27.6	27.7	30.9	31.8	32.5	33.1	32.9	32.0	31.7	31.7
State and Local	13.6	13.0	12.9	13.1	13.7	13.6	13.3	13.2	13.3	13.5	13.5
						Percent of Gross Domestic Product					
National Health Expenditures	8.8	10.9	12.0	13.4	13.3	13.4	13.3	13.1	13.1	13.1	13.2
						Average Annual Percent Growth from Previous Year Shown					
National Health Expenditures	11.7 [3]	10.8	11.7	8.5	5.5	5.7	5.0	4.9	5.4	5.7	6.9
Private	10.2 [3]	11.3	11.7	6.4	2.5	4.7	4.5	5.5	6.8	6.0	6.9
Public	14.8 [3]	10.1	11.7	11.4	9.4	6.9	5.6	4.3	3.7	5.4	7.0
Federal	17.5 [3]	10.1	11.8	12.5	8.8	7.9	6.8	4.3	2.5	4.7	6.9
State and Local	11.5 [3]	10.1	11.4	8.9	10.8	4.5	2.7	4.2	6.8	7.1	7.0
U.S. Population	1.1 [3]	1.0	1.1	1.1	1.0	1.0	0.9	0.9	0.9	0.9	0.9
Gross Domestic Product	8.7 [3]	7.8	6.6	4.6	6.2	4.9	5.6	6.5	5.6	5.5	6.5

[1]July 1 Census resident based population estimates for each year 1980–2000.
[2]U.S. Department of Commerce, Bureau of Economic Analysis.
[3]Average annual growth between 1960 and 1980.

NOTE: Numbers and percents may not add to totals because of rounding.

SOURCE: "Table 1. National Health Expenditures Aggregate and per Capita Amounts, Percent Distribution, and Average Annual Percent Growth, by Source of Funds: Selected Calendar Years 1980–2000," in *National Health Expenditures Tables,* Centers for Medicare & Medicaid Services, Office of the Actuary, National Health Statistics Group, Baltimore, MD [Online] http://www.hcfa.gov/stats/NHE-OAct/tables/t1.htm [Accessed March 26, 2002]

outpatient physical therapy, speech pathology services, home health care services, and medical equipment and supplies.

MEDICARE HEALTH MAINTENANCE ORGANIZATIONS (HMOS). In 1985, Medicare, in an effort to control costs and ensure quality medical care, began offering its beneficiaries a managed care option. Medicare beneficiaries could choose between Medicare managed care insurance and traditional Medicare insurance. In 1985, 44,100 beneficiaries signed up with Medicare health maintenance organizations (HMOs). As of January 1, 2001, about 6.1 million Medicare beneficiaries were enrolled in HMOs.

For monthly pre-paid premiums, HMO enrollees receive benefits not available under Medicare, such as preventive care, routine physical exams, prescription drugs, dental care, eyeglasses, and hearing aids. The HMOs, in turn, receive fixed payments from the Centers for Medicare and Medicaid Services (CMS) (which was known as the Health Care Financing Administration, or HCFA, until June 14, 2001), the federal agency responsible for the management and implementation of the Medicare and Medicaid insurance programs.

PRIVATE HEALTH PLANS FOR MEDICARE BENEFICIARIES. In 1999, for the first time, Medicare offered the senior population other private health plans, including

TABLE 9.2

Consumer Price Index and average annual percent change for all items, selected items, and medical care components, selected years 1960–2000

[Data are based on reporting by samples of providers and other retail outlets]

Items and medical care components	1960	1970	1980	1990	1995	1997	1998	1999	2000
				Consumer Price Index (CPI)					
All items	29.6	38.8	82.4	130.7	152.4	160.5	163.0	166.6	172.2
All items excluding medical care	30.2	39.2	82.8	128.8	148.6	156.3	158.6	162.0	167.3
All services	24.1	35.0	77.9	139.2	168.7	179.4	184.2	188.8	195.3
Food	30.0	39.2	86.8	132.4	148.4	157.3	160.7	164.1	167.8
Apparel	45.7	59.2	90.9	124.1	132.0	132.9	133.0	131.3	129.6
Housing	- - -	36.4	81.1	128.5	148.5	156.8	160.4	163.9	169.6
Energy	22.4	25.5	86.0	102.1	105.2	111.5	102.9	106.6	124.6
Medical care	22.3	34.0	74.9	162.8	220.5	234.6	242.1	250.6	260.8
Components of medical care									
Medical care services	19.5	32.3	74.8	162.7	224.2	239.1	246.8	255.1	266.0
Professional services	- - -	37.0	77.9	156.1	201.0	215.4	222.2	229.2	237.7
Physicians' services	21.9	34.5	76.5	160.8	208.8	222.9	229.5	236.0	244.7
Dental services	27.0	39.2	78.9	155.8	206.8	226.6	236.2	247.2	258.5
Eye glasses and eye care[1]	- - -	- - -	- - -	117.3	137.0	141.5	144.1	145.5	149.7
Services by other medical professionals[1]	- - -	- - -	- - -	120.2	143.9	151.8	155.4	158.7	161.9
Hospital and related services	- - -	- - -	69.2	178.0	257.8	278.4	287.5	299.5	317.3
Hospital services[2]	- - -	- - -	- - -	- - -	- - -	101.7	105.0	109.3	115.9
Inpatient hospital services[2]	- - -	- - -	- - -	- - -	- - -	101.3	104.0	107.9	113.8
Outpatient hospital services[1]	- - -	- - -	- - -	138.7	204.6	224.9	233.2	246.0	263.8
Hospital rooms	9.3	23.6	68.0	175.4	251.2	- - -	- - -	- - -	- - -
Other inpatient services[1]	- - -	- - -	- - -	142.7	206.8	- - -	- - -	- - -	- - -
Nursing homes and adult day care	- - -	- - -	- - -	- - -	- - -	102.3	107.1	111.6	117.0
Medical care commodities	46.9	46.5	75.4	163.4	204.5	215.3	221.8	230.7	238.1
Prescription drugs and medical supplies	54.0	47.4	72.5	181.7	235.0	249.3	258.6	273.4	285.4
Nonprescription drugs and medical supplies[1]	- - -	- - -	- - -	120.6	140.5	145.4	147.7	148.5	149.5
Internal and respiratory over-the-counter drugs	- - -	42.3	74.9	145.9	167.0	173.1	175.4	175.9	176.9
Nonprescription medical equipment and supplies	- - -	- - -	79.2	138.0	166.3	171.5	174.9	176.7	178.1
				Average annual percent change from previous year shown					
All items	...	4.3	8.9	4.7	3.1	2.6	1.6	2.2	3.4
All items excluding medical care	...	4.1	8.8	4.5	2.9	2.6	1.5	2.1	3.3
All services	...	5.6	10.2	6.0	3.9	3.1	2.7	2.5	3.4
Food	...	4.0	7.7	4.3	2.3	3.0	2.2	2.1	2.3
Apparel	...	4.4	4.6	3.2	1.2	0.3	0.1	1.3	1.3
Housing	...	- - -	9.9	4.7	2.9	2.8	2.3	2.2	3.5
Energy	...	2.2	15.4	1.7	0.6	3.0	7.7	3.6	16.9
Medical care	...	6.2	9.5	8.1	6.3	3.1	3.2	3.5	4.1
Components of medical care									
Medical care services	...	7.3	9.9	8.1	6.6	3.3	3.2	3.4	4.3
Professional services	...	- - -	8.9	7.2	5.2	3.5	3.2	3.2	3.7
Physicians' services	...	6.6	9.7	7.7	5.4	3.3	3.0	2.8	3.7
Dental services	...	5.3	8.2	7.0	5.8	4.7	4.2	4.7	4.6
Eye glasses and eye care[1]	...	- - -	- - -	- - -	3.2	1.6	1.8	1.0	2.9
Services by other medical professionals[1]	...	- - -	- - -	- - -	3.7	2.7	2.4	2.1	2.0
Hospital and related services	...	- - -	- - -	9.9	7.7	3.9	3.3	4.2	5.9
Hospital services[2]	...	- - -	- - -	- - -	- - -	- - -	3.2	4.1	6.0
Inpatient hospital services[2]	...	- - -	- - -	- - -	- - -	- - -	2.7	3.8	5.5
Outpatient hospital services[1]	...	- - -	- - -	- - -	8.1	4.8	3.7	5.5	7.2
Hospital rooms	...	13.9	12.2	9.9	7.4	- - -	- - -	- - -	- - -
Other inpatient services[1]	...	- - -	- - -	- - -	7.7	- - -	- - -	- - -	- - -
Nursing homes and adult day care	...	- - -	- - -	- - -	- - -	- - -	4.7	4.2	4.8
Medical care commodities	...	0.7	7.2	8.0	4.6	2.6	3.0	4.0	3.2
Prescription drugs and medical supplies	...	−0.2	7.2	9.6	5.3	3.0	3.7	5.7	4.4
Nonprescription drugs and medical supplies	...	- - -	- - -	- - -	3.1	1.7	1.6	0.5	0.7
Internal and respiratory over-the-counter drugs	...	1.6	7.7	6.9	2.7	1.8	1.3	0.3	0.6
Nonprescription medical equipment and supplies	...	- - -	- - -	5.7	3.8	1.6	2.0	1.0	0.8

- - - Data not available.
... Category not applicable.
[1]Dec. 1986 = 100.
[2]Dec. 1996 = 100.
NOTES: 1982–84= 100, except where noted.

SOURCE: "Table 115. Consumer Price Index and average annual percent change for all items, selected items, and medical care components: United States, selected years 1960–2000," in *Health, United States, 2001*, Centers for Disease Control and Prevention, National Center for Health Statistics, National Vital Statistics System, Hyattsville, MD, 2001

FIGURE 9.1

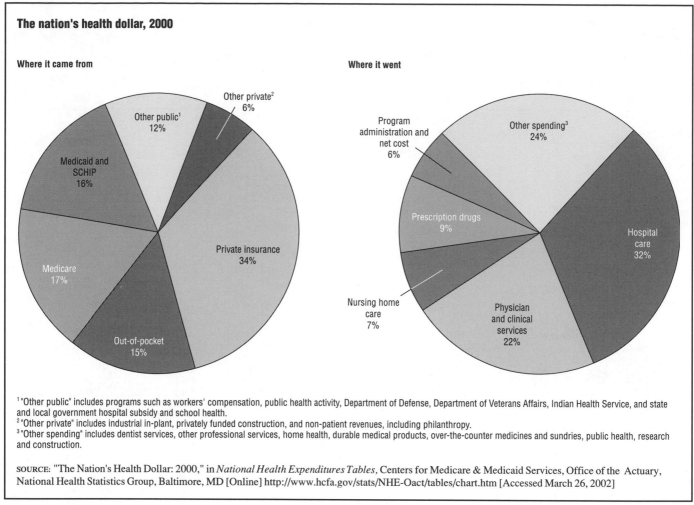

The nation's health dollar, 2000

Where it came from

- Other private[2] 6%
- Other public[1] 12%
- Medicaid and SCHIP 16%
- Medicare 17%
- Out-of-pocket 15%
- Private insurance 34%

Where it went

- Program administration and net cost 6%
- Prescription drugs 9%
- Nursing home care 7%
- Other spending[3] 24%
- Hospital care 32%
- Physician and clinical services 22%

[1] "Other public" includes programs such as workers' compensation, public health activity, Department of Defense, Department of Veterans Affairs, Indian Health Service, and state and local government hospital subsidy and school health.
[2] "Other private" includes industrial in-plant, privately funded construction, and non-patient revenues, including philanthropy.
[3] "Other spending" includes dentist services, other professional services, home health, durable medical products, over-the-counter medicines and sundries, public health, research and construction.

SOURCE: "The Nation's Health Dollar: 2000," in *National Health Expenditures Tables,* Centers for Medicare & Medicaid Services, Office of the Actuary, National Health Statistics Group, Baltimore, MD [Online] http://www.hcfa.gov/stats/NHE-Oact/tables/chart.htm [Accessed March 26, 2002]

preferred provider organizations (PPOs) and provider-sponsored organizations (PSOs). This change, known as Medicare+Choice, is a result of the Balanced Budget Act of 1997 (PL 105-33), aimed at saving Medicare more money. The act is also designed to reduce fraud and abuse. These factors contributed to the reduction of Medicare spending growth from 6.0 percent in 1997 to 2.5 percent in 1998, and 1.5 percent in 1999 (according to CMS statistics). The decline was short-lived, however, and in 2000 Medicare spending grew 5.6 percent.

Recently, several insurance plans have opted out of the Medicare programs, citing escalating costs and inadequate reimbursement. An estimated 934,000 Medicare beneficiaries were dropped by their Medicare HMO plans in 2000 and by December 31, 2001, a total of more than 1.7 million Medicare beneficiaries had lost their HMO plans. Enrollees who were dropped were able to return to traditional Medicare fee-for-service coverage or join other Medicare HMO plans.

Medicaid

The Medicaid health insurance program, enacted under Title XIX ("Grants to States for Medical Assistance

Programs") of the Social Security Act, provides medical assistance to low-income persons, including those with disabilities, or members of families with dependent children. It is jointly financed by federal and state governments. Medicaid coverage includes hospitalization, physicians' services, laboratory fees, diagnostic screenings, and long-term nursing home care.

In 1998, while persons aged 65 and over made up only 9.8 percent of all Medicaid recipients, they received more than one-fourth (28.5 percent) of all Medicaid benefits. The average payment was $10,242 per older adult, compared with $9,095 for the blind and disabled, $1,876 for adults in families with dependent children, and $1,203 for children under the age of 21 years. (See Table 9.4.)

WHO PAYS FOR END-OF-LIFE CARE?

The Committee on Care at the End of Life of the Institute of Medicine (IOM) has reported that the United States has not performed a comprehensive study about the sources of payment for end-of-life care.

According to the IOM committee, nearly three-fourths (74.7 percent) of those who die each year are 65 years and

TABLE 9.3

Medicare enrollees and expenditures and percent distribution, according to type of service, United States and other areas, selected years 1970–99

[Data are compiled by the Health Care Financing Administration]

Type of service	1970	1980	1985	1990	1995	1996	1997	1998	1999[1]
Enrollees					Number in millions				
Total[2]	20.4	28.4	31.1	34.3	37.6	38.1	38.5	38.9	39.2
Hospital insurance	20.1	28.0	30.6	33.7	37.2	37.7	38.1	38.5	38.8
Supplementary medical insurance	19.5	27.3	29.9	32.6	35.6	36.1	36.4	36.8	37.0
Expenditures					Amount in millions				
Total	$7,493	$36,822	$72,294	$110,984	$184,203	$200,337	$213,576	$213,401	$212,959
Total hospital insurance (HI)	5,281	25,577	48,414	66,997	117,604	129,929	139,452	135,771	130,632
HI payments to managed care organizations[3,4]	- - -	7	768	2,654	6,701	11,777	16,338	20,055	21,973
HI payments for fee-for-service utilization	5,281	25,570	47,646	64,343	110,904	118,152	123,115	115,718	108,659
Inpatient hospital	4,827	24,109	44,172	56,922	82,283	86,063	88,694	86,757	85,697
Skilled nursing facility	246	395	548	2,488	9,135	10,900	12,808	13,112	10,755
Home health agency[4]	51	540	1,913	3,661	16,201	17,720	17,671	11,685	7,591
Hospice	...	...	43	325	1,857	1,997	2,082	2,184	2,575
Administrative expenses[5]	157	525	970	947	1,428	1,472	1,860	1,980	2,041
Total supplementary medical insurance (SMI)	2,212	11,245	23,880	43,987	66,599	70,408	74,124	77,630	82,327
SMI payments to managed care organizations[3,4]	26	203	720	2,827	6,610	9,558	10,962	14,273	16,604
SMI payments for fee-for-service utilization[6]	2,186	11,042	23,160	41,160	59,989	60,849	63,163	63,357	65,723
Physician/supplies[7]	1,790	8,187	17,312	29,609	- - -	- - -	- - -	- - -	- - -
Outpatient hospital[8]	114	1,897	4,319	8,482	- - -	- - -	- - -	- - -	- - -
Independent laboratory[9]	11	114	558	1,476	- - -	- - -	- - -	- - -	- - -
Physician fee schedule	- - -	- - -	- - -	- - -	31,660	31,631	31,898	32,447	33,340
Durable medical equipment	- - -	- - -	- - -	- - -	3,689	3,825	4,236	4,040	4,293
Laboratory[10]	- - -	- - -	- - -	- - -	4,255	3,881	3,832	3,574	3,676
Other[11]	- - -	- - -	- - -	- - -	9,861	10,808	12,160	12,320	12,236
Hospital[12]	- - -	- - -	- - -	- - -	8,666	8,638	9,413	8,762	8,771
Home health agency[4]	34	234	38	74	229	242	241	681	1,759
Administrative expenses[5]	237	610	933	1,519	1,629	1,824	1,384	1,534	1,649
				Percent distribution of expenditures					
Total hospital in surance (HI)	100.0	100.0	100.0	100.0	100.0	100.0	100.0	100.0	100.0
HI payments to managed care organizations[3]	- - -	0.0	1.6	4.0	5.7	9.1	11.7	14.8	16.8
HI payments for fee-for-service utilization	100.0	100.0	98.4	96.0	94.3	90.9	88.3	85.2	83.2
Inpatient hospital	91.4	94.3	91.2	85.0	70.0	66.2	63.6	63.9	65.6
Skilled nursing acility facility	4.7	1.5	1.1	3.7	7.8	8.4	9.2	9.7	8.2
Home health agency[4]	1.0	2.1	4.0	5.5	13.8	13.6	12.7	8.6	5.8
Hospice	...	...	0.1	0.5	1.6	1.5	1.5	1.6	2.0
Administrative expenses[5]	3.0	2.1	2.0	1.4	1.2	1.1	1.3	1.5	1.6

older. Medicare covers these older adults during the terminal stage of their lives. Medicaid further covers 13 percent of those older adults who have exhausted their Medicare benefits, as well as poor and disabled younger patients. Health programs under the Department of Veterans Affairs and the Department of Defense also pay for terminal care.

No specific information about the cost of end-of-life care exists for the one-fourth of those who die every year who are under age 65. Such care is more than likely financed by employer health insurance, personal funds, Medicare, and Medicaid. Nonetheless, aside from funds paid out for hospice services, the government has no other information about this group's terminal health care.

Medicare Hospice Benefits

In 1982 Congress created a Medicare hospice benefit program (Tax Equity and Fiscal Responsibility Act, PL 97-248, 122) to provide services to terminally ill patients with six months or less to live. In 1989 the Government Accounting Office (GAO) reported that only 35 percent of eligible hospices were Medicare-certified, in part due to the Health Care Financing Administration's low rates of reimbursement to hospices. That same year, Congress gave hospices a 20 percent increase in reimbursement rates through a provision in the Omnibus Budget Reconciliation Act (PL 101-239, 6005).

Under the Balanced Budget Act of 1997 (PL 105-33), Medicare hospice benefits are divided into three benefit periods:

• An initial 90-day period.

• A subsequent 90-day period.

• An unlimited number of subsequent 60-day periods, based on a patient's satisfying the program eligibility requirements.

TABLE 9.3

Medicare enrollees and expenditures and percent distribution, according to type of service, United States and other areas, selected years 1970–99 [CONTINUED]

[Data are compiled by the Health Care Financing Administration]

Type of service	1970	1980	1985	1990	1995	1996	1997	1998	1999[1]
					Percent distribution of expenditures				
Total supplementary medical insurance (SMI)	100.0	100.0	100.0	100.0	100.0	100.0	100.0	100.0	100.0
SMI payments to managed care organizations[3]	1.2	1.8	3.0	6.4	9.9	13.6	14.8	18.4	20.2
SMI payments for fee-for-service utilization[6]	98.8	98.2	97.0	93.6	90.1	86.4	85.2	81.6	79.8
Physician/supplies[7]	80.9	72.8	72.5	67.3	- - -	- - -	- - -	- - -	- - -
Outpatient hospital[8]	5.2	16.9	18.1	19.3	- - -	- - -	- - -	- - -	- - -
Independent laboratory[9]	0.5	1.0	2.3	3.4	- - -	- - -	- - -	- - -	- - -
Physician fee schedule	- - -	- - -	- - -	- - -	47.5	44.9	43.0	41.8	40.5
Durable medical equipment	- - -	- - -	- - -	- - -	5.5	5.4	5.7	5.2	5.2
Laboratory[10]	- - -	- - -	- - -	- - -	6.4	5.5	5.2	4.6	4.5
Other[11]	- - -	- - -	- - -	- - -	14.8	15.4	16.4	15.9	14.9
Hospital[12]	- - -	- - -	- - -	- - -	13.0	12.3	12.7	11.3	10.7
Home health agency[4]	1.5	2.1	0.2	0.2	0.3	0.3	0.3	0.9	2.1
Administrative expenses[5]	10.7	5.4	3.9	3.5	2.4	2.6	1.9	2.0	2.0

- - - Data not available."
. . . Category not applicable."
[1] Preliminary figures; home health agency expenditures for 1999 reflect annual home health HI to SMI transfer amounts.
[2] Average number enrolled in the hospital insurance and/or supplementary medical insurance programs for the period.
[3] Medicare-approved managed care organizations.
[4] Reflects annual home health HI to SMI transfer amounts for 1998 and later.
[5] Includes research, costs of experiments and demonstration projects, and peer review activity.
[6] Type of service reporting categories for fee-for-service reimbursement differ before and after 1991.
[7] Includes payment for physicians, practitioners, durable medical equipment, and all suppliers other than Independent laboratory, which is shown separately through 1990. Beginning in 1991, those physician services subject to the Physician fee schedule are so broken out. Payments for laboratory services paid under the Laboratory fee schedule and performed in a physician office are included under beginning in 1991. Payments for durable medical equipment are broken out and so labeled beginning in 1991. The remaining services from the category are included in Other.
[8] Includes payments for hospital outpatient department services, for skilled nursing facility outpatient services, for Part B services received as an inpatient in a hospital or skilled nursing facility setting, and for other types of outpatient facilities. Beginning 1991, payments for hospital outpatient department services, except for laboratory services, are listed under "Hospital." Hospital outpatient laboratory services are included in the "Laboratory" line.
[9] Beginning in 1991 those independent laboratory services that were paid under the Laboratory fee schedule (most of independent lab) are included in the line; the remaining services are included in "Physician fee schedule" and "Other" lines.
[10] Payments for laboratory services paid under the Laboratory fee schedule performed in a physician office, independent lab, or in a hospital outpatient department.
[11] Includes payments for free-standing ambulatory surgical center facility services; ambulance services; supplies; free-standing end-stage renal disease (ESRD) dialysis facility services; rural health clinics; outpatient rehabilitation facilities; psychiatric hospitals; and federally qualified health centers.
[12] Includes the hospital facility costs for Medicare Part B services that are predominantly in the outpatient department, with the exception of hospital outpatient" laboratory services, which are included on the "Laboratory" line. The physician reimbursement is included on the "Physician fee schedule" line.
Notes: Table includes service disbursements as of January 2001 for Medicare enrollees residing in Puerto Rico, Virgin Islands, Guam, other outlying areas, foreign" countries, and unknown residence. Totals do not necessarily equal the sums of rounded components.

SOURCE: "Table 135. Medicare enrollees and expenditures and percent distribution, according to type of service: United States and other areas, selected years 1970–99," in *Health United States, 2001*, Centers for Disease Control and Prevention, National Center for Health Statistics, National Vital Statistics System, Hyattsville, MD, 2001.

At the start of each period, the Medicare patient must be recertified as terminally ill. After the patient's death, the patient's family receives up to 13 months of bereavement service.

In 2000, Medicare-certified hospices numbered 2,273, a substantial increase from 31 hospices in 1984, stimulated in part by increased reimbursement rates established by Congress in 1989. Of these hospices, 739 were with home health agencies (HHA), 554 were affiliated with hospitals, 20 with skilled nursing facilities (SNF), and 960 were freestanding hospices. (See Table 9.5.) Medicare covers the expenditures of approximately 60 percent of hospice patients.

Terminally ill Medicare patients who stayed in a hospice spent less money than those who stayed in a hospital or skilled nursing facility. In 1998 a one-day stay in a hospice cost Medicare $113, compared with $482 for a skilled nursing facility and $2,177 for a hospital. (See Table 9.6.) A study conducted by the National Hospice Organization (NHO) in 1995 showed that hospice users in the last month of their lives saved Medicare $2,884 compared with non-hospice users.

The Hospice Association of America (HAA) contends that terminally ill patients often wait too long to enter hospice care. The HAA believes that the difficulty of predicting when death may occur could account for part of the delay, along with the reticence of caregivers, patients, and family to accept a terminal prognosis.

While terminal care is often associated with hospice, very few dying people qualify for Medicare hospice

TABLE 9.4

Medicaid recipients and medical vendor payments, according to basis of eligibility, and race and ethnicity, selected fiscal years, 1972–98

[Data are compiled by the Health Care Financing Administration]

Basis of eligibility and race and ethnicity	1972	1975	1980	1985	1990	1995	1996	1997	1998[1]
Recipients					Number in millions				
All recipients	17.6	22.0	21.6	21.8	25.3	36.3	36.1	34.9	40.6
					Percent of recipients				
Basis of eligibility:[2]									
Aged (65 years and over)	18.8	16.4	15.9	14.0	12.7	11.4	11.9	11.3	9.8
Blind and disabled	9.8	11.2	13.5	13.8	14.7	16.1	17.2	17.6	16.3
Adults in families with dependent children[3]	17.8	20.6	22.6	25.3	23.8	21.0	19.7	19.5	19.5
Children under age 21[4]	44.5	43.6	43.2	44.7	44.4	47.3	46.3	45.3	46.7
Other Title XIX[5]	9.0	8.2	6.9	5.6	3.9	1.7	1.8	6.3	7.8
Race and ethnicity:[6]									
White	---	---	---	---	42.8	45.5	44.8	44.4	41.3
Black	---	---	---	---	25.1	24.7	23.9	23.5	24.2
American Indian or Alaska Native	---	---	---	---	1.0	0.8	0.8	1.0	0.8
Asian or Pacific Islander	---	---	---	---	2.0	2.2	2.1	1.9	2.5
Hispanic	---	---	---	---	15.2	17.2	17.5	14.3	15.6
Unknown	---	---	---	---	14.0	9.6	10.9	14.9	15.5
Vendor payments[7]					Amount in billions				
All payments	$6.3	$12.2	$23.3	$37.5	$64.9	$120.1	$121.7	$124.4	$142.3
					Percent distribution				
Total	100.0	100.0	100.0	100.0	100.0	100.0	100.0	100.0	100.0
Basis of eligibility:									
Aged (65 years and over)	30.6	35.6	37.5	37.6	33.2	30.4	30.4	30.3	28.5
Blind and disabled	22.2	25.7	32.7	35.9	37.6	41.1	42.8	43.5	42.4
Adults in families with dependent children[3]	15.3	16.8	13.9	12.7	13.2	11.2	10.1	9.9	10.4
Children under age 21[4]	18.1	17.9	13.4	11.8	14.0	15.0	14.4	14.1	16.0
Other Title XIX[5]	13.9	4.0	2.6	2.1	1.6	1.2	1.2	2.2	2.6
Race and ethnicity:[6]									
White	---	---	---	---	53.4	54.3	54.1	55.0	54.3
Black	---	---	---	---	18.3	19.2	18.7	18.5	19.6
American Indian or Alaska Native	---	---	---	---	0.6	0.5	0.6	0.6	0.8
Asian or Pacific Islander	---	---	---	---	1.0	1.2	1.1	0.9	1.4
Hispanic	---	---	---	---	5.3	7.3	7.4	6.8	8.2
Unknown	---	---	---	---	21.3	17.6	18.1	18.2	15.7
Vendor payments per recipient[7]					Amount				
All recipients	$358	$556	$1,079	$1,719	$2,568	$3,311	$3,369	$3,568	$3,501
Basis of eligibility:									
Aged (65 years and over)	580	1,206	2,540	4,605	6,717	8,868	8,622	9,538	10,242
Blind and disabled	807	1,276	2,618	4,459	6,564	8,435	8,369	8,832	9,095
Adults in families with dependent children[3]	307	455	662	860	1,429	1,777	1,722	1,809	1,876
Children under age 21[4]	145	228	335	452	811	1,047	1,048	1,111	1,203
Other Title XIX[5]	555	273	398	657	1,062	2,380	2,152	1,242	1,166
Race and ethnicity:[6]									
White	---	---	---	---	3,207	3,953	4,074	4,421	4,609
Black	---	---	---	---	1,878	2,568	2,631	2,798	2,836
American Indian or Alaska Native	---	---	---	---	1,706	2,142	2,298	2,500	3,297
Asian or Pacific Islander	---	---	---	---	1,257	1,713	1,767	1,610	1,924
Hispanic	---	---	---	---	903	1,400	1,428	1,699	1,842
Unknown	---	---	---	---	3,909	6,099	5,603	4,356	3,531

- - - Data not available.

[1] Prior to 1998 recipient counts exclude those individuals who only received coverage under prepaid health care and for whom no direct vendor payments were made during the year. Prior to 1998 vendor payments exclude payments to health maintenance organizations and other prepaid health plans ($19.3 billion in 1998 and $18 billion in 1997). The total number of persons who were Medicaid eligible and enrolled was 41.4 million in 1998, 41.6 million in 1997, and 41.2 million in 1996 (HCFA Medicaid Statistics, Program and Financial Statistics FY1996, FY1997, and FY1998. unpublished).
[2] In 1980 and 1985 recipients included in more than one category. In 1990–96, 0.2–2.5 percent of recipients have unknown basis of eligibility. From 1997 onwards, unknowns are included in Other Title XIX.
[3] Includes adults in the Aid to Families with Dependent Children (AFDC) program.
[4] Includes children in the AFDC program. From 1997 onwards includes foster care.
[5] Includes some participants in the Supplemental Security Income program and other people deemed medically needy in participating states. From 1997 onwards excludes foster care and includes unknown eligibility.
[6] Race and ethnicity as determined on initial Medicaid application. Categories are mutually exclusive.
[7] Vendor payments exclude disproportionate share hospital payments ($16 billion in 1997 and $15 billion in 1998).
Notes: 1972 and 1975 data are for fiscal year ending June 30. All other years are for fiscal year ending September 30.

SOURCE: "Table 138. Medicaid recipients and medical vendor payments, according to basis of eligibility, and race and ethnicity: United States, selected fiscal years 1972–98," in *Health, United States, 2001*, Centers for Disease Control and Prevention, National Center for Health Statistics, National Vital Statistics System, Hyattsville, MD, 2001.

TABLE 9.5

Number of Medicare-certified hospices by auspice, 1984–2000

Year	HHA	HOSP	SNF	FSTG	TOTAL
1984	n/a	n/a	n/a	n/a	31
1985	n/a	n/a	n/a	n/a	158
1986	113	54	10	68	245
1987	155	101	11	122	389
1988	213	138	11	191	553
1989	286	182	13	220	701
1990	313	221	12	260	806
1991	325	282	10	394	1,011
1992	334	291	10	404	1,039
1993	438	341	10	499	1,288
1994	583	401	12	608	1,604
1995	699	460	19	679	1,857
1996	815	526	22	791	2,154
1997	823	561	22	868	2,274
1998	763	553	21	878	2,215
1999	762	562	22	928	2,274
2000	739	554	20	960	2,273

Notes: Home health agency-based (HHA) hospices are owned and operated by freestanding proprietary and nonprofit home care agencies. Hospital-based (HOSP) hospices are operating units or departments of a Hospital. Skilled nursing facility-based (SNF) hospices are operating units or departments of a skilled nursing facility or nursing facility. Freestanding (FSTG) hospices are independent, mostly nonprofit organizations.

SOURCE: "Table 1. Number of Medicare-certified Hospices, by Auspice, 1984-2000," in *Hospice Facts and Statistics,* Hospice Association of America, Washington, DC [Online] http://www.nahc.org/Consumer/hpcstats.html [Accessed March 26, 2002].

TABLE 9.7

Medicare benefit payments, fiscal years 2000 and 2001

	2000 (Estimated)		2001 (Projected)	
	Amount ($millions)	Percent of total	Amount ($millions)	Percent of total
Total Medicare Benefit Payments*	214,868	100.0	237,790	100.0
Part A				
Hospital care	86,566	40.3	93,336	39.3
Skilled nursing facility	10,593	4.9	12,270	5.2
Home health	4,552	2.1	3,566	1.5
Hospice	2,818	1.3	3,037	1.3
Managed Care	21,463	10.0	22,883	9.6
TOTAL	125,992	58.6	135,092	56.8
Part B				
Physician	35,947	16.7	40,209	16.9
Durable medical equipment	4,573	2.1	5,214	2.2
Carrier lab	2,201	1.0	2,334	1.0
Other carrier	7,164	3.3	8,037	3.4
Hospital	8,439	3.9	12,243	5.1
Home health	4,570	2.1	6,761	2.8
Intermediary lab	1,622	0.8	1,773	0.7
Other intermediary	6,013	2.8	6,701	2.8
Managed care	18,348	8.5	19,426	8.2
TOTAL	88,876	41.4	102,698	43.2

Note: Part A data does not include peer review organization payments. Figures may not add to totals due to rounding.

SOURCE: "Table 4. Medicare Benefit Payments, FY 2000 and FY 2001," in *Hospice Facts and Statistics,* Hospice Association of America, Washington, DC [Online] http://www.nahc.org/Consumer/hpcstats.html [Accessed March 26, 2002]

TABLE 9.6

Comparison of hospital, SNF, and hospice Medicare charges, 1995–98

	1995	1996	1997	1998
Hospital inpatient charges per day	$1,909	$2,068	$2,238	$2,177
Skilled nursing facility charges per day	402	443	487	482
Hospice charges per covered day of care	103	106	109	113

Note: Additional years are projected using consumer price index forecasts from the Bureau of Labor Statistics web site.

SOURCE: "Comparison of Hospital, SNF, and Hospice Medicare Charges, 1995-1998," in *Basic Statistics About Hospice,* National Association for Home Care, Washington, DC [Online] http://www.nahc.org/Consumer/hpcstats.html [Accessed April 23, 2002]

TABLE 9.8

Medicaid payments, by type of service, fiscal year 1998

	Amount ($millions)	Percent of Total
Inpatient hospital	21,498.7	15.1
Nursing home	31,892.1	22.4
Physician	6,070.0	4.3
Outpatient hospital	5,759.0	4.0
Home health	9,410.2	6.6
Hospice (b)	325.0	0.2
Prescription drugs	13,521.7	9.5
ICF (MR) services (c)	9,481.7	6.6
Other	44,684.5	31.3
Total payments (a)	**142,642.9**	**100.0**

Notes: (a) Total outlays include hospice outlays plus payments for all service types included, not just the eight service types listed. (b) Hospice outlays come from Form HCFA-64. The federal share of Medicaid's hospice spending is $185.7 million, or 57.1% of the total fiscal year 1998 Medicaid hospice payments. (c) ICF is intermediate care facilities.

SOURCE: "Table 9. Medicaid Payments, by Type of Service, FY98," in *Hospice Facts and Statistics,* Hospice Association of America, Washington, DC [Online] http://www.nahc.org/Consumer/hpcstats.html [Accessed March 26, 2002]

benefits. In 2000 only about 1.3 percent ($2.8 billion) of all Medicare benefit payments went to hospice care. The 2001 projected hospice spending is comparably small ($3.04 billion, or 1.3 percent of the projected $238 billion total Medicare expenditures). (See Table 9.7.)

Medicaid Hospice Benefits

Hospice services also comprise a small portion of Medicaid reimbursements. In 1998 Medicaid reimbursements comprised only 0.2 percent ($325 million) of the total $142.6 billion expenditures. (See Table 9.8.) Providing hospice care under Medicaid is optional for each state. In 1999, 43 states and the District of Columbia offered hospice benefits. (See Table 9.9.)

LONG-TERM HEALTH CARE

Longer life spans and life-sustaining technologies have created an increasing need for long-term care. For some older people, relatives provide the long-term care; however, those who require labor-intensive, round-the-clock care often stay in nursing homes.

Home Health Care

The concept of home health care began as post-acute care after hospitalization, an alternative to longer, costlier hospital stays. Home health care services have grown tremendously since the 1980s, when prospective payment for Medicare patients sharply reduced hospital lengths-of-stay.

In 1972 Medicare extended home care coverage to persons under 65 years of age only if they were disabled or suffered from end stage renal disease (ESRD). Prior to the year 2000, Medicare coverage for home health care was limited to patients immediately following discharge from the hospital. By the year 2000, Medicare covered beneficiaries' home health care services with no requirement for prior hospitalization. There were also no limits to the number of professional visits or to the length of coverage. As long as the patient's condition warranted it, the following services were provided:

- Part-time or intermittent skilled nursing and home health aide services.

- Speech-language pathology services.

- Physical and occupational therapy.

- Medical social services.

- Medical supplies.

- Durable medical equipment (with a 20 percent co-pay).

Over time, the population receiving home care services has changed. Today, much of home health care is associated with rehabilitation from critical illnesses, and fewer users are long-term patients with chronic conditions. Compared with acute care users, the long-term patients are older, more functionally disabled, and more likely to be incontinent.

In 1996, 48 percent of home health users received home health aide services and 42 percent received skilled nursing care. By 1999, home health aide visits dropped to 34 percent and skilled nursing rose to 49 percent. In 1999, the proportion of therapy visits nearly doubled, from 9 percent in 1996 to 16 percent. (See Figure 9.2.) This changing pattern of utilization reflects a shift from longer-term care for chronic conditions to short-term post-acute care.

From 1989 to 1997 annual Medicare spending for home health care rose 30 percent. Relaxed eligibility criteria for home health care, including elimination of the

TABLE 9.9

Number of states offering hospice under Medicaid, 1987–99

Year	Total Number	States Added	States Dropped
1987	6	FL, KY, MI, MN, ND, VT	
1988	15	DE, HI, IL, MA, NE, NY, NC, RI, TX, WI	MN
1989	24	AZ, CA, GA, ID, KS, MO, MT, PA, TN, UT	NE
1990	32	AL, AK, IA, MD, MN, NM, OH, VA, WA	TN
1991	34	CO, MS, TN	AK
1992	35	NJ	
1993	36	DC, WV	AZ
1994	38	OR, WY	
1995	40	AK, SC	
1996	41	AR	
1997	42	IN	
1998	44	AZ, NV	
1999	44		

SOURCE: "Table 10. Number of States Offering Hospice Under Medicaid, 1987-1999," in *Hospice Facts and Statistics,* Hospice Association of America, Washington, DC [Online] http://www.nahc.org/Consumer/hpcstats.html [Accessed March 26, 2002].

requirement of an acute hospitalization before receiving home care, enabled an increased number of beneficiaries to use services. Home health care utilization peaked in 1997 and began to decline during 1998. (See Table 9.10.)

MEDICARE LIMITS HOME CARE SERVICES. The Balanced Budget Act of 1997 (PL 105-33) aimed to cut approximately $16.2 billion from Medicare home care expenditures over a period of five years. The federal government sought to return home health care to its original concept of short-term care, plus skilled nursing and therapy services. According to Medicare's administrator, Nancy-Ann DeParle, some of the 4.8 million Medicare beneficiaries who received home health care would lose certain personal care services, such as assistance with bathing, dressing, and eating.

The Balanced Budget Act sharply curtailed the growth of home-care spending, greatly affecting health care providers. Annual Medicare home health care spending fell 32 percent between 1998 and 1999 in response to tightened eligibility requirements for skilled nursing services, limited per visit payments, and increasingly stringent claims review. (See Table 9.10.) The changes forced many agencies to close and transfer their patients to other home-health companies. Nationwide, it was estimated that 1,200 agencies went out of business during 1998.

Nursing Home Care

Growth of the home health care industry in the early 1990s is only partly responsible for the decline in the number of Americans entering nursing homes. Assisted living and continuing-care retirement communities offer other alternatives to nursing home care. When it is possible, many older adults prefer to remain in the community and receive health care in their homes. There is also a

FIGURE 9.2

Proportion of home health visits by visit type, 1996 and 1999

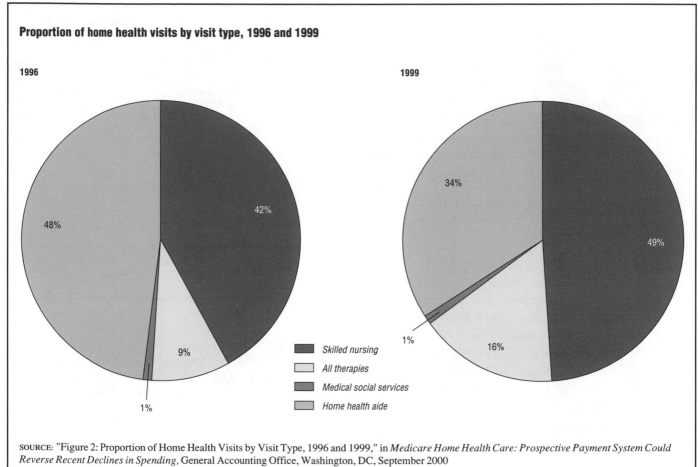

SOURCE: "Figure 2: Proportion of Home Health Visits by Visit Type, 1996 and 1999," in *Medicare Home Health Care: Prospective Payment System Could Reverse Recent Declines in Spending,* General Accounting Office, Washington, DC, September 2000

TABLE 9.10

History of Medicare home health care spending growth, 1985–99

Period	Annual spending rate	Significant change shaping service use
1985-88	1%	Tightened interpretation of coverage criteria; increased emphasis on medical review of home health claims.
1989-97	30%	Loosening of coverage criteria allowed more beneficiaries to receive more services.
1998-99	-32%	IPS limited per visit payments and limited aggregate agency payments; heightened scrutiny of claims; changed qualifying criteria for "skilled" services.

SOURCE: "Table 5. History of Medicare Home Health Care Spending Growth, 1985–99" in *Medicare Home Health Care: Prospective Payment System Could Reverse Recent Declines in Spending,* General Accounting Office, Washington, DC, September 2000.

FIGURE 9.3

Rate of home health care usage among persons 65 years of age and older, 1992–98

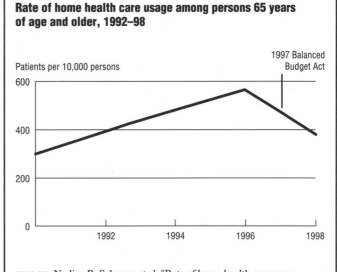

SOURCE: Nadine R. Sahyoun et al, "Rate of home health care usage among persons 65 years of age and older, 1992–1998," in "The Changing Profile of Nursing Home Residents: 1985–1997," in *Trends in Health and Aging,* Centers for Disease Control and Prevention, National Center for Health Statistics, Hyattsville, MD, no. 4, March 2001

---

trend toward healthy aging—more older adults are living longer with fewer disabilities. (See Figure 9.3.)

Still, in 1999 nearly 1.5 million adults age 65 and older were nursing home residents. Most were white (87.1 percent), female (74.2 percent), and more than half (51.5 percent) were 85 years and older. (See Table 9.11.)

Nursing homes provide terminally ill residents with end-of-life services in different ways:

• Caring for patients in the nursing home.

• Transferring patients who request it to hospitals or hospices.

• Contracting with hospices to provide palliative care (care that relieves the pain but does not cure the illness) within the nursing home.

A combination of federal, state, and private monies finance nursing home care. According to the Administration on Aging, in 2000 almost half of the funds came from Medicaid, one-third came from private payment, 10 percent from Medicare, and 5 percent from private insurance.

Patients in a Persistent Vegetative State

In the year 2002, the precise number of patients in a persistent vegetative state (PVS) remained unknown, as no system was in place to count them. However, the most recent estimates ("Persistent Vegetative State and the Decision to Withdraw or Withhold Life Support," *The Journal of the American Medical Association,* vol. 63, no. 3, January 19, 1990) are that there are approximately 15,000 to 25,000 PVS patients in the United States. The costs to maintain such patients range from $2,000 to $10,000 a month, depending on the acuity of care needed (the type, degree, or extent of required services).

The End Stage Renal Disease Program

End stage renal disease (ESRD) is the final phase of irreversible kidney disease, and requires either kidney transplantation or dialysis to maintain life. Dialysis is a medical procedure in which a machine takes over the function of the kidneys by removing waste products from the blood. Medicare beneficiaries with ESRD are high-cost users of Medicare services. In 1972 amendments to the Social Security Act extended Medicare coverage to include ESRD patients.

When the ESRD program was started in 1974, it cost Medicare $229 million. By 1995 (the most recent data available), expenses had risen to nearly $9.3 billion for 264,260 persons, or about 0.9 percent of all patients served by Medicare. This small percentage of patients accounted for about 5.8 percent of all Medicare reimbursements. In 1995 the average cost per ESRD patient was $35,154, approximately seven times higher than for beneficiaries without ESRD ($4,963).

By the year 2000 the fastest growing group of ESRD patients was persons over 65 years of age. The segment of Medicare beneficiaries with a disability or ESRD rose from 9.9 percent in 1977 to 12.7 percent in 1997. This group is projected to grow to 15.6 percent, or 8.8 million beneficiaries, by the year 2017. (See Figure 9.4.)

FIGURE 9.4

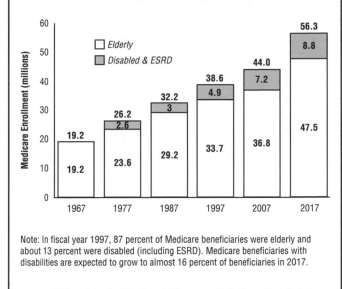

Growth in the number and percent of Medicare beneficiaries with disabilities or end stage renal disease, 1967–2017

Note: In fiscal year 1997, 87 percent of Medicare beneficiaries were elderly and about 13 percent were disabled (including ESRD). Medicare beneficiaries with disabilities are expected to grow to almost 16 percent of beneficiaries in 2017.

SOURCE: "Growth in the Number and Percent of Medicare Beneficiaries with Disabilities or End Stage Renal Disease, 1967–2017," in *A Profile of Medicare: Chart Book 1998,* Health Care Financing Administration, Baltimore, MD [Online] http://www.hcfa.gov/pubforms/chartbk.htm [Accessed April 23, 2002].

PATIENTS WITH TERMINAL DISEASES

Terminal patients often receive high-technology intensive care that simply prolongs the dying process. Studies by the HCFA (now the CMS) found that "medical services generally become much more intense as death approaches." In the United States, the fear of malpractice suits, physicians' training to fight death to the end, and government reimbursement encourage continued medical care at all costs.

Acquired Immunodeficiency Syndrome (AIDS)

The incidence of deaths due to acquired immunodeficiency syndrome (AIDS), the last stage of an infection caused by the human immunodeficiency virus (HIV), showed a marked decline from 1993 to 2000. However, AIDS continues to devastate the American population. As of June 2001 more than 784,000 cases of AIDS and 457,667 total deaths from the disease had been reported to the Centers for Disease Control and Prevention (CDC).

In 2000 the federal government spent $10.9 billion on research, education and prevention, medical care, and cash assistance for HIV/AIDS patients—a 53-fold increase over the $205 million spent in 1985. More than half (58 percent, or $6.3 billion) was spent on medical care. (See Table 9.12.) The per-person cost of AIDS medication was between $12,000 and $70,000 annually, depending on the patient's drug regimen. The costs of

TABLE 9.11

Nursing home residents 65 years of age and over, by selected characteristics, 1973–74, 1985, 1995, and 1999

[Data are based on a sample of nursing home residents]

Age, sex, and race	Residents				Residents per 1,000 population			
	1973–74	1985	1995	1999	1973–74	1985	1995	1999
Age								
65 years and over, age adjusted[1]	. . .	. . .	. . .	. . .	58.5	54.0	45.9	43.3
65 years and over, crude	961,500	1,318,300	1,422,600	1,469,500	44.7	46.2	42.4	42.9
65–74 years	163,100	212,100	190,200	194,800	12.3	12.5	10.1	10.8
75–84 years	384,900	509,000	511,900	517,600	57.7	57.7	45.9	43.0
85 years and over	413,600	597,300	720,400	757,100	257.3	220.3	198.6	182.5
Male								
65 years and over, age adjusted[1]	. . .	. . .	. . .	. . .	42.5	38.8	32.8	30.6
65 years and over, crude	265,700	334,400	356,800	377,800	30.0	29.0	26.1	26.5
65–74 years	65,100	80,600	79,300	84,100	11.3	10.8	9.5	10.3
75–84 years	102,300	141,300	144,300	149,500	39.9	43.0	33.3	30.8
85 years and over	98,300	112,600	133,100	144,200	182.7	145.7	130.8	116.5
Female								
65 years and over, age adjusted[1]	. . .	. . .	. . .	. . .	67.5	61.5	52.3	49.8
65 years and over, crude	695,800	983,900	1,065,800	1,091,700	54.9	57.9	53.7	54.6
65–74 years	98,000	131,500	110,900	110,700	13.1	13.8	10.6	11.2
75–84 years	282,600	367,700	367,600	368,100	68.9	66.4	53.9	51.2
85 years and over	315,300	484,700	587,300	612,900	294.9	250.1	224.9	210.5
White[2]								
65 years and over, age adjusted[1]	. . .	. . .	. . .	. . .	61.2	55.5	45.4	41.9
65 years and over, crude	920,600	1,227,400	1,271,200	1,279,600	46.9	47.7	42.3	42.1
65–74 years	150,100	187,800	154,400	157,200	12.5	12.3	9.3	10.0
75–84 years	369,700	473,600	453,800	440,600	60.3	59.1	44.9	40.5
85 years and over	400,800	566,000	663,000	681,700	270.8	228.7	200.7	181.8
Black[2]								
65 years and over, age adjusted[1]	. . .	. . .	. . .	. . .	28.2	41.5	50.4	55.6
65 years and over, crude	37,700	82,000	122,900	145,900	22.0	35.0	45.2	51.1
65–74 years	12,200	22,500	29,700	30,300	11.1	15.4	18.4	18.2
75–84 years	13,400	30,600	47,300	58,700	26.7	45.3	57.2	66.5
85 years and over	12,100	29,000	45,800	56,900	105.7	141.5	167.1	183.1

. . . Category not applicable.

[1] Age adjusted by the direct method to the year 2000 population standard using the following three age groups: 65–74 years, 75–84 years, and 85 years and over.

[2] Beginning in 1999 the instruction for the race item on the Current Resident Questionnaire was changed so that more than one race could be recorded. In previous years only one racial category could be checked. Estimates for racial groups presented in this table are for residents for whom only one race was recorded. Estimates for visits where multiple races were checked are unreliable due to small sample sizes and are not shown.

Notes: Excludes residents in personal care or domiciliary care homes. Age refers to age at time of interview. Rates are based on the resident population as of July 1. Starting in 1997, population figures are adjusted for net underenumeration using the 1990 National Population Adjustment Matrix from the U.S. Bureau of the Census. Data for additional years are available.

SOURCE: "Table 97. Nursing home residents 65 years of age and over, according to age, sex, and race: United States, 1973–74, 1985, 1995, and 1999," in *Health, United States, 2001,* Centers for Disease Control and Prevention, National Center for Health Statistics, National Vital Statistics System, Hyattsville, MD, 2001.

---

treatment are expected to increase in response to the rising costs of hospitalization, home health care, physician services, and insurance premiums and co-payments.

MEDICAID ASSISTANCE. The financing of health care for AIDS patients has increasingly become the responsibility of Medicaid, the entitlement program that provides medical assistance to low-income Americans. This is due, in large part, to the rising incidence of AIDS among poor people and intravenous drug users—groups least likely to have private health insurance. Further, many patients who might once have had private insurance through their employers lose their coverage when they become too ill to work. These individuals eventually turn to Medicaid and other public programs for medical assistance.

Some people, whose employment and economic condition previously afforded the insurance coverage they needed, find their situation changed once they test positive for HIV. Some may become virtually ineligible for private health insurance coverage. Others require government assistance because insurance companies can declare HIV infection a "pre-existing condition," making it ineligible for payment of insurance claims. In addition, some insurance companies limit AIDS coverage to relatively small amounts.

THE RYAN WHITE COMPREHENSIVE AIDS RESOURCES EMERGENCY (CARE) ACT. Currently, the CARE Act (PL101-381) is the only federal program providing funds specifically for medical and support services for

TABLE 9.12

Federal spending for human immunodeficiency virus (HIV)-related activities, according to agency and type of activity, selected fiscal years, 1985–2000

[Data are compiled from federal government appropriations]

Agency and type of activity	1985	1990	1995	1996	1997	1998	1999	2000[1]
Agency					Amount in millions			
All Federal spending	$205	$3,064	$6,821	$7,522	$8,363	$8,931	$9,966	$10,932
Department of Health and Human Services, total	197	2,620	4,941	5,598	6,367	6,835	7,694	8,488
Department of Health and Human Services discretionary spending, total[2]	109	1,591	2,700	2,898	3,267	3,535	4,094	4,588
National Institutes of Health	66	907	1,334	1,411	1,501	1,604	1,793	2,006
Substance Abuse and Mental Health Services Administration	–	50	24	54	64	70	92	114
Centers for Disease Control and Prevention	33	443	590	584	617	625	657	730
Food and Drug Administration	9	57	73	73	73	73	70	70
Health Resources and Services Administration	–	113	661	762	1,001	1,155	1,416	1,600
Agency for Health Care Policy and Research	–	8	9	6	4	1	2	3
Office of Public Health and Science[3]	–	8	4	4	4	4	12	12
Indian Health Service	–	3	4	3	4	4	4	4
Emergency Fund	...	...	...	...	...	...	50	50
Other Department of Health and Human Services agencies	–	3	2	2				
Health Care Financing Administration	75	780	2,240	2,700	3,100	3,300	3,600	3,900
Social Security Administration[4]	13	249	...	...	...	...	...	...
Social Security Administration[4]	...	...	940	976	1,001	1,061	1,149	1,177
Department of Veterans Affairs	8	220	317	331	332	343	401	457
Department of Defense	–	125	112	98	100	105	86	98
Agency for International Development	–	71	120	115	117	121	135	190
Department of Housing and Urban Development	–	–	171	171	196	204	225	232
Office of Personnel Management	–	21	212	226	241	253	266	27
Other departments	–	7	8	7	9	9	10	11
Activity								
Research	84	1,142	1,589	1,653	1,730	1,831	1,900	2,124
Department of Health and Human Services discretionary spending[2]	83	1,093	1,544	1,619	1,702	1,801	1,869	2,083
Department of Veterans Affairs	1	15	5	6	6	6	7	7
Department of Defense	–	34	40	28	22	24	24	34
Education and prevention	26	486	658	635	685	701	918	1,057
Department of Health and Human Services discretionary spending[2]	25	351	492	476	522	534	739	820
Department of Veterans Affairs	1	31	31	31	31	31	30	33
Department of Defense	–	28	12	11	12	13	10	10
Agency for International Development	–	71	120	115	117	121	135	190
Other	–	5	3	2	3	2	4	4
Medical care	81	1,187	3,462	4,087	4,752	5,134	5,775	6,342
Health Care Financing Administration:								
Medicaid (Federal share)	70	670	1,640	1,600	1,800	1,900	2,100	2,200
Medicare	5	110	600	1,100	1,300	1,400	1,500	1,700
Department of Health and Human Services discretionary spending[2]	–	144	664	803	1,044	1,200	1,487	1,685
Department of Veterans Affairs	6	174	281	294	295	306	364	417
Department of Defense	–	63	60	59	66	68	52	54
Office of Personnel Management	–	21	212	226	241	253	266	279
Other	–	5	5	5	6	7	6	7
Cash assistance	13	249	1,111	1,147	1,197	1,265	1,374	1,409
Social Security Administration:								
Disability Insurance	10	210	640	696	691	726	789	792
Supplemental Security Income	3	39	300	280	310	335	360	385
Department of Housing and Urban Development	–		171	171	196	204	225	232

– Quantity zero.
... Category not applicable.
[1] Preliminary figures.
[2] Department of Health and Human Services discretionary spending is spending that is not entitlement spending. Medicare and Medicaid are examples of entitlement spending.
[3] The Office of the Assistant Secretary for Health prior to fiscal year 1996.
[4] Prior to 1995 the Social Security Administration was part of the Department of Health and Human Services.

SOURCE: "Table 127. Federal spending for human immunodeficiency virus (HIV)-related activities, according to agency and type of activity: United States, selected fiscal years, 1985–2000," in *Health, United States, 2001*, Centers for Disease Control and Prevention, National Center for Health Statistics, National Vital Statistics System, Hyattsville, MD, 2001.

TABLE 9.13

Ryan White CARE (Comprehensive AIDS Emergency) Act Title I Grant Awards, 1993–2001

EMA	Fiscal year 1993	Fiscal year 1994	Fiscal year 1995	Fiscal year 1996	Fiscal year 1997	Fiscal year 1998	Fiscal year 1999	Fiscal year 2000	Fiscal year 2001
Atlanta GA	$5,490,571	$7,488,801	$9,091,331	$9,208,162	$12,632,117	$12,021,454	$13,147,268	$15,507,832	$15,992,692
Austin TX	N/E [1]	N/E	2,124,274	2,398,671	3,337,861	2,856,752	3,175,509	3,575,995	3,922,582
Baltimore MD	3,250,343	3,923,438	4,715,150	8,364,074	10,033,688	12,184,481	13,478,549	15,351,112	16,698,367
Bergen-Passaic NJ	N/E	2,019,121	2,847,639	3,369,095	4,292,593	4,354,291	4,320,176	4,626,995	5,234,104
Boston MA	4,154,744	6,955,035	7,079,242	8,360,436	9,033,443	9,463,130	10,647,381	12,469,255	15,363,160
Caguas PR	N/E	N/E	902,928	1,064,876	1,431,210	1,405,197	1,610,314	1,713,686	1,750,404
Chicago IL	7,390,763	9,625,451	12,099,865	13,164,930	15,741,071	15,995,512	18,227,884	19,003,954	22,963,079
Cleveland-Lorain-Elyria OH	N/E	N/E	N/E	1,384,956	1,877,513	2,459,443	2,933,058	3,107,796	3,384,855
Dallas TX	4,542,034	6,935,644	8,176,385	7,820,653	8,129,583	9,082,217	10,164,078	11,077,000	12,098,406
Denver CO	N/E	3,375,884	3,092,041	3,549,707	4,668,572	4,278,161	4,150,341	4,581,734	4,840,128
Detroit MI	2,091,739	2,849,559	2,406,902	4,405,380	6,087,121	5,628,350	6,585,744	7,234,813	7,612,631
Dutchess Co. NY	N/E	N/E	609,583	581,761	776,847	854,481	1,220,662	1,208,858	1,362,331
Ft. Lauderdale FL	4,591,215	6,814,599	5,091,994	6,584,204	8,312,185	10,128,631	10,810,324	11,437,539	13,816,037
Ft. Worth-Arlington TX	N/E	N/E	N/E	2,255,398	1,902,232	2,618,024	2,935,543	2,968,606	3,298,024
Hartford CT	N/E	N/E	N/E	3,048,467	2,661,473	3,613,029	4,019,409	4,417,574	4,868,180
Houston TX	7,820,319	10,133,592	10,233,981	10,312,524	10,768,697	12,722,479	15,489,996	17,665,434	19,283,756
Jacksonville FL	N/E	N/E	2,418,868	2,725,251	3,762,713	3,443,168	3,683,146	4,175,873	4,799,813
Jersey City NJ	3,618,220	4,140,141	3,770,366	3,767,874	4,600,103	5,320,300	5,015,785	5,541,714	6,167,889
Kansas City MO	N/E	2,655,564	2,726,195	2,514,291	2,884,537	2,622,409	2,952,910	3,064,120	3,386,127
Las Vegas NV [2]	0	0	0	0	0	0	3,402,697	3,689,337	4,455,787
Los Angeles CA	19,190,269	25,441,211	31,037,580	26,313,561	30,227,298	30,637,106	33,540,737	34,683,327	35,020,216
Miami FL	9,716,264	15,258,563	19,195,347	15,156,078	18,863,208	18,472,153	21,248,387	23,450,383	25,385,904
Middlesex Somerset-Hunterdon NJ	N/E	N/E	N/E	2,198,883	1,919,076	2,597,923	2,555,029	2,750,975	2,888,808
Minneapolis-St. Paul MN	N/E	N/E	N/E	1,370,726	1,990,700	2,570,712	2,548,603	2,826,949	3,216,026
Nassau-Suffolk NY	2,012,809	2,886,968	3,895,849	3,683,885	4,697,795	4,939,871	5,632,012	6,118,736	6,532,144
Newark NJ	3,542,848	7,009,180	11,791,405	9,725,848	11,612,530	12,630,257	14,390,269	14,554,092	16,254,538
New Haven CT	N/E	2,136,872	2,711,634	4,002,182	5,336,678	5,348,730	6,100,471	6,261,941	6,944,353
New Orleans LA	1,796,972	3,243,332	3,503,009	2,087,199	4,727,682	4,921,857	5,695,360	5,935,834	6,942,652
New York NY	44,469,219	100,054,267	93,587,184	92,241,697	92,459,373	95,325,334	96,961,856	107,560,148	119,256,891
Norfolk VA [2]	0	0	0	0	0	0	3,665,087	4,089,698	4,736,759
Oakland CA	2,602,816	3,929,287	4,148,299	4,741,595	5,905,961	5,926,194	6,218,532	6,704,657	6,776,406
Orange County CA	1,839,726	2,627,947	3,175,288	3,492,993	4,401,330	3,810,759	4,300,690	4,670,880	4,956,671
Orlando FL	N/E	2,715,587	3,194,835	3,599,489	4,319,349	4,609,839	4,907,180	6,007,600	6,497,014
Philadelphia PA	4,729,230	7,374,936	9,836,096	10,345,478	13,465,328	14,081,773	16,011,451	18,134,011	22,114,655
Phoenix AZ	N/E	2,217,471	2,447,784	2,901,602	3,380,053	3,412,037	3,865,319	5,001,568	6,575,645
Ponce PR	1,280,364	1,176,793	1,908,071	1,685,036	2,183,463	2,200,114	2,487,768	2,460,695	2,607,961
Portland OR	N/E	N/E	2,402,734	2,688,924	3,472,480	3,057,466	3,115,251	3,216,312	3,513,044
Riverside-San Bernardino CA	N/E	2,402,010	2,656,331	4,687,432	5,986,979	5,634,427	6,463,388	6,913,948	6,940,381
Sacramento CA	N/E	N/E	N/E	2,463,814	2,038,827	2,389,370	2,578,873	2,744,171	2,899,765
St. Louis MO	N/E	2,248,247	2,581,330	2,587,364	3,506,350	3,561,850	3,664,771	4,239,080	4,432,316
San Antonio TX	N/E	N/E	1,731,222	2,396,426	3,014,191	2,952,239	3,014,654	3,163,374	3,862,398
San Diego CA	3,761,979	5,233,574	5,628,252	6,592,104	8,198,109	8,452,437	8,872,685	9,071,625	10,577,352
San Francisco CA	18,944,229	27,217,076	39,210,400	35,172,274	37,194,634	36,394,914	36,218,513	35,246,477	35,771,651
San Jose CA	N/E	N/E	N/E	2,275,044	1,992,602	2,445,480	2,486,136	2,612,060	2,866,655
San Juan PR	4,679,777	8,456,057	10,269,416	8,199,506	10,550,845	11,658,912	11,912,865	13,558,330	15,094,482
Santa Rosa-Petaluma CA	N/E	N/E	1,207,605	1,142,456	1,330,630	1,225,807	1,127,018	1,152,406	1,206,194
Seattle WA	2,824,570	3,233,903	4,048,484	4,289,545	5,481,431	5,060,533	5,303,343	5,488,688	5,852,286
Tampa-St. Petersburg FL	2,265,553	3,304,312	4,231,119	4,610,201	6,548,952	6,536,189	7,236,728	8,016,131	8,595,830
Vineland- Millville-Bridgeton NJ	N/E	N/E	340,644	454,338	677,001	594,001	688,648	684,897	807,157
Washington DC	7,447,578	9,328,712	10,713,183	12,763,696	15,838,868	16,710,726	18,322,558	19,903,750	24,507,346
West Palm Beach FL	N/E	3,582,542	3,770,641	3,390,914	5,122,618	5,965,481	6,711,944	7,169,030	7,795,848
TOTALS	**$182,326,998**	**$319,989,000**	**$349,370,000**	**$372,141,000**	**$429,377,900**	**$445,176,000**	**$485,816,900**	**$526,811,000**	**$582,727,700**

[1] "N/E" means the EMA was "not eligible" to receive funding in that fiscal year.
[2] Fiscal year 1999 was the first year of Title I funding.
Note: Fiscal year 1991 total was $86,083,000; Fiscal year 1992 $119,426,000.

SOURCE: "Ryan White CARE Act Title I Grant Awards," Health Resource and Services Administration, HIV/AIDS Bureau, Rockville, MD, 2001 [Online] ftp://ftp.hrsa.gov/hab/fundinghistory.pdf [Accessed April 26, 2002].

HIV/AIDS patients. It was initially passed in 1990 and was reauthorized in 1996 and 2000. Appropriations of CARE funds follow four formulas:

• Under the Title I formula, the federal government provides emergency assistance to metropolitan areas disproportionately affected by the HIV epidemic. To qualify for Title I financing, eligible metropolitan areas (EMAs) must have more than 2,000 cumulative AIDS cases reported during the preceding five years and a population of at least 500,000. In fiscal year (FY) 2001, 51 EMAs in 21 states, the District of

TABLE 9.14

Ryan White CARE (Comprehensive AIDS Emergency) Act Title II Grant Awards, 1991–2000

State	Fiscal Year 1991 - Fiscal Year 1995	Fiscal Year 1996 Total	Fiscal Year 1997 Total	Fiscal Year 1998 Total	Fiscal Year 1999 Total	Fiscal Year 2000 Formula	Fiscal Year 2000 ADAP*	Fiscal Year 2000 Total
Alabama	$4,829,350	$2,756,823	$4,167,971	$5,110,076	$7,294,833	$3,584,510	$4,639,040	$8,223,550
Alaska	500,000	288,443	362,917	444,562	593,491	280,996	363,662	644,658
Arizona	5,707,125	2,260,259	3,496,214	4,553,503	6,281,940	2,639,155	5,237,395	7,876,550
Arkansas	2,819,849	1,369,814	2,050,008	2,505,494	3,313,331	1,625,526	2,103,741	3,729,267
California	101,736,257	36,282,354	57,920,029	73,677,524	95,937,546	32,537,743	74,056,285	106,594,028
Colorado	6,273,190	2,509,154	3,734,969	4,614,053	5,755,742	2,126,738	4,375,239	6,501,977
Connecticut	7,398,150	3,651,778	6,120,430	8,267,209	11,422,933	3,778,961	8,694,101	12,473,062
Delaware	1,655,026	1,259,006	1,942,410	2,429,055	3,065,717	1,501,219	1,942,863	3,444,082
Dist. of Columbia	8,609,687	3,332,588	5,490,772	7,719,573	11,009,761	3,508,473	8,700,340	12,208,813
Florida	62,624,900	25,220,349	41,314,996	53,845,136	73,482,287	27,331,222	56,820,710	84,151,932
Georgia	17,635,309	7,394,151	12,340,139	16,211,799	21,473,723	8,397,826	16,211,619	24,609,445
Hawaii	2,113,003	1,180,678	1,701,733	1,933,618	2,425,061	1,183,240	1,531,338	2,714,578
Idaho	568,982	285,657	362,917	444,562	581,700	278,034	359,828	637,862
Illinois	19,658,478	7,260,236	12,033,969	15,478,545	21,516,441	7,348,535	16,392,905	23,741,440
Indiana	5,035,921	2,762,555	4,301,051	5,362,040	7,161,199	3,405,664	4,407,580	7,813,244
Iowa	1,157,658	613,264	917,406	1,104,116	1,450,320	696,217	901,037	1,597,254
Kansas	2,000,328	1,050,840	1,565,364	1,888,481	2,407,272	1,049,083	1,631,556	2,680,639
Kentucky	2,458,912	1,344,978	2,078,323	2,882,026	4,075,831	2,039,702	2,639,763	4,679,465
Louisiana	10,104,144	4,080,447	6,969,329	9,199,630	13,072,061	5,384,296	9,275,299	14,659,595
Maine	810,055	536,845	719,201	806,854	970,811	459,028	594,070	1,053,098
Maryland	14,021,974	6,521,685	10,948,524	14,847,982	20,672,553	7,081,339	16,544,049	23,625,388
Massachusetts	12,364,148	4,836,051	7,528,256	9,780,533	12,626,775	4,796,709	10,338,436	15,135,145
Michigan	9,295,185	3,897,084	5,814,246	7,690,514	10,452,742	4,063,406	7,773,145	11,836,551
Minnesota	3,220,768	1,249,617	1,878,085	2,365,346	2,995,477	1,057,229	2,371,809	3,429,038
Mississippi	3,479,363	1,868,450	2,760,714	3,623,766	4,995,545	2,589,467	3,351,265	5,940,732
Missouri	9,053,788	3,131,126	4,586,448	5,952,010	7,811,393	2,899,468	5,943,296	8,842,764
Montana	456,197	129,912	201,037	375,524	477,324	250,000	243,995	493,995
Nebraska	923,095	506,277	733,358	931,421	1,206,634	594,386	769,249	1,363,635
Nevada	3,194,245	2,049,946	3,001,392	3,898,380	4,647,952	1,598,090	3,364,738	4,962,828
New Hampshire	642,850	332,092	529,197	651,190	861,790	317,246	610,476	927,722
New Jersey	29,042,291	13,135,111	21,380,789	28,345,926	37,702,846	12,815,241	27,947,200	40,762,441
New Mexico	1,682,335	882,641	1,183,568	1,687,316	2,476,155	1,169,997	1,514,200	2,684,197
New York	103,550,023	38,324,520	64,354,160	87,884,362	127,095,837	42,636,690	95,825,514	138,462,204
North Carolina	8,016,460	4,810,589	7,053,271	8,657,402	11,672,934	5,810,860	7,526,237	13,337,097
North Dakota	419,872	107,243	124,390	145,189	175,060	100,000	83,474	183,474
Ohio	9,109,982	4,668,106	7,316,497	8,953,866	11,834,654	5,120,326	7,742,270	12,862,596
Oklahoma	3,581,484	1,656,387	2,282,191	2,890,518	3,902,893	1,867,782	2,417,266	4,285,048
Oregon	4,318,167	1,684,631	2,749,308	3,438,455	4,333,257	1,603,248	3,119,691	4,722,939
Pennsylvania	17,227,187	7,991,467	12,944,947	16,937,81	23,632,455	9,309,084	17,587,661	26,896,745
Rhode Island	1,585,172	1,083,242	1,548,831	1,843,025	2,354,312	1,122,008	1,452,093	2,574,101
South Carolina	7,019,356	4,516,376	6,622,883	8,161,966	10,934,388	5,775,847	7,475,048	13,250,895
South Dakota	500,000	112,536	138,843	161,507	205,084	101,714	131,638	233,352
Tennessee	5,770,766	3,757,915	5,736,623	7,230,546	9,818,153	4,998,883	6,469,509	11,468,392
Texas	44,589,664	16,132,517	25,697,515	35,149,403	50,244,224	18,736,047	38,195,998	56,932,045
Utah	1,677,559	810,043	1,251,524	1,542,931	2,083,114	1,057,785	1,368,976	2,426,761
Vermont	503,727	279,529	342,140	404,394	488,047	250,000	260,156	510,156
Virginia	8,798,087	5,365,718	8,116,678	10,452,242	13,099,292	5,277,831	9,567,364	14,845,195
Washington	8,192,474	3,154,250	4,898,005	6,404,980	8,333,780	3,036,562	5,983,248	9,019,810
West Virginia	774,743	446,290	740,356	937,140	1,422,541	616,555	846,071	1,462,626
Wisconsin	3,429,155	1,840,433	2,579,528	3,054,537	3,812,983	1,847,729	2,394,773	4,242,502
Wyoming	444,037	113,650	137,940	169,038	196,506	100,000	105,536	205,536
Guam	16,937	4,970	11,608	11,052	19,652	16,916	21,893	38,809
Puerto Rico	31,723,832	9,376,181	12,920,475	16,793,353	23,401,013	8,248,605	17,399,027	25,647,632
Virgin Islands	170,167	157,300	191,323	222,010	624,305	290,702	376,020	667,110
Totals	**$612,491,414**	**$250,405,164**	**$397,895,000**	**$520,074,000**	**$709,904,300**	**$266,314,000**	**$528,000,000**	**$794,314,000**

*AIDS Drug Assistance Program.

SOURCE: "Ryan White CARE Act Title II Grant Awards," Health Resource and Services Administration, HIV/AIDS Bureau, Rockville, MD, 2001 [Online] ftp://ftp.hrsa.gov/hab/fundinghistory.pdf [accessed April 20, 2002]

Columbia, and Puerto Rico received almost $583 million. (See Table 9.13.)

• Under the Title II formula, funds are provided to state governments. Ninety percent of Title II funds are allo-

cated based on AIDS patient counts, while 10 percent are distributed through competitive grants to public and nonprofit agencies. Since FY 1991, states have received nearly $3.3 billion. In addition, states receive funding to support AIDS Drug Assistance Programs

FIGURE 9.5

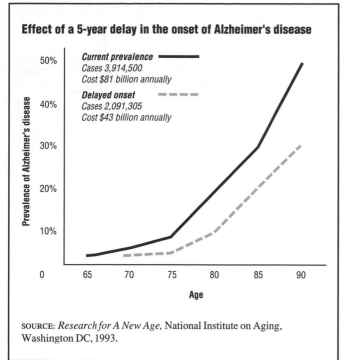

Effect of a 5-year delay in the onset of Alzheimer's disease

Current prevalence
Cases 3,914,500
Cost $81 billion annually

Delayed onset
Cases 2,091,305
Cost $43 billion annually

SOURCE: *Research for A New Age,* National Institute on Aging, Washington DC, 1993.

(ADAPs). ADAPs provide medication to low-income HIV patients who are uninsured or underinsured. In 2000 alone, the federal government provided $528 million for ADAPs funds and more than $266 million for improved health care and support services for HIV/AIDS patients, totaling over $794 million. (See Table 9.14.)

• Title III funds are designated for Early Intervention Services (EIS) and Planning. EIS grants support outpatient HIV services for low-income people in existing primary care systems, and Planning grants aid those working to develop HIV primary care.

• Title IV programs focus on the development of assistance for women, infants, and children.

Cancer

Cancer, in all its forms, is very expensive to treat. Compared with other diseases, there are more options for cancer treatment, more adverse side effects that require treatment, and a greater potential for unrelieved pain. According to the American Cancer Society, hospitalization accounts for about 76 percent of cancer expenditures, while physician and other medical fees account for 18 percent.

Generally, the younger a cancer patient is, the higher the treatment cost. Younger people often fight the disease longer than older people. Most of these expenses occur at the end of life. Hospitalization for the initial phase of treatment costs only 38 percent as much as terminal care. In addition, physician charges for terminal care may be as much as three times higher than charges for initial treatment.

Some experts claim that if more cancer patients were offered hospice care or made advance directives limiting futile treatment—especially high-technology medical interventions—the costs of end-of-life cancer care would be dramatically reduced.

MEDICARE, CLINICAL TRIALS, AND CANCER. Historically, younger patients have had greater access to the newest experimental drugs or procedures, in part because some health plans have been willing to cover all or a portion of the costs associated with clinical trials (research studies that offer promising new anti-cancer drugs and treatment to patients enrolled). Policies vary, and some plans decide whether they will pay for clinical trials on a case-by-case basis. Some health plans limit coverage to patients for whom no standard therapy is available. Others cover clinical trials only if they are not much more expensive than standard treatment, and many choose not to cover any costs involved with clinical trials.

On June 7, 2000, President Bill Clinton revised Medicare payment policies to enable beneficiaries to participate in clinical trials. Prior to this policy change, many older adults were prevented from participating in clinical trials because they could not afford the costs associated with the trials.

Alzheimer's Disease

According to the National Institute on Aging (NIA), about 4 million Americans currently suffer from some form of dementia (conditions characterized by memory loss, behavior and personality changes, and decreasing thinking abilities), and at least 360,000 new cases will occur each year. Care and treatment of persons suffering from dementia costs the United States as much as $100 billion each year. NIA researchers, while hoping to ultimately eliminate Alzheimer's disease (the single-most common cause of dementia), are currently investigating ways to delay the onset of debilitating symptoms. A five-year delay in the onset of Alzheimer's disease decreases the prevalence of the disease, reducing suffering and health care costs. (See Figure 9.5.)

THE COST OF DYING IN AMERICA

According to the Alliance for Aging Research, in *Seven Deadly Myths: Uncovering the Facts About the High Cost of the Last Year of Life* (Washington, D.C., 1997), there are several misconceptions about the cost of health care for older adults at the end of life:

• Contrary to popular belief, older people do not generally receive heroic, high-technology medical treatments at the end of life. Only 3 percent of terminally ill Medicare patients receive costly, aggressive care. Furthermore, the older the patient, the less likely he or she is to receive aggressive care when dying.

- A majority of older adults do not die in hospitals. The percentage of the elderly dying in hospitals decreases with age. In fact, the SUPPORT researchers, who conducted the largest-ever study of the care of critically ill and dying patients, found that estimated hospital costs for patients 80 and older were approximately $7,000 lower than for patients under the age of 50.

- It is commonly assumed that aggressive care for older adults is futile and a waste of money, since they are going to die anyway. Medicare data show that of patients who incur the most expenses, half die and the other half survive.

- Advance directives do not guarantee that physicians will honor patients' end-of-life preferences. Advance directives may be of limited usefulness if they are written in vague terms and lack specificity. For example, physicians may be reluctant to withhold a specific life-prolonging measure if a patient's advance directive simply states a preference not to prolong dying. Further, when physicians are unable or reluctant to accurately predict when patients are near the end of life, they may be unwilling to comply with advance directives.

- Limiting end-of-life care for the elderly does not save significantly on Medicare costs. While data reveal that 27 to 30 percent of Medicare expenditures are for terminal care, the approximately 3 percent of high-cost Medicare patients account for less than 1 percent of total annual health care costs.

- The aging of America has not yet become a major factor in the rising cost of health care. HCFA analysts found that general price inflation and health sector-specific inflation have been responsible for increased health care costs. In fact, the HCFA projects that between 1965 and 2005, the growing elderly group will add less than 1 percent to the annual growth of personal health care costs. They predict that only after 2010, when baby boomers start turning 65, will aging be a major factor in health care spending.

- The Alliance observes that both the popular media and academic literature tend to associate America's aging with economic disasters. Cross-cultural studies indicate that countries such as Japan, which has experienced a dramatic rise in the aging population, show no parallel increase in health care spending.

While all of these are promising findings, it is as grave a mistake to underestimate the challenge posed by population aging as it is to depict it as an inevitable disaster. One of the most important tasks now is to address the crucial issues surrounding optimal health care services and health care costs at the end of life, while there is still time to develop effective interventions. It is critical that we conduct the research, gather the data, and develop policies and practices for end-of-life care based on evidence and ethics rather than misconceptions.

CHAPTER 10

OLDER ADULTS

THE LONGEVITY REVOLUTION

The United States is on the threshold of a "longevity revolution." Dr. Robert N. Butler, the first director of the National Institute of Aging and chairman of the International Longevity Center, observed that during the twentieth century, life expectancy rose further and faster than during the entire period from ancient Rome (275 B.C.E., when life expectancy was about 26 years) through the year 1900.

The combination of better sanitation (safe drinking water, food, and disposal of waste), improved medical care, and reduced death rates for infants, children, and young adults accounts for this tremendous increase. Life expectancy in the United States in 1900 was 49 years; by 1971 this life expectancy had increased to almost 69 years. In *Putting Aging on Hold: Delaying the Diseases of Old Age* (1995), the American Federation for Aging Research and the Alliance for Aging Research projected that for persons born in the year 2000, life expectancy, with optimal nutrition and exercise, would be 85 years.

THE AGING OF AMERICA

As of 2000 there were 35 million people in the United States 65 years and older, comprising nearly 13 percent of the population. The Alliance for Aging Research (AAR) calculated that every day during 2002, approximately 6,000 people in the United States will celebrate their sixty-fifth birthday. From just 4 percent of the total population in 1900, those 65 years of age and older are projected to account for 20 percent of the population, or 79 million people, in the year 2050. (See Table 10.1 and Table 10.2.)

Baby Boomers

Children born during the post-World War II "baby boom" (1946–64) will begin turning 65 in the year 2011.

TABLE 10.1

Population by age, 1990–2050
[In thousands. As of July 1. Resident population]

Year	Total	Under 5 years	5 to 13 years	14 to 17 years	18 to 24 years	25 to 34 years	35 to 44 years	45 to 64 years	65 years and over	85 years and over	100 years and over
Estimate											
1990	249,402	18,849	31,996	13,311	26,826	43,139	37,766	46,280	31,235	3,057	37
Projections **Middle series**											
1995	262,820	19,591	34,378	14,773	24,926	40,863	42,514	52,231	33,543	3,634	54
2000	274,634	18,987	36,043	15,752	26,258	37,233	44,659	60,992	34,709	4,259	72
2005	285,981	19,127	35,850	16,986	28,268	36,306	42,165	71,113	36,166	4,899	101
2010	297,716	20,012	35,605	16,894	30,138	38,292	38,521	78,848	39,408	5,671	131
2020	322,742	21,979	38,660	16,965	29,919	42,934	39,612	79,454	53,220	6,460	214
2030	346,899	23,066	41,589	18,788	31,826	42,744	44,263	75,245	69,379	8,455	324
2040	369,980	24,980	43,993	19,844	34,570	45,932	44,159	81,268	75,233	13,552	447
2050	393,931	27,106	47,804	21,207	36,333	49,365	47,393	85,862	78,859	18,223	834

SOURCE: Jennifer Cheesman Day, "Population by Age, 1990–2050" in *Population Projections of the United States by Age, Sex, Race, and Hispanic Origin: 1995–2050* U.S. Bureau of the Census, Washington, DC, 1996.

TABLE 10.2

Percent distribution of the population by age, 1990–2050

[In percent. As of July 1. Resident population]

Year	Total	Under 5 years	5 to 13 years	14 to 17 years	18 to 24 years	25 to 34 years	35 to 44 years	45 to 64 years	65 years and over	85 years and over	100 years and over
Estimate											
1990	100.0	7.6	12.8	5.3	10.8	17.3	15.1	18.6	12.5	1.2	0.0
Projections											
Middle series											
1995	100.0	7.5	13.1	5.6	9.5	15.5	16.2	19.9	12.8	1.4	0.0
2000	100.0	6.9	13.1	5.7	9.6	13.6	16.3	22.2	12.6	1.6	0.0
2005	100.0	6.7	12.5	5.9	9.9	12.7	14.7	24.9	12.6	1.7	0.0
2010	100.0	6.7	12.0	5.7	10.1	12.9	12.9	26.5	13.2	1.9	0.0
2020	100.0	6.8	12.0	5.3	9.3	13.3	12.3	24.6	16.5	2.0	0.1
2030	100.0	6.6	12.0	5.4	9.2	12.3	12.8	21.7	20.0	2.4	0.1
2040	100.0	6.8	11.9	5.4	9.3	12.4	11.9	22.0	20.3	3.7	0.1
2050	100.0	6.9	12.1	5.4	9.2	12.5	12.0	21.8	20.0	4.6	0.2

SOURCE: Jennifer Cheesman Day, "Percent Distribution of the Population by Age, 1990–2050" in *Population Projections of the United States by Age, Sex, Race, and Hispanic Origin: 1995–2050,* U.S. Bureau of the Census, Washington, DC, 1996.

Baby boomers, the largest single generation in the history of the United States, will help swell the over-65 population to approximately 40 million in 2011. (See Table 10.1.)

The Oldest Old

Americans aged 85 and older account for the most rapidly growing age group in the population. Predictions vary as to how fast this "oldest old" segment of the population is increasing. In their official report to the White House Conference on Aging (*Putting Aging on Hold: Delaying the Diseases of Old Age,* 1995), the American Federation for Aging Research (AFAR) and the Alliance for Aging Research (AAR) concluded that predictions by the Bureau of the Census are quite conservative compared to those given by private entities.

The Census Bureau's mid-range prediction is that there will be between 18 and 19 million "oldest old" by the year 2050. (See Table 10.1.) Other demographers forecast more than twice the Census Bureau's estimated numbers of oldest old. They predict that by mid-century, as many as 48.7 million Americans will be over age 85. Even the Census Bureau's high-range predictions allow that there might be 27.3 million people 85 and over in the U.S. by 2050.

LEADING CAUSES OF DEATH AMONG THE ELDERLY

More than six out of every ten persons aged 65 and over died from heart attacks (diseases of the heart), cancer (malignant neoplasms), or stroke (cerebrovascular diseases) in 1999. (See Table 10.3.)

Coronary Heart Disease

Coronary heart disease (CHD) is the leading cause of death in the United States, and remains the leading cause of death among older Americans. Approximately four out of five persons who die of CHD are aged 65 years and older. Generally, women have less incidence of heart disease than men do until they turn 65, at which point their numbers approach those of men. In 1999, 607,265 persons aged 65 and older died of heart disease. (See Table 10.3.) The risk of dying from heart disease increases greatly after age 65. The death rate from CHD in 1999 for those 75 to 84 years old (1,861.8 deaths per 100,000 population) was more than two and one-half times the rate for those 65 to 74 years old (709.5 per 100,000). For those 85 years and older, the death rate rose sharply to 6,032.5 deaths per 100,000 population. (See Table 10.4.)

Since the 1970s, deaths from heart disease have consistently declined. (See Table 10.4.) Several factors account for this, including better control of hypertension (high blood pressure) and cholesterol levels in the blood. The *Baltimore Longitudinal Study of Aging,* "America's longest running scientific examination of human aging," found that even at the end of life, high cholesterol continues to be a risk factor in heart disease. Changes in lifestyle, such as physical exercise and a healthy diet, help decrease the incidence of heart disease. The expanding use of trained mobile emergency personnel (paramedics) in most urban areas has also contributed to the decrease, and widespread use of cardiopulmonary resuscitation (CPR) and new drugs have increased the likelihood of surviving an initial heart attack.

Until the 1990s, almost all research on heart disease focused on white, middle-aged males. Experts agree that more research as well as prevention efforts should be directed toward women, racial and ethnic minorities, and older adults. Researchers recognize that post-menopausal women are at increased risk for heart disease. One in three women over age 65 suffers from heart disease. According to the American Heart Association, 38 percent of women

TABLE 10.3

Leading causes of death and numbers of deaths, according to age, 1980 and 1999

[Data are based on the National Vital Statistics System.]

Age and rank order	1980 Cause of death	Deaths	1999 Cause of death	Deaths
Under 1 year				
...	All causes	45,526	All causes	27,937
1	Congenital anomalies	9,220	Congenital malformations, deformations and chromosomal abnormalities	5,473
2	Sudden infant death syndrome	5,510	Disorders related to short gestation and low birthweight, not elsewhere classified	4,392
3	Respiratory distress syndrome	4,989	Sudden infant death syndrome	2,648
4	Disorders relating to short gestation and unspecified low birthweight	3,648	Newborn affected by maternal complications of pregnancy	1,399
5	Newborn affected by maternal complications of pregnancy	1,572	Respiratory distress of newborn	1,110
6	Intrauterine hypoxia and birth asphyxia	1,497	Newborn affected by complications of placenta, cord and membranes	1,025
7	Unintentional injuries	1,166	Unintentional injuries	845
8	Birth trauma	1,058	Bacterial sepsis of newborn	691
9	Pneumonia and influenza	1,012	Diseases of circulatory system	667
10	Newborn affected by complications of placenta, cord, and membranes	985	Atelectasis	647
1–4 years				
....	All causes	8,187	All causes	5,249
1	Unintentional injuries	3,313	Unintentional injuries	1,898
2	Congenital anomalies	1,026	Congenital malformations, deformations and chromosomal abnormalities	549
3	Malignant neoplasms	573	Malignant neoplasms	418
4	Diseases of heart	338	Assault (homicide)	376
5	Homicide	319	Diseases of heart	183
6	Pneumonia and influenza	267	Influenza and pneumonia	130
7	Meningitis	223	Certain conditions originating in the perinatal period	92
8	Meningococcal infection	110	Septicemia	87
9	Certain conditions originating in the perinatal period	84	In situ neoplasms, benign neoplasms and neoplasms of uncertain or unknown behavior	63
10	Septicemia	71	Chronic lower respiratory diseases	54
5–14 years				
...	All causes	10,689	All causes	7,595
1	Unintentional injuries	5,224	Unintentional injuries	3,091
2	Malignant neoplasms	1,497	Malignant neoplasms	1,012
3	Congenital anomalies	561	Assault (homicide)	432
4	Homicide	415	Congenital malformations, deformations and chromosomal abnormalities	428
5	Diseases of heart	330	Diseases of heart	277
6	Pneumonia and influenza	194	Suicide	244
7	Suicide	142	Chronic lower respiratory diseases	139
8	Benign neoplasms	104	In situ neoplasms, benign neoplasms, and neoplasms of uncertain or unknown behavior	101
9	Cerebrovascular diseases	95	Influenza and pneumonia	93
10	Chronic obstructive pulmonary diseases	85	Septicemia	77
15–24 years				
...	All causes	49,027	All causes	30,656
1	Unintentional injuries	26,206	Unintentional injuries	13,656
2	Homicide	6,537	Assault (homicide)	4,998
3	Suicide	5,239	Suicide	3,901
4	Malignant neoplasms	2,683	Malignant neoplasms	1,724
5	Diseases of heart	1,223	Diseases of heart	1,069
6	Congenital anomalies	600	Congenital malformations, deformations and chromosomal abnormalities	434
7	Cerebrovascular diseases	418	Chronic lower respiratory diseases	209
8	Pneumonia and influenza	348	Human immunodeficiency virus (HIV) disease	198
9	Chronic obstructive pulmonary diseases	141	Cerebrovascular diseases	182
10	Anemias	133	Influenza and pneumonia	179

Death and Dying

TABLE 10.3

Leading causes of death and numbers of deaths, according to age, 1980 and 1999 [CONTINUED]

[Data are based on the National Vital Statistics System.]

Age and rank order	1980 Cause of death	Deaths	1999 Cause of death	Deaths
25–44 years				
...	All causes	108,658	All causes	130,322
1	Unintentional injuries	26,722	Unintentional injuries	27,121
2	Malignant neoplasms	17,551	Malignant neoplasms	20,734
3	Diseases of heart	14,513	Diseases of heart	16,666
4	Homicide	10,983	Suicide	11,572
5	Suicide	9,855	Human immunodeficiency virus (HIV) disease	8,961
6	Chronic liver disease and cirrhosis	4,782	Assault (homicide)	7,437
7	Cerebrovascular diseases	3,154	Chronic liver disease and cirrhosis	3,709
8	Diabetes mellitus	1,472	Cerebrovascular diseases	3,154
9	Pneumonia and influenza	1,467	Diabetes mellitus	2,524
10	Congenital anomalies	817	Influenza and pneumonia	1,402
45–64 years				
...	All causes	425,338	All causes	391,953
1	Diseases of heart	148,322	Malignant neoplasms	135,748
2	Malignant neoplasms	135,675	Diseases of heart	99,161
3	Cerebrovascular diseases	19,909	Unintentional injuries	18,924
4	Unintentional injuries	18,140	Cerebrovascular diseases	15,215
5	Chronic liver disease and cirrhosis	16,089	Chronic lower respiratory diseases	14,407
6	Chronic obstructive pulmonary diseases	11,514	Diabetes mellitus	13,832
7	Diabetes mellitus	7,977	Chronic liver disease and cirrhosis	12,005
8	Suicide	7,079	Suicide	7,977
9	Pneumonia and influenza	5,804	Human immunodeficiency virus (HIV) disease	5,056
10	Homicide	4,019	Septicemia	4,399
65 years and over				
...	All causes	1,341,848	All causes	1,797,331
1	Diseases of heart	595,406	Diseases of heart	607,265
2	Malignant neoplasms	258,389	Malignant neoplasms	390,122
3	Cerebrovascular diseases	146,417	Cerebrovascular diseases	148,599
4	Pneumonia and influenza	45,512	Chronic lower respiratory diseases	108,112
5	Chronic obstructive pulmonary diseases	43,587	Influenza and pneumonia	57,282
6	Atherosclerosis	28,081	Diabetes mellitus	51,843
7	Diabetes mellitus	25,216	Alzheimer's disease	44,020
8	Unintentional injuries	24,844	Unintentional injuries	32,219
9	Nephritis, nephrotic syndrome, and nephrosis	12,968	Nephritis, nephrotic syndrome and nephrosis	29,938
10	Chronic liver disease and cirrhosis	9,519	Septicemia	24,626

... Category not applicable.

Notes: Cause of death code numbers in 1980 are based on the *International Classification of Diseases, 9th Revision* (ICD–9). Starting in 1999 cause of death code numbers are based on ICD–10.

SOURCE: "Leading causes of death and numbers of deaths, according to age: United States, 1980 and 1999" in *Health United States, 2001,* Centers for Disease Control and Prevention, National Center for Health Statistics, National Vital Statistics System, Hyattsville, MD, 2001

who have heart attacks die within the first year, compared with only 25 percent of men.

Cancer

Cancer (malignant neoplasms) is the second leading cause of death among older adults. In 1999, 390,122 people aged 65 and older died of cancer. (See Table 10.3.) The risk of developing many cancers increases with age and varies by race and ethnicity. (See Table 10.5 and Table 10.6.)

For example, the older a man gets, the more likely he is to develop prostate cancer. The chance of a fatality from prostate cancer also rises with age. The American Cancer Society (*Cancer Facts & Figures 2002,* Atlanta, Georgia, 2002) reports that each year more than three-quarters of

men newly diagnosed with prostate cancer are more than 65 years old. The probability of developing prostate cancer is less than one in 10,000 men who are younger than 40, one in 48 for 40- to 59-year-olds, and one in 8 for men ages 60 to 79. (See Table 10.5.)

Stroke

Stroke (cerebrovascular diseases) is the third leading cause of death and the principal cause of serious disability among older adults, and its incidence increases markedly with age. In 1999, 148,599 persons aged 65 and older died of a stroke. (See Table 10.3.) In 1999 the death rate from stroke for those aged 65 to 74 years of age was 132.2 deaths per 100,000 population. This rate more than triples for each successive decade of age, to 472.8 deaths from stroke per 100,000 population for ages 75 to 84, and

TABLE 10.4

Death rates for diseases of the heart, according to sex, race, Hispanic origin, and age, selected years 1950–99

[Data Are Based On The National Vital Statistics System]

Sex, race, Hispanic origin, and age	1950[1]	1960[1]	1970	1980	1990	1995	1996	1997	1998	Comparability modified 1998	1999[2]
All persons					Deaths per 100,000 resident population						
All ages, age adjusted	586.8	559.0	492.7	412.1	321.8	296.3	288.3	280.4	272.4	268.5	267.8
All ages, crude	355.5	369.0	362.0	336.0	289.5	280.7	276.4	271.6	268.2	264.4	265.9
Under 1 year	3.5	6.6	13.1	22.8	20.1	17.1	16.6	16.4	16.1	15.9	13.7
1–4 years	1.3	1.3	1.7	2.6	1.9	1.6	1.4	1.4	1.4	1.4	1.2
5–14 years	2.1	1.3	0.8	0.9	0.9	0.8	0.9	0.8	0.8	0.8	0.7
15–24 years	6.8	4.0	3.0	2.9	2.5	2.9	2.7	3.0	2.8	2.8	2.8
25–34 years	19.4	15.6	11.4	8.3	7.6	8.5	8.3	8.3	8.3	8.2	8.1
35–44 years	86.4	74.6	66.7	44.6	31.4	32.0	30.5	30.1	30.5	30.1	30.3
45–54 years	308.6	271.8	238.4	180.2	120.5	111.0	108.2	104.9	101.4	100.0	97.7
55–64 years	808.1	737.9	652.3	494.1	367.3	322.9	315.2	302.4	286.9	282.8	274.3
65–74 years	1,839.8	1,740.5	1,558.2	1,218.6	894.3	799.9	776.2	753.7	735.5	725.1	709.5
75–84 years	4,310.1	4,089.4	3,683.8	2,993.1	2,295.7	2,064.7	2,010.2	1,943.6	1,897.3	1,870.4	1,861.8
85 years and over	9,150.6	9,317.8	7,891.3	7,777.1	6,739.9	6,484.1	6,314.5	6,198.9	6,009.6	5,924.3	6,032.5
Male											
All ages, age adjusted	697.0	687.6	634.0	538.9	412.4	372.7	360.7	349.6	336.6	331.8	328.1
All ages, crude	423.4	439.5	422.5	368.6	297.6	282.7	277.4	272.2	268.0	264.2	263.8
Under 1 year	4.0	7.8	15.1	25.5	21.9	17.5	17.4	18.0	16.2	16.0	13.8
1–4 years	1.4	1.4	1.9	2.8	1.9	1.7	1.4	1.5	1.5	1.5	1.3
5–14 years	2.0	1.4	0.9	1.0	0.9	0.8	0.9	0.9	1.0	1.0	0.8
15–24 years	6.8	4.2	3.7	3.7	3.1	3.6	3.3	3.6	3.5	3.5	3.4
25–34 years	22.9	20.1	15.2	11.4	10.3	11.4	11.0	10.8	10.8	10.6	10.6
35–44 years	118.4	112.7	103.2	68.7	48.1	47.2	44.2	43.7	44.0	43.4	43.3
45–54 years	440.5	420.4	376.4	282.6	183.0	168.6	161.8	157.7	152.2	150.0	145.7
55–64 years	1,104.5	1,066.9	987.2	746.8	537.3	465.4	453.8	434.6	411.1	405.3	391.6
65–74 years	2,292.3	2,291.3	2,170.3	1,728.0	1,250.0	1,102.3	1,065.0	1,031.1	997.3	983.1	961.6
75–84 years	4,825.0	4,742.4	4,534.8	3,834.3	2,968.2	2,615.0	2,529.4	2,443.6	2,377.2	2,343.4	2,308.9
85 years and over	9,659.8	9,788.9	8,426.2	8,752.7	7,418.4	7,039.6	6,834.0	6,658.5	6,330.6	6,240.7	6,313.3
Female											
All ages, age adjusted	484.7	447.0	381.6	320.8	257.0	239.7	234.1	228.1	223.1	219.9	220.9
All ages, crude	288.4	300.6	304.5	305.1	281.8	278.8	275.5	271.1	268.3	264.5	268.0
Under 1 year	2.9	5.4	10.9	20.0	18.3	16.7	15.7	14.7	16.1	15.9	13.6
1–4 years	1.2	1.1	1.6	2.5	1.9	1.5	1.4	1.2	1.3	1.3	1.1
5–14 years	2.2	1.2	0.8	0.9	0.8	0.7	0.8	0.7	0.7	0.7	0.6
15–24 years	6.7	3.7	2.3	2.1	1.8	2.2	2.0	2.4	2.1	2.1	2.2
25–34 years	16.2	11.3	7.7	5.3	5.0	5.6	5.6	5.8	5.8	5.7	5.6
35–44 years	55.1	38.2	32.2	21.4	15.1	17.1	16.8	16.5	17.3	17.1	17.6
45–54 years	177.2	127.5	109.9	84.5	61.0	56.0	56.9	54.3	52.8	52.1	51.9
55–64 years	510.0	429.4	351.6	272.1	215.7	193.9	189.3	182.1	173.9	171.4	167.5
65–74 years	1,419.3	1,261.3	1,082.7	828.6	616.8	557.8	543.8	529.4	522.6	515.2	503.2
75–84 years	3,872.0	3,582.7	3,120.8	2,497.0	1,893.8	1,715.2	1,674.7	1,616.6	1,579.5	1,557.1	1,562.5
85 years and over	8,796.1	9,016.8	7,591.8	7,350.5	6,478.1	6,267.8	6,108.0	6,013.7	5,876.6	5,793.2	5,913.8
White male											
All ages, age adjusted	700.2	694.5	640.2	539.6	409.2	368.4	358.2	346.9	333.2	328.5	324.7
All ages, crude	433.0	454.6	438.3	384.0	312.7	297.9	293.3	287.7	283.1	279.1	278.8
45–54 years	423.6	413.2	365.7	269.8	170.6	155.7	149.8	145.4	140.2	138.2	134.7
55–64 years	1,081.7	1,056.0	979.3	730.6	516.7	443.0	431.8	411.2	388.1	382.6	367.6
65–74 years	2,308.3	2,297.9	2,177.2	1,729.7	1,230.5	1,080.5	1,049.5	1,015.1	981.3	967.4	942.1
75–84 years	4,907.3	4,839.9	4,617.6	3,883.2	2,983.4	2,616.1	2,536.0	2,453.7	2,381.5	2,347.7	2,313.9
85 years and over	9,950.5	10,135.8	8,818.0	8,958.0	7,558.7	7,165.5	7,014.5	6,829.7	6,478.8	6,386.8	6,462.1
Black male											
All ages, age adjusted	639.4	615.2	607.3	561.4	485.4	449.2	426.3	414.0	407.8	402.0	398.9
All ages, crude	346.2	330.6	330.3	301.0	256.8	244.2	234.8	230.8	230.5	227.2	226.9
45–54 years	622.5	514.0	512.8	433.4	328.9	317.1	297.7	293.7	282.7	278.7	267.6
55–64 years	1,433.1	1,236.8	1,135.4	987.2	824.0	757.8	740.9	727.8	699.9	690.0	690.3
65–74 years	2,139.1	2,281.4	2,237.8	1,847.2	1,632.9	1,482.9	1,381.3	1,335.4	1,312.7	1,294.1	1,294.0
75–84 years[3]	4,106.1	3,533.6	3,783.4	3,578.8	3,107.1	2,881.4	2,762.0	2,641.6	2,649.3	2,611.7	2,560.2
85 years and over	- - -	6,037.9	5,367.6	6,819.5	6,479.6	5,985.7	5,675.4	5,538.7	5,446.7	5,369.4	5,433.3

TABLE 10.4

Death rates for diseases of the heart, according to sex, race, Hispanic origin, and age, selected years 1950–99 [CONTINUED]

[Data Are Based On The National Vital Statistics System]

Sex, race, Hispanic origin, and age	1950[1]	1960[1]	1970	1980	1990	1995	1996	1997	1998	Comparability modified 1998	1999[2]
American Indian or Alaska Native male[4]					Deaths per 100,000 resident population						
All ages, age adjusted	---	---	---	320.5	264.1	230.5	228.0	234.4	219.5	216.4	211.7
All ages, crude	---	---	---	130.6	108.0	110.4	110.7	116.8	113.2	111.6	109.7
45–54 years	---	---	---	238.1	173.8	151.4	157.5	171.8	151.8	149.6	131.8
55–64 years	---	---	---	496.3	411.0	403.2	404.9	427.2	402.5	396.8	346.3
65–74 years	---	---	---	1,009.4	839.1	918.5	778.0	828.1	793.6	782.3	866.1
75–84 years	---	---	---	2,062.2	1,788.8	1,534.9	1,546.5	1,513.8	1,274.0	1,255.9	1,428.4
85 years and over	---	---	---	4,413.7	3,860.3	2,308.7	2,660.1	2,764.2	2,800.9	2,761.1	2,181.3
Asian or Pacific Islander male[5]											
All ages, age adjusted	---	---	---	286.9	220.7	247.2	208.8	204.5	197.9	195.1	196.7
All ages, crude	---	---	---	119.8	88.7	96.9	97.3	97.4	98.3	96.9	99.2
45–54 years	---	---	---	112.0	70.4	73.4	75.4	72.1	72.9	71.9	64.0
55–64 years	---	---	---	306.7	226.1	214.3	220.7	218.3	210.8	207.8	202.8
65–74 years	---	---	---	852.4	623.5	605.8	581.2	585.1	522.7	515.3	523.1
75–84 years	---	---	---	2,010.9	,642.2	1,680.5	1,534.8	1,432.1	1,493.0	1,471.8	1,459.2
85 years and over	---	---	---	5,923.0	4,617.8	6,372.3	4,338.0	4,392.5	4,110.7	4,052.3	4,229.6
Hispanic male[6]											
All ages, age adjusted	---	---	---	---	270.0	246.8	232.8	223.9	213.8	210.8	212.7
All ages, crude	---	---	---	---	91.0	87.5	85.8	83.9	84.9	83.7	86.0
45–54 years	---	---	---	---	116.4	103.0	98.7	96.2	96.0	94.6	94.7
55–64 years	---	---	---	---	363.0	306.0	310.0	276.9	274.0	270.1	268.7
65–74 years	---	---	---	---	829.9	750.0	725.7	737.2	706.6	696.6	690.6
75–84 years	---	---	---	---	1,971.3	1,734.5	1,688.6	1,628.7	1,522.0	1,500.4	1,527.7
85 years and over	---	---	---	---	4,711.9	4,699.7	4,078.6	3,844.6	3,641.9	3,590.2	3,658.0
White, non-Hispanic male[6]											
All ages, age adjusted	---	---	---	---	413.6	370.6	362.0	351.9	338.3	333.5	329.5
All ages, crude	---	---	---	---	336.5	322.0	318.9	315.0	309.8	305.4	305.5
45–54 years	---	---	---	---	172.8	157.5	152.1	148.5	142.8	140.8	137.2
55–64 years	---	---	---	---	521.3	448.0	435.1	418.1	393.5	387.9	371.9
65–74 years	---	---	---	---	1,243.4	1,088.3	1,056.4	1,025.1	991.7	977.6	952.0
75–84 years	---	---	---	--	3,007.7	2,635.6	2,559.8	2,477.3	2,411.2	2,377.0	2,342.5
85 years and over	---	---	---	---	7,663.4	7,166.3	7,109.2	6,954.2	6,604.4	6,510.6	6,589.0
White female											
All ages, age adjusted	478.0	441.7	376.7	315.9	250.9	233.6	228.6	222.9	217.6	214.5	215.5
All ages, crude	289.4	306.5	313.8	319.2	298.4	297.4	294.2	289.8	286.8	282.7	286.6
45–54 years	141.9	103.4	91.4	71.2	50.2	45.9	46.9	44.9	43.4	42.8	42.8
55–64 years	460.2	383.0	317.7	248.1	192.4	173.1	167.8	162.5	153.9	151.7	149.5
65–74 years	1,400.9	1,229.8	1,044.0	796.7	583.6	526.3	515.1	500.7	493.8	486.8	474.3
75–84 years	3,925.2	3,629.7	3,143.5	2,493.6	1,874.3	1,689.8	1,652.9	1,595.9	1,556.3	1,534.2	1,534.8
85 years and over	9,084.7	9,280.8	7,839.9	7,501.6	6,563.4	6,352.6	6,211.4	6,108.0	5,971.4	5,886.6	6,006.4
Black female											
All ages, age adjusted	536.9	488.9	435.6	378.6	327.5	309.3	302.4	294.7	291.9	287.8	290.5
All ages, crude	287.6	268.5	261.0	249.7	237.0	231.1	229.0	224.2	224.6	221.4	224.0
45–54 years	525.3	360.7	290.9	202.4	155.3	143.1	144.7	134.8	132.9	131.0	128.3
55–64 years	1,210.2	952.3	710.5	530.1	442.0	384.9	388.4	364.8	361.5	356.4	336.1
65–74 years	1,659.4	1,680.5	1,553.2	1,210.3	1,017.5	933.7	890.0	871.6	858.8	846.6	832.7
75–84 years[3]	3,499.3	2,926.9	2,964.1	2,707.2	2,250.9	2,163.1	2,097.7	2,030.5	2,044.8	2,015.8	2,070.1
85 years and over	---	5,650.0	5,003.8	5,796.5	5,766.1	5,614.8	5,493.6	5,542.5	5,373.1	5,296.8	5,525.6

1,606.7 deaths per 100,000 population for those 85 years of age and older. (See Table 10.7.)

Stroke is also responsible for late-life dementia, which, together with Alzheimer's disease, accounts for 90 percent of all dementia (the other 10 percent are reversible dementias caused by conditions such as head injury, alcoholism, and pernicious anemia). While death rates from stroke have declined since the 1960s, approximately one-third of stroke survivors suffer severe disabilities and require continued care. Though many admissions involve multiple diagnoses, it is estimated that approximately 180,000 older adults are admitted annually to nursing homes as a result of stroke.

DEMENTIA

Older people with mental problems were once labeled "senile." Only in recent years have researchers found that

TABLE 10.4

Death rates for diseases of the heart, according to sex, race, Hispanic origin, and age, selected years 1950–99 [CONTINUED]

[Data Are Based On The National Vital Statistics System]

Sex, race, Hispanic origin, and age	1950[1]	1960[1]	1970	1980	1990	1995	1996	1997	1998	Comparability modified 1998	1999[2]
American Indian or Alaska Native female[4]					Deaths per 100,000 resident population						
All ages, age adjusted	- - -	- - -	- - -	175.4	153.1	145.8	141.6	141.1	137.8	135.8	138.3
All ages, crude	- - -	- - -	- - -	80.3	77.5	87.0	86.7	88.6	89.0	87.7	91.0
45–54 years	- - -	- - -	- - -	65.2	62.0	69.2	61.1	59.7	49.4	48.7	51.4
55–64 years	- - -	- - -	- - -	193.5	197.0	210.2	192.5	172.8	183.3	180.7	183.4
65–74 years	- - -	- - -	- - -	577.2	492.8	503.3	512.8	473.8	440.3	434.0	464.3
75–84 years	- - -	- - -	- - -	1,364.3	1,050.3	1,045.6	1,030.0	1,115.2	1,019.8	1,005.3	1,067.5
85 years and over	- - -	- - -	- - -	2,893.3	2,868.7	2,209.8	2,108.8	2,019.5	2,348.9	2,315.5	2,069.4
Asian or Pacific Islander female[5]											
All ages, age adjusted	- - -	- - -	- - -	132.3	149.2	153.2	127.8	123.3	120.9	119.2	121.5
All ages, crude	- - -	- - -	- - -	57.0	62.0	68.2	66.8	66.9	67.3	66.3	70.1
45–54 years	- - -	- - -	- - -	28.6	17.5	21.6	17.2	18.8	18.4	18.1	18.7
55–64 years	- - -	- - -	- - -	92.9	99.0	93.0	82.3	80.5	70.5	69.5	76.6
65–74 years	- - -	- - -	- - -	313.3	323.9	294.9	282.0	272.8	282.9	278.9	271.2
75–84 years	- - -	- - -	- - -	1,053.2	1,130.9	1,063.0	1,009.8	944.0	880.9	868.4	943.2
85 years and over	- - -	- - -	- - -	3,211.0	4,161.2	4,717.9	3,394.7	3,326.2	3,385.5	3,337.4	3,273.8
Hispanic female[6]											
All ages, age adjusted	- - -	- - -	- - -	- - -	177.2	162.5	151.4	151.1	145.8	143.7	146.5
All ages, crude	- - -	- - -	- - -	- - -	79.4	78.9	77.0	78.3	77.7	76.6	79.0
45–54 years	- - -	- - -	- - -	- - -	43.5	32.0	31.3	31.5	31.0	30.6	30.7
55–64 years	- - -	- - -	- - -	- - -	153.2	137.3	125.1	129.5	122.4	120.7	118.1
65–74 years	- - -	- - -	- - -	- - -	460.4	402.4	387.6	391.9	399.8	394.1	357.5
75–84 years	- - -	- - -	- - -	- - -	1,259.7	1,150.1	1,152.8	1,102.4	1,071.1	1,055.9	1,091.5
85 years and over	- - -	- - -	- - -	- - -	4,440.3	4,243.9	3,673.8	3,748.7	3,499.1	3,449.4	3,696.2
White, non-Hispanic female[6]											
All ages, age adjusted	- - -	- - -	- - -	- - -	252.6	234.9	230.7	225.1	220.1	217.0	218.1
All ages, crude	- - -	- - -	- - -	- - -	320.0	321.4	318.9	315.6	313.6	309.1	314.2
45–54 years	- - -	- - -	- - -	- - -	50.2	46.6	47.5	45.7	44.2	43.6	43.6
55–64 years	- - -	- - -	- - -	- - -	193.6	173.6	169.0	163.9	155.3	153.1	150.9
65–74 years	- - -	- - -	- - -	- - -	584.7	529.1	518.0	504.0	496.2	489.2	479.2
75–84 years	- - -	- - -	- - -	- - -	1,890.2	1,697.8	1,663.5	1,609.4	1,571.1	1,548.8	1,548.6
85 years and over	- - -	- - -	- - -	- - -	6,615.2	6,384.5	6,285.4	6,176.4	6,054.4	5,968.4	6,088.7

- - - Data not available.
[1]Includes deaths of persons who were not residents of the 50 states and the District of Columbia.
[2]Starting with 1999 data, cause of death is coded according to ICD–10. To estimate change between 1998 and 1999, compare the 1999 rate with the comparability - modified rate for 1998.
[3]In 1950 rate is for the age group 75 years and over.
[4]Interpretation of trends should take into account that population estimates for American Indians increased by 45 percent between 1980 and 1990, partly due to better enumeration techniques in the 1990 decennial census and to the increased tendency for people to identify themselves as American Indian in 1990.
[5]Interpretation of trends should take into account that the Asian population in the United States more than doubled between 1980 and 1990, primarily due to immigration.
[6]Excludes data from states lacking an Hispanic-origin item on their death certificates.

Notes: Age-adjusted rates are calculated using the year 2000 standard population starting with *Health, United States, 2001*. For data years shown, code numbers for cause of death are based on the then current revision of the *International Classification of Diseases* (ICD). Age groups were selected to minimize the presentation of unstable age-specific death rates based on small numbers of deaths and for consistency among comparison groups. The race groups, white, black, Asian or Pacific Islander, and American Indian or Alaska Native, include persons of Hispanic and non-Hispanic origin. Conversely, persons of Hispanic origin may be of any race. Bias in death rates results from inconsistent race identification between the death certificate (source of data for numerator of death rates) and data from the Census Bureau (denominator); and from undercounts of some population groups in the census. The net effects of misclassification and under coverage result in death rates estimated to be overstated by 1 percent for the white population and 5 percent for the black population; and death rates estimated to be understated by 21 percent for American Indians, 11 percent for Asians, and 2 percent for Hispanics.

SOURCE: "Death rates for diseases of the heart, according to sex, race, Hispanic origin, and age: United States, selected years 1950–99" in *Health United States, 2001*, Centers for Disease Control and Prevention, National Center for Health Statistics, National Vital Statistics System, Hyattsville, MD, 2001.

physical disorders can cause progressive deterioration of mental and neurological functions. These disorders produce symptoms that are collectively known as "dementia." Symptoms of dementia include loss of language functions, inability to think abstractly, inability to care for oneself, personality change, emotional instability, and loss of a sense of time or place.

Dementia has become a serious health problem in developed countries, including the United States, because older adults are living longer. In 2000 the Federal Interagency Forum on Aging-Related Statistics estimated that approximately 10 percent of those older 65 years of age, 20 percent of those older than 75 years of age, and nearly 36 percent of persons over 85 years of age suffer from dementia.

TABLE 10.5

Probability of developing invasive cancers over selected age intervals, by sex, 1996–98*

		Birth-39	40-59	60-79	Birth to Death
All sites†	Male	1.45 (1 in 69)	8.33 (1 in 12)	32.3 (1 in 3)	43.48 (1 in 2)
	Female	1.92 (1 in 52)	9.09 (1 in 11)	20.0 (1 in 5)	38.25 (1 in 3)
Bladder‡	Male	0.024 (1 in 4234)	0.42 (1 in 236)	2.38 (1 in 42)	3.45 (1 in 29)
	Female	Less than 1 in 10,000	0.13 (1 in 760)	0.64 (1 in 156)	1.12 (1 in 89)
Breast	Female	0.44 (1 in 229)	4.17 (1 in 24)	7.14 (1 in 14)	12.5 (1 in 8)
Colon &	Male	0.07 (1 in 1508)	0.87 (1 in 115)	4.00 (1 in 25)	5.88 (1 in 17)
rectum	Female	0.06 (1 in 1719)	0.69 (1 in 145)	3.03 (1 in 33)	5.55 (1 in 18)
Leukemia	Male	0.16 (1 in 627)	0.21 (1 in 483)	0.81 (1 in 124)	1.43 (1 in 70)
	Female	0.12 (1 in 810)	0.15 (1 in 671)	0.47 (1 in 212)	1.04 (1 in 96)
Lung &	Male	0.03 (1 in 3060)	1.12 (1 in 89)	5.88 (1 in 17)	7.69 (1 in 13)
bronchus	Female	0.03 (1 in 3099)	0.86 (1 in 116)	4.00 (1 in 25)	5.88 (1 in 17)
Melanoma	Male	0.13 (1in 769)	0.50 (1 in 199)	0.97 (1 in 103)	1.72 (1 in 58)
of skin	Female	0.19 (1 in 508)	0.38 (1 in 261)	0.49 (1 in 201)	1.22 (1 in 82)
Non-Hodgkin's	Male	0.17 (1 in 591)	0.48 (1 in 208)	1.23 (1 in 81)	2.08 (1 in 48)
lymphoma	Female	0.08 (1 in 1311)	0.32 (1 in 317)	0.98 (1 in 102)	1.75 (1 in 57)
Prostate	Male	Less than 1 in 10,000	2.08 (1 in 48)	12.5 (1 in 8)	16.67 (1 in 6)
Uterine cervix	Female	0.18 (1 in 567)	0.35 (1 in 288)	0.28 (1 in 354)	0.85 (1 in 117)
Uterine corpus	Female	0.05 (1 in 2097)	0.72 (1 in 138)	1.64 (1 in 61)	2.70 (1 in 37)

*For those free of cancer at beginning of age interval. Based on cancer cases diagnosed during 1996-1998. The 1 in statistic and the inverse of the percentage may not be equivalent due to rounding. †Excludes basal and squamous cell skin cancers and in situ carcinomas except urinary bladder. ‡Includes invasive and in situ cancer cases.

SOURCE: "Probability of Developing Invasive Cancers Over Selected Age Intervals, by Sex, US, 1996–1998" in *Cancer Facts & Figures 2002,* American Cancer Society, Atlanta, GA, 2002. Copyright, American Cancer Society, Inc. Reprinted by permission.

Alzheimer's Disease

Alzheimer's disease (AD) is the single-most common cause of dementia. It is a progressive, degenerative disease that attacks the brain and results in severely impaired memory, thinking, and behavior. First described in 1906 by the German neuropathologist Alois Alzheimer, the disorder may strike people in their forties and fifties, but most victims are over age 65.

Dr. Alzheimer's autopsy of a severely demented 55-year-old woman revealed deposits of "neuritic plaques" and "neurofibrillary tangles." The latter characteristic, the presence of twisted and tangled fibers in the brain cells, is the anatomical hallmark of the disease.

SYMPTOMS. AD has been described as "a dementia of gradual onset and progressive decline." Mild or early AD is not easily distinguishable from the characteristics of normal aging—mild episodes of forgetfulness and disorientation. Gradually, the AD patient may experience confusion; language problems, such as trouble finding words; impaired judgment; disorientation in place and time; and changes in mood, behavior, and personality. The speed with which these changes occur varies, but eventually the disease leaves patients unable to care for themselves.

In the terminal stages of AD, patients require care 24 hours a day. They no longer recognize family members or themselves, and need help with simple daily activities, such as eating, dressing, bathing, and using the toilet. Eventually, they may become incontinent, blind, and unable to communicate. The course of the disease varies widely—some patients die within a few years of diagnosis, while others have lived as long as 25 years.

PREVALENCE. In *Alzheimer's Disease: Estimates of Prevalence in the United States* (Washington, D.C., 1998) the U.S. General Accounting Office (GAO) reported that the prevalence rates of Alzheimer's disease increase dramatically with age, doubling approximately every five years until age 85, when the rate begins to slow down. While AD can strike as early as the third, fourth, or fifth decade of life, 90 percent of victims are more than 65 years old when it becomes apparent. In 1999, 44,020 deaths from AD were reported for those 65 and older. (See Table 10.3.) Studies show a somewhat higher prevalence rate among women than among men. (See Table 10.8.)

DEPRESSION

Of the more than 35 million older Americans, approximately 6 million suffer from depression and 1 million of these suffer from severe depression. Family members and health care professionals often fail to recognize depression among the elderly. Since older people usually suffer from comorbidity (the presence of more than one chronic illness at one time), depression may be masked by the symptoms of other disorders.

The older adult suffering from depression may mistakenly think that depression is simply a reaction to an illness, loss, or a consequence of aging. Many sufferers fail to divulge their depression because of the stigma older generations may attach to mental illness.

TABLE 10.6

Cancer incidence and mortality rates* by site, race, and ethnicity, 1992–98

Incidence	White	Black	Asian/Pacific Islander	American Indian/Alaskan Native	Hispanic†
All Sites					
Males	470.4	596.8	327.7	227.7	319.7
Females	354.4	337.6	252.1	186.3	237.7
Total	401.4	445.3	283.4	202.7	270.0
Breast (female)	115.5	101.5	78.1	50.5	68.5
Colon & rectum					
Males	51.4	57.7	47.3	33.5	35.2
Females	36.3	44.7	31.0	24.6	23.2
Total	42.9	50.1	38.2	28.6	28.4
Lung & bronchus					
Males	69.6	107.2	51.9	44.3	36.0
Females	43.6	45.7	22.7	20.6	18.7
Total	54.7	71.6	35.5	31.0	26.0
Prostate	144.6	234.2	82.8	47.8	103.4

Incidence	White	Black	Asian/Pacific Islander	American Indian/Alaskan Native	Hispanic†
All Sites					
Males	203.2	297.7	125.6	125.3	128.8
Females	138.0	166.6	82.4	90.8	84.3
Total	164.5	218.2	101.2	105.4	102.6
Breast (female)	24.3	31.0	11.0	12.4	14.8
Colon & rectum					
Males	20.6	27.3	12.9	11.9	13.0
Females	13.9	19.6	8.9	8.9	8.0
Total	16.8	22.8	10.7	10.3	10.2
Lung & bronchus					
Males	67.8	96.2	33.8	41.8	30.5
Females	34.6	33.6	15.1	20.9	10.9
Total	48.8	59.1	23.3	30.1	19.3
Prostate	22.4	53.1	9.8	14.0	15.9

*Per 100,000, age-adjusted to the 1970 US standard population. †Hispanics are not mutually exclusive from whites, blacks, Asian/Pacific Islanders, and American Indian/Alaskan Natives.

Note: Incidence data are from the 11 Surveillance, Epidemiology, and End Results (SEER) areas; mortality data are from all states except data for Hispanics; data for Hispanics include deaths that occurred in all states except Connecticut, Louisiana, New Hampshire, and Oklahoma.

SOURCE: "Incidence and Mortality Rates* by Site, Race, and Ethnicity, US, 1992–1998" in *Cancer Facts & Figures 2002,* American Cancer Society, Atlanta, GA, 2002. Copyright, American Cancer Society, Inc. Reprinted by permission.

Suicide

According to Dr. Barry D. Lebowitz, chief of the Adult and Geriatric Treatment and Preventive Intervention Research Branch of the National Institute of Mental Health, almost all older people who commit suicide suffer from depression. Most suicidal older adults visit their primary care physician during the month before ending their lives, and approximately 40 percent visit the doctor in the week before committing suicide, though frequently for chronic health problems rather than depression. However, their depression has apparently not been accurately diagnosed or effectively treated. The Alliance for Aging Research (AAR) reports that the tremendous shortage of physicians specializing in geriatrics (the medical subspecialty devoted to older adults) includes those in the field of psychiatry, known as geropsychiatrists. In 2002 there were about 9,500 certified geriatricians practicing in the United States.

Depression is especially common in nursing homes. A survey (Thomas J. Mattimore, et al., "Surrogate and Physician Understanding of Patients' Preferences for Living Permanently in a Nursing Home," *Journal of the American Geriatrics Society,* vol. 45, no. 7, July 1997) found that some older people would rather die than live permanently in a nursing home. Further, some older adults commit "silent suicide." Feeling lonely, abandoned, or suffering financial woes, they end their lives by nonviolent means such as starving themselves, failing to take prescribed medication, or ingesting large amounts of drugs. This type of suicide, as a result of depression, is different from that committed by the terminally ill who, not wishing to prolong the dying process, refuse life-sustaining medical treatment.

In the United States, the suicide rate generally increases with age. In 1999 the "oldest old" (85 years and

TABLE 10.7

Death rates for cerebrovascular diseases, according to sex, race, Hispanic origin, and age, selected years 1950–99

[Data Are Based On The National Vital Statistics System]

Sex, race, Hispanic origin, and age	1950[1]	1960[1]	1970	1980	1990	1995	1996	1997	1998	Comparability modified 1998	1999[2]
All persons					Deaths per 100,000 resident population						
All ages, age adjusted	180.7	177.9	147.7	96.2	65.3	63.8	63.0	61.7	59.5	63.0	61.8
All ages, crude	104.0	108.0	101.9	75.0	57.8	60.0	60.1	59.6	58.5	61.9	61.4
Under 1 year	5.1	4.1	5.0	4.4	3.8	5.8	6.2	7.0	7.8	8.3	2.7
1–4 years	0.9	0.8	1.0	0.5	0.3	0.4	0.3	0.4	0.4	0.4	0.3
5–14 years	0.5	0.7	0.7	0.3	0.2	0.2	0.2	0.2	0.2	0.2	0.2
15–24 years	1.6	1.8	1.6	1.0	0.6	0.5	0.5	0.5	0.5	0.5	0.5
25–34 years	4.2	4.7	4.5	2.6	2.2	1.8	1.8	1.7	1.7	1.8	1.5
35–44 years	18.7	14.7	15.6	8.5	6.4	6.5	6.3	6.3	5.9	6.2	5.7
45–54 years	70.4	49.2	41.6	25.2	18.7	17.6	17.9	16.9	16.5	17.5	15.5
55–64 years	194.2	147.3	115.8	65.1	47.9	46.0	45.3	44.3	42.5	45.0	41.3
65–74 years	554.7	469.2	384.1	219.0	144.2	137.0	135.3	134.7	129.8	137.4	132.2
75–84 years	1,499.6	1,491.3	1,254.2	786.9	498.0	480.4	476.0	461.0	454.3	481.0	472.8
85 years and over	2,990.1	3,680.5	3,014.3	2,283.7	1,628.9	1,630.5	1,606.9	1,578.6	1,494.7	1,582.6	1,606.7
Male											
All ages, age adjusted	186.4	186.1	157.4	102.2	68.5	66.1	65.1	63.8	59.9	63.4	62.4
All ages, crude	102.5	104.5	94.5	63.4	46.7	47.9	48.0	47.7	46.2	48.9	48.4
Under 1 year	6.4	5.0	5.8	5.0	4.4	6.3	6.5	7.6	9.0	9.5	3.3
1–4 years	1.1	0.9	1.2	0.4	0.3	0.4	0.3	0.5	0.3	0.3	0.3
5–14 years	0.5	0.7	0.8	0.3	0.2	0.2	0.2	0.2	0.2	0.2	0.2
15–24 years	1.8	1.9	1.8	1.1	0.7	0.5	0.5	0.6	0.6	0.6	0.5
25–34 years	4.2	4.5	4.4	2.6	2.1	1.9	1.7	1.7	1.7	1.8	1.6
35–44 years	17.5	14.6	15.7	8.7	6.8	7.0	6.7	6.5	6.2	6.6	5.9
45–54 years	67.9	52.2	44.4	27.2	20.5	19.8	20.0	19.2	18.4	19.5	17.1
55–64 years	205.2	163.8	138.7	74.6	54.3	53.3	52.4	51.4	49.4	52.3	47.6
65–74 years	589.6	530.7	449.5	258.6	166.6	155.6	154.5	152.9	145.4	153.9	149.0
75–84 years	1,543.6	1,555.9	1,361.6	866.3	551.1	516.1	507.6	487.9	473.7	501.6	494.5
85 years and over	3,048.6	3,643.1	2,895.2	2,193.6	1,528.5	1,532.1	1,508.1	1,496.2	1,341.8	1,420.7	1,455.5
Female											
All ages, age adjusted	175.8	170.7	140.0	91.7	62.6	61.4	60.8	59.5	58.2	61.6	60.5
All ages, crude	105.6	111.4	109.0	85.9	68.4	71.5	71.8	71.0	70.2	74.3	73.8
Under 1 year	3.7	3.2	4.0	3.8	3.1	5.2	5.9	6.3	6.6	7.0	2.0
1–4 years	0.7	0.7	0.7	0.5	0.3	0.3	0.3	0.3	0.4	0.4	0.3
5–14 years	0.4	0.6	0.6	0.3	0.2	0.2	0.2	0.2	0.2	0.2	0.2
15–24 years	1.5	1.6	1.4	0.8	0.6	0.4	0.4	0.5	0.4	0.4	0.5
25–34 years	4.3	4.9	4.7	2.6	2.2	1.7	1.8	1.7	1.8	1.9	1.5
35–44 years	19.9	14.8	15.6	8.4	6.1	6.0	5.8	6.2	5.7	6.0	5.6
45–54 years	72.9	46.3	39.0	23.3	17.0	15.5	15.9	14.7	14.6	15.5	14.0
55–64 years	183.1	131.8	95.3	56.8	42.2	39.4	38.8	37.9	36.3	38.4	35.5
65–74 years	522.1	415.7	333.3	188.7	126.7	122.0	119.9	119.9	117.1	124.0	118.5
75–84 years	1,462.2	1,441.1	1,183.1	740.1	466.2	457.8	455.6	443.4	441.5	467.5	458.2
85 years and over	2,949.4	3,704.4	3,081.0	2,323.1	1,667.6	1,668.8	1,646.2	1,611.8	1,558.0	1,649.6	1,670.6
White male											
All ages, age adjusted	182.1	181.6	153.7	98.7	65.5	63.1	62.6	61.4	57.5	60.9	60.0
All ages, crude	100.5	102.7	93.5	63.1	46.9	48.5	49.0	48.7	47.2	50.0	49.7
45–54 years	53.7	40.9	35.6	21.7	15.4	14.8	15.2	14.6	14.2	15.0	13.0
55–64 years	182.2	139.0	119.9	64.0	45.7	44.6	43.4	42.2	40.8	43.2	39.6
65–74 years	569.7	501.0	420.0	239.8	152.9	143.3	141.8	141.5	134.6	142.5	138.0
75–84 years	1,556.3	1,564.8	1,361.6	852.7	539.2	502.0	498.9	479.5	464.0	491.3	485.1
85 years and over	3,127.1	3,734.8	3,018.1	2,230.8	1,545.4	1,544.7	1,532.9	1,525.9	1,360.6	1,440.6	1,475.5
Black male											
All ages, age adjusted	228.8	238.5	206.4	142.0	102.2	96.4	93.1	88.4	86.1	91.2	87.4
All ages, crude	122.0	122.9	108.8	73.0	53.0	50.8	50.1	48.3	47.4	50.2	47.7
45–54 years	211.9	166.1	136.1	82.1	68.4	64.0	62.1	59.8	55.6	58.9	51.0
55–64 years	522.8	439.9	343.4	189.7	141.7	133.8	137.5	135.5	129.1	136.7	123.3
65–74 years	783.6	899.2	780.1	472.3	326.9	290.9	291.9	274.3	255.4	270.4	264.0
75–84 years[3]	1,504.9	1,475.2	1,445.7	1,066.3	721.5	699.2	652.1	598.6	620.1	656.6	634.9
85 years and over	- - -	2,700.0	1,963.1	1,873.2	1,421.5	1,386.3	1,325.9	1,278.1	1,233.1	1,305.6	1,343.1

TABLE 10.7

Death rates for cerebrovascular diseases, according to sex, race, Hispanic origin, and age, selected years 1950–99 [CONTINUED]

[Data are based on the National Vital Statistics System]

Sex, race, Hispanic origin, and age	1950[1]	1960[1]	1970	1980	1990	1995	1996	1997	1998	Comparability modified 1998	1999[2]
American Indian or Alaska Native Male[4]					Deaths per 100,000 resident population						
All ages, age adjusted	---	---	---	66.4	44.3	44.6	40.3	40.8	34.0	36.0	40.7
All ages, crude	---	---	---	23.1	16.0	20.1	18.7	18.5	16.6	17.6	19.9
45–54 years	---	---	---	*	*	28.4	19.9	0.0	17.6	18.6	17.0
55–64 years	---	---	---	72.0	39.8	45.7	42.9	49.4	53.5	56.6	37.4
65–74 years	---	---	---	170.5	120.3	153.1	139.1	112.5	109.8	116.3	144.8
75–84 years	---	---	---	523.9	325.9	290.1	319.4	324.0	257.8	273.0	353.6
85 years and over	---	---	---	1,384.7	949.8	748.8	550.4	707.9	450.2	476.7	510.5
Asian or Pacific Islander male[5]											
All ages, age adjusted	---	---	---	71.4	59.1	73.6	59.5	61.8	57.3	60.7	58.0
All ages, crude	---	---	---	28.7	23.3	28.6	27.0	28.8	28.1	29.8	28.6
45–54 years	---	---	---	17.0	15.6	17.3	19.5	18.3	16.9	17.9	18.2
55–64 years	---	---	---	59.9	51.8	62.1	55.3	57.7	56.0	59.3	52.0
65–74 years	---	---	---	197.9	167.9	162.3	161.4	160.3	160.9	170.4	141.8
75–84 years	---	---	---	619.5	483.9	571.8	430.0	524.0	456.5	483.3	472.4
85 years and over	---	---	---	1,399.0	1,196.6	1,801.5	1,348.7	1,219.4	1,149.6	1,217.2	1,248.4
Hispanic male[6]											
All ages, age adjusted	---	---	---	---	46.5	48.4	45.7	43.6	42.9	45.4	44.6
All ages, crude	---	---	---	---	15.6	17.1	16.8	16.6	17.3	18.3	17.8
45–54 years	---	---	---	---	20.0	20.5	23.1	20.4	22.3	23.6	20.0
55–64 years	---	---	---	---	49.2	46.1	50.7	52.6	52.9	56.0	45.5
65–74 years	---	---	---	---	126.4	132.0	114.5	134.5	123.8	131.1	131.9
75–84 years	---	---	---	---	356.6	349.2	347.5	304.2	295.5	312.9	332.5
85 years and over	---	---	---	---	866.3	994.0	866.3	784.1	790.6	837.1	829.5
White, non-Hispanic male[6]											
All ages, age adjusted	---	---	---	---	66.3	63.0	62.8	61.8	57.8	61.2	60.5
All ages, crude	---	---	---	---	50.6	52.2	52.9	53.0	51.2	54.2	54.2
45–54 years	---	---	---	---	14.9	14.1	14.2	13.9	13.2	14.0	12.2
55–64 years	---	---	---	---	45.1	43.8	42.0	41.0	39.4	41.7	38.7
65–74 years	---	---	---	---	154.5	142.9	141.7	140.9	134.4	142.3	137.4
75–84 years	---	---	---	---	547.3	506.3	503.9	485.2	470.1	497.7	490.7
85 years and over	---	---	---	---	1,578.7	1,546.9	1,555.6	1,558.1	1,386.7	1,468.2	1,506.6
White female											
All ages, age adjusted	169.7	165.0	135.5	89.0	60.3	59.3	58.9	57.8	56.4	59.7	58.7
All ages, crude	103.3	110.1	109.8	88.6	71.6	75.8	76.1	75.5	74.7	79.1	78.7
45–54 years	55.0	33.8	30.5	18.6	13.5	12.7	12.7	11.6	11.2	11.9	10.9
55–64 years	156.9	103.0	78.1	48.6	35.8	33.5	33.3	31.8	31.3	33.1	29.7
65–74 years	498.1	383.3	303.2	172.5	116.1	112.4	110.0	111.2	108.4	114.8	109.9
75–84 years	1,471.3	1,444.7	1,176.8	728.8	456.5	448.6	445.7	436.4	433.0	458.5	450.3
85 years and over	3,017.9	3,795.7	3,167.6	2,362.7	1,685.9	1,683.6	1,673.1	1,638.8	1,584.0	1,677.1	1,692.6
Black female											
All ages, age adjusted	238.4	232.5	189.3	119.6	84.0	80.9	78.8	76.0	75.2	79.6	78.1
All ages, crude	128.3	127.7	112.2	77.8	60.7	60.3	59.6	57.9	57.8	61.2	60.0
45–54 years	248.9	166.2	119.4	61.8	44.1	36.4	38.6	38.6	39.9	42.2	36.0
55–64 years	567.7	452.0	272.4	138.4	96.9	85.4	82.8	84.0	76.5	81.0	78.5
65–74 years	754.4	830.5	673.5	361.7	236.7	221.2	216.0	204.6	197.0	208.6	200.3
75–84 years[3]	1,496.7	1,413.1	1,338.2	917.5	595.0	591.0	585.7	580.1	558.0	581.7	582.1
85 years and over	---	2,578.9	2,210.5	1,891.6	1,495.2	1,564.7	1,436.2	1,429.7	1,396.6	1,478.7	1,559.0

older) accounted for the highest rate—19.2 suicides per 100,000 people. Men aged 65 and older had a higher rate (32.1 suicides per 100,000 persons), with the oldest old men (85 years and older) most likely to commit suicide (55 per 100,000 persons). In contrast, the rate among women 65 years and older was 4.3 suicides per 100,000 persons, and that among women 85 and over was 4.1 suicides per 100,000 persons. (See Table 6.1 in Chapter 6.)

By race, white men over the age of 75 had the highest rate—40.8 suicides per 100,000 persons for those 75 to 84 years, and 59.7 per 100,000 persons for those 85 years and older. One generally held theory about the very high rates of suicide among white men aged 75 and over is that they have traditionally been in positions of power and thus have great difficulty adjusting to a life they may consider useless or diminished.

TABLE 10.7

Death rates for cerebrovascular diseases, according to sex, race, Hispanic origin, and age, selected years 1950–99 [CONTINUED]

[Data are based on the National Vital Statistics System]

Sex, race, Hispanic origin, and age	1950[1]	1960[1]	1970	1980	1990	1995	1996	1997	1998	Comparability modified 1998	1999[2]
American Indian or Alaska Native female[3]				Deaths per 100,000 resident population							
All ages, age adjusted	---	---	---	51.2	38.4	40.3	42.0	38.5	39.9	42.2	38.5
All ages, crude	---	---	---	22.0	19.3	23.8	25.4	24.3	25.4	26.9	25.6
45–54 years	---	---	---	*	*	*	24.6	*	18.8	19.9	14.4
55–64 years	---	---	---	*	40.7	43.5	29.7	49.4	47.5	50.3	47.1
65–74 years	---	---	---	128.3	100.5	112.3	127.7	109.0	126.4	133.8	92.5
75–84 years	---	---	---	404.2	282.0	321.7	351.1	319.7	324.6	343.7	310.3
85 years and over	---	---	---	1,095.5	776.2	697.3	700.0	570.0	618.1	654.4	675.4
Asian or Pacific Islander female[5]											
All ages, age adjusted	---	---	---	60.8	54.9	53.4	51.0	49.1	45.6	48.3	48.2
All ages, crude	---	---	---	26.4	24.3	24.9	27.5	27.8	26.4	28.0	28.8
45–54 years	---	---	---	20.3	19.7	16.2	16.2	14.0	11.4	12.1	15.7
55–64 years	---	---	---	43.7	42.1	39.1	36.3	40.7	31.0	32.8	41.6
65–74 years	---	---	---	136.1	124.0	103.3	111.2	109.3	113.4	120.1	107.1
75–84 years	---	---	---	446.6	396.6	405.2	408.3	408.9	388.8	411.7	366.2
85 years and over	---	---	---	1,545.2	1,395.0	1,432.5	1,236.8	1,097.8	1,006.4	1,065.6	1,173.5
Hispanic female[6]											
All ages, age adjusted	---	---	---	---	43.7	40.1	37.7	36.9	36.0	38.1	36.3
All ages, crude	---	---	---	---	20.1	20.0	19.6	19.6	19.6	20.8	19.9
45–54 years	---	---	---	---	15.2	15.1	15.3	12.7	14.2	15.0	12.0
55–64 years	---	---	---	---	38.5	35.6	35.2	32.4	30.1	31.9	29.2
65–74 years	---	---	---	---	102.6	98.2	90.1	96.8	93.0	98.5	92.6
75–84 years	---	---	---	---	308.5	287.0	283.9	286.3	279.1	295.5	280.0
85 years and over	---	---	---	---	1,055.3	931.2	837.8	771.6	755.3	799.7	803.1
White, non-Hispanic female[6]											
All ages, age adjusted	---	---	---	---	61.0	59.6	59.4	58.3	57.1	60.5	59.6
All ages, crude	---	---	---	---	77.2	81.9	82.6	82.4	81.9	86.7	86.7
45–54 years	---	---	---	---	13.2	12.4	12.4	11.3	10.9	11.5	10.6
55–64 years	---	---	---	---	35.7	32.9	32.7	31.4	31.1	32.9	29.5
65–74 years	---	---	---	---	116.9	112.2	110.5	111.4	108.8	115.2	110.4
75–84 years	---	---	---	---	461.9	452.0	449.5	440.9	438.3	464.1	457.1
85 years and over	---	---	---	---	1,714.7	1,698.4	1,701.0	1,668.2	1,615.6	1,710.6	1,728.9

- - - Data not available.
*Based on fewer than 20 deaths.
[1]Includes deaths of persons who were not residents of the 50 states and the District of Columbia.
[2]Starting with 1999 data, cause of death is coded according to ICD–10. To estimate change between 1998 and 1999, compare the 1999 rate with the comparability-modified rate for 1998.
[3]In 1950 rate is for the age group 75 years and over.
[4]Interpretation of trends should take into account that population estimates for American Indians increased by 45 percent between 1980 and 1990, partly due to better enumeration techniques in the 1990 decennial census and to the increased tendency for people to identify themselves as American Indian in 1990.
[5]Interpretation of trends should take into account that the Asian population in the United States more than doubled between 1980 and 1990, primarily due to immigration.
[6]Excludes data from states lacking an Hispanic-origin item on their death certificates.

Notes: Age-adjusted rates are calculated using the year 2000 standard population starting with *Health, United States, 2001*. For data years shown, code numbers for cause of death are based on the then current revision of the *International Classification of Diseases* (ICD). Age groups were selected to minimize the presentation of unstable age-specific death rates based on small numbers of deaths and for consistency among comparison groups. The race groups, white, black, Asian or Pacific Islander, and American Indian or Alaska Native, include persons of Hispanic and non-Hispanic origin. Conversely, persons of Hispanic origin may be of any race. Bias in death rates results from inconsistent race identification between the death certificate (source of data for numerator of death rates) and data from the Census Bureau (denominator); and from undercounts of some population groups in the census. The net effects of misclassification and under coverage result in death rates estimated to be overstated by 1 percent for the white population and 5 percent for the black population; and death rates estimated to be understated by 21 percent for American Indians, 11 percent for Asians, and 2 percent for Hispanics.

SOURCE: "Death rates for cerebrovascular diseases, according to sex, race, Hispanic origin, and age: United States, selected years 1950–99" in *Health United States, 2001*, Centers for Disease Control and Prevention, National Center for Health Statistics, National Vital Statistics System, Hyattsville, MD, 2001.

OLDER WOMEN

Women Live Longer...

The AAR observes that since women live longer than men, "the face of the worldwide longevity revolution is predominantly a female face." In the United States, women tend to outlive men by five to seven years. (See Table 10.9.) In 2000 there were 85 males ages 65–69 for every 100 females of the same age. As both sexes age, the gap widens. For those age 80 and over, there are only 52 males for every 100 females (See Table 10.10.) The U.S Census Bureau found that in 2000, more than two-thirds of all people older than 85 were women—there were approximately 3 million women, compared with 1.2 million men.

...But Older Women Have More Chronic Diseases

Older women are more likely than men of the same age to suffer from chronic conditions, such as arthritis, osteoporosis and related bone fractures, AD, and incontinence. Women are also more likely to have more than one chronic disorder at a time (comorbidity). In *One Final Gift: Humanizing the End of Life for Women in America*, the AAR reported that within the same age group, more women than men have functional and cognitive disabilities.

WHAT IS GERIATRICS?

Geriatrics is the medical subspecialty concerned with the prevention and treatment of diseases in the elderly. In 1909 Dr. Ignatz L. Nascher coined the term geriatrics from the Greek "geras" (old age) and "iatrikos" (physician). Geriatricians are physicians trained in internal medicine or family practice who obtain additional training and certification in the diagnosis and treatment of older adults. Geriatricians rely on the findings of researchers and gerontologists (non-physician professionals who conduct scientific studies of aging and older adults) to help older adults "maintain the highest possible degree of function and independence and avoid unnecessary and costly institutionalization."

Gerontology was unheard of before the nineteenth century, when most people died at an early age. Those who reached old age accepted their deteriorating health as a part of aging. In the early twentieth century, gerontology was born when scientists began to investigate the pathological changes accompanying the aging process.

A Shortage of Geriatricians

According to the AAR and the American Geriatrics Society, the United States currently needs at least 20,000 geriatricians to care for the 36 million older adults. In *Will You Still Treat Me When I'm 65?* (Washington, D.C., May 1996), the AAR reported that the 6,784 primary care physicians then trained in geriatrics (out of 684,414 doctors nationwide) were barely one-third of the needed number. In 2002 certified geriatricians numbered only 9,500—still less than half of the estimated need. Similarly, the AAR reported in 1996 that the United States has less than one-fourth (approximately 500) of the 2,100 academic physician-scientists needed to teach in medical schools and conduct aging-related research. The Alliance estimates that by 2030, the demand for geriatric services will increase to 36,000 geriatricians.

While many developed countries have recognized the need for more geriatrics education, the United States continues to lag in offering geriatrics courses in its medical schools. The latest review of the curricula of the 126 medical schools in the nation (as cited in the 1996 AAR report *Will You Still Treat Me When I'm 65?*) showed only 14 schools with required coursework in geriatrics.

Specialized Care

Physicians who specialize in geriatrics are trained to recognize characteristics that differentiate older patients from other age groups. Geriatricians also realize that aging is not a disease, and that declining health does not necessarily accompany aging. Furthermore, in geriatrics, diseases may manifest symptoms different from those found in a younger person. Frequently, older patients have several co-existing chronic disorders, some of which may be caused by psychological and/or socioeconomic problems.

What is more important is that geriatricians and other caregivers realize that aging does not change the basic personality. The *Baltimore Longitudinal Study of Aging* has found that psychological stereotypes—that some people become crankier with age while others mellow with age—have been disproved by scientific studies. (Longitudinal investigations involve studying changes in the same individuals over time, as they grow older.) This finding is significant for health professionals because a personality change may signal a change in a patient's health. For example, experts have found that personality change may be an early indication of dementia.

Finally, it is vital for geriatricians and others involved in providing health and social services to older adults to appreciate that their values and beliefs may be quite different from those of their patients. Today's older adults grew up in an era that was quite different—they may have seen the advent of air travel, automobiles,

TABLE 10.8

Alzheimer's Disease prevalence rates for men and women ages 65–95, all severity levels

Age	Men		Women	
	Rate[a]	95-percent confidence interval[b]	Rate[a]	95-percent confidence interval[b]
65	0.6%	0.6, 0.7	0.8%	0.7, 0.9
70	1.3	1.2, 1.5	1.7	1.5, 1.9
75	2.7	2.5, 3.0	3.5	3.2, 3.8
80	5.6	5.2, 6.0	7.1	6.7, 7.5
85	11.1	10.3, 11.9	13.8	13.2, 14.5
90	20.8	19.2, 22.4	25.2	24.0, 26.5
95	35.6	32.9, 38.3	41.5	39.3, 43.8

[a]The rates were estimated by logistic regression model.
[b]The 95-percent confidence interval is a pair of values between which the true rate is likely to fall 95 percent of the time.

SOURCE: "AD Prevalence Rates for Men and Women Ages 65–95, All Severity Levels," in *Alzheimer's Disease: Estimates of Prevalence in the United States*, U.S. General Accounting Office, Washington, DC, 1998.

TABLE 10.9

Life expectancy at birth, at 65 years of age, and at 75 years of age, by selected characteristics, selected years, 1900–99

[DATA ARE BASED ON THE NATIONAL VITAL STATISTICS SYSTEM]

Specified age and year	All races Both sexes	All races Male	All races Female	White Both sexes	White Male	White Female	Black Both sexes	Black Male	Black Female
At birth				Remaining life expectancy in years					
1900[1,2]	47.3	46.3	48.3	47.6	46.6	48.7	[3]33.0	[3]32.5	[3]33.5
1950[2]	68.2	65.6	71.1	69.1	66.5	72.2	60.7	58.9	62.7
1960[2]	69.7	66.6	73.1	70.6	67.4	74.1	63.2	60.7	65.9
1970	70.8	67.1	74.7	71.7	68.0	75.6	64.1	60.0	68.3
1980	73.7	70.0	77.4	74.4	70.7	78.1	68.1	63.8	72.5
1985	74.7	71.1	78.2	75.3	71.8	78.7	69.3	65.0	73.4
1990	75.4	71.8	78.8	76.1	72.7	79.4	69.1	64.5	73.6
1991	75.5	72.0	78.9	76.3	72.9	79.6	69.3	64.6	73.8
1992	75.8	72.3	79.1	76.5	73.2	79.8	69.6	65.0	73.9
1993	75.5	72.2	78.8	76.3	73.1	79.5	69.2	64.6	73.7
1994	75.7	72.4	79.0	76.5	73.3	79.6	69.5	64.9	73.9
1995	75.8	72.5	78.9	76.5	73.4	79.6	69.6	65.2	73.9
1996	76.1	73.1	79.1	76.8	73.9	79.7	70.2	66.1	74.2
1997	76.5	73.6	79.4	77.1	74.3	79.9	71.1	67.2	74.7
1998	76.7	73.8	79.5	77.3	74.5	80.0	71.3	67.6	74.8
1999 preliminary	76.7	73.9	79.4	77.3	74.6	79.9	71.4	67.8	74.7
At 65 years									
1900–1902[1,2]	11.9	11.5	12.2	- - -	11.5	12.2	- - -	10.4	11.4
1950[2]	13.9	12.8	15.0	- - -	12.8	15.1	13.9	12.9	14.9
1960[2]	14.3	12.8	15.8	14.4	12.9	15.9	13.9	12.7	15.1
1970	15.2	13.1	17.0	15.2	13.1	17.1	14.2	12.5	15.7
1980	16.4	14.1	18.3	16.5	14.2	18.4	15.1	13.0	16.8
1985	16.7	14.5	18.5	16.8	14.5	18.7	15.2	13.0	16.9
1990	17.2	15.1	18.9	17.3	15.2	19.1	15.4	13.2	17.2
1991	17.4	15.3	19.1	17.5	15.4	19.2	15.5	13.4	17.2
1992	17.5	15.4	19.2	17.6	15.5	19.3	15.7	13.5	17.4
1993	17.3	15.3	18.9	17.4	15.4	19.0	15.5	13.4	17.1
1994	17.4	15.5	19.0	17.5	15.6	19.1	15.7	13.6	17.2
1995	17.4	15.6	18.9	17.6	15.7	19.1	15.6	13.6	17.1
1996	17.5	15.7	19.0	17.6	15.8	19.1	15.8	13.9	17.2
1997	17.7	15.9	19.2	17.8	16.0	19.3	16.1	14.2	17.6
1998	17.8	16.0	19.2	17.8	16.1	19.3	16.1	14.3	17.4
1999 preliminary	17.7	16.0	19.1	17.8	16.1	19.2	16.0	14.3	17.3
At 75 years									
1980	10.4	8.8	11.5	10.4	8.8	11.5	9.7	8.3	10.7
1985	10.6	9.0	11.7	10.6	9.0	11.7	10.1	8.7	11.1
1990	10.9	9.4	12.0	11.0	9.4	12.0	10.2	8.6	11.2
1991	11.1	9.5	12.1	11.1	9.5	12.1	10.2	8.7	11.2
1992	11.2	9.6	12.2	11.2	9.6	12.2	10.4	8.9	11.4
1993	10.9	9.5	11.9	11.0	9.5	12.0	10.2	8.7	11.1
1994	11.0	9.6	12.0	11.1	9.6	12.0	10.3	8.9	11.2
1995	11.0	9.7	11.9	11.1	9.7	12.0	10.2	8.8	11.1
1996	11.1	9.8	12.0	11.1	9.8	12.0	10.3	9.0	11.2
1997	11.2	9.9	12.1	11.2	9.9	12.1	10.7	9.3	11.5
1998	11.3	10.0	12.2	11.3	10.0	12.2	10.5	9.2	11.3
1999 preliminary	11.2	9.9	12.1	11.2	10.0	12.1	10.4	9.2	11.1

- - - Data not available.

[1] Death registration area only. The death registration area increased from 10 states and the District of Columbia in 1900 to the coterminous United States in 1933.
[2] Includes deaths of persons who were not residents of the 50 states and the District of Columbia.
[3] Figure is for the all other population.

Notes: Beginning in 1997 life table methodology was revised to construct complete life tables by single years of age that extend to age 100. Previously abridged life tables were constructed for five-year age groups ending with the age group 85 years and over.

SOURCE: "Table 28. Life expectancy at birth, at 65 years of age, and at 75 years of age, according to race and sex: United States, selected years 1900–99," in *Health, United States, 2001,* Centers for Disease Control and Prevention, National Center for Health Statistics, National Vital Statistics System, Hyattsville, MD, 2001.

telephones, television, Medicare, and Social Security. The United States was previously largely rural and opportunities for college education were more limited, especially for women. Young people were stricken by polio (a viral infection that can cause paralysis and death), antibiotics had not yet been discovered, and hospitals were seen as places where people went to die. By understanding cultural and societal influences affecting older adults, health professionals will be better able to reduce the functional impact of illness in old age and treat all patients, including those at the end of life, with respect and compassion.

TABLE 10.10

Sex ratio for population 25 years and over by age, 2000 and 2030

(Men per 100 women)

Country	2000						2030					
	25 to 54 years	55 to 64 years	65 to 69 years	70 to 74 years	75 to 79 years	80 years and over	25 to 54 years	55 to 64 years	65 to 69 years	70 to 74 years	75 to 79 years	80 years and over
United States	98	91	85	79	72	52	98	92	89	86	81	64

SOURCE: Adapted from Kevin Kinsella and Victoria A. Velkoff, "Table 6. Sex Ratio for Population 25 Years and Over by Age: 2000 and 2030," in *An Aging World: 2001,* series P95/01-1, U.S. Census Bureau, U.S. Government Printing Office, Washington, DC, 2001.

CHAPTER 11
PUBLIC OPINION ABOUT LIFE AND DEATH

LIFE AFTER DEATH

Since the dawn of history, many people have believed that human beings do not disappear into oblivion upon their death. Numerous religions and cultures teach that the physical body may cease to exist, but that some element of the human person goes on to what many call the "afterlife." Between 1972 and 1982, when the Roper Center for Public Opinion Research asked the American public, "Do you believe there is life after death?," 70 percent believed in an afterlife, while 20 percent did not. In 1996, when the Roper Center asked the same question, 73 percent of respondents said yes, and 16 percent said no.

A 1997 poll conducted by the Gallup Organization for the Nathan Cummings Foundation and the Fetzer Institute, as published in "A Roper Center Data Review: Facing Death" (*Public Perspective*, March/April 2001), revealed similar results. Sixty-seven percent of those polled said they believed they would exist in some form after their death, and of those, 83 percent expressed optimism that existence in the afterlife is a positive experience, as opposed to negative or neutral. (See Figure 11.1 and Figure 11.2.) Further, nearly three-quarters (72 percent) of those who believe they will exist in an afterlife also feel they will experience spiritual growth after death. (See Figure 11.3.)

FIGURE 11.1

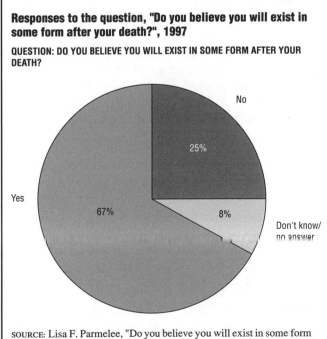

Responses to the question, "Do you believe you will exist in some form after your death?", 1997

QUESTION: DO YOU BELIEVE YOU WILL EXIST IN SOME FORM AFTER YOUR DEATH?

SOURCE: Lisa F. Parmelee, "Do you believe you will exist in some form after your death?" in "Afterworld" in "A Roper Center Data Review: Facing Death" in *Public Perspective,* March/April 2001. Data from a survey by the Gallup Organization for the Nathan Cummings Foundation and Fetzer Institute, May 1997. © Public perspective, a publication of the Roper Center for Public Opinion Research, University of Connecticut, Storrs. Reprinted by permission.

FIGURE 11.2

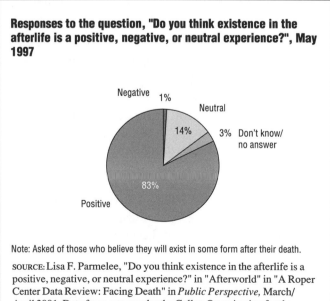

Responses to the question, "Do you think existence in the afterlife is a positive, negative, or neutral experience?", May 1997

Note: Asked of those who believe they will exist in some form after their death.

SOURCE: Lisa F. Parmelee, "Do you think existence in the afterlife is a positive, negative, or neutral experience?" in "Afterworld" in "A Roper Center Data Review: Facing Death" in *Public Perspective,* March/April 2001. Data from a survey by the Gallup Organization for the Nathan Cummings Foundation and Fetzer Institute, May 1997. © Public Perspective, a publication of the Roper Center for Public Opinion Research, University of Connecticut, Storrs. Reprinted by permission.

FIGURE 11.3

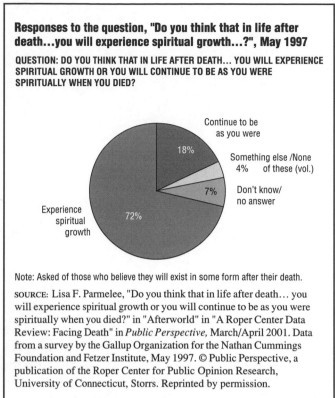

Responses to the question, "Do you think that in life after death...you will experience spiritual growth...?", May 1997

QUESTION: DO YOU THINK THAT IN LIFE AFTER DEATH... YOU WILL EXPERIENCE SPIRITUAL GROWTH OR YOU WILL CONTINUE TO BE AS YOU WERE SPIRITUALLY WHEN YOU DIED?

- Continue to be as you were — 18%
- Something else /None of these (vol.) — 4%
- Don't know/ no answer — 7%
- Experience spiritual growth — 72%

Note: Asked of those who believe they will exist in some form after their death.

SOURCE: Lisa F. Parmelee, "Do you think that in life after death... you will experience spiritual growth or you will continue to be as you were spiritually when you died?" in "Afterworld" in "A Roper Center Data Review: Facing Death" in *Public Perspective,* March/April 2001. Data from a survey by the Gallup Organization for the Nathan Cummings Foundation and Fetzer Institute, May 1997. © Public Perspective, a publication of the Roper Center for Public Opinion Research, University of Connecticut, Storrs. Reprinted by permission.

Because so many people believe in an afterlife and anticipate a spiritual life after death, it is not surprising that more than half of respondents expressed concern about "not being forgiven by God" (57 percent), "not reconciling with others" (56 percent), and "dying when ... removed or cut off from God or a higher power" (51 percent). About half (49 percent) worried about "not being forgiven by someone for something." (See Figure 11.4.)

CLONING TO ACHIEVE IMMORTALITY

The cloning of animals has raised the question— are humans next? Following the February 1997 announcement of this scientific achievement from the Roslin Institute in Edinburgh, Scotland, the Gallup Poll asked respondents if they thought the cloning of human beings would be a good thing or a bad thing. Nearly 9 of 10 Americans (87 percent) thought the cloning of humans would be a bad thing. Asked about the morality of human cloning, the same majority (88 percent) indicated that the cloning of human beings would be morally wrong.

A March 1998 online survey of more than 350 people by Cyber Dialogue, a New York City online research company, found that two-thirds (67 percent) of the American public were somewhat opposed or very opposed to the cloning of human beings. In November 2001 a CNN/*USA Today*/Gallup Poll reported that 88 percent of Americans disapproved of cloning to produce a human being. There was a more favorable response to cloning intended to find treatments for certain diseases—more than half of the respondents (54 percent) approved of cloning for medical research purposes.

CONCERNS ABOUT DEATH

Americans say they are not afraid of death. In a 1999 survey conducted by the *Los Angeles Times* (as reported in "A Roper Center Data Review: Facing Death," *Public Perspective*, March/April 2001), 83 percent said they were not afraid to die. Fear of death seems to decline with advancing age. Among young adults ages 18–44, 18 percent said they were afraid to die, while 79 percent were unafraid. Among respondents age 65 and over, only 7 percent reported a fear of death, while 90 percent said they were not afraid. (See Figure 11.5.)

In the same survey, about half of the respondents (49 percent) said they very seldom think about death and 10 percent claimed they never think at all about their own deaths. (See Figure 11.6.) A September 2000 survey found that the largest proportion of respondents (38 percent) think about their own deaths just a few times each year. (See Figure 11.7.)

Fearful Aspects of Dying

Although they may not fear death or spend much time thinking about their own deaths, Americans are fearful about some aspects of dying. In a survey conducted by Yankelovich Partners/*Time*/CNN (as reported in "A Roper Center Data Review: Facing Death," *Public Perspective*, March/April 2001), two-thirds of respondents expressed much or some concern about dying in pain. Another two-thirds said they were "very fearful" or "somewhat fearful" of leaving loved ones behind, and 43 percent of respondents were "very fearful" or "somewhat fearful" about dying alone. (See Figure 11.8.)

The 1997 Gallup Organization survey (cited in the same Roper Center Data Review) reveals that when they think about their own death, the majority of Americans (70 percent) express some or a great deal of concern about "not having the chance to say goodbye to someone." Similar proportions of respondents also feared causing loved ones stress and inconvenience (64 percent), and worried about how their families or loved ones would be cared for (65 percent). (See Figure 11.4.)

The same survey found that nearly three-quarters of respondents (73 percent) fear the possibility of being in a persistent vegetative state before dying, and more than two-thirds (67 percent) are afraid they will suffer "great physical pain" before death. About half (49 percent) are concerned about having others make medical decisions for them, and 41 percent are concerned about being in the hospital while dying. (See Figure 11.4.)

FIGURE 11.4

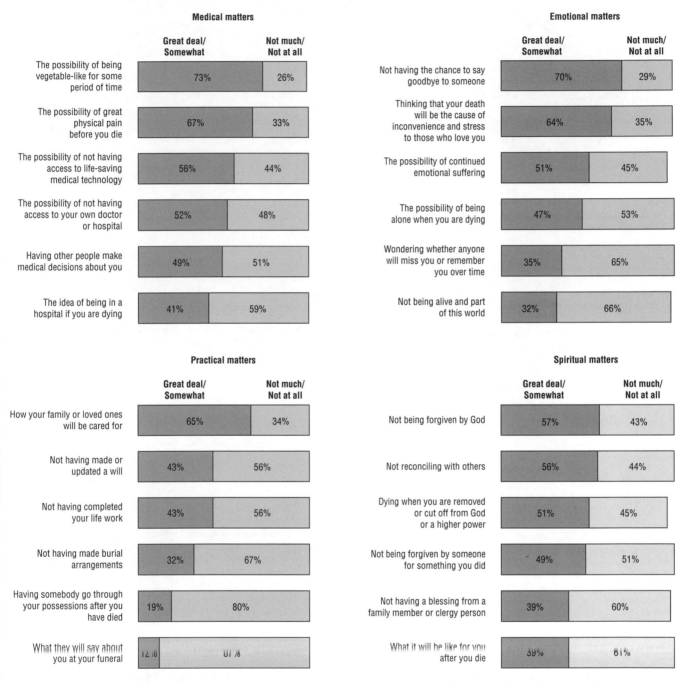

Responses to the question, "How much, if at all, does each of these [medical/emotional/practical/spiritual] matters worry you when you think about your own death...?", May 1997

QUESTIONS: ...HOW MUCH, IF AT ALL, DOES EACH OF THESE [MEDICAL/EMOTIONAL/PRACTICAL/SPIRITUAL] MATTERS WORRY YOU WHEN YOU THINK ABOUT YOUR OWN DEATH... A GREAT DEAL, SOMEWHAT, NOT MUCH, OR NOT AT ALL?

Medical matters

	Great deal/ Somewhat	Not much/ Not at all
The possibility of being vegetable-like for some period of time	73%	26%
The possibility of great physical pain before you die	67%	33%
The possibility of not having access to life-saving medical technology	56%	44%
The possibility of not having access to your own doctor or hospital	52%	48%
Having other people make medical decisions about you	49%	51%
The idea of being in a hospital if you are dying	41%	59%

Emotional matters

	Great deal/ Somewhat	Not much/ Not at all
Not having the chance to say goodbye to someone	70%	29%
Thinking that your death will be the cause of inconvenience and stress to those who love you	64%	35%
The possibility of continued emotional suffering	51%	45%
The possibility of being alone when you are dying	47%	53%
Wondering whether anyone will miss you or remember you over time	35%	65%
Not being alive and part of this world	32%	66%

Practical matters

	Great deal/ Somewhat	Not much/ Not at all
How your family or loved ones will be cared for	65%	34%
Not having made or updated a will	43%	56%
Not having completed your life work	43%	56%
Not having made burial arrangements	32%	67%
Having somebody go through your possessions after you have died	19%	80%
What they will say about you at your funeral	12%	87%

Spiritual matters

	Great deal/ Somewhat	Not much/ Not at all
Not being forgiven by God	57%	43%
Not reconciling with others	56%	44%
Dying when you are removed or cut off from God or a higher power	51%	45%
Not being forgiven by someone for something you did	49%	51%
Not having a blessing from a family member or clergy person	39%	60%
What it will be like for you after you die	39%	61%

SOURCE: Lisa F. Parmelee, "Hypothetical Questions" in "A Roper Center Data Review: Facing Death" in *Public Perspective,* March/April 2001. Data from a survey by the Gallup Organization for the Nathan Cummings Foundation and Fetzer Institute, May 1997. © Public perspective, a publication of the Roper Center for Public Opinion Research, University of Connecticut, Storrs. Reprinted by permission.

The Yankelovich Partners/*Time*/CNN survey found that the majority of people (73 percent) would prefer to die at home rather than in a hospital, hospice, or nursing home. Despite these expressed wishes to die at home, less than half (43 percent) believed they were likely to die at home—28 percent thought they were likely to die in a hospital, nursing home, or hospice. (See Figure 11.9.)

FIGURE 11.5

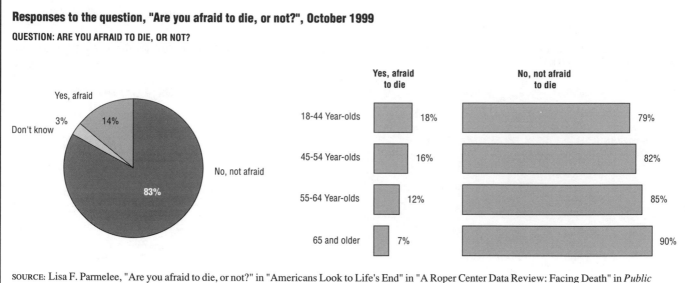

Responses to the question, "Are you afraid to die, or not?", October 1999

QUESTION: ARE YOU AFRAID TO DIE, OR NOT?

SOURCE: Lisa F. Parmelee, "Are you afraid to die, or not?" in "Americans Look to Life's End" in "A Roper Center Data Review: Facing Death" in *Public Perspective,* March/April 2001. Data from a survey by the *Los Angeles Times,* October 20-23, 1999. © Public perspective, a publication of the Roper Center for Public Opinion Research, University of Connecticut, Storrs. Reprinted by permission.

FIGURE 11.6

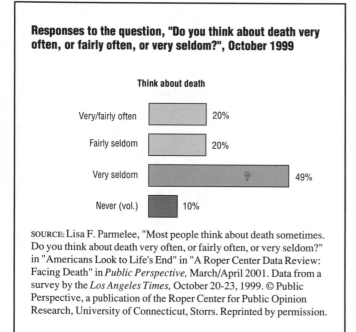

Responses to the question, "Do you think about death very often, or fairly often, or very seldom?", October 1999

SOURCE: Lisa F. Parmelee, "Most people think about death sometimes. Do you think about death very often, or fairly often, or very seldom?" in "Americans Look to Life's End" in "A Roper Center Data Review: Facing Death" in *Public Perspective,* March/April 2001. Data from a survey by the *Los Angeles Times,* October 20-23, 1999. © Public Perspective, a publication of the Roper Center for Public Opinion Research, University of Connecticut, Storrs. Reprinted by permission.

FIGURE 11.7

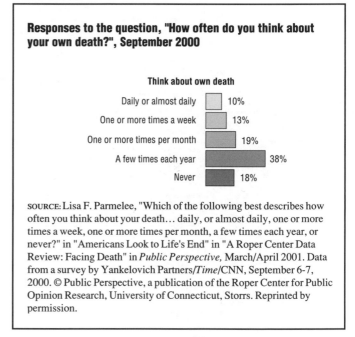

Responses to the question, "How often do you think about your own death?", September 2000

SOURCE: Lisa F. Parmelee, "Which of the following best describes how often you think about your death... daily, or almost daily, one or more times a week, one or more times per month, a few times each year, or never?" in "Americans Look to Life's End" in "A Roper Center Data Review: Facing Death" in *Public Perspective,* March/April 2001. Data from a survey by Yankelovich Partners/*Time*/CNN, September 6-7, 2000. © Public Perspective, a publication of the Roper Center for Public Opinion Research, University of Connecticut, Storrs. Reprinted by permission.

The Seriously Ill Have Different Concerns

When patients with advanced chronic illnesses were asked in 1999 whether they agreed or strongly agreed about the importance of a variety of end-of-life issues, their concerns were quite different from the general population. While dying at home appears to be a priority for many Americans, only 35 percent of the seriously ill named dying at home as a priority, making it last on their list of concerns. Their top priorities were being kept clean (99 percent), having a nurse with whom they felt comfort-

able (97 percent), knowing what to expect about their physical conditions (96 percent), trusting their physician (94 percent), and being free of pain (93 percent). (See Figure 11.10.)

Seriously ill patients also felt it was very meaningful to have someone who would listen to them (95 percent), and more than nine out of ten said it was important to them to maintain both their dignity (95 percent) and sense of humor (93 percent). Almost all believed it was vital to name someone to make decisions for them if they became

FIGURE 11.8

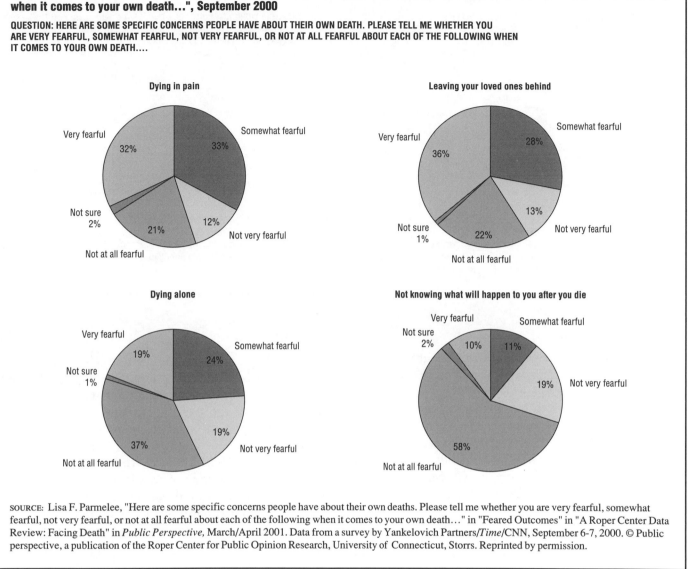

Responses to the question, "Are you very fearful, somewhat fearful, not very fearful, or not at all fearful about each of the following when it comes to your own death...", September 2000

QUESTION: HERE ARE SOME SPECIFIC CONCERNS PEOPLE HAVE ABOUT THEIR OWN DEATH. PLEASE TELL ME WHETHER YOU ARE VERY FEARFUL, SOMEWHAT FEARFUL, NOT VERY FEARFUL, OR NOT AT ALL FEARFUL ABOUT EACH OF THE FOLLOWING WHEN IT COMES TO YOUR OWN DEATH....

SOURCE: Lisa F. Parmelee, "Here are some specific concerns people have about their own deaths. Please tell me whether you are very fearful, somewhat fearful, not very fearful, or not at all fearful about each of the following when it comes to your own death..." in "Feared Outcomes" in "A Roper Center Data Review: Facing Death" in *Public Perspective,* March/April 2001. Data from a survey by Yankelovich Partners/*Time*/CNN, September 6-7, 2000. © Public perspective, a publication of the Roper Center for Public Opinion Research, University of Connecticut, Storrs. Reprinted by permission.

unable to make them (98 percent), and to have their financial affairs in order (94 percent). They did not wish to be a burden to their families (89 percent) or to society (81 percent). (See Figure 11.10.)

While only half of seriously ill respondents felt it was important to be able to discuss their spiritual beliefs with their physicians (50 percent), more than two-thirds (69 percent) wished to meet with a clergy member, and 85 percent valued prayer. The highest spiritual priority for seriously ill patients was coming to peace with God (89 percent). (See Figure 11.10.)

GETTING OLDER

Living to 100

National surveys of the adult population by the Alliance for Aging Research (AAR) have found that

Americans would generally like to live longer. In 2001, 6 in 10 Americans (63 percent) said they would like to live to be 100 years old. Men (68 percent), and those aged 18–36 (69 percent) were more likely to want to live to be 100 years old. (See Figure 11.11.) These findings are similar to AAR studies from 1991 and 1996.

Although a majority of Americans would like to live to be 100 years old, not all expect to get their wish. Nonetheless, 90 percent of people completing an online survey, and 60 percent of those who responded by telephone, expected to live to be at least 80 years old. More than half (62 percent) of those surveyed online said they expected to live to be at least 90 years old. (See Figure 11.12.) Earlier AAR surveys, conducted in 1991, 1992, and 1996, also showed that more than half of the respondents (56, 58, and 51 percent, respectively) thought they would live to be at least 80 years old.

FIGURE 11.9

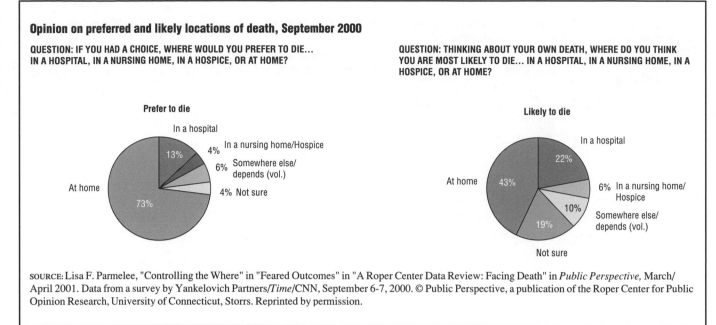

Opinion on preferred and likely locations of death, September 2000

QUESTION: IF YOU HAD A CHOICE, WHERE WOULD YOU PREFER TO DIE...
IN A HOSPITAL, IN A NURSING HOME, IN A HOSPICE, OR AT HOME?

QUESTION: THINKING ABOUT YOUR OWN DEATH, WHERE DO YOU THINK
YOU ARE MOST LIKELY TO DIE... IN A HOSPITAL, IN A NURSING HOME, IN A
HOSPICE, OR AT HOME?

SOURCE: Lisa F. Parmelee, "Controlling the Where" in "Feared Outcomes" in "A Roper Center Data Review: Facing Death" in *Public Perspective,* March/April 2001. Data from a survey by Yankelovich Partners/*Time*/CNN, September 6-7, 2000. © Public Perspective, a publication of the Roper Center for Public Opinion Research, University of Connecticut, Storrs. Reprinted by permission.

Concerns About Aging

The aging of the baby boomers, and the growing number of people living longer, have focused much attention on concerns that come with aging. The AAR survey found that while Americans want to live longer, more than half of respondents to the online survey were concerned about living in a nursing home (51 percent) and disease (61 percent) in old age. Becoming a financial burden to their children (45 percent) and remaining attractive (46 percent) worried less than half of those surveyed. (See Figure 11.13.)

Nursing Homes Get Mixed Reviews

During 2001, *The NewsHour with Jim Lehrer,* the Harvard School of Public Health, and The Henry J. Kaiser Family Foundation conducted a national survey about nursing homes. Among other questions, participants were asked about their willingness to accept moving into a nursing home.

Of the 1,309 adults surveyed, a little less than half (47 percent) said they would not like, but would accept, having to move into a nursing home if they could not care for themselves at home, while 43 percent felt that moving into a nursing home would be totally unacceptable. Only 10 percent of the survey respondents felt they would accept it as the best thing for themselves. A majority felt that nursing homes are understaffed, often neglect or abuse residents, and that nursing home residents are lonely. About half (45 percent) felt that nursing homes make most people who move into them worse off than before. Further, 86 percent of respondents believed that "most people who stay in a nursing home never go home."

SUICIDE

A 1998 National Opinion Research Center survey found that 61 percent of respondents approved of suicide if a person had an incurable disease, but only a small minority approved of it if the person had gone bankrupt (10 percent), had dishonored his or her family (10 percent), or was simply tired of living (16 percent). In comparison, the same poll from 1977 found that a much lower percentage of people (38 percent) thought suicide was acceptable if one had an incurable illness. Suicide in other situations was also found less acceptable in the 1977 survey than in the 1998 survey. (See Figure 11.14.)

PHYSICIAN-ASSISTED SUICIDE

Many advocates of physician-assisted suicide believe that people who are suffering from uncontrollable pain should be allowed to end their lives with a lethal dose of medication prescribed by their doctor. Dr. Marcia Angell, for example, former executive editor of *The New England Journal of Medicine,* claims that "those with cancer, AIDS, and other neurologic disorders may die by inches and in great anguish, despite every effort of their doctors and nurses." She believes that if all possible palliative efforts have failed to provide pain relief, then physician-assisted suicide should be permitted.

Public Support

In March 2002, 40 percent of respondents to an ABC News/Beliefnet poll thought that doctors should be legally permitted to help terminally ill patients commit suicide by giving them prescriptions for lethal drugs,

FIGURE 11.10

Responses to the question, "What do you believe to be the most important considerations at the end of a person's life?", 1999

QUESTION: WE ARE INTERESTED IN LEARNING WHAT YOU BELIEVE, FROM YOU EXPERIENCE, TO BE THE MOST IMPORTANT CONSIDERATIONS AT THE END OF A PERSON'S LIFE. AT THE END OF EACH STATEMENT, PLEASE CIRCLE THE RATING WHICH BEST REFLECTS YOU FEELINGS.

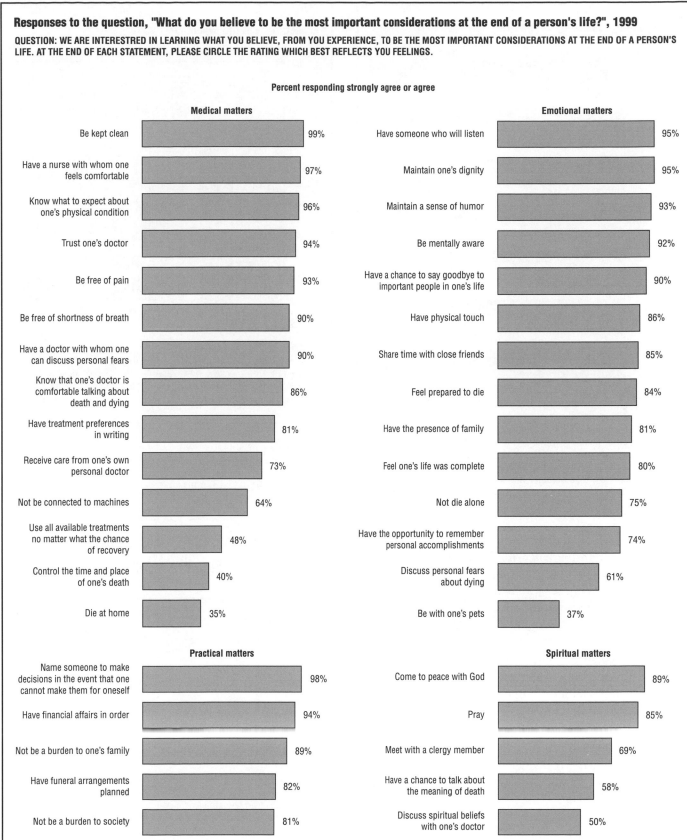

Percent responding strongly agree or agree

Medical matters

Be kept clean	99%
Have a nurse with whom one feels comfortable	97%
Know what to expect about one's physical condition	96%
Trust one's doctor	94%
Be free of pain	93%
Be free of shortness of breath	90%
Have a doctor with whom one can discuss personal fears	90%
Know that one's doctor is comfortable talking about death and dying	86%
Have treatment preferences in writing	81%
Receive care from one's own personal doctor	73%
Not be connected to machines	64%
Use all available treatments no matter what the chance of recovery	48%
Control the time and place of one's death	40%
Die at home	35%

Emotional matters

Have someone who will listen	95%
Maintain one's dignity	95%
Maintain a sense of humor	93%
Be mentally aware	92%
Have a chance to say goodbye to important people in one's life	90%
Have physical touch	86%
Share time with close friends	85%
Feel prepared to die	84%
Have the presence of family	81%
Feel one's life was complete	80%
Not die alone	75%
Have the opportunity to remember personal accomplishments	74%
Discuss personal fears about dying	61%
Be with one's pets	37%

Practical matters

Name someone to make decisions in the event that one cannot make them for oneself	98%
Have financial affairs in order	94%
Not be a burden to one's family	89%
Have funeral arrangements planned	82%
Not be a burden to society	81%

Spiritual matters

Come to peace with God	89%
Pray	85%
Meet with a clergy member	69%
Have a chance to talk about the meaning of death	58%
Discuss spiritual beliefs with one's doctor	50%

Note: Sample of 340 seriously ill patients who were randomly selected from the National Veterans Affairs Patient Treatment File database. Criterion for selection was hospitalization within the past year for an advanced chronic illness.

SOURCE: Lisa F. Parmelee, "Closer to Real" in "A Roper Center Data Review: Facing Death" in *Public Perspective,* March/April 2001. Data from a survey by Karen E. Steinhauser et al., Program on the Medical Encounter & Palliative Care, March-August 1999. © Public perspective, a publication of the Roper Center for Public Opinion Research, University of Connecticut, Storrs. Reprinted by permission.

FIGURE 11.11

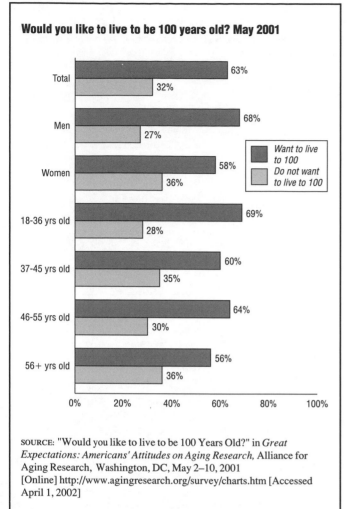

Would you like to live to be 100 years old? May 2001

Legend:
- Want to live to 100
- Do not want to live to 100

Category	Want to live to 100	Do not want to live to 100
Total	63%	32%
Men	68%	27%
Women	58%	36%
18-36 yrs old	69%	28%
37-45 yrs old	60%	35%
46-55 yrs old	64%	30%
56+ yrs old	56%	36%

SOURCE: "Would you like to live to be 100 Years Old?" in *Great Expectations: Americans' Attitudes on Aging Research,* Alliance for Aging Research, Washington, DC, May 2–10, 2001 [Online] http://www.agingresearch.org/survey/charts.htm [Accessed April 1, 2002]

FIGURE 11.12

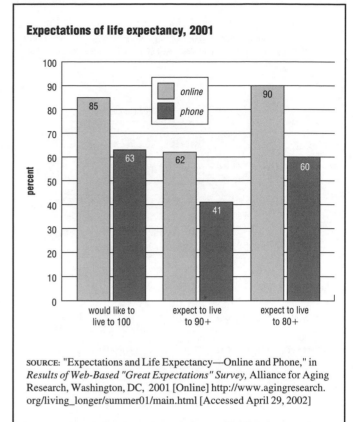

Expectations of life expectancy, 2001

Legend:
- online
- phone

	online	phone
would like to live to 100	85	63
expect to live to 90+	62	41
expect to live to 80+	90	60

SOURCE: "Expectations and Life Expectancy—Online and Phone," in *Results of Web-Based "Great Expectations" Survey,* Alliance for Aging Research, Washington, DC, 2001 [Online] http://www.agingresearch.org/living_longer/summer01/main.html [Accessed April 29, 2002]

FIGURE 11.13

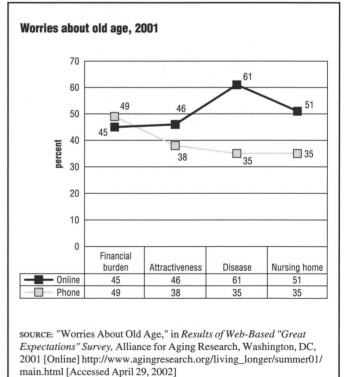

Worries about old age, 2001

	Financial burden	Attractiveness	Disease	Nursing home
Online	45	46	61	51
Phone	49	38	35	35

SOURCE: "Worries About Old Age," in *Results of Web-Based "Great Expectations" Survey,* Alliance for Aging Research, Washington, DC, 2001 [Online] http://www.agingresearch.org/living_longer/summer01/main.html [Accessed April 29, 2002]

compared with 48 percent who disapproved. When the survey specified that eligible patients "would have to be diagnosed as having less than six months to live, get a second opinion from another doctor,... ask for the drugs three times [and] there would be a 15-day waiting period before the prescription could be filled," a slightly higher percentage (46 percent) supported legalizing physician-assisted suicide. Still, 48 percent of respondents felt that even with these added safeguards, physician-assisted suicide should be illegal.

Personal Consideration

Just as the public is divided about the right of patients to physician-assisted suicide, so it is divided about suicide as a personal option. A 1997 survey asking whether respondents could imagine a situation where they might seek physician-assisted suicide found that half (50 percent) could conceive of asking a doctor to help them painlessly end their lives. (See Figure 11.15.)

A 1999 *Los Angeles Times* survey found only 12 percent of respondents said they had ever considered suicide, while 86 percent claimed never to have consid-

ered it. (See Figure 11.16.) Nonetheless, Americans believe that suicide will claim more lives in the future. The majority (68 percent) of respondents to a 1999

FIGURE 11.14

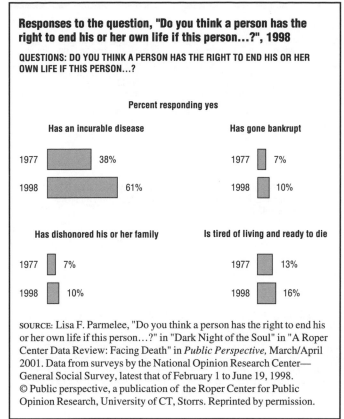

Responses to the question, "Do you think a person has the right to end his or her own life if this person...?", 1998

QUESTIONS: DO YOU THINK A PERSON HAS THE RIGHT TO END HIS OR HER OWN LIFE IF THIS PERSON...?

Percent responding yes

Has an incurable disease

| 1977 | 38% |
| 1998 | 61% |

Has gone bankrupt

| 1977 | 7% |
| 1998 | 10% |

Has dishonored his or her family

| 1977 | 7% |
| 1998 | 10% |

Is tired of living and ready to die

| 1977 | 13% |
| 1998 | 16% |

SOURCE: Lisa F. Parmelee, "Do you think a person has the right to end his or her own life if this person...?" in "Dark Night of the Soul" in "A Roper Center Data Review: Facing Death" in *Public Perspective*, March/April 2001. Data from surveys by the National Opinion Research Center—General Social Survey, latest that of February 1 to June 19, 1998. © Public perspective, a publication of the Roper Center for Public Opinion Research, University of CT, Storrs. Reprinted by permission.

FIGURE 11.15

"Can you imagine any situation where you yourself might want your doctor to end your own life intentionally by some painless means if you requested it?", May 1997

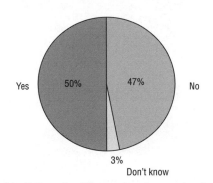

Yes 50% No 47% Don't know 3%

SOURCE: Lisa F. Parmelee, "Can you imagine any situation where you yourself might want your doctor to end your own life intentionally by some painless means if you requested it?" in "Dark Night of the Soul" in "A Roper Center Data Review: Facing Death" in *Public Perspective*, March/April 2001. Data from a survey by the Gallup Organization for the Nathan Cummings Foundation and Fetzer Institute, May 1997. © Public Perspective, a publication of the Roper Center for Public Opinion Research, University of Connecticut, Storrs. Reprinted by permission.

FIGURE 11.16

Responses to the question, "At any time in your life, have you considered suicide, or not?", October 1999

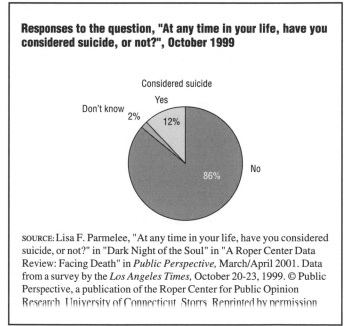

Considered suicide Yes 12% Don't know 2% No 86%

SOURCE: Lisa F. Parmelee, "At any time in your life, have you considered suicide, or not?" in "Dark Night of the Soul" in "A Roper Center Data Review: Facing Death" in *Public Perspective*, March/April 2001. Data from a survey by the *Los Angeles Times*, October 20-23, 1999. © Public Perspective, a publication of the Roper Center for Public Opinion Research, University of Connecticut, Storrs. Reprinted by permission.

Harris Interactive survey thought suicide would kill more people ten years in the future than it does today. (See Figure 11.17.)

The Supreme Court and Public Opinion on Physician-Assisted Suicide

PUBLIC OPINION PRIOR TO SUPREME COURT DECISION ON PHYSICIAN-ASSISTED SUICIDE. On June 23 and 24, 1997, just a few days before the Supreme Court ruling on assisted suicide (brought on by the cases *Washington et al. v. Harold Glucksberg* and *Dennis C. Vacco, Attorney General of New York et al. v. Timothy E. Quill et al.*), the Gallup Poll asked if doctors should be allowed by law to help a patient commit suicide if that patient is incurably ill and suffers from severe pain. More than half (57 percent) of the respondents supported physician-assisted suicide for incurable patients in severe pain, compared with about one-third (35 percent) who opposed it.

PUBLIC OPINION AFTER THE SUPREME COURT DECISION ON PHYSICIAN-ASSISTED SUICIDE. In July 1997, a few weeks after the Supreme Court ruled that there is no constitutional right to physician-assisted suicide, the Harris Poll asked the public if they agreed or disagreed with the Supreme Court decision. Almost two-thirds of respondents (65 percent) disagreed with the decision. Younger people were more likely to favor physician-assisted suicide, with those 25 to 29 years old most strongly (73 per-

cent) in favor of it. People 65 years old and older were least likely to support assisted suicide (55 percent).

In August 1997 a majority (68 percent) of respondents to a Harris Poll thought that "the law should allow doctors to comply with the wishes of a dying patient in severe distress who asks to have his or her life ended." In 1982 only about half (53 percent) of the respondents had agreed with the same statement.

FIGURE 11.17

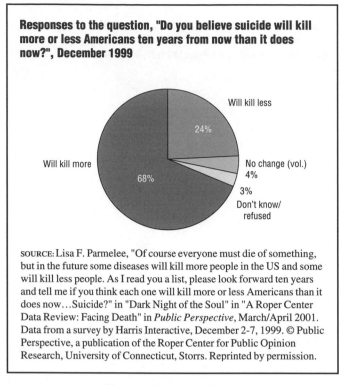

Responses to the question, "Do you believe suicide will kill more or less Americans ten years from now than it does now?", December 1999

Will kill less 24%

Will kill more 68%

No change (vol.) 4%

3% Don't know/ refused

SOURCE: Lisa F. Parmelee, "Of course everyone must die of something, but in the future some diseases will kill more people in the US and some will kill less people. As I read you a list, please look forward ten years and tell me if you think each one will kill more or less Americans than it does now…Suicide?" in "Dark Night of the Soul" in "A Roper Center Data Review: Facing Death" in *Public Perspective*, March/April 2001. Data from a survey by Harris Interactive, December 2-7, 1999. © Public Perspective, a publication of the Roper Center for Public Opinion Research, University of Connecticut, Storrs. Reprinted by permission.

TABLE 11.1

Opinion on physician assisted suicide, December 2001

"DO YOU THINK THAT THE LAW SHOULD ALLOW DOCTORS TO COMPLY WITH THE WISHES OF A DYING PATIENT IN SEVERE DISTRESS WHO ASKS TO HAVE HIS OR HER LIFE ENDED, OR NOT?"

	Should %	Should Not %	Not Sure %
2001	65	29	6
1997	68	27	4
1993	73	24	3
1987	62	32	4

"IN 1997, THE U.S. SUPREME COURT RULED THAT INDIVIDUALS DO NOT HAVE A CONSTITUTIONAL RIGHT TO DOCTOR-ASSISTED SUICIDE. DO YOU AGREE OR DISAGREE WITH THIS DECISION?"

	Agree %	Dis- agree %	Not Sure %
2001	32	63	4
1997	32	65	3

"IN 1994, PEOPLE IN OREGON VOTED ON A PROPOSITION THAT WOULD ALLOW DOCTOR-ASSISTED SUICIDES FOR PATIENTS WITH LESS THAN SIX MONTHS TO LIVE. DOCTORS WOULD BE ALLOWED TO HELP PATIENTS TO COMMIT SUICIDE— BUT ONLY IF ALL OF THE THREE FOLLOWING CONDITIONS WERE MET: (A) THE PATIENT REQUESTS IT THREE TIMES. (B) THERE IS A SECOND OPINION FROM ANOTHER DOCTOR. (C) THERE IS A 15-DAY WAITING PERIOD FOR THE PATIENT TO CHANGE HIS OR HER MIND. WOULD YOU FAVOR OR OPPOSE SUCH A LAW IN YOUR STATE?"

	%
Favor	61
Oppose	34
Not sure	5

"THIS PROPOSITION, ALLOWING PHYSICIAN-ASSISTED SUICIDE, WAS APPROVED BY A MAJORITY IN OREGON. ATTORNEY GENERAL ASHCROFT RECENTLY MOVED TO OVERRULE THE PROPOSITION, WHICH HE SAYS IS NOW ILLEGAL. DO YOU THINK ATTORNEY GENERAL ASHCROFT WAS RIGHT OR WRONG TO DO THIS?"

	%
Right	35
Wrong	58
Not sure	7

SOURCE: "Do you think the law should allow doctors to comply with the wishes of a dying patient in severe distress who asks to have his or her life ended, or not?" and "In 1997, the U.S. Supreme Court ruled…" The Polling Report, Inc. [Online] http://www.pollingreport.com/ health1.htm#AssistedSuicide [accessed April 1, 2002]. Data from "2-to-1 Majorities Continue to Support Rights to Both Euthanasia and Doctor-Assisted Suicide: Clear Majority Also Believes (When Asked) That Attorney General Ashcroft is Wrong to Oppose Oregon Proposition Allowing Physician-Assisted Suicide," THE HARRIS POLL®, released January 9, 2002, Harris Interactive®.

In December 2001, 65 percent of respondents to a Harris Poll felt "the law should allow doctors to comply with the wishes of a dying patient in severe distress who asks to have his or her life ended." Similarly, there was little change in public perception of the constitutionality of physician-assisted suicide from 1997 to 2001: 63 percent of those polled in late 2001 disagreed with the Supreme Court's 1997 decision. (See Table 11.1.)

OREGON PHYSICIAN-ASSISTED SUICIDE LAW

In 1994 Oregon became the first jurisdiction in the world to legalize physician-assisted suicide, with its Death with Dignity Act. Under the Act, Oregon law permits physician-assisted suicide for patients with less than six months to live. Patients must request physician assistance three times, receive a second opinion from another doctor, and wait 15 days to allow time to reconsider.

Before the Death with Dignity Act could take effect, though, opponents of the law succeeded in obtaining an injunction against it. Three years later, in November 1997, Oregon's legislature let the voters decide whether to repeal or retain the law. Voters reaffirmed the Death with Dignity Act. In August 1997, prior to voters' reaffirmation of Oregon's physician-assisted suicide law, about 7 in 10 people (69 percent) surveyed by the Harris Poll indicated they would approve of a similar law allowing physician-assisted suicide in their state. Asked again in 2001 whether they would favor or oppose such a law in their own state, 61 percent of respondents indicated they favored such legislation. (See Table 11.1.)

Using Federally-Controlled Drugs for Assisted Suicide

After the Death with Dignity Act took effect in November 1997, the Drug Enforcement Administration (DEA) announced that "delivering, dispensing, or prescribing a controlled substance with the intent of assisting a suicide" would be a violation of the federal Controlled Substances Act (PL 91-513). Then-Attorney General Janet Reno overruled DEA administrator Thomas Constantine, who had made the above statement.

In October 2000, U.S. Attorney General John Ashcroft overturned Reno's ruling, in an attempt to again allow the DEA to act against physicians who prescribe lethal drugs under Oregon's physician-assisted suicide law. In December 2001 the Harris Poll asked adults nationwide whether they considered Attorney General Ashcroft's effort to overrule the proposition right or wrong. More than half of respondents (58 percent) believed his action was wrong. (See Table 11.1.) On April 17, 2002, U.S. District Judge Robert E. Jones agreed, noting that "[t]o allow an attorney general—an appointed executive...—to determine the legitimacy of a particular medical practice ... would be unprecedented and extraordinary." Jones' ruling reaffirmed the Death with Dignity Act.

IMPORTANT NAMES AND ADDRESSES

AARP (formerly the American Association of Retired Persons)
601 E St., NW
Washington, DC 20049
(202) 434-2560
FAX: (202) 434-2588
(800) 424-3410
E-mail: member@aarp.org
URL: http://www.aarp.org/

Aging with Dignity
P.O. Box 1661
Tallahassee, FL 32302-1661
(850) 681-2010
FAX: (850) 681-2481
(888) 5-WISHES
E-mail: fivewishes@agingwithdignity.org
URL: http://www.agingwithdignity.org

Alliance for Aging Research
2021 K St., NW, Suite 305
Washington, DC 20006
(202) 293-2856
FAX: (202) 785-8574
E-mail: info@agingresearch.org
URL: http://www.agingresearch.org

Alzheimer's Association
919 N. Michigan Ave., Suite 1100
Chicago, IL 60611-1676
(312) 335-8700
FAX: (312) 335-1110
(800) 272-3900
E-mail: info@alz.org
URL: http://www.alz.org/

American Cancer Society
2200 Century Pkwy., Suite 950
Atlanta, GA 30345
(404) 816-4994
FAX: (404) 315-9348
(800) ACS-2345
URL: http://www.cancer.org/

Centers for Disease Control and Prevention
1600 Clifton Rd.
Atlanta, GA 30333
(404) 639-3534
(800) 311-3435
URL: http://www.cdc.gov

Children's Hospice International
901 N. Pitt St., Suite 230
Alexandria, VA 22314
(703) 684-0330
FAX: (703) 684-0226
(800) 24-CHILD
E-mail: chiorg@aol.com
URL: http://www.chionline.org/

**Division of Transplantation
Health Resources and Services
Administration
U.S. Department of Health and
Human Services**
5600 Fishers Ln.
Parklawn Bldg., Room 7C-22
Rockville, MD 20857
(301) 443-7577
E-mail: dfcrcomm@hrsa.gov
URL: http://www.hrsa.gov/OSP/dot/
dotmain.htm

The Hastings Center
21 Malcolm Gordon Rd.
Garrison, NY 10524-5555
(845) 424-4040
FAX: (845) 424-4545
E-mail: mail@thehastingscenter.org
URL: http://www.thehastingscenter.org/

The Hemlock Society USA
P.O. Box 101810
Denver, CO 80250-1810
(303) 639-1202
FAX (303) 639-1224
(800) 247-7421
E-mail: email@hemlock.org
URL: http://www.hemlock.org

International Task Force on Euthanasia and Assisted Suicide
P.O. Box 760
Steubenville, OH 43952
(740) 282-3810
URL: http://www.iaetf.org/

March of Dimes Birth Defects Foundation
1275 Mamaroneck Ave.
White Plains, NY 10605
(888) MODIMES
URL: http://www.modimes.org/

National Association for Home Care (formerly Hospice Association of America)
228 7th St., SE
Washington, DC 20003
(202) 547-7424
FAX: (202) 547-3540
URL: http://www.nahc.org/

The National Council on Aging
409 3rd St., SW, Suite 200
Washington, DC 20024
(202) 479-1200
FAX: (202) 479-0735
E-mail: info@ncoa.org
URL: http://www.ncoa.org/

The National Hospice and Palliative Care Organization
1700 Diagonal Rd., Suite 625
Alexandria, VA 22314
(703) 837-1500
FAX: (703) 837-1233
E-mail: info@nhpco.org
URL: http://www.nhpco.org/

**National Institute on Aging
National Institutes of Health
U.S. Department of Health
and Human Services**
Bethesda, MD 20892
(301) 496-4000

(800) 222-2225
webmaster@nia.nih.gov
URL: http://www.nih.gov/nia/

National Right to Life Committee
512 10th St., NW
Washington, DC 20004
(202) 626-8800
E-mail: NRLC@nrlc.org
URL: http://www.nrlc.org/

Older Women's League (OWL)
666 11th St. NW, Suite 700
Washington, DC 20001
(202) 783-6686
FAX: (202) 638-2356
(800) 825-3695
E-mail: owlinfo@owl-national.org
URL: http://www.owl-national.org/

The Park Ridge Center for the Study of Health, Faith, and Ethics
211 E. Ontario St., Suite 800
Chicago, IL 60611-3215
(312) 266-2222
FAX (312) 266-6086
URL: http://www.prchfe.org/

Partnership for Caring (formerly Choice in Dying)
1620 Eye St., NW, Suite 202
Washington, DC 20006
(202) 296-8071
FAX: (202) 296-8352
Hotline: (800) 989-9455
E-mail: pfc@partnershipforcaring.org
URL: http://www.partnershipforcaring.org/

United Network for Organ Sharing (UNOS)
1100 Boulders Pkwy., Suite 500
P.O. Box 13770
Richmond, VA 23225-8770
(804) 330-8576
Hotline: (888) TXINFO1
URL: http://www.unos.org/

United States Conference of Catholic Bishops (USCCB)
Secretariat for Pro-Life Activities
3211 4th St., NE
Washington, DC 20017-1194
(202) 541-3070
URL: http://www.nccbuscc.org/

Visiting Nurse Associations of America
11 Beacon St., Suite 910
Boston, MA 02108
(617) 523-4042
FAX: (617) 227-4843
E-mail: vnaa@vnaa.org
URL: http://www.vnaa.org/

RESOURCES

The President's Commission for the Study of Ethical Problems in Medicine and Biomedical and Behavioral Research was the first group to conduct a major government study on death. The Commission's reports, *Defining Death: Medical, Legal and Ethical Issues in the Determination of Death* (1981), *Making Health Care Decisions: The Ethical and Legal Implications of Informed Consent in the Patient-Practitioner Relationship* (1982), and *Deciding to Forego Life-Sustaining Treatment* (1983) have set the standards for many medical and bioethical debates.

The National Center for Health Statistics (NCHS) of the Centers for Disease Control and Prevention (CDC), in its annual publication *Health, United States, 2001* (2001), provides a statistical overview of the nation's health. The NCHS periodical *National Vital Statistics Reports* supplies detailed U.S. birth and death data for 1999 and 2000. The CDC reports on nationwide health trends in *Advance Data, Morbidity and Mortality Weekly Report, HIV/AIDS Surveillance Report* and *Trends in Health and Aging* (2001). The Centers for Medicare & Medicaid Services (formerly known as the Health Care Financing Administration), Office of the Actuary, National Health Statistics Group, reports on the nation's health care spending.

The U.S. Census Bureau publishes a wide variety of demographic information on American life. *Population Projections of the U.S. by Age, Sex, Race, and Hispanic Origin, 1995–2050* (1996) and *An Aging World: 2001* (2001) provide information on aging. The U.S. General Accounting Office (GAO), the investigative arm of Congress, provides a report on *Alzheimer's Disease: Estimates of Prevalence in the United States* (1998).

The Alliance for Aging Research (AAR) promotes scientific research in human aging and conducts educational programs to increase communication and understanding among professionals who serve the elderly. Particularly useful among its data are *Seven Deadly Myths: Uncovering the Facts About the High Cost of the Last Year of Life* (1997), *One Final Gift: Humanizing the End of Life for Women in America* (1998), and *Great Expectations: Americans' Attitudes on Aging Research* (2001).

Partnership for Caring (formerly Choice in Dying) provides a national hotline to help patients, families, and health care professionals during end-of-life crises. It also offers other materials and services relating to end-of-life medical care and decision-making, including advance directives and physician-assisted suicide.

The United Network for Organ Sharing (UNOS) manages the national transplant waiting list, maintains data on organ transplants, and distributes organ donor cards. Valuable information on these topics is available in the *2000 Annual Report of the U.S. Scientific Registry for Transplant Recipients and the Organ Procurement and Transplantation Network: Transplant Data: 1990–1999*.

The National Right to Life Committee provides a *Resolution on Euthanasia* and alternative living will, while the Hemlock Society USA provides *The Provisions of the Oregon Death with Dignity Act* and the society's *General Principles and Objectives*. The National Conference of Catholic Bishops (NCCB) includes helpful information in its *Life at Risk (A Chronicle of Euthanasia Trends in America)*, published ten times annually by the Secretariat for Pro-Life Activities.

The Hospice Association of America and the National Hospice Organization both collect much data about hospice care, and the ABA Commission on Legal Problems of the Elderly has published information relating to advance directives. For cancer statistics, a premier source is the American Cancer Society's *Cancer Facts & Figures—2002*.

The Journal of the American Medical Association (Chicago), *The New England Journal of Medicine* (Boston), the *Journal of the American Geriatrics Society* (New York), the *Annals of Internal Medicine* (Philadelphia), and the *Lancet* (London, England), are all journals that frequently publish studies dealing with life-sustaining treatment, medical ethics, and medical costs.

The Gallup Organization (Princeton, New Jersey), Harris Interactive (New York), and the Roper Center for Public Opinion Research (University of Connecticut) have all conducted opinion polls on various topics related to death and dying, as has the Polling Report, Inc. The Henry J. Kaiser Family Foundation (Menlo Park, California) has conducted the *National Survey on Nursing Homes* (1998).

INDEX